SLAYER SLANG

A Buffy the Vampire Slayer Lexicon

Slayer Slang

A Buffy the Vampire Slayer Lexicon

by

MICHAEL ADAMS

OXFORD UNIVERSITY PRESS

2003

Oxford University Press

Oxford   New York   Auckland   Bangkok   Buenos Aires   Cape Town
Chennai   Dar es Salaam   Delhi   Hong Kong   Istanbul   Karachi
Kolkata   Kuala Lumpur   Madrid   Melbourne   Mexico City
Mumbai   Nairobi   São Paulo   Shanghai   Taipei   Tokyo   Toronto

Published by Oxford University Press, Inc.
198 Madison Avenue, New York, New York, 10016
http://www.oup-usa.org

Oxford is a registered trademark of Oxford University Press

Book design by T. Kellers
Set in Joanna
Jacket design by David Stevenson

Library of Congress Cataloging-in-Publication Data

Adams, Michael, 1961–
    Slayer slang : a Buffy the vampire slayer lexicon / by Michael Adams.
        p. cm.
    Includes bibliographical references and index.
    ISBN 0-19-516033-9 (hardcover : alk. paper)
        1. Buffy, the vampire slayer (Television program)—
    Miscellanea. I. Title.
PN 1992.77.B84 A34 2003
791.45'72—dc21   2003004781

Printing number: 9 8 7 6 5 4 3 2

Printed in the United States of America on acid-free paper

Contents

This book is dedicated to the writers
of Buffy the Vampire Slayer
who gave us slayer slang,
to the actors who brought it to life,
and to the many writers and speakers,
especially the Bronzers and Betarers,
who have made so much of it.

Introduction

I t is tempting, of course, to write such an introduction in fluent
Buffinese: "I am not unproud...." But, for your sake and my own, I
resist.

When I joined the writing staff of *Buffy the Vampire Slayer*, the show
was entering its third year on the air, and, as a fan, I was already an
admirer of the distinctive uses of language on the show. I showed up for
work eagerly anticipating my dive into the linguistic world of Buffy.
Looking back now through my first draft of my first script written for
the show, my eye falls on the words *über-Mom*, *mom-buttons*, and in a
coinage that never made it to the air, *loafer-whiffle* (the sound Giles's
shoes make). Now, in the show's seventh year, I find I enjoy the creative
language just as much. The first draft of my most recent script contains
belly-button-centric, *chock-full-o-sanity*, and, believe it or not, *vomit-watch*.
How much fun is my job? Lots of much.

Creative compounds are only one of the ways in which the study of
language overlaps with the study of the Culture of Buffy. Before I entered
the world of television writing, I was a student in the graduate Linguistics program at U.C. Berkeley. I studied metaphor—a kind of subslice of
semantics that should have proven impractical. It has served me very
well at Buffy however, where the problems and emotions of our young
characters are physicalized every week as demons and such. The same
mechanisms that dictate the rules of metaphor in language are at work
in our scripts. For example, there is a productive metaphor for causation

in English in which AFFECTING someone is understood as TOUCHING them. Examples illustrating this include I *got to him*, I *reached him*, and *His situation touched me*. On Buffy we used this metaphor in the script *Same Time, Same Place*, in which Willow's fears of not being able to "connect" with her friends manifested themselves as a magical situation in which Willow was unable to touch them.

There are other, more peripheral ways in which my job at *Buffy* reminds me of my time spent studying language. I enjoy selecting demon names—I like them to sound unlike English, and unlike each other. The Fyarl demon and the Mfashnik demon are two that I am very fond of. In the script *A New Man*, I was also able to write some of the Fyarl language, and we learn that "Fllewn?" is a sensible question.

I also take great joy in scripted wordless exclamations like Joss's "Humnoo?" from the script *Lessons* and my own "Bleah gukguk yeee," Xander's expression of disgust in *Same Time, Same Place*.

Also, I enjoy giving the actors grammatically or phonologically complex lines. When Willow is caught drawing an occult symbol in *Gingerbread*, she defends herself:

WILLOW (nervous): A doodle. I do doodle. You too. You do doodle too.

And I like the following exchange, from Drew Greenberg's script *Him*.

WILLOW: Damn love spell. I've tried every anti-love-spell spell I can find.
ANYA: Even if you found the right one, guy would probably just do an anti-anti-love-spell-spell spell.
WILLOW: What?

Buffy gets humor out of juxtaposing casual language with dramatic import in this line from *Doublemeat Palace*, when she's convinced that the Doublemeat Medley is made of people:

BUFFY: The beefy layer is definitely people! Probably not the chickeny part! But who knows? Who knows?!

I've also been lucky to have the opportunity to write for a Troll who spoke in a stilted style and all capital letters, and to get to write British slang for Spike and sometimes Giles over the years. Buffy is absolutely FULL of fun stuff for a lover of language.

Let us assume, then, that the field of linguistics might have reason to be interested in Buffy. But what exactly IS Buffy? As someone on the inside, I want to address this. It's important to realize that the Buffy universe is not monolithic. It is created by many different individuals. Buffy is a story told by a staff, a group of writers, usually numbering six or seven in a given season, with members of the group coming and going over the years, and frequently with layers of rewriting imposing one staff member's words over another's. The only thing that gives us coherence is that we're all writing segments of the same story and that we're all doing our darnedest to do a Joss Whedon impersonation. This is what gives Buffy its consistent sound.

Joss is Buffy's father, the creator and show-runner, the king of us. Much of the way the Buffy characters speak is a result of the way he speaks. For example, he has told me that his use of the distinctive Buffyword *sitch* dates at least back to his college days. He also cites its use as a verb, as in *sitch me* ('bring me up to date on the situation'). Joss's idiolect is rich in such truncated forms including the exotic *nesse* (for 'necessary').

He also makes frequent use of the double negative (*not untalented*) and the extension of metaphors (*it's not pointless, it's pointy*). The speech of Buffy and her friends is an amplified version of his own speech. And it doesn't end with the fictional characters; the Buffy writers inevitably end up not only writing like Joss, but talking like him as well.

It all begins with Joss. But it doesn't end there. With so many of us laboring over so many years, and with so many fans writing about the show, and indulging in creative fanfic, together we have extended the language of the Buffyverse. For example, above I used the phrase "lots of much." Although I may be wrong, to my knowledge this has never appeared on the show. BUT IT COULD. To my ears it clearly falls into the universe of Potential Buffyisms. It follows the patterns established on the show over the years. Being a Buffy writer means, of course, living in the world of Potential Buffyisms all the time, coining and truncating and compounding our way through a script, all the time creating new data for others to study. It is an odd sitch.

Also, if you would like to get really dizzy, imagine how the writer feels when she is AWARE that the words she writes are becoming part of the

Buffyspeak database. Does the observer affect the outcome? I guess I hope so, because cool.

As I write this, we are nearing the end of the natural lifespan of the show, and we the writers find ourselves growing conscious of the body of work we are all partly responsible for. We helped shape characters who now live in other media—comic books, fanfic, novels...they will outlive our contributions to the show. The distinctive use of language obviously lives on with them, and will continue to do so, written by others. It will be hard for us to let go, to see it continue in other ways, in other hands. I will be interested to see if the Buffy way of speaking will change as it gets farther from Joss's orbit.

But I'm getting into the world of speculation. I don't have to answer these questions. I don't even have to understand anything about the inner workings of Buffyspeak. All I have to do is write. As any linguist knows, being fluent in a language and understanding the mechanisms of that language are two completely different things.

For example, I know that the following is an acceptable exchange...

> XANDER: Is he throwing a tasteful British wiggins?
> BUFFY: With extra wig.

...but I'm not the one who has to analyze it.
I leave that to the author of this work.

JANE ESPENSON
Co-Executive Producer, *Buffy the Vampire Slayer*

Preface

This book attempts several things at once, perhaps reflecting foolish ambition; yet this may be the only study of slayer slang ever written, so it seemed appropriate to explain as much as possible about the vocabulary and speech practices associated with, if not always original to, *Buffy the Vampire Slayer*. First, it is an exercise in philology, the presentation and analysis of language in a particular literary text or group of related texts; in this guise, the book is an aid to understanding and enjoying the television show and the many, many texts derived from it. Second, the glossary that makes up half of the book records many, though by no means all, items of slayer slang. Entries in the glossary illustrate the micro-histories of the words registered there with quotations, a service to lexicographers and linguists for whom the quotations constitute useful raw material. Fans of the show, I hope, will find the glossary fun to browse. Third, the chapters that precede the glossary not only describe slayer slang but explore its relations to American slang and general American English. I have tried very hard to make the linguistics and language history presented here accessible to general readers, especially Buffy fans, while preserving material and argument of use to linguists, lexicographers, and historians of American English. Slayer slang seems to me a wonderful opportunity for just folks to think about language seriously without sacrificing any fun; I hope that professionals, bereft of jargon and parenthetical references, will nonetheless find the book useful and also a pleasant excursion through a delightful lexicon.

I would like to thank the President and Trustees of Albright College for granting me a sabbatical leave to finish this book. I owe several friends and colleagues debts for help with particular words, for citations I had otherwise overlooked (or about which I never would have known), and for references and Buffy-related material, among them Mary Blockley, Al Cacicedo, Guillaume de Syon, Matt Goldsborough, Larry Horn, Bill King, Erin McKean, and Tim Redding. I hope that I haven't forgotten anyone, but I probably have, and I apologize for any oversights. Connie Eble, the late Robert Chapman, and Jesse Sheidlower have provided welcome support and encouragement throughout the project. Hosea L. Baker did a splendid job of helping me to check and correct quotations from printed material. The Linguistics Discussion Group of the University of Iceland gave very helpful advice after they heard me present my research as far as it had developed by February 2001.

This is my chance to apologize to my colleagues at Albright College, especially Gary Adlestein, Mary Jane Androne, Richard Androne, Jeff Barker, Al Cacicedo, Guillaume de Syon, Lynn Morrow, John Pankratz, and Jeff Woodward, not to mention the many students at Albright College, the University of Iceland, and Duke University, who tolerated my five-year obsession with slayer slang. The same goes for my mother, Dorothy Fisher, who at least pretended to listen as I rattled on interminably about the language of a television show she could bear to see only once. Elizabeth Price put up with a lot while I was writing this book, but every Tuesday evening she sat beside me to watch the latest episode, companionship for which I am grateful beyond telling.

My greatest obligation, however, is to my friend and editor Erin McKean, who published the article "Slayer Slang" in *Verbatim: The Language Quarterly* and then encouraged me to write the book, finally guiding me, ever so patiently and wisely, through to publication. Martin Coleman, Marina Padakis, and Charles Carson, all of them remarkably keen-eyed, saved me from countless errors and inconsistencies, for which I thank them. In addition, Marina Padakis compiled the index. Together they are responsible for much of what is good about this book; I fear that I alone am responsible for its deficiencies.

MICHAEL ADAMS
10 February 2003
Durham, North Carolina

CHAPTER I

Slayer Slang

Buffy the Vampire Slayer entered stage left, with a whimper. Joss Whedon, a versatile screenwriter whose credits include *Alien: Resurrection*, *Toy Story*, and *Speed*, introduced Buffy the Vampire Slayer in the eponymous feature film (1992), but many considered the film so bad that it looked as though the Buffyverse would end then, without a bang. As we have learned since, however, Whedon is something of a genius, not only persistent and ambitious, but brave. Who else has written and produced an essentially silent hour-long episode of television (*Hush*, which aired on 14 December 1999); who else recently has produced and written (both text and music) a 90-minute musical episode occasionally reminiscent of Sondheim but recognizably his own (*Once More, With Feeling*, which aired on 10 November 2001)? Propelled by talent and sheer determination, and in spite of earlier setbacks, *Buffy the Vampire Slayer* (henceforth *Buffy* or *BTVS*) made its television debut on 10 March 1997, and the Buffyverse was re-created, with a big bang; this year, it completes its seventh and final season, a long run for any television show. At the end of its fifth season, it entered syndication: A feature of the UPN Network's regular season, *Buffy* reruns appear nightly on the FX Network and weekly on FOX. Few hour-long hybrids of drama and comedy, especially those about Slayers and the vampires they slay, have ever been so successful.

The series opens with a formulaic introduction to vampire slayers, of which Buffy is only the most recent: "As long as there have been demons, there has been the Slayer. One girl in all the world, a Chosen One, born with the strength and skill to hunt vampires and other deadly creatures ... to stop the spread of their evil. When one Slayer dies, the next is called and trained by the Watcher." Buffy is a reluctant slayer: Vampires interfere with her cheerleading career and her social life. After burning her Los Angeles high school to the ground during a prom in order to kill the vampires who attempted to turn the event into a blood-fest, Buffy Summers moves to Sunnydale, California. Unable to escape her destiny as a Slayer, however, she encounters her new Watcher, Rupert Giles, who poses as Sunnydale High School's librarian. Sunnydale, we discover in the first episode, is located on a Hellmouth, and vampires roam the streets freely after dark, bent on nothing less than the destruction of this world.

Though her identity should be secret, a few friends know Buffy as the Slayer and assist her: Willow Rosenberg, her best friend, is a brilliant computer nerd who once loved her childhood friend, Xander Harris; Xander, clever enough, though an underachiever, has a crush on Buffy, but has always loved Willow; Cordelia Chase is rich, popular, acid-tongued, and unaccountably in love with her boyfriend, Xander; Oz, incidentally a werewolf, is usually just Willow's boyfriend and plays guitar in a band; and Buffy falls in love with Angel, a reformed vampire who turns bad again, and whom Buffy is forced to kill at the end of the second season. By twists of plot too convoluted to rehearse here, a rival slayer named Faith appears in the third season, a high school dropout, horny, leathered, and tattooed. Faith turns bad, survives a Buffy-induced coma, and is, perhaps, redeemed by a resurrected Angel.

By the time Buffy gets to college, Giles is no longer her official Watcher, but the proprietor of a magic shop. Willow has discovered that she's a witch. Oz leaves. Cordelia departs for Los Angeles to become an actress, but ends up first a secretary and then a partner in Angel Investigations. Willow discovers that she's a lesbian by falling in love with another lesbian witch, Tara. Xander, foiled by his SAT scores, takes a job in construction, becomes a successful contractor, and almost marries a vengeance demon, Anya, who sacrifices immortality to be with him, a choice she regrets when he deserts her at the altar. Buffy continues to slay vampires and demons, goes to class, gets drunk, and falls in love with Riley Finn, a soldier who leads a clandestine squad of demon hunters attached to a government project, the Initiative, under the supervision of Buffy's psychology professor. The relationship doesn't work out.

An ancient order of monks transforms a supernatural force called The Key into a person, Dawn, whom they place under the Slayer's protection by convincing everyone (Buffy, Mrs. Summers, and all of Buffy's associates) that Dawn is, and always has been, Buffy's sister. Glory, a goddess bent on world domination, needs The Key in order to achieve her goal, and she almost wins it, until Buffy sacrifices herself instead of Dawn— Glory needs Dawn's blood for a ritual, but Buffy realizes that, if they're sisters, her blood will do as well as Dawn's. Willow then brings Buffy back from the dead by means of magic. Buffy, who has been in Heaven, finds it hard to adjust to life in Sunnydale, so she has a torrid affair with Spike, a vampire and longtime resident in the story's arc, but, unlike Angel, a soulless one. Slaying doesn't pay the bills, so she takes a job at Doublemeat Palace, a local fast-food joint. Jonathan, one of Buffy's high school classmates, and once her great admirer, teams up with Warren and Andrew, and the three of them become the Slayer's "nemesises." After some amusing high jinks, Warren attempts to kill Buffy, but kills Tara instead; Willow, by now a recovering magic addict, falls off the wagon, flays Warren, and almost ends the world but, under Xander's loving influence, turns back toward good at the last moment.

Slayer, witch, werewolf, vampire, commando, contractor, vengeance demon, supernatural force incarnate—in other words, they are all average kids, in average relationships, battling the forces of adolescent evil, personified, in Sunnydale at least, by vampires, demons, and monsters. They are also particularly adept speakers of American English, especially of slang. After her self-sacrifice, Buffy is buried under a headstone that reads "She Saved the World. A Lot." What does it mean for American English that the world's protector, its thoroughly contemporary American savior, is a rapid-fire quipster, a hip teen who knows the language of her place and time, but who, by virtue of her role as Slayer, however hesitantly accepted, is necessarily an unacknowledged hero, an essentially normal person whose destiny casts her out of the mainstream, whose status paradoxically erases her status in the conventional world? Buffy needs slang, as means of shrugging off millennial expectations, as a weapon, and as an expression of personality officially denied her by her role: in a sense, she IS slang, as are those who associate with her.

Slayer Phenomena

From the outset, *Buffy the Vampire Slayer* has had a fairly large following; it was, for five years, the most popular show on the WB Network, with an audience primarily of teens and twenty-somethings, but including plenty of thirty-something viewers as well. Fans of the show have proven extraordinarily dedicated to it: they support a *Buffy* industry that produces the obligatory action figures, calendars, T-shirts, posters, trading cards, jewelry, shot glasses, and an interactive video game; the show has inspired nearly 75 novels and novelizations, more than 100 comic books and graphic novels, a quarterly magazine, and a dozen or so thick books about the show, at least two of which are now in their second editions. Dozens of magazines have published even more dozens of articles about *Buffy* and its stars, and Web activity surrounding the show has been phenomenal, to say the least. Homage to *Buffy* is both more frequent and more sincere than those who live outside the Buffyverse can imagine easily.

Almost from the beginning, B*TVS* captured a large audience for a show on a minor network, the fledgling WB. By the third season, its season-long audience had settled at around 4.5 million viewers nationwide, though its draw in urban centers for particular episodes was considerably greater: the Season Three premiere attracted more than 9 million viewers in New York, 8 million in Los Angeles, and 7 million in Chicago. When the show moved from the WB to UPN in 2001, it had maintained that average, and, as recently as 17 December 2002, the episode Bring on the Night played to 4 million fans, constituting 6% of television viewers during that time slot. These numbers are well above the current average ratings for the UPN overall (2.5 million viewers at a 4% share of the total television viewing audience), as well as for the WB (2.9 million viewers at a 5% share). *Buffy* hardly competes with the top 20 rated shows (many of which approach 10 million viewers, and the most popular of which exceed even that benchmark by several million), but *Buffy's* audience is nonetheless large enough to stir up interest and to develop and disseminate its variety of American slang.

Fans of the show have long bemoaned the lack of respect paid to *Buffy* in the awards competitions, especially the Emmys: It has received a few technical awards and a few nominations in what are usually considered the more important categories, like writing and acting, but awards in those categories have not been forthcoming. The Academy's apparent snubs are balanced not only by a devoted audience—those who read the novels and participate on posting boards and collect the comics—but by persistent critical acclaim. Ken Tucker, television critic for *Entertainment Weekly*, has been its most vocal champion, frequently calling it the best show on television (a judgment with which I wholeheartedly agree, as, apparently, does Dean Valentine, president and CEO of UPN, who acquired the show in 2001). Tucker managed to negotiate a 24-page spread on the show in *Entertainment Weekly* (1 October 1999), complete with articles, sidebars on interesting aspects of the show (like wardrobe), a lively episode guide, and an excellent glossary of characteristic terms, "Buffy A to Z," compiled by Megan Howard.

Why is the show so good? Tucker's commentary in the issue makes a compelling case: "[W]ith remarkable speed, *Buffy* became that rare kind of TV programming: a show whose characters grew only more complex (and—rarer still—not even necessarily more likable), and one in which episodes began adding up to a rich, expansive mythology that could accommodate any comment Whedon and company wanted to make on contemporary culture." As a show about adolescents, *Buffy* naturally appeals to adolescents, who like the image of themselves reflected in the show, for "[t]ime and time again, Buffy (as smartly played by Sarah Michelle Gellar) takes on heavy-duty, life and death responsibilities, giving the lie to the current cliché of adolescents as self-absorbed, workphobic louts," but, as Tucker also notes, "an awful lot of grown-ups [are] utterly entranced and *moved* by this show," and he attributes their fascination to the fact that "*Buffy* is about adolescents whose form and content are never themselves adolescent—the exact opposite of *Seinfeld* and scores of lesser shows that idealize the notion of prolonging teen sensibilities well into adulthood." Whereas *Seinfeld* was flamboyantly about nothing, *Buffy* is packed with content. Sure, there are "the yuks, satire, and pop-culture effluvia that make Buffy a fun watch," but "there is one salient quality that distinguishes [it] from all the teeming teen shows" on television, namely, "*respect*: respect for the series' young protagonists, but also, more broadly, for life—for its preciousness and its precariousness." As a result, Tucker's daughter Hannah notes in a sidebar, Buffy appeals to an unusually broad audience. Bickering about who controls the remote dissolves, and families, if only for an hour, are brought together rather than split into demographics: "[O]nce a week in my very own home," she writes, "two teenage girls and their father sit in front of the TV for the purposes of watching (get this) *the same show*."

The sentiment has often been repeated on The Bronze and Bronze: Beta posting boards, about which a few words must be said. Activity on these boards is remarkable, another significant Slayer phenomenon. There are, of course, as on all posting boards, insipid "drive-by" posts in all lowercase letters—"i love buffy, do u?" and that sort of thing—but the insipid have their place among us, and the Bronzers and Betarers, who have built a thriving Net community over the last few years, welcome them affably enough. Lowercase thirteen-year-olds are joined by articulate college students, Ph.D.–certified college professors, and others from all corners of the working world. They discuss many things on the boards, arising from their friendships, their common interests, and even the cultures of the boards themselves, but also frequently about Buffy. The Buffy-related discussions, in my experience, are informed and intelligent and sometimes even eloquent, all of which should give pause to those who deride communication on the Internet, and I have learned a great deal and thought more deeply about the show by lurking on the boards to collect material for the glossary. And, as the glossary shows, the role of the posting boards in establishing, developing, and disseminating slayer slang has been profound.[1]

But the posting boards are by no means the only slayer venues on the Internet. A simple search on any engine will bring up more than 37,000 matches for "Buffy the Vampire Slayer," and hundreds of these are sites dedicated to the show or to its stars.[2] *Yahoo! Internet Life* reported that, in 1999, "Sarah Michelle Gellar and her nocturnal brigade from the WB

---

[1] *The Bronze and Bronze: Beta were/are official posting boards, sponsored respectively by the network home to Buffy. When the show left the WB Network for UPN in 2001, there was a hiatus of several months before Bronze: Beta was up and running. Both boards are notably cohesive and a case study in cyber-civics; along such lines, Amanda Zweerink and Sarah N. Gatson, in "www.buffy.com: Cliques, Boundaries, and Hierarchies in an Internet Community" (2002), consider some of the boards' problems, as well as their contributions to the Buffyverse.*

Network's *Buffy the Vampire Slayer* created the most traffic and buzz at the Net's top TV hub," and in October of the same year, *Premiere* ranked Gellar seventh among actresses with the biggest Web presence, with more than 135 sites devoted to her at that time. The point, I'm sure, is gradually becoming clear: not long after *Buffy* arrived on the scene, it was ubiquitous, a television and cultural phenomenon adored by its fans and, by others, not easily ignored.

The show's stars are all, as slayer slang would have it, hotties, so they naturally grace many magazine covers; *Buffy* has, in fact, received an extraordinary level of coverage in magazines of every kind. Of course, entertainment magazines devoted to fantasy and science fiction have included stories about the show frequently (*Spectrum: The Magazine of Television, Film & Comics, Cinefantastique, RetroVision, Sci-Fi TV, Sci-Fi Teen, Femmes Fatales: The Luscious Ladies of Horror, Fantasy & Science Fiction, Cinescape, Starburst: The Premiere Magazine of Sci-Fi Entertainment, Dreamwatch: Fantastic Entertainment*, and *X-Posé: Exploring Fantastic Movies and TV*, to name a few), but *Buffy* (and, as its icon, Sarah Michelle Gellar) has been the darling of mainstream entertainment magazines as well, including *TV Guide* (at least one exclusive cover [19–25 February 2000] for Gellar), *Rolling Stone* (two covers for Gellar [2 April 1998 and 11 May 2000]), and, as mentioned above, *Entertainment Weekly* (three more exclusive covers for Gellar [1 October 1999, 7 September 2001, and 26 February 2003], as well as many shared covers). Articles in the magazines above are at least ostensibly about the show, but many other magazines, "lifestyle" magazines, focus on the stars instead, and here again the variety of coverage is astonishing: Gellar appears modishly kohleyed on the cover of the very hip *Nylon* (January/February 2000), but she and her female co-stars are featured in the much more staid *In Style*

---

² I hope that readers will forgive me for not working through the matches to determine exactly how many websites are in the list. Experience tells me that many of the matches are duplicates; nevertheless, I have visited hundreds of clearly *Buffy*-related sites and feel confident about that vague estimate. Some of the websites are essentially ephemeral, single pages of homage to the show or one of its stars; on the other hand, some are quite elaborate—full-service sites— including picture galleries, episode guides, news, links to other sites, and extensive collections of quotations from episodes of the show (for example, see perhaps the best of the general *Buffy* sites, **www.buffyguide.com**).

(November 1998); Gellar was one of the short-lived pseudo-political magazine *George*'s choices for "The 20 Most Fascinating Women in Politics: Women Who Rule" (September 1998), but she has also grinned from the cover of *Glamour* (October 2000) and every other style/fashion magazine for teens and young women. And *Buffy* finds its way into special-interest magazines as well: collectors encounter "Once Bitten: 50 Facts about Moore Action Collectibles' *Buffy the Vampire Slayer* Toys That You Never Knew" in *Toyfare* (November 1999); librarians muse over "Bibliographic Good vs. Evil in Buffy the Vampire Slayer" in *American Libraries* (September 1999), and readers of *Out* (August 2001) can enjoy "Hannigan's Shenanigans," complete with photos of Alyson Hannigan, *Buffy*'s Willow Rosenberg, vamping for her lesbian fans. To repeat my earlier point, *Buffy* is everywhere and appeals to a broad variety of people, well beyond the show's dedicated fans, for a broad variety of reasons. More than most television shows, *Buffy* has influenced American culture, and because language is so central to the show's appeal, we might consider slayer slang's potential influence on American slang and its relation to American English generally.

Magazines need faces and fit bodies to sell magazines and the products advertised within, but fascination with *Buffy* is not all a matter of image, market, and (to be frank) sex. Many of the magazines discover in *Buffy* significant contemporary issues, beyond the eternal ones that Tucker, better than anyone else, has isolated in the *Buffy* culture. Some of these appeal particularly to adolescents, like seeing events in the show as a loose allegory of high school life, clearly one of the show's intended bases. Joss Whedon had it in mind as early as the 1992 film: "'To me, high school *was* a horror movie,' he is quoted as saying. And did I mention sex? "*Buffy* is one of the most sexually blunt shows on the air and, for its family-hour time slot, almost subversively so. … 'It's something we deal with,' says Whedon, 'because it's something that's on people's minds.'" As Emma Forrest points out, "Though television means nothing, it also means everything. *Buffy the Vampire Slayer* is about a character who challenges every weary, dangerous notion of adolescent female sexuality." Sexuality bleeds into politics, as women are redefined according to "girl power." In "The 20 Most Fascinating Women in Politics," *George* insisted that "Sarah Michelle Gellar represents real girl power, the kind that can kung-fu the undead back into oblivion … but what she's really taking on is the regular assortment of challenges that threaten to suck the lifeblood out of teenage girls, like a suffocating school hierarchy and a sexual double standard." And if one doesn't watch Buffy in order to deal with high school, sexuality, or life and death, one can enjoy it for its robust play with language, for "The show's appeal lies in the smart-mouthed writing and dark, anything-goes story lines"; yet "The Buffy series, while keeping all the delightfully campy dialogue, the action, and the humor, finally became the true horror show Whedon envisioned when he first penned the original script to the 1992 movie." In other words, if people were honest, Buffy would appeal to all of them, for one reason or another.

For such recent phenomena, Buffy and the Buffyverse have stimulated a surprising amount of intellectual interest. Harper's (July 1999) excerpted an article titled "The Buffy Files," by Tracie McMillan and Oscar Owens, published in The Activist earlier that year. According to a headnote, The Activist is "the magazine of the young Democratic Socialists," and the authors attempt to show that Buffy, "in which high school students meet during their lunch period to organize the defense of their town against vampires, could just as easily be about 'a high school feminist or social-ist club.'" Harper's then proceeded to print a series of "socialist under-tones the authors found in selected episodes of the program." One won-ders whether Hannah Tucker ever considered the show radical political discourse! But the fact that Tucker, her father, and McMillan and Owens can watch it for such different reasons, draw widely different conclu-sions from the same episodes, and all come away satisfied citizens of the Buffyverse, is part of Buffy's magic.

Recently, two collections of essays about Buffy and the Buffyverse have appeared: Reading the Vampire Slayer: An Unofficial Critical Companion to Buffy and Angel, edited by Roz Kaveney (2001), and Fighting the Forces: What's at Stake in Buffy the Vampire Slayer, edited by Rhonda V. Wilcox and David Lavery (2002), who are also the editors of Slayage: The Online International Journal of Buffy Studies.[3] The journal was chosen by USA

---

[3] The full range of intellectual interest in Buffy can best be displayed by listing these books' contents here. Reading the Vampire Slayer: Roz Kaveney, "'She Saved the World. A Lot.': An Introduction to the Themes and Structure of Buffy and Angel"; Boyd Tonkin, "Entropy as

Today (14 February 2002) as one of their "Hot Picks," a fact that once again illustrates Buffy's phenomenal versatility: after all, USA Today is hardly America's highbrow newspaper, but the journal is intellectually serious, and that it would be a "Hot Pick" surely says something about the impact BTVS has had on American culture. Intellectual work can be serious and fun at the same time, of course, and, among other fun aspects of the show, the scholarly journal and books are fully aware of slayer jargon, slayer slang, and slayer style, and some of the authors actually invent items of slayer slang—they may work in the ivory tower, but, at the onset of the twenty-first century, the ivory tower not only has TV, it has cable.

Demon: Buffy in Southern California"; Brian Wall and Michael Zryd, "Vampire Dialectics: Knowledge, Institutions and Labour"; Steve Wilson, "'Laugh, Spawn of Hell, Laugh'"; Karen Sayer, "'It Wasn't Our World Anymore. They Made It Theirs': Reading Space and Place"; Zoe-Jane Playden, "'What You Are, What's to Come': Feminisms, Citizenship and the Divine"; Anne Millard Dougherty, "Just a Girl: Buffy as Icon"; Dave West, "'Concentrate on the Kicking Movie': Buffy and East Asian Cinema"; Esther Saxey, "Staking a Claim: The Series and Its Slash Fan-Fiction"; and Ian Shuttleworth, "'They Always Mistake Me for the Character I Play!': Transformation, Identity and Role-Playing in the Buffyverse (and a Defense of Fine Acting)."

Fighting the Forces incorporates an even broader range of interests: Camille Bacon-Smith, "The Color of the Dark in Buffy the Vampire Slayer"; Rhonda V. Wilcox, "'Who Died and Made Her the Boss?': Patterns of Mortality in Buffy"; Elyce Rae Helford, "'My Emotions Give Me Power': The Containment of Girls' Anger in Buffy"; Patricia Pender, "'I'm Buffy, and You're…History': The Postmodern Politics of Buffy"; Farah Mendelsohn, "Surpassing the Love of vampires; or, Why (and How) a Queer Reading of the Buffy/Willow Relationship Is Denied"; J. P. Williams, "Choosing Your Own Mother: Mother-Daughter Conflicts in Buffy"; Karen Eileen Overbey and Lahney Preston-Matto, "Staking in Tongues: Speech Act as Weapon in Buffy"; Lynne Edwards, "Slaying in Black and White: Kendra as Tragic Mulatta in Buffy"; Mary Alice Mooney, "The Undemonization of Supporting Characters in Buffy"; Gregory Erickson, "'Sometimes You Need a Story': American Christianity, Vampires, and Buffy"; Catherine Siemann, "Darkness Falls on the Endless Summer: Buffy as Gidget for the Fin de Siècle"; Anita Rose, "Of Creatures and Creators: Buffy does Frankenstein"; Diane DeKalb-Rittenhouse, "Sex and the Single Vampire: The Evolution of the Vampire Lothario and Its Representation in Buffy"; Elizabeth Krimmer and Shipa Ruval, "'Digging the Undead': Death and Desire in Buffy"; Donald Keller, "Spirit Guides and Shadow Selves: From the Dream Life of Buffy (and Faith)"; Tanya Krzywinska, "Hubble-Bubble, Herbs, and Grimoires: Magic, Manichaeanism, and Witchcraft in Buffy"; Sarah E. Skwire, "Whose Side Are You on, Anyway? Children, Adults, and the Use of Fairy Tales in Buffy"; Kristina Busse, "Crossing the Final Taboo: Family, Sexuality, and Incest in Buffyverse Fan Fiction"; S. Renee Dechert, "'My Boyfriend's in the Band!' Buffy and the Rhetoric of Music"; Justine Larbalestier, "Buffy's Mary Sue Is Jonathan: Buffy Acknowledges the Fans"; Amanda Zweerink and Sarah N. Gatson, "www.buffy.com: Cliques, Boundaries, and Hierarchies in an Internet Community"; and David Lavery, "Afterword: The Genius of Joss Whedon."

Buffy the Vampire Slayer is remarkable television at the center of a universe of interests not unlike the world in which we live, in spite of the vampires and demons: it captivates the 14-year-old and the 50-year-old, the political and the literary, the thoughtful and the vacuous; it is an allegory of American high school and teen social life; it asserts girl power; it is humor and pathos, death and duty and another day, love and hatred, and is so incredibly complex, complex enough to represent the experience of living in this world, which, if we're honest, is not what most television is about. Whether your culture is popular or elite, Buffy has influenced it, and because Buffy is so linguistically potent, its cultural influence amounts, in part, to influence on American speech. Millions of Americans, those within the Buffyverse, are enthusiastic users of slayer slang. And although slayer slang isn't the legal tender of standard American English, it is cultural currency: some who hear it wrinkle their brows, test the paper, and hold the watermarks up to the light; in the end, they are forced to accept it as the way at least some of us talk now.

Slayer Jargon

According to Walter Nash in *Jargon: Its Uses and Abuses*: "'[J]argon' denotes the terminology of some profession, occupation, or pursuit." In medieval England, guilds were called *mysteries* because, in order to be a glover or a goldsmith, for instance, one had to possess special knowledge of leather or gold, gloves or jewelry, the trade secrets one wouldn't discuss with those outside the guild. Jargon is allied to mystery: it expresses the uniqueness of a profession or pursuit, what sets it apart from others; supposedly, only those who follow the profession or pursuit will know the language of the guild, though jargon occasionally seeps into general use. For instance, servers in restaurants use terms like *on a wait* 'have customers waiting for tables', *in the weeds* 'swamped, overwhelmed', and *deuce* 'table with two place-settings' among themselves in order to facilitate their work and to express professional camaraderie; the rest of us, though we may recognize such terms, don't use them. On the other hand, *eighty-six* 'out of (something)', as in "The nine-inch nails are eighty-sixed," has migrated from restaurant jargon into American slang;

and we all know and use terms like *busboy* or *busser*, even though they apply only in restaurant contexts.

Like any other profession, vampire slaying has its own lexicon, the core items of which the glossary includes, though most slayer jargon is excluded; for example, I have not entered names of any demon species from the show (with the oblique exceptions of **bezoar** and **vengeance demony**), nor *The Master*, *The Anointed One*, or *sire* 'turn (someone) into a vampire', etc. I have included those terms central to slaying or other pursuits within the Buffyverse, like **bezoar**, **Bronze**, **dust**, **Hellmouth**, **Scooby Gang**, **slay**, **Slayer**, **Slayerette**, **stake**, **undead**, **vamp**, and **Watcher**. Most of these are "productive" terms, words from which other words develop, and some of the subsequent words walk over the line from slayer jargon into slayer slang; the fact that others do not suggests some fundamental differences between jargon and slang as varieties of American English.[4]

Slayer jargon occurs at three levels. The primary level, first-order slayer jargon, consists of terms essential to the slaying enterprise, for instance, **Slayer** and **Watcher**. **Slayer** is a tricky term which itself contains a hierarchy of meanings. In the first instance, it is the title of the one girl chosen in all the world to fight vampires and other demons, and in this sense is always capitalized. But Buffy dies (temporarily) in the episode *Prophecy Girl* and another Slayer (or slayer), Kendra, is called; when Kendra dies on the edge of the vampire Drusilla's razor-sharp fingernail, Faith is called. So there are Slayers and there are slayers: if the title applies to Buffy only, as the Chosen One (Kendra and Faith never take that appellation as their own), then there are more slayers than Slayers; if the title applies to any slayer who is called, there must be slayers who never hear the call and don't become THE Slayer, or even A Slayer. Surely, past slayers who are not the present Slayer but who, like Buffy, saved the world a lot in their own times and places deserve the capital S. And, as a result, **Slayer** is far more often capitalized than not, even when used attributively or in compounds or blends, though the variation in use indicates an

---

[4] In their now classic article "Is Slang a Word for Linguists?," Bethany K. Dumas and Jonathan Lighter characterize jargon and the relationship between jargon and slang much as I do here; I am sure that I am indebted to their insights, which were inscribed indelibly on my blank slate when I began to study slang seriously.

implicit awareness on the parts of at least some that **Slayer** is usually pure jargon but at other times verges on a common noun for anyone who kills vampires.

Certainly, *slayer* is not the universal term for one who kills vampires professionally; *vampire hunter*, for instance, is an alternative. Vampire hunters other than Slayers fight alongside the Slayers, though they don't share the title or the dignity it confers: Willow, Xander, Giles, Cordelia, Oz, Tara, Dawn, and even Spike (a vampire himself), in essence, the **Scooby Gang**, kill vampires and other demons and protect the world as though they are slayers, though they aren't. Vampires inhabit universes other than the Buffy one, and those who kill them elsewhere bear no title. Yet *BTVS* appears to have influenced the jargon of those other universes: In *John Carpenter's Vampires: Los Muertos* (2002), written and directed by Tommy Lee Wallace, Derek (played by Jon Bon Jovi), the film's vampire hunter, asks his government control, "Why do I need to pose as an archaeologist?" to which he receives the answer, "The Mexican government has not yet recognized Vampire Slayer as a legitimate occupation." With Buffy so much in the air for so many years, it's difficult to imagine that the show didn't contribute to Wallace's use of the term, though he uses *vampire hunter* and *hunter* otherwise throughout the film. While *vampire slayer* and *Slayer* are hardly household words, but remain essentially jargon, they have entered public consciousness enough that, if we suddenly suffered a plague of vampires, citizens would turn frantically to *Slayer* in the Yellow Pages.

Hellmouth, a place-name, and **Watcher**, another title, behave much like **Slayer**. Like **Slayer** each is, in a sense, invariant. The first episode of the show (10 March 1997) was titled *Welcome to the Hellmouth*, and, from that point forward, evidence as reflected in the glossary most often implies that Sunnydale, California is on THE Hellmouth, that there are no others. This is true even in situations where technically the term has generalized, for instance, when Buffy asks in *Reptile Boy* (13 October 1997), "Who needs a social life when they've got their very own Hellmouth?": such a sentence supposes that others might have such a Hellmouth, though she is clearly talking about herself and HER Hellmouth; nonetheless, as opposed to other uses of the term, nothing in the sentence suggests that there might be only one Hellmouth. And by the episode *I Only Have Eyes for You* (28 April 1998), Principal Snyder can claim, "I'm doing everything I can, but you people have to realize [...] that we are on a Hellmouth," and the indefinite article clearly implies that the one on which Sunnydale sits is not the only one, but an example of a type of thing. So there is THE **Hellmouth**, jargon as concrete as THE **Slayer**, and there are **hellmouths**, jargon whose reference has loosened a bit, like **slayers**. **Watcher** follows the same pattern, referring most concretely to THE Slayer's Watcher, THE Watcher, but also denoting a class of people who were or are Watchers, like those who sit on the Watchers' Council.

Jargon generally does not develop as aggressively as slang, because it is not in the interest of jargon users that it would: jargon is necessarily precise, it's language about a job used to get the job done, and a loosening of reference or lexical adaptation interferes with precision. It is hardly surprising, then, that **Watcher** contributes to other jargon terms, like *Watchers' Council* and *Watchers' Journals*, that it occasionally contributes to names adopted by posting board participants, and that it shifts into an attributive noun, but otherwise develops little and unremarkably: the glossary includes only one quotation in which **Watcher** applies to someone other than a "real" Watcher (see sense 1.c), and **pre-Watcher**, **Superwatcher**, **Watcherly**, and **Watcher-napping**, each represented by a single quotation, together hardly amount to an adventure in language.

Hellmouth proves a more flexible item of slayer slang, though not much, and only because, unlike *Watcher*, *Hell* (or *hell*) already means things in English far and away from the core proper noun, the place-name antonym for *Heaven*. Thus, besides the predictable shift into an attributive noun, **Hellmouth** shifts semantically to mean anything resembling the torture of Hell (as in "Escape rerun HELLmouth by reading a new Buffy tale each week this summer at *Buffy's European Summer Vacation*" or "I actually still have my original AOHellmouth acct.") or to serve as an expletive (as in "I know in advance that there's no way in hellmouth I'll figure out those *Matrix* codes without some serious help"). So jargon **Hellmouth** develops into slang **Hellmouth**, but in relatively few instances, and never far removed from previously established slang.

A Slayer **slays** the **undead**, and these elements of first-order slayer jargon are similarly restrained, though each develops more flamboyantly than **Watcher** and **Hellmouth**. As a verb, **slay** predictably shifts into adjective and noun senses, and the name for the activity of killing vampires and other demons, **slaying**, also extends naturally, almost necessarily, from the term for the action, though **slayage**, a slangier term for the same thing, is less obvious. Even less expected is the shift from the sense 'killing vampires and other demons' to that of 'defeat something other than vampires, as though one were a Slayer of it', a metaphorical development that crosses into slang and shows that Buffyfans, once in a while, make even slayer jargon their own. Cleverness intrudes when Xander replaces **Slayer** with **Slaymaster General**, or when Little Willow, perhaps the most famous participant on the Bronze posting board, names her website the **Slayground**, or another Bronzer waves good-bye to the board with **slay you later**.

Undead also leads to inventive forms, though it mostly exists as collective noun, attributive noun, and adjectives, as it has continuously from its inception in Bram Stoker's *Dracula* (1897). One can't help but admire Buffy's caustic ingenuity, though, when she introduces **Undead-American** during an argument with Angel, acknowledging what she presumes are his "ethnic" sensitivities. And even though the context supplied in the glossary is somewhat opaque, **unDead Sea Scrolls** invites an appreciative smile as well. Beyond these forms, **undead** contributes to slayer slang by setting an example: the un- in **undead** inspires a wide range of other words (see Chapter 2). Like **Slayer**, though already well-entrenched in vampire literature, **undead** is a more familiar term because of Buffy, though it remains predominantly jargon, rather than slang.

While none of these terms set off an avalanche of new words, they aren't the most restrictive items of first-order slayer jargon: compared to them, **Chosen One** and **Old Ones** are inelastic. The former suggests the extent to which the Slayer is also a savior, dedicated not only to **slayage**, as Buffy would say, but to world **saveage**. It originates in Biblical ἐκλεκτός, another name for the Messiah, as in "And the people stood by, watching; but the rulers scoffed at [Jesus], saying, 'He saved others; let him save himself, if he is the Christ of God, his Chosen One!'" (Luke 23:35). **Chosen One** begat two parallel forms. The first of these, *Anointed One*, has a similarly Biblical character and is introduced in the episode *Never Kill a Boy on the First Date* (31 March 1997), when the Master reads from

The Book of Aurelius, a sort of vampire Book of the Apocalypse: "There will be a time of crisis, of worlds hanging in the balance. And in this time shall come the Anointed, the Master's great warrior. The Slayer will not know him, will not stop him. And he will lead her to hell. As it is written, so shall it be. Five will die, and from their ashes the Anointed One shall rise. The Order of Aurelius shall greet him and usher him to his immortal destiny. As it is written, so shall it be." The second may refer to Lucifer/Satan, the Biblical antagonist of the Biblical Chosen One, and appears in Christopher Golden and Nancy Holder's novel *Out of the Madhouse* (1999, p. 178): "A merry chase he had led me for almost a century. Fulcanelli, base servant of the Fallen One." **Old Ones** is borrowed from the demonology of the American horror writer H. P. Lovecraft, and while, like **Chosen One**, it is borrowed on occasion as a posting board handle, it is otherwise unproductive.

By contrast with the above terms, **Slayer** is unusually productive. First, it lends itself to other jargon, like **Slayer Handbook**, which originates in the show, and **Slayer's bag**, **Slayer's Litany**, and **Slayer sense**, which appear (sometimes much more persistently than the glossary can demonstrate) in novels based on the show. Such forms raise an interesting question. **Slayer** is the core item of slayer jargon, and **Slayer Handbook** was conceived by Marti Noxon, one of the show's writers, for the episode *What's My Line, Part 2* (24 November 1997), and so clearly belongs to slayer jargon, as well. But the hazard of fictional jargon for a fictional profession is that it does not develop naturally, but rather in authors' imaginations, and authors not associated with the show seem to feel the need, as well as the license, to develop slayer jargon beyond what the show's writers imagined. We may wonder, then, who defines the slaying profession, and whether some items of slayer jargon are more authentic than others, and those others' "imitations" of slayer jargon rather than the real thing. In the real world, for a real profession, the problem can't arise; but slayer jargon is real language from a fictional world developed by more than one author and, as a result, has some eccentric characteristics.

But plenty of slang develops from **Slayer**, as well, and one may wonder why, given the relatively shallow development of other slayer jargon. Of course, **Slayer** is what the Buffyverse is all about; the title of the show is

Buffy the Vampire Slayer. Thus, everyone from writers to fans pays more attention to **Slayerness** than to **Watcherness*,[5] and **Slayer**-based items are more likely to emanate from their keyboards. Sound and word structure probably have something to do with it, too: **Slayer** is barely a two-syllable word, and **Slayerness** much less cumbersome than **Chosen Oneness*; in some cases, /r/ is an easier sound on which to combine another word-part than /th/, and **Hellmouthdom* a helluva mouthful compared to **Slayerdom**. Thus forms like **Slayercam, Slayeresque, Slayerette, Slayerhood, Slayerish, Slayerism, Slayerpalooza, Slayersville**, and even **Slayer-o-meter** (but not **Chosen One-o-meter* or **Watcher-o-meter*) are plausible, perhaps even predictable. And some **Slayer** slang is clever, like **inner Slayer** for the 'essential person of a Slayer', by analogy with *inner child*, and extension of the term to mean 'one who dominates in some activity', as in Cordelia's famous retort in the episode *Halloween* (27 October 1997), "Look, Buffy, you may be hot stuff when it comes to demonology or whatever, but when it comes to dating, I'm the Slayer," and Buffy's challenge in Nancy Holder's novel *The Evil That Men Do* (2000, p. 298), "Who died and made you Slayer slayer?"

As Nash points out, "Any study of [jargon] needs to take some account of the interplay of *shop talk* and *show talk*; jargon links the callings people follow with the impressions they try to create." Quips like those above, so typical of discourse in the Buffyverse, support his view, as do slangy synonyms for other items of first-order slayer jargon, namely, **dust, stake**, and **vamp**. Such words simultaneously reflect several motives. First, they come from familiarity with slaying, which, practiced night after night, becomes routine and prompts casual vocabulary. Second, American teenagers inevitably resist the stuffiness of old-world jargon, as Buffy does practically from the moment she is called: in the episode *Welcome to the Hellmouth* (10 March 1997), Giles reminds her that "Into each generation a Slayer is born, one girl, in all the world, a Chosen One, born with the...," and Buffy wearily responds, "...the strength and skill to hunt the vampires, to stop the spread of evil, blah,

---

[5] Throughout this book, including the glossary, asterisks indicate that the form following is unattested. Unattested forms may be hypothetical (for instance, **Buffed typeface** assumes the verb form **Buffy*, for which there is, however, no evidence) or simply invented for purposes of illustration.

blah, blah. I've heard it, okay?" A reluctant Slayer may finally accept her destiny, but will insist on doing so on her own terms. Third, vampire slaying is a terrible business, the Slayer's burden heavy, the challenges she and her friends face constant and endless; thrust into the situation, one might respond to danger and fear with flippancy. As Giles admonishes Buffy in the episode *Gingerbread* (12 January 1999), "I'm aware of your distaste for studying vibratory stones, but as it's part of your training, I'd appreciate your glib-free attention." Perhaps that's too much to ask. I, for one, willingly allow our heroine as much glib as she needs to save the world. Again.

Though fresh-sounding, **dust** and **stake** cleave to the pattern of restrained development established by **slay**. All three develop into nouns for the activity of killing vampires—**slaying**, **dusting**, and **staking**—and all three also develop into nouns for an episode of killing—a vampire deserves a good **dusting** or a good **staking**, and sometimes a Slayer yearns for a good **slay**. Though there is no *dustage, **stakage** follows **slayage**, and **non-slayey** leads to **dusty** and **stakey**. Like **slay**, **dust** shifts to a general meaning, in which something other than a vampire goes down, as in this from Zoe-Jane Playden's "'What You Are, What's to Come': Feminisms, Citizenship, and the Divine": "My invitation, therefore, is to come on patrol with a select group of Slayers, to join Buffy, the Scoobies, and feminist thinkers, and to help in doing the dusting." And like **slay**, **stake** ends up incorporated in a common catch phrase, the former in **Slay you later** 'see you later', the latter in **Stake that** 'take that (with a stake)'. **Vamp**, on the other hand, yields many more forms: the noun is used attributively and also shifts into an adjective, not only to mean 'vampire' but something metaphorically 'undead'; it shifts into verbs, **vamped** and **vamping**, meaning 'turn (someone) into a vampire', the former subsequently shifting into the semantically related adjective and the latter into a noun for the 'state of being turned into a vampire'. And the list of developments goes on, with **bedvamp**, as in "Don't let the bedvamps bite," **henchvamp**, **nonvamp**, **Supervamp**, **vampdom**, **vamped out**, **vamp-face**, **vamp-goon**, **vampnap** 'abduct a vampire', **vamp-snuffing**, and more, including the unavoidable **vampy**, parallel to **dusty**, **non-slayey**, and **stakey**.

Dust, **stake**, and **vamp** rest on the cusp of first-order slayer jargon: They are terms for professional matters, but they are not terms used by

Slayers from time immemorial. They are terms of their place and time, jargon that sounds like slang, more like **Slayerette** and **Scooby Gang**, the most important items of second-order slayer jargon. These aren't first-order terms because they belong less to slaying than to Buffy's unique brand of it: Slayers are supposed to work alone, and there is no traditional term for a band of slayer friends, because, before Buffy, Slayers never had any. But just as Buffy alters the terms on which the Slayer slays, she opens lexical gaps that Willow and Xander happily fill with new terms. Willow introduces **Slayerette** in the episode *The Witch* (17 March 1997): "You're the Slayer, and we're, like, the Slayerettes," but the term had more or less run its course by 2001: it was somewhat debased by a term it influenced, **Cordettes**, the name given to that coven of popularity, Cordelia's friends, before she became a Slayerette herself; and it does bear an unfortunate resemblance to *majorette*, suggesting that what became the Scooby Gang served a cosmetic purpose, supportively twirling batons while Buffy staked vamps, an image not only unflattering, but contrary to fact.

Scooby Gang, introduced by Xander in the episode *What's My Line*, *Part 1* (17 November 1997), became popular for several reasons. Slayer slang (and much conversation in the Buffyverse) trades regularly on popular culture; and **Scooby Gang** is more fun than **Slayerettes**, partly because it is more susceptible to development. **Scooby Gang** is shortened to **Scoobies** and the even more familiar **Scoobs**, and **Scooby** is easier to use as an attributive noun than **Slayerette**. While **Scooby-centric** and **Scooby ganger**, though not destined for frequent use, are plausible, *Slayerette-centric and *Slayeretter are for all intents and purposes impossible. In other words, **Scooby Gang** becomes the dominant synonym because users of slayer slang can do things with it, and, as the glossary suggests, it has been used both more frequently than **Slayerette** and in a wider variety of contexts. Like **Slayerette**, though, **Scooby Gang** is a puzzling term: if those who assist her are the Gang, is the Slayer the Buffyverse's Scooby Doo?

Third-order slayer jargon, while the language of an occupation in the Buffyverse, namely, participation on the official posting board, is not jargon of the slaying profession. Three items, **Bronze**, **Beta**, and **bezoar** are most prominent in this class of slayer jargon. **The Bronze** is the name of the club to which Buffy and the Scooby Gang resort after hours, and the posting board was originally named after that club. When *BTVS* left the WB Network for UPN, Warner Brothers withdrew its support for the board, and it took some months to reestablish the Buffyverse's online community; the board's second iteration is called the **Bronze: Beta**, which participants quickly shortened to **Beta**. Those on the board became **Bronzers** (their counterparts on the **Beta** sometimes call themselves **Betarers**), who spent hours weekly, sometimes daily, **Bronzing**, or having **Bronzey** fun in **Bronzerdom**.

Each posting board, within the Buffyverse or without, is governed by a certain etiquette, and occasionally someone's behavior would be **unBronzian**. Such a person came to be called a **bezoar**, easily the most interesting item of slayer jargon. The term appears in only one episode of the show, *Bad Eggs* (12 January 1998), as the name of a sort of dinosaur demon whose offspring hatch from eggs. The posting board adopted **bezoar** as a pun: a **bezoar** is a 'bad egg; rude or offensive person'. *Bezoar*, however, is not a recent invention: it entered Middle English via Old French *bezahar*, in turn from Arabic *bāzahr*, and ultimately from Persian *pādzahr* (*pād-* 'protector', from Avestan *pātar*). One swallowed a bezoar, a sort of hairball, to mitigate the effects of poison; specific poisons could only be slowed by specific bezoars. It seems unlikely that Marti Noxon, who wrote *Bad Eggs*, or any of those, like Joss Whedon, who could have influenced the episode's script, reinvented this uncommon, historically sedimented word; rather, one suspects that Noxon, who knows a great deal about the occult and its history, had encountered the word in its original sense, liked the sounds, and chose it as a demon moniker.[6]

Activity on the **Bronze** requires that one learn posting-board jargon, some of it typical of all boards, some local to the **Bronze** and the **Beta**. For instance, people like me visit the board without *posting* and *lurk*

---

[6] Currently, bezoar is an unexpectedly familiar term, not only in the Buffyverse, but courtesy of J. K. Rowling's Harry Potter books: according to Harry's professor Snape, in *Harry Potter and the Sorcerer's Stone* (New York: Scholastic, 1998, p. 138), "A bezoar is a stone taken from the stomach of a goat and it will save you from most poisons." Chronology makes Rowling's potential influence on Noxon problematic: Rowling's book was copyrighted in 1997, but the book was issued in the United States in 1998; Bad Eggs aired on 12 January 1998, but the script must have been written somewhat earlier. Unless Noxon read the book before it was released in the U.S., one must conclude that both Rowling and Noxon "rediscovered" the term at about the same time, a remarkable coincidence.

instead, reading the *posts* of others. Participants may log on illicitly while at work; on the **Bronze** and the **Beta**, at least, work is known as *whup* (as in *big whup*, one supposes), and if the boss comes by unexpectedly, the shirker in question may sign off quickly with *poof*. Interestingly, following a word-formative practice emphasized in the show, these terms rapidly developed alternate forms: **postage**, **lurkage**, **whuppage**, and **poofage**. In other words, third-order jargon got slanged. Whereas **Chosen One** and **Watcher**, terms at the heart of Slayer mythology, and **dust** and **stake**, terms central to the practice of slaying, have resisted development, jargon removed once or twice from the center easily mingles with slayer slang.

Slayer Slang

Karen Eileen Overbey and Lahney Preston-Matto, in their excellent article, "Staking in Tongues: Speech Act as Weapon in Buffy," conclude that

> Buffy is able to survive longer than the other Slayers because she is embedded in language and because she embodies language. It is a very particular language, with its own vernacular, but it behaves like all languages in that it creates, it compiles, it translates, it follows well-defined rules, it draws on shared knowledge, and it must be wielded with precision in order to be effective.... Any Slayer can brandish a weapon, but for Buffy the Vampire Slayer, the tongue is as pointed as the stake.

Of course, when Overbey and Preston-Matto say that Buffy has survived longer than other Slayers, they mean that the character doesn't end up dead (or, at least, not permanently dead); but the show has survived, even prospered, against all odds, and its success derives in large part from the show's language.

Buffy has introduced new slang terms and phrases in nearly every episode, many of them formed in the usual ways, some of them at the crest of new formative tendencies (for further discussion of which, see Chapter 2). The show incorporates familiar slang, too; the familiar and newly coined slayer slang together compose a particularly vivid snapshot of current American teen slang. Undoubtedly, most slayer slang will prove ephemeral, not that there's anything wrong with that; indeed, short-lived terms and tendencies are often significant in their time and can influence the course of American English, though once they disappear, we may not see the connections between them and what follows them (see Chapter 4). Some items of slayer slang, however, steadily intrude on everyday speech and may be here to stay, not only as slang, but as standard American English (see Chapter 3).

While much of the show's slang reproduces the current teen lexicon—good fortune for slang lexicographers, who comb the media for words generally spoken, and then only recently—*Buffy the Vampire Slayer* not only invents slang, but intends to do so. As Sarah Michelle Gellar, the actress who plays Buffy, explained to *Rolling Stone* (2 April 1998), "'Let me tell you how un-Buffy I am.... For the first episode, I come in and yell, "What's the sitch?" I did not know what "sitch" meant. I still have to ask Joss, "What does this mean?" because I don't speak the lingo. I think he makes it up half the time.' 'The slang? I make it all up,' says Whedon cheerfully," though Gellar more accurately estimates the show's linguistic creativity. Once America's busiest teen, Gellar surely knows plenty of slang, and her ignorance of Whedon's lingo is one index of its novelty. Viewers recognize and appreciate the show's characteristic innovation: while playing the *Buffy the Vampire Slayer* Drinking Game (for which the official shot glasses come in handy), viewers are invited to drink whenever "Buffy utters a 'Buffy-ism,'" though we are told that this category "Does not include CBSs (Cute Buffy Sayings) like: 'Goodbye stakes, hello flying fatalities.'" According to the rules, CBSs deserve two sips where **Buffy-isms** warrant only one, but the game neatly distinguishes the show's lexicon from its discourse.

Buffy employs plenty of familiar slang, some recorded in dictionaries and some not. A few terms have been around for a long time. The oldest item is probably **otherwhere** 'elsewhere', as when Buffy says, in the episode *Band Candy* (10 November 1998), "Also, I think she [Joyce Summers] wanted me otherwhere." Though absent from dictionaries, Mark Twain recorded a form of *otherwhere* in *A Tramp Abroad* (1880): "I saw no idiots there, but the captain said, 'Because of late years the government has taken to lugging them off to asylums and otherwheres.'" It seems unlikely that the show's writers borrowed the item from Twain; more likely, they reinvented the term, which is, after all, composed of common and semantically associated parts.

But David Greenwalt undoubtedly borrowed **five-by-five**, in the sense 'good, satisfied' (metaphorically the dimensions of *square* 'fine, in agreement, in accord', as in "Everything's *square*" or "It's all right, we're *square*"), from well-established American slang: the *Historical Dictionary of American Slang* records the term from the 1940s, as an item of U.S. military slang, and the dictionary's most recent citation for the word is dated 1983, suggesting that, though infrequently, speakers continue to use it. Greenwalt imported **five-by-five** to the Buffyverse in the episode *Faith, Hope, and Trick* (13 October 1998), when Faith says, "Hey, as long as you don't go scratchin' at me or humpin' my leg, we're five-by-five, ya know?"; subsequent use in Doug Petrie's *Revelations* (17 November 1998) provides lexically useful context: "How are you?" Buffy asks Faith, to which she responds, "Five-by-five." "I'll interpret that as good," glosses Buffy in turn, and very near *HDAS*'s 'perfect, fine'. **Five-by-five** so absolutely belongs to Faith that, when Faith and Buffy switch bodies in the episode *Who Are You?* (29 February 2000), and Faith responds to Joyce Summers's "Are you sure you're okay?" with an automatic "Five-by-five," the irony chills viewers to the bone.

If Faith's idiosyncratic slang veers toward the ancient and the obscure, other characters favor the teen mainstream: "Don't worry, I can **deal**," Buffy assures her companions; "So, you're not *down* with Angel," she acknowledges of Spike, once Angel's rival among Sunnydale vampires; "That's the sound she makes when she's speechless with **geeker** joy," Xander explains of Willow; "Great," says Willow, "I'll give Xander a call. What's his number? Oh, yeah, 1-800-I'm dating a *skanky ho*"; "You just went O.J. on your girlfriend," Buffy remarks to one unfortunate; "My egg *went postal* on me," she explains after a monster hatches from it. Buffy, just like any real American teen, develops crushes on **hotties**, but if the love is unrequited, the situation, *like, totally heinous, Buffy*, far from abject, *chills*. Maybe she'll stay at home on Saturday and *veg* rather than indulge the boy's unromantic *riff*. If the **hottie** in question asks her out again, she might see an *upside* and be *good to go*, or she might ask herself, *"What's up with that?,"* refuse him sarcastically with archaic, and therefore insincere, slang, like "Wow, you're a *dish*," and then **bail**. *Whatever*, you get the idea.

All of the forms above have been uttered in episodes of the show, though not all appear in the glossary;[7] all have been fairly popular items of American slang, either at one point or another during the show's run or throughout it; they are familiar to parents and teachers and others who wouldn't use them; no one would mistake them for slang that Whedon and Company had made up. Some less familiar items of slayer slang may seem new, and, indeed, they are relatively fresh; but the writers have plucked them from their favorite movies. When, in the 1992 film, Buffy responds to her first Watcher's request that she accompany him to the cemetery, "What's your damage?," she echoes a line from the dark comedy classic *Heathers* (1989), written by Daniel Waters and directed by Michael Lehmann. Perhaps Whedon merely reflected popular usage, though I have found no evidence for the pre-*Heathers* popularity of **damage** meaning 'problem'; or perhaps he independently developed the relevant sense of *damage*. Chances are that he knew the film well and consciously or unconsciously borrowed the term. "All I want to do is graduate from school, go to Europe, marry Christian Slater, and die," Buffy says in the *Slayer* film; her crush on Slater probably grew from his compellingly mischievous performance in *Heathers*. Slayer slang's **much**, considered briefly later in this chapter and extensively in Chapters 2 and 3, also (as far as I can tell) first appeared in *Heathers* and is also used, rather ineptly, in the 1992 film, though brilliantly and powerfully afterwards. The coincidence, that two terms apparently new in *Heathers* appear practically at the creation of the Buffyverse, argues that both are borrowed rather than reinvented.

Similarly, Marti Noxon may have been influenced, again either consciously or unconsciously, by Paul Thomas Anderson's film *Boogie Nights* (1997), in which a character says, "You hear that bass? Right? You hear

---

[7] *While I could not include every item slayer slang shares with American teen slang or general American slang, hindsight insists that* chill, *clipped from* chill out, *should have been registered, as parallel with* **bail** *and* **deal** *and several other similar forms. As Buffy would say, following Cher in Amy Heckerling's film* Clueless (1995), "*Oops! My* **bad**."

it? It kicks. It turns. It curls up your belly, makes you wanna freaky-deaky? Got it?" Here, *freaky-deaky* is a verb meaning 'go crazy'; Noxon appears to have shifted the verb into an adjective and also shifted the meaning slightly, from *crazy* 'wild' to something more like *crazy* 'weird'. Her **freaky-deaky** occurs in the episode *All Men Are Beasts* (20 October 1998): "[Buffy:] 'Oh, boy, Faith and her nutty books.' [Giles:] 'Exploring Demon Dimensions and History of Acathla.' [Buffy:] 'Yeah, and she still listens to heavy metal. Freaky-deaky.'" The whimsical reduplication, which sounds like a caught-off-guard, on-the-spot creation, is Buffy's attempt to cover for the fact that she, not Faith, is unexpectedly hitting the books—she doesn't want to raise Giles's expectations. And Whedon may have borrowed Willow's "Oh, great! I'm so the **Net Girl**" (*Lie to Me*, 3 November 1997) from "Virtuality," a song on Rush's album *Test for Echo* (Atlantic, 1996):

> Net boy, net girl
> Send your signal 'round the world;
> Let your fingers walk and talk
> And set you free.
> Net boy, net girl
> Send your impulse 'round the world;
> Put your message in a modem
> And throw it in the Cyber Sea.

The combining forms -*girl* and -*guy* are so prevalent in slayer slang, however, and Willow's proclivity for research on the Internet so obvious, that, in this case, Whedon may have rederived the term.

A related term, **girly girl**, seems to have been in the air, though not dispersed as widely as forms like **chill** and **deal**, rather than borrowed from a particular text: "Don't forget, you're supposed to be a girly girl, like the rest of us," Willow reminds Buffy in the episode *Phases* (27 January 1998). This item probably imitates *manly man*, a parallel form of which both writers and viewers are probably aware; certainly it occurred to Tracey Forbes when writing *Where the Wild Things Are* (25 April 2000): "Oh, who's the puffed up manly man?" *Manly man* is at least as old as Chaucer's description of the Monk in the General Prologue to *The Canterbury Tales*. Not all similar words admit similar reduplication: there are no *guyly guys or *boyly boys, so **girly girl** is a less predictable form than the simplicity of its elements would suggest. Though unrecorded elsewhere, **girly girl** is in general use. For instance, Natalie Maines, in the magazine Q (July 1999, p. 36/1), thus compares the Spice Girls to her own group, the Dixie Chicks: "'We're musicians and they're entertainers, but we're very girly girls,' she concedes, fiddling with her hair extensions. 'We like to play dress-up.'" On MTV's reality-based series, *The Real World: Hawaii* (1999), a cast member remarks, "I was definitely the girly girl of the house," a comment prompted by a kiss between two of her female housemates, one an acknowledged lesbian, so that the sense seems to be 'straight girl', a specialized meaning that assumes general awareness of the term and its more common meaning.

But the show does more than merely capture current teen slang; rather, it is endlessly, if unevenly, inventive. Thus Buffy, only tentatively supporting the romance budding between Xander and Cordelia in *Bewitched, Bothered, and Bewildered* (10 February 1998), assures them, "I'm glad that you guys are getting along, **almost really**." Vampires, apparently cast into fashion limbo on the day they become undead, are often marked by their unstylish wardrobes. "Look at his jacket," says Buffy of one them, in *Welcome to the Hellmouth* (10 March 1997). "It's dated?" asks Giles, to which Buffy responds, "It's **carbon-dated**." When Cordelia dumps him in *Bewitched, Bothered, and Bewildered*, Xander asks a young, not awfully proficient witch to cast a love spell on Cordelia; when it backfires and affects everyone BUT Cordelia, he muses to Giles, "Every woman in Sunnydale wants to make me her **cuddle-monkey**."[8]

Most of us are lucky if we're carefree, but the Slayer thinks in grander terms: "I don't have a destiny," she retorts in *Becoming, Part 1* (12 May 1998), when reminded of her cosmic role, "I'm **destiny-free**." When bitten by his infant nephew, Oz is shocked to learn, in *Phases* (27 January 1998), that he belongs to a family of werewolves: "It's not every day you find out you're a werewolf," he explains, "That's fairly **freaksome**." In

---

[8] This last form is not quite original. Though cuddle-bunny is the only form entered in slang dictionaries, cuddle + ANIMAL TYPE appears to be an active species of combination in American English, for instance, as reflected in "'Must you eat like a beast cuddle bear?'" from James Hynes's The Lecturer's Tale (New York: Picador, 2001, p. 168).

spite of the lunar cycle, Oz's popularity, his social position, is intact, but not everyone in high school is so lucky, as Cordelia, ever alert on such matters, points out: "Doesn't Owen realize he's **hitting a major backspace** by hanging out with that loser?" (*Never Kill a Boy on the First Date*, 31 March 1997). Teens map their own linguistic territory, as opposed to their parents', with slang, and sometimes "improve" earlier slang to stake their own generation's claim. In *When She Was Bad* (15 September 1997), Cordelia complains to a petulant Buffy, "Whatever is causing the Joan Collins 'tude, deal with it. Embrace the pain, spank your **inner moppet**, whatever, but get over it." Cordelia's coinage puts her divorced parents' pop-psychological jargon in its place.

With vampire slaying and other important teen responsibilities imminent in *Innocence* (20 January 1998), Buffy and her cohort are forced to do a **round robin**, which, as Willow glosses, is "where everybody calls everybody else's mom and tells them they're staying at everybody's house." Slang for Sunnydale teens, as for teens worldwide, serves as a transgressive code. Fun abounds for average teenagers, who **round robin** to party in the Sunnydale graveyard, but, as the Slayer who inevitably saves them from rising vampires ruminates in *What's My Line?, Part 1* (17 November 1997), "It's all **mootville** for me." Instead, she's forced to play miniature golf with her mother's boyfriend; when she cheats and the boyfriend, actually a robot who makes people like him by lacing baked goods with pleasant sedatives, overreacts, she admits, "Yeah, I kicked my ball in, **put me in jail**, but he totally **wigged**" (*Ted*, 8 December 1997). Man or robot, the prospect of a boyfriend for Mom unsettles her: "You know how dispiriting it is for me to even contemplate you grownups having **smoochies**" (*Halloween*, 27 October 1997), a sentiment echoed in the hearts and minds, at least, of teen viewers everywhere.

Lest the show seem "cleaner" than other adolescent TV, sex comes up frequently, especially regarding Buffy's relationship with Angel. Angel, though a vampire, had regained his soul, but when he and Buffy have sexual relations, her first, he finally experiences true happiness, the trigger that fires his soul back to Hell. Given the plot on its own terms, and the way in which the story metaphorically represents one take on adolescent sexual experiment (whatever boys say before sex, they're monsters afterwards, sex kills, etc.), references to sex in the early episodes are, for the most part, predictably innocent, though that changes dramatically in Season Four and from then on. When Faith arrives in Sunnydale in Season Three, she is already sexually active, her sexual language potent and notably absent from the dictionary record: "Bet you and Scott have been up here **kicking the gear shift**," she remarks to Buffy as they hunt vampires on Lovers' Lane; unable to leave the subject alone, she asks, "Do you ever catch kids doing the **diddy** out here?" (*All Men Are Beasts*, 20 October 1998). Faith's sexual references aren't always euphemistic and lighthearted, however. At her earthiest, in *Bad Girls* (9 February 1999), she grunts: "I mean, I'm sorry, it's just, all this sweating nightly, side-by-side action, and you never put in for a little after-hours **unh**?"

It is difficult to imagine the value of such terms to the show, embedded as they are in a rich and dynamic context, context that resists excerption. Meaning, then, is sometimes difficult to isolate, but not the sociolinguistic importance of slayer slang: every major character on the show coins or derives terms to reflect subtly his or her social and psychological experience. The result is clever, precise, and expressive, as the language of adults, slang or other, naturally cannot be. Neither Buffy nor any of her associates is, as Oz denominates a particularly dim bulb in *Phases* (27 January 1998), "a master of the **single entendre**,"[9] and the show's continual use of slang, not to mention its running commentary on the English language, successfully dignifies teen language and the range of teen experience for which it speaks.

Evidence already quoted proves that the English language often occupies the writers' minds, and thus it often occupies the characters' minds, as well. *Buffy the Vampire Slayer* is an especially language-conscious television show. The characters are backhanded definers ("Man, that's like, I don't know, that's moxie, or something"), bemused grammarians (in one episode, Willow struggles to determine whether one should say *slayed* or *slew*), amateur etymologists ("'The whole nine yards'—what does it mean? This is going to bother me all day"), or self-conscious stylists ("Again, so many words. Couldn't we just say, 'We be in trouble?...

---

[9] *The earliest known use of* **single entendre** *seems to be that of playwright George S. Kaufman, who reportedly said to Howard Dietz, about Dietz's play* Between the Devil (1937), *"I understand your new play is full of single entendre."*

Gone.' Notice the economy of phrasing. 'Gone.' Simple, direct."), whatever the situation demands. "Apparently Buffy has decided that what's wrong with the English language is all those pesky words," Xander remarks in one episode. But the problem may not be the absolute number of words so much as the plethora of inadequately expressive ones. As the show continually demonstrates, teens dissatisfied with the language they inherit can invent a language in which the words are not pesky but relevant.

Besides contributing items to the slang lexicon, slayer slang intensifies current formative practices in slang: it glories in them, certainly, but it also constitutes, by exaggerating them, a critique of those practices. For instance, the writers acknowledge that slang increasingly trades on references to popular culture by shifting proper names into other parts of speech, both verbs and adjectives. Thus Xander asks in *Puppet Show* (5 May 1997), "Does anyone feel like we've been **Keyser Sozed**?" after the character in *The Usual Suspects* when he means 'tricked, manipulated'. Afraid that Halloween will get out of hand, Xander remarks in *Halloween* (27 October 1997), "Halloween quiet? I figured it would have been a big ole vamp **Scareapalooza**," from the alternative rock festival *Lollapalooza*; similarly he argues in *The Wish* (8 December 1998), "Look, you wanna do **Guiltapalooza**, fine, but I'm done with that."

Xander is not the only character who watches television and rents videos. Concerned about the robot boyfriend's influence over her mother, Buffy worries to Willow, in *Ted* (8 December 1997), that "Mom has been totally different since he's been around." "Different like happy?" Willow asks. "No," says Buffy, "like **Stepford**." Men, Faith surmises, in a different conversation, are the less dynamic sex. "Every guy, from **Manimal** to **Mr. I-Loved-The English Patient** has beast in him," she warns Buffy in *All Men Are Beasts* (3 November 1998), not that Buffy takes Faith's judgments at face value. Sometimes, as in *Doppelgangland* (23 February 1999), she's sympathetic: "I know Faith's not gonna be on the cover of **Sanity Fair**, but she had it rough." At other times, she's less inclined to be charitable. Buffy's mother, who likes Faith, questions Buffy's mounting criticism in the episode *Faith, Hope, and Trick* (13 November 1998): "Does anybody else think Faith is creepy?" "No," Buffy concedes, "but I'm the one getting **single-white-femaled** here."

Buffy even memorializes some of her school assignments in slayer slang. In *Band Candy* (10 November 1998), she resists door-to-door candy sales to support the marching band as diplomatically as she can: "I'm sure we love the idea of going all **Willy Loman**, but we're not in the band." Buffy is not a particularly diligent student and seems not to have understood much about *Death of a Salesman* from Cliffs Notes, but literature is not the primary source of her vocabulary, anyway. She hears patterns in language and reproduces them in slayer slang. For instance, though inattentive during chemistry class, she remembers the sound of phrases like "oxidation reduction reaction" and bends the sound to suit her own slangy purposes: "Before we were going out," her almost b' ;friend Scott muses in *Homecoming* (3 November 1998), "you seemed so full of life, like a force of nature. Now you just seem distracted all the time." "I'm getting better, honest," Buffy reassures him, "In fact, from here on, you're going to see a **drastic distraction reduction. Drastic distraction reduction**...try saying that ten times fast." Or maybe this phrase is less a deft malapropism than imitation psychoanalytic jargon, for it's Faith, not Buffy, who resists therapeutic regimens: "I don't wanna get all **twelve-steppy**," she warns in *Enemies* (16 March 1999), while admitting that she may be an overly enthusiastic killer, a candidate for Slayers Anonymous.

Buffy seems especially attracted to words with a retro sound: in *Faith, Hope, and Trick* (13 October 1998), a vampire forever trapped in seventies garb is **Slut-o-rama**, her boyfriend **Disco Dave**; and while trying to reassure Xander that she's his reliable friend in *The Wish* (8 December 1998), she sounds a bit like a late-night television commercial: "I'm here for you Xand. I'm **Support-o-gal**." When Faith admires her for her pent-up anger, Buffy demurs: "I mean, you really got some quality rage going," Faith congratulates her in *Homecoming* (3 November 1998), "Really gives you an edge." "**Edge Girl**. Just what I always wanted to be," says Buffy, fusing contemporary "Edge" culture with the much earlier *It girl*. Of course, this impressive range of cultural reference reflects not Buffy's command of twentieth-century cultural history, but the combined allusive tendencies of several writers and directors. Such collaboration has established *BTVS* as the mint in which items of current teen slang are struck, mass-produced, and then passed nationwide.

The show likes to push certain formative tendencies to the extreme and, in such mimicry, aptly describes current slang, though particular items thus produced are unlikely to enter the general slang lexicon. For instance, like the core English lexicon, slang considers -*free* a more or less infinitely productive suffix. *Carefree*, formed to replace an archaic sense of *careless*, begat such forms as *guilt-free*, a synonym for *guiltless*, and such forms in turn begat a tribe of advertising words, like *sugar-free*, that have gradually superseded their -*less* counterparts. Buffy and her companions variously describe themselves as **destiny-free**, **move-free**, and, most interesting in this list, **fester-free** and **glib-free**, which push the envelope a little by combining *free* with verbs and adjectives, previously unlikely parts of speech.

The prefix *un-* is similarly productive: something that isn't *cool* also isn't **warm*, but is *uncool*; a soft drink that contains no cola isn't called, say, **citrusade*, but the *Un-cola*. By analogy, then, in *Inca Mummy Girl* (6 October 1997), Buffy admonishes Giles, "C'mon, Giles, budge. No one likes an **unbudger**," and Willow can say of Giles in *Halloween* (27 October 1997), "Actually, he was **unmad**." Though not especially clever or descriptive, such words may reflect meanings inadequately conveyed in the standard lexicon: when one is **unmad**, one certainly isn't angry, but there's no reason to assume that one is happy, either; so the word mediates two common emotional states, and thus identifies a third. Such unusual uses of the prefix *un-* are reinforced by vocabulary specific to vampires. In *Lovers' Walk* (24 November 1998), Drusilla, a recurring vampire character, sends her erstwhile boyfriend, Spike, what Cordelia, in *Revelations* (17 November 1998), calls a **dump-o-gram**, and he petulantly observes, "Yeah, I've got an **unlife**, you know," not a comment on how empty his life will be once she's left it, but an apt description of a vampire's very existence. At least since Bram Stoker's *Dracula* (1897), vampires have been called the *Undead*, any vampire could be called *an undead*, and vampires have been attributively *undead*. Parallels with **unmad** are obvious: **undead** and **unlife** signify the state that is NEITHER dead NOR alive.

While prefix *un-* precisely distinguishes exotic states from familiar ones, other prefixes reflect adolescent attitudes best in muddier meanings. In "I Do," the hit single from her album *Firecracker* (Geffen, 1997), Lisa Loeb sings, "I'm tired of overthinking." I suppose that one can think too much or too often about a particular subject at a particular time, yet I am unconvinced that *overthinking* is possible in general; rather, I suspect that the word reflects a frequent adolescent concern, sometimes recovered by adults, an unwillingness to think as hard as certain situations in life demand or deserve. In the same year, in the episode *Halloween* (27 October 1997), Buffy would say of a character that "He's not exactly one to overshare." **Overshare**, formed along the same lines as *overthink*, compactly and neutrally expresses the act of being stingy (with things or information, etc.), for which standard English has no word, and for which the slang lexicon in the past depended on pejoratives, like *jew*. But this meaning is produced at the level of the sentence, primarily as a matter of tone, namely, sarcasm. In any literal sense, it's difficult to conceive what it would mean for someone to **overshare**, or how an observer could judge that, though one had shared adequately, that is, just short of *oversharing*, one somehow had shared too little. Imprecise or illogical words usually express psychologically imprecise states, like hopes, fears, and disappointments, but this criticizes neither such words nor their speakers, because the words perfectly convey incompletely rationalized but nonetheless real experiences. As Buffy says in *Welcome to the Hellmouth* (10 March 1997), "Can you vague that up for me?"[10]

Slayer slang, like all slang, is notable for a sort of casual efficiency, what many language purists decry as verbal laziness. Many of the examples above show that slayer slang is as synthetic, as complicating, as it is efficient, but the efficiency is there, too, for instance in forms like the adjective **genius**, as in Cordelia's "I mean, whose genius idea was that?" from the episode *I Only Have Eyes for You* (28 April 1998) either clipped from *ingenious* and respelled, or a shift of noun *genius* into an adjective. One way or the other, **genius** is a shorter than usual form of the adjective. Willow and Oz sometimes employ elliptical items, like **still**, that

---

[10] In the *Winter* 1998 issue of the official Buffy the Vampire Slayer *magazine, an uneven glossary (pp. 50–51), enters* **vague up** *as* *vogue up *'make more attractive', but I have listened to the line on videotape several times and arrive at this form, instead. The more recently published Script Book: First Season, Volume 1 (New York: Pocket Books, 2000, p. 33) confirms my transcription.*

also participate in the general tendency to abbreviate forms, for instance, "So I'd still, if you'd still." "I'd still. I'd very still," from *Phases* (27 January 1998), a speech habit perhaps once again learned from *Heathers* (1988), which includes elliptical *very*, as in "How very" and "Don't worry, Ram's been so sweet lately, consoling me and stuff—it'll be very," or formed by analogy with the now ubiquitous elliptical *with*, as in "I'm going to the movies, do you want to go with?"

Sometimes shortening is so extreme as to be impenetrable without considerable cultural knowledge, for example in **W/Xness**, a form developed, not by the show, but on the Bronze posting board (2 June 2001): "After all these seasons without even a shred of W/Xness." Here the puzzled reader must recognize *W* as an initial for *Willow* and the X as an initial for *Xander*; but a great deal of the term's semantic content is condensed into the /. The slash stands for 'imagined in a romantic or sexual relationship with' and originated with a genre of fan fiction (that is, fiction based on characters and other aspects of a television show, written by fans of that show) called slash fiction. According to Justine Larbalestier,

> Slash fiction—so called because of the slash between the two characters linked—is fanfic in which two characters not explicitly romantically or sexually linked in a show are brought together. Originally a *Star Trek* phenomenon, the first slashed pair was Kirk/Spock...the earliest examples of the genre were all same-sex couples and were a means of opening up the universe of the show—*Star Trek* was a heterosexual universe; slashing highlighted the unspoken possibilities that existed between Kirk and Spock, turning homosocial love into homosexual desire. This has long extended to any pairing not directly posited by a show.

So the posting board participant does nothing new in slashing Willow and Xander, but, for the uninitiated, the hidden background to slash and the radical shortening is bound to confuse, and, in a situation like **W/X**, suffixation with -*ness* is downright disorienting, since the suffix makes sense only if you know the meaning of the base to which it attaches.

Buffy's writers shift adjectives to nouns more frequently than is generally the case. Sometimes the shift operates on a slang item, as in "Just seeing the two of you kissing after everything that happened, I leaned towards the **postal**" (*Revelations*, 17 November 1998). But such shifts mostly reinvigorate common items from the standard lexicon: "If Angel's doing something wrong," Xander insists, "I want to know—'cause it gives me a **happy**" (*Lie to Me*, 3 November 1997); "Stop with the **crazy**; go talk to Angel," Willow suggests in *Enemies* (17 March 1999); "Relax, Will," Buffy reassures her in *Becoming, Part 1* (12 May 1998), "I was making with the **funny**"; "What's with the **grim**?" asks Xander in *Gingerbread* (12 January 1999); "Love makes you do the **wacky**," Buffy pronounces in *Some Assembly Required* (22 September 1997), and isn't it the truth?

All of this linguistic activity—creation, development, and dissemination—reminds us that, while slayer slang may provide a snapshot of current American teen slang, slang and language generally demand a moving picture. As Buffy would say, slayer slang "is all part of the glamorous world of vampire slayage" (*Out of Mind, Out of Sight*, 19 May 1997). But already it belongs not only to that world, or even only to the Buffyverse, as some of the "unchosen" have already begun to prove.

Slayer Style

It's not polite to belch publicly, not even around friends, unless, of course, it's the sort of "eructation" about which Walt Whitman writes in "Slang in America":

> Slang, or indirection, [is] an attempt of common humanity to escape from bald literalism, and express itself illimitably, which in the highest walks produces poets and poems, and doubtless in pre-historic times gave the start to, and perfected, the whole immense tangle of the old mythologies....slang, too, is the wholesome fermentation or eructation of those processes eternally active in language, by which froth and specks are thrown up, mostly to pass away, though occasionally to settle permanently and chrystallize [sic].

Many language purists take a less charitable view of linguistic burping and hope that the froth and specks, the words and perhaps even the processes thus thrown up in slang, indeed will pass away, not that there's anything wrong with that, unless one believes that the only good words are old words.[11]

As James Sledd has argued, though, slang is perhaps somewhat more disruptive than mere bad manners, and the conservatives among us have good reason to question, even to resist, slang:

> When a teacher warns his students against slang, he reaffirms his allegiance to the social order that created him. Typically slang is a para-code, a system of substitutes for statusful expressions which are used by people who lack conventional status and do not conduct important affairs of established communities. Slang flourishes in the areas of sex, drinking, narcotics, racing, athletics, popular music, and other crime—a "liberal" language of things done as ends in themselves by gentlemen who are not gentlemen and dislike gentility. Genteel pedagogues must naturally oppose it, precisely because slang serves the outs as a weapon against the ins. To use slang is to deny *allegiance* to the existing order, either jokingly or in earnest, by refusing even the words which represent convention and signal status; and those who are paid to preserve the status quo are prompted to repress slang as they are prompted to repress any other symbol of revolution.

Whitman and Sledd propose quite different but, in fact, complementary, versions of slang. For Whitman, slang, at its best, is art; art demands style, and style is an individuating quality of language, as well as of any other artistic medium. Sledd views slang as the linguistic activism of one community within, yet apart from, another; so, while slang may characterize the individual speaker, its cohesive force, the way it draws the statusless together and constructs focused opposition toward the conventionally statusful, is ultimately important. In other words, because Whitman and Sledd are both right, slang is the agent simultaneously of cultural opposition, cohesion within a dissenting language community, and individual style within that community.

Slayer slang illustrates slang's complexity, the blend of Whitman's and Sledd's perspectives as just described, particularly well: though the show has an unusually wide demographic, most of its viewers, thus most us-

---

[11] *Dumas and Lighter, in "Is Slang a Term for Linguists?," provide an excellent synopsis of language purists' various aversions to slang.*

ers of slayer slang, are too young to have achieved "conventional status" or "conduct the important affairs of established communities." As a result, they have established their own community, the Buffyverse, the world of all things Buffy. Fluency in slayer slang not only indicates membership in that community, but, like gravity in the physical universe, is one of the forces that holds the Buffyverse together; citizens of the Buffyverse position themselves within the community by means of slayer style, the poetic or individuating use of slayer slang. Belonging to the group and asserting individuality within that group are partners, as Sledd would say, in the same crime: style distinguishes slayer slang from mainstream English, and its users operate within preexisting parameters, yet their individual styles motivate change within slayer slang, leading recursively to revised parameters and new distinctions between slayer slang and general American English.

Slayer slang is more complicated, and thus more interesting, than we might guess. Fourteen-year-olds share the official Buffy posting board (originally The Bronze, now Bronze: Beta) with college students and college professors; erstwhile parents converse with other people's children about Buffy themes and other stuff; posters from the States share worldviews with Buffyholics from Canada, Germany, and Singapore. Hannah Tucker watches the show with her father and younger sister. Tucker's account flouts conventional wisdom, for as Rebecca Wiseman advises in Queen Bees & Wannabes,

> **Don't use the slang your daughter uses.** There's nothing more ridiculous to a teen than an adult who tries to be hip by using teen slang. Slang changes so fast that it's impossible to keep up anyway. Nevertheless, some parents think that if they use it, they'll relate to their daughter better. Not true. It only looks like you're trying too hard—and there's nothing worse to a teen. If she uses a word you don't understand, ask her to explain it to you. She may laugh at how clueless you are, but it demonstrates that you respect and are interested in what she has to say and how she describes her world.

Since they not only watch the show with him, but actually ENJOY doing so, it's reasonable to assume that Hannah and her sister talk with Ken about **Slayers** and **Watchers** and **Hellmouths, slayage** and world **saveage**. If that gives Ken a big **happy**, the girls won't **wig**: rather than laugh at his cluelessness, they would welcome him as another member of the slayer slang–speaking community. Thus slayer slang is unexpectedly problematic, for it is hard to identify a common ground of dissent for teenage daughters and their much older, conventionally important father; and, since heterogeneity in this context could amount to entropy, slayer slang faces a greater-than-usual burden, as it attempts to center the Buffyverse and hold it together over time and space, but also as it simultaneously, almost paradoxically, allows speakers the freedom to assert individual styles.

Given the extraordinary burden slayer slang faces, then, we search for mechanisms to explain its success. Common interest in all things Buffy, articulated in slayer jargon, is undoubtedly a factor: no one outside the Buffyverse will know that "As long as there have been demons, there has been a Slayer. One girl in all the world, a Chosen One, born with the strength and skill to hunt vampires and other deadly creatures…to stop the spread of their evil. When one Slayer dies, the next is called and trained by the Watcher." **Slayer**, **Chosen One**, and **Watcher**, while formed from common enough English words, clearly have special meanings here, as do **dust** and **stake**, **Scooby Gang**, **undead** for all those demons, especially vampires, who are the living dead, and **vamp** as the familiar term (the term you would use if you **dusted** them every day) for vampire. Like verbal passports, such terms identify those who flash them in conversation as citizens of the Buffyverse.

Thus slayer jargon sometimes develops into slayer slang, even very clever, memorable slang. So, in the episode *When She Was Bad* (15 September 1997), **undead** yields **Undead-American**, as in "You're a vampire. Or is that an offensive term? Should I say 'Undead-American'?" and (from a somewhat cryptic exchange on the official posting board [24 July 2002]), **unDead Sea Scrolls**: "Judas: Don't worry. I'm sure that as soon as those pertinent unDead Sea Scrolls are publicized, you'll be vindicated and Satan will stop chewing on you." **Hellmouth** is appropriated on the posting board for quite other meanings, for instance, as a simple expletive ("Hey, I was born in L.A.…so what in the Hellmouth am I doing in Seattle?" [29 April 1999]) and as an oblique one ("I actually still have my AOl Hellmouth acc[oun]t" [1 September 2000]). It's safe to say that no one outside the Buffyverse would immediately understand these forms, at least, not with the specialized meanings first developed in slayer jargon. So, in slayer slang, the Buffyverse secedes from general American English, and both jargon and slang are the badges by which one rebel recognizes another—anyone who sticks with slayer jargon and never develops slayer slang effectively will speak with an "accent" and invite curiosity, if not suspicion.

Speakers of slayer slang, like users of American slang generally, create new words on the fly by shifting a familiar word from its accustomed grammatical function to a new one: "I cannot believe," Buffy says in one episode, "that you of all people are trying to **Scully** me." As Eve V. Clark and Herbert H. Clark pointed out several years ago, however, there is a semantic problem represented in this particular sort of shift, from proper name to verb, because the name itself is merely referential, not definable: what meaning shifts along with the function, from noun to verb, in the case above? There must be an intermediate, unarticulated step in the development of such a word, when the speaker derives from the name a common noun with a meaning, before shifting that intermediate noun into the verb. But with what meaning should the word be endowed? Which is Dana Scully's essential characteristic, the one that an auditor surely will associate with the verbed name, her scientific skepticism or her religious piety? For such nonce-words to be comprehensible, speaker and auditors must share certain cultural knowledge (about *The X-Files* for instance), but must also agree on what counts about the person whose name ends up a verb.

Similarly, use of slayer slang **much**, shifted from adverb to adjective and even to noun, sometimes requires shared knowledge and perspective: in a sidebar in *Mademoiselle* (December 1998), Q laments, "My ex-fiancé is getting married in two weeks. Now I realize I still love him. Should I tell him?" and A responds, "Meanwhile, *My Best Friend's Wedding*/*Friends* much?" One can understand the response only if one (a) can identify the essential similarity between the film and television show and (b) will accept the use of **much** to modify a compound proper name, essentially in its adverbial sense. In other words, for some of the most general items of slayer slang, as opposed to slayer jargon, the speech community using them must cohere sufficiently to make sense of them. But, in spite of the fact that *Mademoiselle* had a large readership, the sentence quoted from it surely is not meant to be acceptable to all: it transgresses against statusful norms, and it trades on in-group semantics, in-group syntax, and even what one might call the in-group cognition necessary for agreement on semantic and syntactic meaning.

We share cultural knowledge and perspective most readily within our own respective generations; slayer slang's attempt to ameliorate the effects of generational difference, to build a type of super-speech community, certainly distinguishes it from the run of American slang. But generation matters, even in the Buffyverse. Among many formative tendencies, slayer slang habitually clips verb phrases inherited, for the most part, from the 1960s, like **bail** (out), **bug** (out), **creep** (out), **deal** (with), **freak** (out), **hang** (out), **show** (up), **team** (up), and **wig** (out), as well as adjective phrases developed from them, like **freaked** (out), **messed** (up), and **wigged** (out). Both phrasal and clipped forms are generally available from the outset, but the phrasal forms predominated until the mid-1990s, when younger folk preferred the clipped forms in order to distinguish themselves from the type of person (for instance, their parents and teachers) who would deploy the phrasal forms of their own youth, hoping to prove, as Wiseman fears, that they are down with the language of youth today. Buffy adapted to the trend smoothly: though it by no means excluded use of the phrases, it legitimated (or re-legitimated) the clipped forms, which clearly express a style. There is something subtly different between the psychologies of one who says that she can *deal with* (something) and one who says that she can *deal*; *hanging out with* (someone) is subtly different from *hanging*. Perhaps speakers of the clipped forms exhibit a certain self-sufficiency, swallowing the transactional nature of their behavior; or perhaps they are too casual, or too cool, or perhaps being too cool is being too casual to say what goes without saying. So far, I can depend only on my ear to make the distinction, but I think that Buffy's younger sister Dawn reverts to the phrasal forms, in her generational turn attempting to distinguish herself as a Y against the Xs.

To clip or not to clip—sometimes that is the question, and it is answered in part as a matter of style, of the speaker's choice to sound a certain way, to project a certain attitude. But we affiliate with others partly because we like the way they sound, or because we are attracted to or challenged by their attitude, and, when slang expresses the attitude, we are tempted to join the rebellion it represents, though, in a commodified and marketed culture, clipping is probably no more effective as a challenge to the status quo than the Gap revolution, striped sweaters that will show those with conventional status and responsibilities just how monochromatic they really are. Some aspects of current American slang bother language purists just because they accomplish so little semantically. Slayer slang is replete with words taking the suffixes *-age*, *-ness*, and *-y* (I have collected more than 200 forms among them, about 100 with *-y* alone, and this only scratches the surface of forms produced), but what do such suffixed forms supply that isn't already available in American English? If someone is engaged in **drinkage**, she's just *drinking*; and the difference between the professions of **slayage** and **slay-ing** is purely morphological, unless one takes the social and stylistic values of slang seriously enough to justify redundant forms.

It seems to me that developing a "system" of redundant forms serves cohesion within a given speech community: the forms fill no lexical gap, they aren't NECESSARY, in a formal semantic sense; but they do communicate group identity, and their use in certain situations fosters relationships within the group. Redundant suffixation and related processes in slang may be atavistic tendencies, a linguistic remnant of primate grooming, the very grooming that Robin Dunbar has argued cogently led to language use in the first place:

> The conventional view is that language evolved to enable males to do things like coordinate hunts more effectively. This is the "there's a herd of bison down by the lake" view of language. An alternative view might be that language evolved to enable the exchange of highfalutin stories about the supernatural or the tribe's origins. The hypothesis I am proposing is diametrically opposed to ideas like these, which formally or informally have dominated everyone's thinking in disciplines from anthropology to linguistics and paleontology. In a nutshell, I am suggesting that language evolved to allow us to gossip.

Of course, it is ill-advised, if not dangerous, to gossip with just anyone; the gossip's rule of thumb is to gossip within an established relationship, and nurture intimacy with gossip. If repetitive and supposedly unnecessary use of the *-age* suffix constitutes the code by which a group of speakers marks its array of mutual relationships, then it certainly serves a purpose. As Dunbar says of -*age*'s prehistory, "It seemed that, after all, a grunt was not just a grunt."

Nearly every instance of slang that holds the Buffyverse together is, in the first instance, an exercise in the speaker's individual style—or maybe I shouldn't say "in the first instance," because were there not a slayer slang that cohered before the individual speech act, no one would attempt a stylish interpretation of it. Again, slang and style, though not the same thing, are two sides of the same coin and, at every toss, each has an even chance of turning up. One could view this as a paradox, but it isn't really, because slang does originate in a sense of style, someone's decision to dissent from convention at a certain moment in a certain way, only to discover that, sometimes, individuating style is the source of a new convention; the more conventional a style of speech becomes, the less useful it is as slang, on both Whitman's and Sledd's terms, which explains why slang is generally, but not absolutely, ephemeral.

Consider, for instance, the case of **much**, described earlier. It's not strange, in colloquial speech, for **much** to collocate with verbs in brief interrogative sentences, like "Walk much?" or "Cook much?," usually sarcastic commentary on perceived ineptitude. But, as far as we can tell, **much** first collocates with adjectives in such sentences in the film *Heathers* (1989), released a few years before the Buffy film and a decade before the television show first aired. Nonetheless, **much** + ADJECTIVE (not to mention **much** + NOUN, as in the example above) is distinctive slayer slang, and the queen of **much** is Cordelia Chase, a rich, snobby, and very style-conscious foil to Buffy, who, much to her own chagrin, gradually becomes one of Buffy's inner circle.

Tact is not Cordelia's style. As she says in the episode *Killed by Death* (3 March 1998) "Tact is just not saying true stuff. I'll pass." Her use of *much* reflects that opinion, as well as a tendency to dismiss others' legitimate concerns, and a latent sense of inconvenience at being asked the question to which she responds: in *The Harvest* (10 March 1997), Buffy asks "How did he die?" and Cordelia responds, as if to say "Don't ask me!" with "I don't know"; Buffy, however, has a job to do, so continues indelicately, "Well, are there any marks?" to which Cordelia replies, "Morbid much?" One wouldn't think that others would aspire to Cordelia's obnoxious verbal style, yet they do, almost immediately, first other characters on the show, then representations of those characters in novels based on the show, and finally speakers on the very edge of the Buffyverse, whose use indicates that **much** has passed from slayer slang to general American slang, from which it will very likely move, eventually, into mainstream use.

Similarly, Buffy is the original -*age* and -*y* suffixer, the one who establishes those tendencies within slayer slang. Buffy's **slayage** and world **saveage** express her whimsy and impose a distance between her teenage life and the horrible, incomprehensible duties of Slayer. But she doesn't long possess those suffixes exclusively: she sets the example, which, as the Slayer, she naturally would; but -*age* and -*y* suffixed forms very quickly come to characterize the whole Scooby Gang, serving as the adhesive that binds them together. If, night after night, you slay vampires, you need to know who your friends are, and you know who they are because they speak the same language. Though Buffy uses the -*y* suffix first and memorably, by the end of the show's sixth season, Willow and Xander, her closest companions, aren't far behind. Use of the suffixes generalizes to every corner of the Buffyverse, where slayer slang, originating in slayer style, serves the social purposes described earlier. Indeed, Bronzers and Betarers, participants on the official posting boards, are responsible for a super-majority of -*age* suffixed forms I have collected.

Buffy's Slayer style is more persistently individual in other types of slayer slang. For instance, she leads in -*ness* suffixation, with 5 of 13 forms recorded from the show included in the glossary, though Xander speaks 4 of them, Willow 3, and Oz and Cordelia are each responsible for 1 item. But the situation is slightly more complicated than the numbers immediately suggest: **Slayerness**, though first uttered by Buffy in the episode *Choices* (4 May 1999), is repeated by Buffy magically transposed into Faith's body in *Who Are You?* (29 February 2000); and **sadness** comes from Jonathan, in the early seasons Buffy's fan, in the fifth and sixth seasons ostensibly one of Buffy's "nemesises," but, by the time he uses the -*ness* form, clearly once again on Buffy's side. In other words, **Slayerness** from the mouth of Eliza Dushku is really a Buffy utterance in *Who Are You?*, and **sadness** is a sympathetic form, Jonathan's imitation of Buffy's style. So -*ness* belongs to Buffy, at roughly twice the rate that

Xander uses it and much more frequently than any other character does.

Buffy is even more specifically characterized by her tendency to form new words from pop cultural sources, sometimes by generalizing or adapting a name and more often by verbing one. Of 32 such words included in the glossary, from both the television show and novels based on the show, Buffy is responsible for 18, Xander for 6, Willow for 3, Cordelia and Faith for 2 each, and Oz and Riley for 1 each.[12] From **Scully** (7 April 1997) to **David Lynch**, as in "So that's why time went all David Lynch" (5 February 2002), Buffy is the queen of such shifts, as surely as Cordelia is queen of shifted **much**. Although **round robin** was actually used by Willow, in the episode *Innocence* (20 January 1998), it is interesting that a glossary of Buffy terms published in the official magazine (Winter 1998) attributed the term to Buffy, perhaps suggesting that fans already associated semantic and functional shifts with the Slayer's repartee.

Of course, *Buffy the Vampire Slayer* is a fiction, and the characters exhibit verbal styles that originate in the verbal styles of the show's writers, a somewhat amusing fact, since several of the writers are Buffyatrics. As with the Scoobies, -y suffixation identifies, not a single writer's style, but the style of the whole Whedon Gang, the core group of the show's writers, including Whedon himself, Marti Noxon, Doug Petrie, David Fury, Jane Espenson, and, with regard to -y suffixing, Rebecca Kirshner. Whedon certainly initiates the process, in the show's first season (1997) but Noxon adopts it soon thereafter, as early as 12 January 1998, several months before Espenson joins in, on 10 November 1998.

But originating a form does not make it one's own, at least, not forever—remember that **much** is at least as old as *Heathers*, but it is undoubtedly one of the features most characteristic of slayer slang. Raw numbers suggest that -y is less characteristic of Whedon's style than the

---

[12] *Buffy gives us* **Be Kind—Rewind, Andy Sipowicz, Carrie** (twice), **David Lynch,** *do a* **William Burroughs, Exorcist twist, Lifetime TV, Mod Squad, Psych 101, Sabrina, Sanity Fair, Scully,** *single-white-femaled,* **spider sense, Stepford, Village People, Wild Bunch,** *and* **Willy Loman;** *Xander is credited with* **Dawson's Creek, Felicity, Full Monty, Gene and Roger, Keyser Soze,** *and the very productive* **Scooby Gang;** *Willow provides* **Jimmy Hoffa, round robin,** *and* **Sherlock;** *Faith introduces* **Mr. I-Loved-The-English Patient** *and* **twelve-steppy** *and Cordelia* **007** *and* **inner moppet;** *Oz contributes* **Waco** *and Riley* **Clark Kent.**

styles of the other writers: within the material collected here, Noxon employs the suffix 11 times, with Petrie on her heels at 10; Espenson follows with 9, Kirshner with 8, Fury with 7, and Whedon with a mere 6, roughly half the number of forms created by Noxon. Use of -y appears to be marginally more characteristic of Noxon's style than those of the others, and we have reason to accept the validity of this measure: in an interview with *Entertainment Weekly*, Noxon was quoted as saying, "We're going to get *Buffy* back to a lighter, less angsty place." *Angsty* may prove that -y suffixation is natural to Noxon, an element of her own slangy style, though the quotation's late date (13 September 2002) does not exclude the possibility that Noxon's style has been influenced by her work on the show.

Raw numbers aren't the only relevant ones, however. One might consider intensity of use, as well, and doing so attributes -y to the style of other authors. Whedon's low raw figure is even less impressive when one considers the number of episodes he has written over the years and that his 6 forms occur across 5 different episodes; Noxon has also written many episodes, and her 11 forms are spread over 8 episodes, whereas Petrie's 10 are concentrated in 6 (a greater degree of intensity, in other words); Kirshner, who has written many fewer episodes than the others, places 8 forms in only 3 episodes, a concentration of use that might justify the claim that she, though first a student of Whedon's and Noxon's style, finally makes -y a particularly significant feature of her own.

In any event, slayer style, first the literary style of the show's writers, becomes a public example as the style of the show's characters, and ultimately composes the style of the entire Buffyverse, as slayer slang becomes, not only the means to community, but finding an individual voice within that community.

References

Accounts of Whedon's career and the origins of *Buffy the Vampire Slayer* can be found in Christopher Golden and Nancy Holder, *The Watcher's Guide* (New York: Pocket Books, 1998); Kathleen Tracy, *The Girl's Got Bite: The Unofficial Guide to Buffy's World* (Los Angeles: Renaissance Books, 1998); N. E. Genge, *The*

Buffy Chronicles: The Unofficial Companion to Buffy the Vampire Slayer (New York: Three Rivers Press, 1998), and Nikki Stafford's wonderfully revised and expanded Bite Me!: An Unofficial Guide to the World of Buffy the Vampire Slayer (Toronto: ECW Press, 2002). On ratings and importance in the television market, see "Buffy Delivers Hot Ratings," in *Buffy the Vampire Slayer*, the official magazine (Winter 1998), p. 14; Jeff Jensen, on p. 64 of the extensive Buffy spread in *Entertainment Weekly* (7 September 2001); and, for Dean Valentine's opinion, Jeffrey Epstein's "Hannigan's Shenanigans," in Out (August 2001), p. 53. For Web presence, see "The E*List," in *Premiere* (October 2000), p. 70; and "Year on the Net," in *Yahoo! Internet Life* (January 2000), p. 106/1. Zweerink and Gatson's essay can be found in Rhonda V. Wilcox and David Lavery, ed., *Fighting the Forces: What's at Stake in* Buffy the Vampire Slayer (Lanham, MD: Rowman & Littlefield, 2002), pp. 239–249. Buffy found its way into Scott Brick's "Once Bitten," in *Joyfare* (November 1999), pp. 40–46; and Graceanne DeCandido's "Bibliographic Good vs. Evil in *Buffy the Vampire Slayer*," in *American Libraries* (September 1999), pp. 44–47. On Buffy and sexuality, see Tracy's *The Girl's Got Bite*, p. 1; Mim Udovitch's "What Makes Buffy Slay," *Rolling Stone* (10 May 2001), pp. 60–66; Emma Forrest's "Interview with the Vampire Slayer," *Nylon* (January 2000), pp. 60–65; Debbie Stoller's "Sarah Michelle Gellar," in "The 20 Most Fascinating Women in Politics: Women Who Rule," *George* (September 1998), pp. 110–112; Jancee Dunn's "Love at First Bite," *Rolling Stone* (2 April 1998), pp. 40–45; and Genge's *The Buffy Chronicles*, p. xiv. For highbrow Buffy, see, for excerpts from the article by McMillan and Owens, *Harper's* (July 1999), pp. 35–36; Roz Kaveney, ed., *Reading the Vampire Slayer: An Unofficial Critical Companion to Buffy and Angel* (New York: Tauris Parke, 2001); and Wilcox and Lavery, as cited above. *Slayage: The Online International Journal of Buffy Studies*, also edited by Wilcox and Lavery, resides at **www.slayage.tv**. For a thorough survey of jargon, see Walter Nash, *Jargon: Its Uses and Abuses* (Cambridge, MA: Blackwell, 1993); the first quotation from Nash appears on p. 4, the second on p. 7. The items of restaurant jargon listed and many others are discussed in my article, "The Server's Lexicon: Inquiries into Current Restaurant Jargon" *American Speech* (Spring 1988), pp. 57–83. Dumas and Lighter's "Is Slang a Word for Linguists?" was published in *American Speech* (Spring 1978), pp. 5–17. For an account of Little Willow, "Net Goddess of the Buffyverse," see Stafford (2002), cited above, pp. 149–156. Overbey and Preston-Matto's essay can be found in Wilcox and Lavery, cited above, pp. 73–84. Gellar and Whedon are quoted from Jancee Dunn's "Love at First Bite," cited above. Versions of the drinking game are available at sites all over the World Wide Web. Howard Teichman reports Kaufman's quip in *George S. Kaufman: An Intimate Portrait* (New York: Atheneum, 1972), p. 119. Justine Larbalestier's "Buffy's Mary Sue is Jonathan: Buffy Acknowledges the Fans," is among the articles in Wilcox and Lavery, cited above, pp. 227–238. Walt Whitman's seminal "Slang in America," originally publihsed in 1885, is still available in *The English Language: Essays by*

Linguists and Men of Letters, 1858—1964, edited by W. F. Bolton and David Crystal (Cambridge: Cambridge University Press, 1969), pp. 54—58; the quoted passage is on the last page. James Sledd's article, "On Not Teaching English Usage," appeared in the *English Journal* (1965), pp. 698—703; Mark Halpern, whose article "The End of Linguistics" is discussed in Chapter 4, would undoubtedly consider Sledd "dangerous"—all the more true because he is right. Dumas and Lighter's article is cited earlier. Rebecca Wiseman considers the social plight of American girls in *Queen Bees & Wannabes* (New York: Crown, 2002); the quotation is from p. 61. Eve V. Clark and Herbert H. Clark discuss the cognitive and semantic difficulties that arise "When Nouns Surface as Verbs," in the journal *Language* (1979), pp. 767—811. Robin Dunbar outlines his theory of language's pre-history in *Grooming, Gossip, and the Evolution of Language* (Cambridge, MA: Harvard University Press, 1996); I quote from pages 79 and 47, in that order. Throughout this chapter, and the subsequent ones, precise references are given only to those quotations illustrating particular words but not found in the glossary; if information about a quotation seems incomplete, you'll find more about it in the glossary under the word in question. Much of this chapter is adapted from my article "Slayer Slang," published in two parts in *Verbatim: The Language Quarterly* (Summer/Autumn 1999), with the generous permission of that journal's editor.

CHAPTER 2

Making Slayer Slang

E nglish is full of words, but the processes by which they form are relatively few. Slang forms according to the same processes as mainstream English, but it bends those processes a little in order to resist convention or the linguistic status quo. Essentially all English word-formative processes operate within slayer slang; but slayer slang, both as an engine driving the formation of new words and as a social lexicon, a style of language use, depends very much on the processes by which it is made and the novel ways in which it handles what are, by and large, the tools with which we craft new words in English.

The least potent process in slayer slang is borrowing. English has borrowed a lot of words from other languages over the centuries; French and Latin each contributed approximately 25% of English vocabulary, and English has adopted and adapted words from other languages regularly, sometimes from quite unexpected points on the globe: *tango* from Ibibio (Nigeria), *boomerang* from Dharuk (Australia), *jaguar* from Guaraní (Paraguay), and *sequoia* from Cherokee. American slang borrows much less frequently than mainstream English (though there is some intra-language borrowing, mainly from African American English slang into general American slang), and slayer slang includes only one or two borrowed forms, the German prefix *über-* (discussed further below) and perhaps the suffix in a Bronze handle, *Buffyenta*, which may reflect contact with American Spanish or Yiddish, depending on whether one interprets the item as suffixed (*Buffy* + *-ienta*) or a blend (*Buffy* + *yenta*).

Outright coinage is similarly minimal in slayer slang, but that also is no surprise, as English words aren't often newly minted, but instead

develop from already existing words. Still, slayer slang admits a few innovations, or at least near-innovations: **ooginess** may be reanalyzed from
uglies or *ooky* (or perhaps by both, in a mixed etymology); the first
element of **oogly-booglies** derives even more transparently from *uglies*,
but reduplication spins the term away from anything recorded in dictionaries; **unh**, in both the senses 'fuck' and 'thrust, as with a stake' underscores the tendency for coinages in English to imitate and lexicalize
sounds.[1] **Eeuch**, as in "Did you just eeuch my name?" from the episode
Tabula Rasa (13 November 2001), coins a word from a visceral reaction.
Bitca and **riddichio**, reanalyzed from *bitch* and *ridiculous* respectively,
are not, strictly speaking, coinages.

   Since its origin in Germanic dialects two millennia past, English has
favored compounding as a way of creating new words, and slayer slang
offers many compounds, like **beefstick**, **Buffyfan**, **Buffyland**, **Buffytime**,
Buffy Paradigm, **Buffy Syndrome**, **Slayground**, **Cave-Slayer**, **Slayer-eyes**,
Slayer Handbook, **Slayer-patrol**, **Slayer sense**, and **slayer slang** itself,
and **vampface**. Sometimes compounded elements look like suffixes and
combine frequently with other words; these forms, if they are used like
suffixes often enough, actually become suffixes in time. Such is the case
with *-holic* (as in **Buffyholic**), abstracted originally from *alcoholic*, and
-iatric (as in **Buffyatric**), originally abstracted from *geriatric*. Abstracted
from *robot* some years ago, *-bot* speeds down a road towards the same
fate, with a pit-stop in slayer slang just long enough to produce **Buffybot**;[2]
and *-cam*, clipped from *camera* (as in **Slayercam**), has traveled a similar

---

[1] **Unh** *bears an interesting resemblance to* fuck, *for which it serves as a euphemistic synonym
in one sense; in another sense, it means 'thrust', which, we suspect, on the evidence of cognates
in other Germanic languages, is the etymological meaning for* fuck, *though we cannot be sure,
as* fuck *is not recorded in English until roughly* 1500.

[2] *Although* -bot *is unattested as a combining form in major commercial and slang dictionaries, its use is increasingly accepted: witness the television show BattleBots (Comedy Central),
in which robots engage in battle with one another, controlled remotely by their inventors. Hasbro,
Inc., the toy manufacturer, will soon, according to their website, release Battling Bots, which
apparently frees the previously bound combining form. Both terms are trademarks, which probably explains why* -bot *hasn't found its way into dictionaries yet.* -Bot *was productive well
before it entered slayer slang in* 2001: Urkelbot *occurred in an episode of the comedy series
News Radio; I have seen the episode only as a rerun and cannot identify it, but Phil Hartman
played Bill McNeill in the episode, so it must have aired no later than* 12 May 1998, *before
Hartman was killed.*

distance, also at an impressive velocity. Some nouns, like *girl* and *thing*, essentially become *-girl* and *-thing*, illimitably flexible combining forms used much more frequently, both generally and in slayer slang, than any of the others listed above (as in **Edge Girl**, **Hacker Girl**, **Net Girl**, *Sitting Target Girl*, and all of the items recorded at *-thing*). And some verbs become nouns just so that they can be compounded with other nouns, for instance, *speak* or *-speak* in **bezoar-speak** and **Buffyspeak**.

While new terms result from combining, they also develop in the opposite direction, by shortening. We have already considered the importance of clipped phrases like **bail** (out) and **deal** (with) to slayer slang in Chapter 1.[3] There are other clippings, too, most notably **sitch**, which has a continuous history in slayer slang, from the film version of *Buffy* (1992) onward, but also some collected for, but not included in, the glossary, like *mist* 'mistake', *neg* 'no', and *pos* 'yes'. The first occurs in the episode *Something Blue* (30 November 1999), in which Willow says, "I interrupted. You've got apples. My mist," a somewhat adventurous but implausible synonym for **bad**; the other two appear in the same passage of Richie Tankersley Cusick's novelization of *The Harvest* (1997, p. 18). None of them caught on. And although there are no acronyms in slayer slang, there is a suffixed alphabetism (or initialism), **W/Xness**.

One cannot say that blends abound in slayer slang, but there are several of them, and they are particularly memorable, either because they are clever, obtrusive (or both), or central to the Buffy lexicon. **Buffyverse** (*Buffy* + *universe*) belongs to the last category, while *AOHellmouth* (*AOL* + *Hellmouth*), **Buffinator** (*Buffy* + *Terminator*), **Buffivor** (*Buffy* + *Survivor*), **Buffypedia** (*Buffy* + *encyclopedia*), **deadfill** (*dead* + *landfill*), **Spuffy** (*Spike* + *Buffy*), **unDead Sea Scrolls** (*undead* + *Dead Sea Scrolls*), **bedvamp** (*bedbug* + *vamp*), and **vampnap** (*vamp* + *kidnap*) belong to the other categories, according to one's taste. Besides **Buffyverse**, **manimal** is the best known of slayer slang blends, not because it's clever or unique, but because it occurred indelibly as part of Faith's philosophy: "Every guy, from Manimal right on down to Mr.-I-Loved-*The English Patient*, has

---

[3] *One can find the following forms clipped from phrasal verbs in the glossary:* **bail, bug, creep, deal, flake, freak, hang, show, team,** *and* **wig;** **freaked, messed,** *and* **wigged** *are clipped from phrases formed on participial adjectives.*

beast in him." **Manimal** has also been productive, having spawned the posting board handle **humanimal** (*human* + *manimal* or *human* + *manimal*).

All of the forms listed above, and the operation of the accompanying processes within slayer slang, are interesting enough, but not as interesting or as revealing about the special characteristics of slayer slang, those that simultaneously challenge and influence mainstream American slang: prefixes (and prefixing), suffixes (and suffixing), and words that undergo a functional shift (and the process of shifting). These are the terms (and processes) through which the Buffyverse coheres, and also those in which adherents of Buffy assert a slayer style.

The Attraction of Prefixes

When it comes to prefixes, slayer slang employs a few of the usual suspects: *de-* in **defreak**; *non-* in **non-mathy**, **non-slayey**, and **non-vamp**; *pre-* in **pre-posy**, **pre-Slayer**, **pre-Watcher**, and *pre-here* (which I heard on a rerun episode of *Angel* before I could record the quotation); *re-* in **repostage**, and *semi-* in **semi-Scooby**. All of these prefixes occur much less frequently in slayer slang than they do in American English generally. *Super-*, though quite popular in slang contexts ("What are you, super-professor?," "You're supermom!," "Get away from me, supergeek!"), plays only a bit part in slayer slang, in **supervamp** and **super-Watcher**—ultimately, it is upstaged by its exotic German cousin, *über-*.

But if slayer slang, for the most part, casts very few instances of relatively few prefixes, two others, *not-* and *über-*, play prominent roles, while *un-* plays the lead. Partly to save space, partly because it does not clearly originate in *Buffy*, and partly because it also isn't otherwise prevalent in American slang, I removed the evidence for *not-* from the glossary. I had collected six forms: *not-auntie* (26 June 1999) and *not-birthday* (13 October 1999) both appeared on the Bronze; the first instance of *not-* prefixing in the television show also occurred on 13 October 1999, in the episode *Faith, Hope, and Trick*, in which Buffy complains, "Plus, at school today, she was making eyes at my not-boyfriend." David

Greenwalt's script for the episode was written before influence from the posting board examples quoted above was possible, though he might have been influenced by earlier posting board activity; yet it is clear that the posting board forms were not influenced by the show. On 8 December 1999, I encountered *not-daughter* and *not-mom* in mutually referential posts on the Bronze. And then *not-* apparently disappeared from the *Buffy* record until 12 February 2002, in the episode *Older and Far Away*: "I assume that this was an act of kindness," Buffy says. "That'll help with the not-throttling."

As John Algeo once remarked, "Words have continued to come into, and pass out of, vogue along with hemlines, hair lengths, and folk heroes." *Über-* is currently voguish in American slang, and slayer slang, though not a slave to trends, is nonetheless always conscious of them, and hasn't overlooked it.[4] *Über-* is more persuasively an item of slayer slang than *not-*. Though words prefixed with *über-* entered American slang before *Buffy* first aired, **übersuck**, the earliest form in the glossary, is from the episode *Inca Mummy Girl* (6 October 1997). **Übervampire** surfaced in a Dark Horse Comic (October 1999), and in the same month, a glossary of slayer slang in *Entertainment Weekly* registered *übersuck*, which suggests that the glossary's compiler, at least, saw the word as characteristic of the show's adventurous language. So did Gilman and Sherman in their novel *Visitors* (1999), in which Buffy remarks to Giles, "Hey, Oz may be the überslacker sometimes, but he takes the music seriously" (p. 115). **Überevil** is heard in the episode *Goodbye, Iowa* (15 February 2000), and later in the year, **überachiever** appears in Nancy Holder's *The Watcher's Guide, Volume 2*. As an element of **übernerd**, the prefix made its way into a December 2001 article about Buffy in the entertainment magazine *Starburst*. Finally, in 2002, *über-* spread itself among many quite distinct, though more or less *Buffy*-related, media: **übercreepy** figured in the film *Scooby Doo*, starring Sarah Michelle Gellar, and the film reflects the television cartoon's durable appeal, reinforced,

---

[4] *The dictionary record fails to reflect the fact that American English has, for some time, borrowed the German combining form über- 'over, above; ultimate, prototypical' to express the sense 'super-'; but the prefix contributes to many nonce-formations, as in the following headline from Premiere (April 2001): "Behind every Oscar talent, there's an über-agent at work" (p. 22).*

in part, by the invention of the **Scooby Gang**. Later in the year, in one of the show's many memorable lines, Xander warns Willow, "You may be a hopped-up überwitch, but this carpenter can drywall you into the next century" (*The Grave*, 21 May); still later, **überexcited** popped up in conversation on the Bronze (28 July). Unlike not-, über- clearly entered the Buffyverse through the show, and then spread among a variety of media continuously over several years—among prefixes, and without denying its rising popularity in general American slang, über- is undeniably a slayer slang prefix.

Preeminent among the slayer slang prefixes, though, is un-, a staple English prefix, but not one especially preferred in American slang. Un- is significant, not merely because it participates in more slayer slang than any other prefix (though it does—nearly three times as much as über-, and more than four times as much as not-), and not only because some words formed with un- are thematically central to the Buffyverse (though **undead** and **unlife** certainly are), but because slayer slang un- breaks rules.

Edna Andrews recently itemized the rules for un-, not throughout the history of English, but for current use.[5] For instance, "The most obvious points regarding verbs prefixed by un- are: (1) each verb is transitive (except for the obsolete *unbe*); (2) in most cases, the verb in question in nonprefixed form may double as a noun," but these rules do not apply

[5] *To be fair, though Andrews's explanation of un- fails to account for its use in slayer slang, Andrews cannot be held responsible: after all, her article, published in 1986, could not anticipate language that hadn't yet developed. She drew her information from Webster's Ninth New Collegiate Dictionary (1983) and Webster's New World Dictionary of the American Language (1968—now 35 years old), and neither these nor any other dictionaries at the time included the forms recorded in the glossary. They did not even include* **undead**: *The American Heritage Dictionary of the English Language, Fourth Edition (2000) finally entered it, but only as an adjective (it was not in The American Heritage Dictionary of the English Language, Third Edition [1993]); Merriam-Webster's New Collegiate Dictionary, Tenth Edition (1993) entered it, but only as a noun; Merriam-Webster's New International Dictionary of the English Language, Third Edition (1961) entered* **undead** *as a plural noun but defines it as 'vampire'; the Oxford English Dictionary, Second Edition (1989) defines it as an adjective meaning "Not dead; alive. Also, not quite dead but not fully alive, dead-and-alive. In vampirism, clinically dead but not yet at rest." The information provided in the glossary should convince lexicographers to refine their treatment of* **undead**, *in all of its senses, in future editions of their dictionaries.*

in the case of slayer slang's **unlive**. And more profoundly, un- in slayer slang sometimes ignores the following expectation: "un- cannot prefix adjectives denoting the ABSENCE of a particular quality (cf. *unafraid* but not *unempty)." But the un- of **undead** *adj* (in sense 3) and related forms, such as **Undead-American, unDead Sea Scrolls,** as well as **unlazy,** does precisely that. And, finally, "A general invariant meaning for un- as a verbal prefix can be stated as follows: a CANCELLATION of the original state such that minimal change occurs—a simple reversal. In adjectives, un- reverses the lexical meaning of the adjective and has no implication that the opposite state has any validity within the given speech situation." Andrews's rule for verbs (for which a good example would be *unravel*—something was raveled, then it isn't, and that's the only change indicated by the un-) is ironically true: **unlive** represents an exaggeratedly "minimal" change: When one *unlives,* one does nearly everything one does when alive, except actually BE alive.

A number of adjectival forms with un- included in the glossary do satisfy Andrews's expectations, **unbad,** for instance, and **unbeating, unbendy, uncomputered, undreaming, unfun, ungood, unminiony, unmixy, unquality, unscrolled,** and **untopicy**: all of these mean simply the opposite of the root; **uncomputered** means 'lacking a computer' where *computered would mean 'having a computer', **unmixy** means 'incompatible' where *mixy would mean 'compatible', etc. But other forms, like **undead** *adj,* certainly do not, because vestiges of the opposite quality ARE present: if you think of the undead as the "living dead," slayer slang's transgression in this regard will be obvious. And in context, a number of other forms also seem to break this rule. How does one parse Joss Whedon's comment (13 January 2002) that he is "not unlazy," that he does "procrastinate"? Apparently, he's not really energetic (or unlazy), yet the syntactic decision to be "not unlazy," rather than "not energetic," manages to imply a state between energy and laziness, rather like the state between death and life captured in the term *undead.* Similarly, in the episode *After Life* (9 October 2001), when Tara reassures Willow, "You don't have to be brave. I still love you. If you're worried, you can be worried," Willow responds, "Well, I'm not unworried," we are left to consider that she is SORT OF worried, but not worried enough to say that she REALLY IS worried. Through such forms, characters articulate the grayness of the Buffyverse, its constant liminality; and the un- of slayer slang is interesting partly because, contrary to accepted practice in which un- is a one-way prefix, it nonetheless manages to have things both ways.

Similarly, in both Golden and Holder's *Child of the Hunt* (1998) and Gilman and Sherman's *Deep Water* (2000), Buffy describes her relationship with Angel to herself as an **unrelationship**, though this does not mean that they don't have a relationship—rather, it means that they both do, and do not, have one. One of the best things about the Buffyverse is that it does not uncomplicate complicated things. Another is its daring challenges to linguistic "rules" or "tendencies": un- is approximately 85% an adjective prefix, 13% a verb prefix, and only 2% a noun prefix (*unreason, unrest, untruth,* and *unwisdom* are the only examples that come to mind); yet slayer slang includes eight nouns under un-: **unbudger, unchipperness, undead** (in senses 1 and 2), **undeath, unfun** (in sense 1), **unlife,** and **untopicyness,** besides **unrelationship.** While **Undead-American** and **unDead Sea Scrolls** are nouns, they are not included here because the element *undead* in those compounds is an adjective; and perhaps the two forms suffixed with *-ness* should not be included, either. But even with these exceptions, un- combines with nouns more frequently in slayer slang than in general American English, and **undead** n is prominent and productive well beyond the norm even in slayer slang, where its only rivals are **Slayer** and **Buffy,** with **(the) Bronze, (the) Hellmouth, Scooby Gang, slay, vamp, Watcher,** and the **wig** system following a length or two behind.

Nouns prefixed with un-, together with un- prefixed verbs and adjectives that break semantic rules, then, are significant items of the *Buffy* lexicon, one of many bloodless revolutions waged by slayer slang against the linguistic status quo. But the forms that subscribe to the rules are revolutionary by association: most of them wouldn't have been created unless **undead** had been at the core of the vocabulary, and even a form like **unwindy,** to which *-y* rather than un- has newly been affixed, is implicated in the slayer slang un-. **Undead** is like a magnet, attracting to it any number of adjectives shaved from the English lexicon and then newly charged with peculiar significance. To a lesser extent, the same is true of *über-*, and perhaps even *not-*.

Happy Endings: The Suffix and Slayer Slang

One naturally assumes that, were slayer slang to accomplish anything new with English suffixes, the suffixes themselves would be new. It is difficult, however, to make up suffixes—how would anybody understand them? The closest we come is to abstract parts of preexisting words and use them as suffixes, like -*holic* from *alcoholic* and -*atric* from *geriatric*. Slayer slang does employ such suffixes, but infrequently: **Buffyholic** and **Buffyatric** are the only items to use the forms just mentioned, even though such combining forms verging on suffixes are increasingly productive in English. Slayer slang has abstracted -*palooza*, probably from *Lollapalooza*, the name of a rock festival organized annually from 1990 to 1998, rather than from *lollapalooza*, which the *Historical Dictionary of American Slang* defines as "something that is an extraordinary example of its kind."[6] But the form only leads to a few items, employed very infrequently: **buttonpalooza**, **Guiltapalooza**, **Scareapalooza**, **Slayerpalooza**, and **Wiccapalooza**.

In fact, slayer slang is much more subversive than when first meets the eye (or ear), because it prefers to stretch the application of well-established English suffixes and sometimes stretches them thin. Many time-honored suffixes are handled in traditional ways, however: **Bronzerdom**, **Buffdom**, and **Slayerdom**, to each of which -*dom* attributes to the root a 'realm' or 'domain', as it has to nouns since Old English. The *Oxford English Dictionary, Second Edition* (1989, henceforth OED2), sv -**dom**, notes that "The number of these derivatives has increased in later times, and -*dom* is now a living suffix, freely-employed to form nonce-derivatives," and H. L. Mencken had observed the increased use of -*dom* in American English in *The American Language* (1936), all of which goes to show that slayer slang's use of -*dom* is commonplace.

Other older English suffixes also contribute minimally to slayer slang, without disrupting established patterns of use: -*ish* (which, in one sense,

---

[6] The use of -*palooza* yet again exemplifies slayer slang's tendency to trade on popular culture, and most BTVS viewers would connect the form to the rock festival, even though, vaguely, they know that the more general form exists; the likelihood of the association is suggested in John Vornholt's novel, *Coyote Moon* (1998, p. 2): "'Okay, so tonight wasn't Lollapalooza at the Bronze.'"

gives us English, an Old English word, though not the oldest), in the sense 'belonging to a person or thing; characteristic of a person or thing' yields **break and enterish, Buffyish, Hellmouthish**, and **Slayerish**; the very old diminutive -*kin* (which we have never located in an Old English text but appears early in Middle English), provides **buffkin**, while -*let*, a somewhat later diminutive, borrowed from French, contributes **bitcalet**, and -*ette*, a related form, generates **Cordette** and **Slayerette**, terms central to the Buffy lexicon; -*less*, like -*dom*, originally an independent word in Old English, has been used only as a suffix since Middle English, and, though quite common in English generally, offers up only **Buffyless** in slayer slang; -*ville*, a comparatively recent suffix abstracted from the French word *ville* 'town', meaning 'imaginary place' or 'quality suggested by the root word', is mildly more productive than those listed above (**booksville, dateville, dustville, Hellsville, mootville, scrollsville**, and **Slayersville**); similarly, -*fest*, to mean 'outstanding occasion', abstracted from the free noun *fest* 'festival', yields **bite-fest, Slayerfest, suckfest**, and **vid-fest**; -*free*, already a combining form in Old English and increasingly popular in current English, is responsible for several items: **ash-free, blood-free, crack whore–free, destiny-free, fester-free, geek dance–free, glib-free, Miata-free, move-free, pants-free, rumble-free, spoiler-free, stake-free**, and **vamp-free**. As I will argue in the next chapter, all of these suffixes (with the exception of -*free*) are important to the development of the roots to which they are attached and help to ensure the durability of the root and associated forms, though they are unexceptional in themselves.

But slayer slang does not always play by the rules, nor could it and still be slang: when it flouts the linguistic status quo, slayer slang is great fun for the Buffyverse's ins, not least because they are, at least sometimes, those Sledd identifies as the outs; they enjoy irritating supposedly responsible speakers of English while consolidating an edgy group identity with other like-minded fans of Buffy. Again, to wreak the most havoc, slayer slang resorts, not to anything especially newfangled, but to suffixes that most responsible speakers of English think are under control, apparently innocuous suffixes like -*ness*, -*age*, and -*y*.

For those who have appointed themselves to preserve the "purity" of English, however, -*ness* is far from innocent, but one of the usual suspects in crimes against the language. The OED, quite correctly dedicated to describing the language historically, does not lay down laws for the proper use of -*ness*; but one might take its entry for -*ness* as outlining the historical parameters for its use, the parameters on which our expectations are founded. According to OED2, "In O[ld] E[nglish] -*nes* is the suffix most usually attached to adjectives and past participles to form substantives expressing a state or condition.... A large number of these survive in middle and modern English, and new formations of the same type have been continually made in all periods of the language, it being possible to add the suffix to any adjective or participle, whatever its form or origin may be." This is the familiar -*ness* of *bitterness* and *hardness*, though OED2 points out that -*ness* also has combined often with compound adjectives (*selfconceitedness* and *water-tightness*, for instance) and even with adjectival phrases (like *used-upness* and *up-to-dateness*). "[F]ew of the latter, however," the entry notes, "are in established or serious use, and most of them are of recent introduction. This is also the case with formations on pronouns, adverbs, etc., as in I-*ness, me-ness, whatness; whyness, withoutness, nowness, everydayness*, etc." There are, in addition, some "[u]ses of the suffix somewhat varying from those mentioned above...such as FORCENESS, MILKNESS, WILDERNESS, WITNESS," so uses of -*ness* have never been absolutely predictable.

Though not intended as such, if observers of the language take the OED's entry for -*ness* as a set of rules, they will encounter many alleged violations in written, not to mention spoken, English. Theodore Williams compiled some outraged responses to illicit use, though he made it clear that he did not agree with them. A sample of those comments will help to explain why slayer slang's use of -*ness* might not meet with universal approval. My favorite was excerpted from Time (11 May 1962):

> Now comes an equally formidable enemy: -*ness* [equally as much a "barbarism" as *businesswise, dollarwise, salewise*, and *weatherwise*] denoting "state, quality, or condition." It is not the friendly suffix of *greatness, goodness, loveliness* (properly forming abstract nouns from adjectives) or even Loch Ness, but a whole new invasion of language.... Teacher Foote [Professor Dorothy

N. Foote of San Jose State College] reports that -ness added to nouns, pronouns, verbs, and phrases—a custom thought until now to be mostly whimsical, as in *whyness*, and *everydayness*—has become popular among distinctly
unjocose people.

Schoolmarm much? But Robert E. Morsberger was equally exercised,
even if he chose a different metaphor to convey his distaste: "Our language itself demonstrates…grotesque mutations in truncated, telescoped
words and words with extra inflationary growths on the suffix end." If
-ness is not a formidable, barbaric enemy, it is a cancer on healthy English. At least Richard Altick's objection was primarily aesthetic:

> Good judges of English style strongly object to the overuse of nouns in
> modern writing, not merely because their cumulative weight can overtax
> the single verb or two that the sentence may contain. They also point out
> that many of the favorite nouns used by businessmen, lawyers, and other
> kinds of more or less specialized writers end in -tion, -ity, -ment, -ness, and
> -ance. Words ending in these suffixes are not notably lovely in sound, and if
> used to excess they grate upon the ear.

But you can see how Altick's comment challenges slayer slang: if lawyers
and such, those Sledd surely had in mind as those who possess "conventional status" and "conduct the important affairs of established communities," are already a step over the -ness line, users of slayer slang, from
writers of the show to fans, must go a step further.

Of course, some of the furor over -ness and similarly dangerous suffixes
has abated since the 1960s; for good or ill, we've become as permissive
about suffixes as about everything else in American culture. One expects
current views, like that of Robert W. Burchfield, in the eminently easy-
going *The New Fowler's Modern English Usage* (1996), to be more moder-
ate: "It is worth noting that -ness is a strong living suffix (used esp. to
form nonce-words). In recent years I have noted numerous examples of
such formations that are either not in the *OED* or marked as rare: e.g.
accidentalness (I. Murdoch, 1989), *energizedness* (New Yorker, 1986),
familyness (Newsweek, 1992), *unimpressedness* (New Yorker, 1990)." Interestingly, Burchfield's sources underscore the suffix's establishedness; the

examples, mostly ADJECTIVE + -ness, conform to expectations raised by the entry in OED2.

In slayer slang, -ness is a significant suffix: it distinguishes 32 entries or subentries in the glossary, a significant proportion of the items registered there; but it is also one of the suffixes in which slayer slang is either playful or wicked, depending on one's perspective.[7] Several of the items are conventional enough, for instance, **activeness, patheticness,** and **weirdness,** simply ADJECTIVE + -ness. But many items, even those formed on adjectives, are unusual, for a variety of reasons. Since we know that -ness forms with nouns on occasion, *mathness, *neat freakness, and *doubleshiftness are all possible words, but slayer slang has suffixed the roots into adjectives before resuffixing them with -ness into nouns, arriving at **mathiness, neat-freakishness,** and **double-shiftiness,** instead. Context suggests some word-play in the latter item, as Buffy is suspicious about the reasons for her having to pull a *double shift*, so finds the situation shifty 'shady', as well as shifty 'pertaining to a work shift'. Verbs only rarely combine with -ness, so *driveness is unlikely and suffixing the verb into adjectiveness, as **driveyness,** is probably the only way to make -ness suffixing acceptable. All of these examples demonstrate what Morsberger considered vicious "extra inflationary growths on the suffix end" of words, and even though word length may not be a reason to proscribe a newly formed word, Morsberger notices that "excessive" or "unnatural" word length can signal jargon or slang, and part of the appeal (or the horror) of such forms as **neat-freakishness** or **double-shiftiness** is their relative length, the automatic recognition on the part of speakers and listeners that the forms are already compounds, and so are less likely to take -ness than shorter, or less complex, words. The same effect is achieved by **unchipperness** and **untopicyness,** especially in the second case, where the three affixes (un-, -y, and -ness) overwhelm the

---

[7] *Because the forms are not always evident in the glossary, it may be useful to list them here:* activeness, afterness, AIMness, bad guyness, badness, Buffyness, coolness, double-shiftiness, driveyness, foulness, geekiness, gladness, going outness, hottiness, manness, machoness, mathiness, neat-freakishness, ooginess, patheticness, sadness, Slayerness, Spuffyness, sticking upness, timeliness, unchipperness, untopicyness, vagueness, veinyness, W/Xness, weirdness, *and* whupness.

noun, and multiple affixation, rather than the root's meaning, characterizes the word.

Sometimes the novel aspect of a -ness form isn't rampant accumulation of word parts, but its role in syntax, in the structure of sentences. A
few slayer slang items place the -nessed form in an "absolute" position.
So, though *timely* 'occurring at an appropriate time' is already familiar
to English speakers, and *timeliness* is an attested form, slayer slang's **timeliness** is a bit different: as Xander says in the episode *Bargaining* 1 (2
October 2001), "It's time? Like time time? With the timeliness?" Usually, we are interested in the timeliness OF something; we don't concern
ourselves with timeliness as an abstract quality. Here, 'appropriateness' is
captured by the first two questions, while the abstractness of *timeliness* is
abstracted from itself as a result of its position in the sentence, and from
the grammatical constraint signified by the definite article. **Gladness** serves
a similar function, with a slight difference, as it represents not only a
state of affairs, but the emotional state of its speaker, as when, in the
episode *Phases* (27 January 1998), Oz asks, out of concern for what he
may have done in his werewolf phase, "Is everybody okay? Did anyone
get bitten or scratched?," and Willow answers, "No, we're fine," and Oz
responds, "Gladness."

Coolness, in its first sense, 'acceptableness', is also used as an absolute,
parallel to **gladness**. Yet it challenges our expectations a bit more, because the root means not 'somewhere between warm and cold', but
'excellent', a slang sense; **gladness** forms on the standard, historical sense
of *glad*. Similarly, **sadness** forms on *sad*, not in the sense 'sorrowful, un-
happy', but in a more recent slang sense 'awkward, unfortunate, pathetic': as Jonathan says to Andrew in *Two to Go* (21 May 2002), "You're
looking for implants?...You are sadness personified," which shifts the
word's meaning and asserts its abstractness simultaneously, though not
"absolutely." Slayer slang updates some adjectives in its -ness forms, both
semantically and in the roles such words play in English sentences.

OED2 reports that -ness frequently combines with nouns and pronouns in order to bring out an essential quality, like *I-ness* or *me-ness*,
the process that bothers some language conservatives. So **Buffyness** and
Slayerness are not surprising forms. Acknowledging this, users of slayer
slang challenge expectations by affixing -ness to unusual nouns, so that

resultant forms seem strange enough to vex mainstream observers and are opaque enough to belong to those who live in the Buffyverse: **whupness** forms on *whup*, the Bronze and Bronze: Beta term for 'work' or 'responsibility outside activity on the posting board'; **AIMness** applies the suffix, unexpectedly, to an acronym; and **W/Xness** is even more involuted, really a very complex idea compacted into a single term, since it means 'state of wishing that Willow and Xander would have a romantic relationship', where the slash is the most meaningful part of the word. **5 by 5ness** is a similar case—though formed on an adjective, the word is unusual because **five by five** is a metaphorical way of saying 'square', which is a metaphorical way of saying of saying 'in accord, true, all right'. If the root of a -nessed form is already periphrastic, a circumlocution, then the suffixed form will seem shocking, at least to those not fluent in slayer slang.

Though VERB + -ness is rarer than combinations of the suffix with adjectives and nouns, they have been recorded. Users of slayer slang know this, not by looking in dictionaries, but intuitively, as native speakers of English, and, unwilling to settle for anything established, however tenuously, they find a way to stretch even this category of -ness forms, by combining -ness, not with simple verbs, but with verb phrases, thus **going outness** and **sticking-upness**. Word length and complexity obviously militate against the immediate acceptance of these forms, but so does abstractness applied to contextually specific roots: "Thanks for sticking up for me," writes a Betarer, "even if there was no sticking-upness needed" (31 July 2002). And the slanginess of such forms is even clearer when a Bronzer doubts the validity of his or her diction: "[S]low board…must be Friday night going out-ness (if that's a word)" (1 September 2000). We are even more reluctant to -ness adverbs and prepositions than we are verb phrases, so **afterness** is, for purely grammatical reasons, a bothersome combination.

Slayer slang's use of -ness, then, is interesting for several reasons: it trades on a formative tendency long-established in English use; it applies that tendency in ways typical of jargon and slang, ways that have bothered those invested in the linguistic status quo for some time; it takes what those conservatives find unusual, new, and mildly offensive and makes it more unusual, newer, and incrementally more offensive;

and it demonstrates that, in only seven years, a speech community can push the envelope in every aspect of its application, just enough to reinforce the exclusive habits of that speech community by alienating just enough of those who adhere to more traditional patterns—morphological, semantic, and syntactic—of -ness suffixation.

As Sledd would have it, slayer slang's use of -ness is "revolutionary," everyday rebellion against linguistic constraints imposed by other speakers, usually statusful speakers, both historically and in the present day. Rebellion can take various forms, and the dynamics of -age are quite different from those of -ness. The suffix -age entered English later than -ness, borrowed from Old French, from which -age forms were adopted into Middle English; while Anglo-French remained the prestige language in England (until roughly 1400), new -age forms were created in it, passed along to Middle English, and naturalized, until the process itself was naturalized and English began to produce its own -age suffixed words. Many common English nouns form with -age, some of them (like *advantage, damage, foliage, language, marriage, message, savage,* and *voyage*) so basic to our vocabulary that most of us don't recognize them as suffixed forms, especially since the roots were not naturalized. Over the last millennium, English has accumulated an extensive list of words ending in -age: *baggage, bondage, cleavage, luggage, mileage, parsonage, parentage, passage, pilgrimage, tonnage,* and *usage* are just a few. Connie C. Eble, in *Slang & Sociability*, notes that -age has for years been popular in American slang, generating such forms as *foodage, fundage, rainage, scoopage,* and *studyage*. As with -ness, many -age forms are likely to be nonce-words, created instrumentally, to serve a particular purpose in a particular conversation, but not repeated until familiar and then authorized by dictionaries.

If -age is so well-established, in English generally and even in American slang, how can it contribute to slayer slang's unique character, not to mention Sledd's revolution? The number of historical and recorded nonce-forms alone limits its potential to disrupt American speech, but that isn't the only force pulling the suffix back from the edge. Perhaps because it had been in natural English use for centuries before -age entered the language, our expectations for -ness may be narrower than those for

-*age*, more etymological: it has always and only been used to alter roots into abstract nouns; slang challenges, not the result of -*ness* suffixation, but expectations for what roots legitimately take the suffix. Yet this is a recipe for rebellion, if anyone decides to mix supposedly incompatible ingredients: we immediately notice the slangy flavor of items cooked to suit the taste of a self-conscious group, rather than to satisfy the bland palate of general English. Some, of course, would replace "bland" with "refined," but variety is the spice of life, and, by definition, slang promotes variety.

By contrast, -*age* is a flexible suffix: it combines freely with both nouns and verbs and it does so to several different results. Whereas -*ness* in all of its manifestations resolves into one sense, the *American Heritage Dictionary of the English Language*, Fourth Edition (2000, henceforth *AHD4*), analyzes -*age* into 6 different senses, 8 if we include subsenses:

> -**age** *suff.* **1a.** Collection; mass: *sewerage.* **b.** Amount: *footage.* **2.** Relationship, connection: *parentage.* **3.** Condition; state: *vagabondage.* **4a.** An action: *blockage.* **b.** Result of an action: *breakage.* **5.** Residence or place of: *vicarage.* **6.** Charge or fee: *cartage.*

As a result of its flexibility, use of -*age* surprises us less than use of -*ness*. In fact, slayer slang employs -*age* in the least surprising ways: the 55 examples included in the glossary distribute among only 4 of the 8 senses—1a, 3, 4a, and 4b—and one of those—sense 3—contributes to only a few items of slayer slang.[8] The pattern reflects relative proportions of the various senses in general English vocabulary, as well as in American slang, though items formed with -*age* in the other senses are not beyond the imagination: *stakage* need not mean either a collection or mass of stakings or action of killing vampires with wooden stakes, but

---

[8] *For easy reference, the following list collects all of the -age forms collected in the glossary:* agreeage, AIMage, appearage, blood-coughage, breakage, Christian Baleage, clearage, clueage, Dewage, downage, drinkage, droppage, Ewanage, flingage, Jossage, kickage, kissage, linkage, lurkage, meetage, missage, moveage, pluggage, poofage, postage, poundage, punnage, quotage, saveage, scorage, scrollage, sighage, signage, slayage, slayerage, sliceage, slowage, sparkage, spoilage, spoilerage, stakage, stealage, suckage, swappage, taggage, thuddage, topicage, vibage, viewage, VIPage, visitage, watchage, weirdage, whuppage, and wiggage.

the number of stakes used in a particular episode of slayage, as under sense 1b; *Scoobyage might capture the friendship among members of the Scooby Gang, under sense 2, as might *gangage, had **Gang** (sv **Scooby Gang**) enjoyed greater currency; *Spikeage might have referred to Spike's crypt, under sense 5; and, because when demons play poker they play for cats, *cattage could be the price of anteing up, under sense 6. Sense 3 would admit many forms apparently not created in slayer slang (though, admittedly, I simply might not have encountered them), most notably *vampage.

Slayer slang's -age is impressive, not only for the number of words it contributes to the lexicon, but for the way in which it helps to bind members of the Buffyverse to one another, as discussed in Chapter 1. Far more productive than -ness, -age is a hyperactive suffix in slayer slang, generating forms more rapidly than in American slang or in general American English, which suggests that -age forms in slayer slang are semantically less important than in English generally, that is, the words thus supplied usually do not fill gaps in current vocabulary; instead, they perform an important social function within the speech community that uses slayer slang. Indeed, those who police English complain about -aged words, just because they are so often redundant.[9] Slayer slang, I fear, won't unruffle their feathers: if someone needs **poundage**, he just needs a good pounding; if someone is addicted to **punnage**, she uses a lot of puns. In other words, inflected forms of words, like participles and plurals, much "nearer" to the root than -age, usually supply our lexical needs and no -ageing is required. Necessity is always accompanied by assumptions, however, and to call a redundant form "unnecessary" or "needless" is to presume that one can accurately gauge "the need." The need for -age in slayer slang is social, not lexical, and a matter of style, though admittedly not the style one reads about in style guides.

---

[9] They are what Wilson Follett called "needless words," or what Erik Wensberg, revising Follett's Modern American Usage: A Guide, called "unnecessary words." Neither Follett nor Wensberg mentions -age specifically in their entries, but Wensberg reveals an opinion on the suffix by cutting one of Follett's sentences: "Surplusage is common with such words as factor, field, and NATURE"—perhaps Wensberg thought the same of -age and chose to correct what he saw as Follett's bad example. Usage itself, we must assume, is neither needless nor unnecessary.

Slayer slang stretches -*age* somewhat beyond the established bound-aries of its use: for instance, **sparkage** refers, not literally to ignition, but to the metaphorical spark of romance between girl and boy; as with -*ness*, -*age* attaches to new senses of old words, catching us off guard. This tendency fuses with another atypical of -*age* forms in general English or even American slang, a magnifying, sometimes microscopic, particularity of reference. Many of the -*aged* roots in slayer slang are common English words with newly specialized senses, senses associated with activity in the Buffyverse or one of its galaxies, like the Bronze and Bronze: Beta posting boards: **downage** (as when a computer networked system is down); **droppage** (what you do to HTML tags, a.k.a **taggage**); **postage** (not what you put on your mail but what you put on the post-ing board); **linkage** (as in the Buffy-related links you pass along to other posting board participants); **lurkage** (the unsocial activity of **scrollage** without **postage**), etc. These terms could be used by participants on any posting board, but **spoilage** and **spoilerage** (referring to **postage** that reveals details about recent or upcoming episodes, *spoilers*, that would *spoil* the fun of watching the episode oneself) are useful only on a post-ing board dedicated to a television serial; **VIPage** is appropriate only to a television series–related board on which stars occasionally post; **poofage** and **whuppage** are comprehensible only to those participating on the Bronze or Bronze: Beta, as they are formed on the jargon of those boards.

Many words suffixed with -*age* in slayer slang form on roots much more specific than expected in American English, even in slang, in which the purpose of -*age* is to take a general term, noun or verb, to the level of a mass or collective noun: *baggage* or *sewerage*, *blockage* or *breakage*—specificity arises in the "oblique" senses of -*age*, those unusual or un-known in slayer slang, the ones that generate *parentage* or *vicarage* or *linage*. **Drinkage** fits the accustomed semantic pattern of -*age*, as described in *AHD4*; **Dewage** does not, to the extent that proper names are not usually roots of -*aged* words. *Lustage* would parallel **kissage** and **meetage**; but **Ewanage** 'discussion about Ewan McGregor' and **Christian Baleage** 'lusting after Christian Bale' resemble *language* and *mileage* only after magnifying the referential domain by several degrees. Even **slayage** and **stakage** are narrower terms in the Buffyverse than they are in general American English.

Ewanage and **Christian Baleage** are not only formed on very precise roots, but pack so much information into the resulting words that they bulge with meaning: **Ewanage** does not refer to Ewans in the mass, nor does it refer to Ewan McGregor in the mass; rather it assumes 'discussion about' without articulating it, and the same is true of 'lusting after' in **Christian Baleage**. The lust, explicit in the latter and implicit in the former, was understood by participants in what, though posted on the Bronze, were really private conversations. **Jossage** means not Josses in the mass, but a collection of information about Joss Whedon; **blood-coughage** means a mass of *blood-coughs, or coughing that expectorates blood. Erin McKean, this book's editor, proposed another bulgy -*age* word in an interview with the *Chicago Tribune* (12 June 2002): "She saw a possible future dictionary entry in 'thrubbage'—referring to the thigh rubbage people experience in hot months when they wear shorts."[10] Would the term apply to the chafing of thighs in winter months? Apparently not. And the blend of thigh and *rubbage* is itself ambitious. The referent, qualified by a great deal of assumed information, is more specific than can be conveyed comfortably in a single word. Of course, many of us put up with discomfort for the sake of style—if the shoe doesn't quite fit, wear it anyway.

Redundancy has its problems: -*ness* suffixed words in slayer slang distribute fairly evenly among the years from 1998 to 2002; -*age* suffixed forms do not. Of 54 -*aged* words recorded in the glossary, 38 appeared in 1999 and 2000. In 1997 and 1998, Buffy lit a fuse (**slayage, missage, kissage, saveage, sliceage,** and **sparkage**); subsequently, use of the suffix exploded throughout the Buffyverse. For a while, the hyperactive use of -*age* served a social purpose, but eventually, by 2001, it had burned out

---

[10] McKean is a Buffyholic, and one can ascribe her liking for the term (which was coined, or at least suggested, by Jodi White of New York, who proposed it on the "What's Your Word?" segment of the Public Radio Internatioal program The Next Big Thing on 26 May 2002) confidently to the slayer slang proclivity for -age; I collected many other -age forms from general media while compiling the glossary (for instance, flakeage, as in "My flakeage rate is pretty low…but I am pretty ruthless; I don't like a excuses at all…a girl flakes that's it," quoted from the message board at **www.collegescream.com** [11 August 2001], and boilage, as in "Now we have obtained boilage. It's time to integrate the cocoa powder," quoted from an episode of Alton Brown's Food Network show Good Eats (13 February 2002), but could not, in good conscience, include them, as there is no reason to believe, given the history of -age in English and in American slang, that the forms were influenced by slayer slang.

from overuse, perhaps because its versatility limited its potential. Or, if you prefer, styles change. While slayer slang would always need a styling suffix, -*age* was superseded. In order for it to serve the same social purposes, its replacement had to be established already as a feature of slayer slang, but it needed to be more flexible than -*ness*, more interesting, and ultimately more disruptive, than -*age*.

Because it satisfies such requirements, -*y* has become the ultimate slayer slang suffix. Its prominence is due partly to the sheer accumulation of forms, about 100 items in the glossary, depending on how one counts, but, one might argue, the large number of forms reflects -*y*'s suitability.[11] But its distribution among the years covered by the glossary is revealing, too. The glossary records more -*y* forms than -*age* or -*ness* forms for all but one year: 5 in 1997 (versus 2 and 1 for -*age* and -*ness*, respectively), 7 in 1998 (rather than 5 and 4), 14 in 1999 (compared to 21 and 6), 15 in 2001 (as opposed to 4 and 7), and 33 in 2002 (far outdistancing 5 and 8). The comparative figures are significant: one sees that, while firmly established as part of slayer slang from the outset, -*y* gains incredible currency just as -*age* winds down; though the number of -*y* suffixed words increases by a factor of 2 in 1999, -*age* maintains its ascendency for that year, but their relative frequency reverses in 2000, after which -*age* contributes to the lexicon negligibly, while -*y* replaces it as the hyperactive suffix. Indeed, I did not record all possible -*y* forms from 2001 and 2002, given limitations of space, and my impression from notes taken during the seventh season (items from which are not in-

---

[11] For handy reference, here is a list of the glossary's -*y* forms: *Angely, angsty, avoidy, bitey, bookwoormy, brainwashy, Bronzey, broody, cardboardy, cartoony, checky, chickeny, commandery, couply, crayon-breaky, demony, depressedy, developmenty, diggy, discipliny, double-shiftiness, Dracy, driveyness, dusty, eaty, fangy, fevery, fighty, fortressy, frowny, geekiness, girl-powery, glowery, griefy, groiny, hackery, haunty, heart of darknessy, huntery, judgy, kitteny, knifey, lizardy, matchy, mathiness, metaphory, melty, murdery, necklacey, non-mathy, non-slayey, non-vengeance demony, out-of-the-loopy, passiony, pointy, pokey, posty, punctury, rampagey, ranty, researchy, revealy, rinsey, roby, rumbly, rushy, samey, secret agenty, shrimpy, skulky, slippy, snoozey, stammery, stay iny, stompy, stiff upper-lippy, stakey, stretchy, stripy, surfacey, topicy, trancey, twelve-steppy, twitchy, unbendy, unminiony, unmixy, unwindy, vampiry, vampy, veiny, wakey-girl, whispery, wicca-y, wiggy, witchy, wolfy,* and *wrathy.* I have not included **hottie** in this list, because, though the word plays an important role in slayer slang, it clearly predates the show, precisely in the sense illustrated by the glossary. I exclude **untopicy** and **untopicyness** because they are clearly formed on **topicy**; even though **veininess** occurred in an episode of the show some months before another episode introduced **veiny**, I have included the latter here, as the more basic form.

cluded in the glossary) is that -*age* has all but disappeared and -*y* remains productive. In other words, -*y* has assumed the mantle of slayer slang's social suffix since 2000.

Like -*ness* and -*age*, -*y* is embedded deep in the history of English, but it carries fewer constraints. OED2 summarizes -*y* (sv -*y* suffix[1]) as follows:

> The general sense of this suffix is 'having the qualities of' or 'full of' that which is denoted by the n[oun] to which it is added.... As early as the 13th c[entury] this suffix began to be used with verb-stems to express the meaning 'inclined or apt to' do something, or 'giving occasion' to a certain action.... From the early years of the 19th cent[ury] the suffix has been used still more freely in nonce-words designed to connote such characteristics of a person or thing as call for condemnation, ridicule, or contempt.

Of course, these count as definitions, but they offer the suffix a great deal more latitude than that allowed -*ness*, for instance, which can only raise its root to abstractness; and OED2's treatment of -*y* is much less specific than *AHD4*'s treatment of -*age*, which suggests that -*y* operates more fluidly than the other suffix. This doesn't mean that -*y* doesn't mean lots of things, but only that the meaning it adds to a root, beyond what the OED defines, is less easily generalized, less easily pinned down into subsenses, than meanings of -*age*. In this opinion, *AHD4* (sv -*y*[1] *suff*) more or less concurs: "1. Characterized by; consisting of: *clayey*. 2a. Like: *summery*. b. To some degree; somewhat; rather: *chilly*. 3. Tending toward; inclined toward: *sleepy*." All of this leads to one conclusion: -*y* has a lot of semantic room in which to maneuver.

To be an effective slang suffix, however, there have to be some "rules" or "acceptability standards" about use of -*y*, rules or standards that can be bent a bit, if not broken. And there are, some of them resembling those we apply to -*ness* and -*age*. For instance, we generally like to join -*y* with simple roots: we don't raise an eyebrow at forms from noun roots such as *messy*, *milky*, or *windy*, or those from verb roots such as **bendy**, **stretchy**, or **unwindy**; we say *shadowy* and *willowy* without tripping over our tongues for fear of disapproval. But three syllables is about as far as we like to go. Just as we accept **neat-freakishness** and **Christian Baleage** only reluctantly, if at all, we notice immediately that **commandery**, crayon-breaky, developmenty, discipliny, girl-powery, heart of darknessy, vengeance demony, out-of-the-loopy, secret agenty, stiff upper-lippy, and **unminiony** are strangely long.[12] Length is not the only aberration we hear: we usually keep our inevitably unstressed suffixes close to a word's stressed syllable, easy enough in the case of one-syllable roots; but in cases like **crayon-breaky, developmenty, discipliny,** and **girl-powery**, there's a lot more unstress than stress. Occasionally, we are surprised by an unlikely sequence of sounds, as in **wicca-y.**

Slayer slang, beyond questions of word length and distribution of stress, also challenges our assumptions about what types of words take the -y suffix. Historically, the OED tells us, -y took hold of nouns and turned them into adjectives, but the nouns have been common, for the most part, not proper, so **Angely** and **Dracy** are, according to historical patterns, unpredictable, though technically no rules have been broken. And while OED2 and AHD4 agree that -y can attach to verbs as well as nouns, no one expects it on the ends of adjective roots, such as **depressedy, out of the loopy,** or **samey.** (Note that some items are all the more surprising because they bend more than one rule.) Then, some words, for reasons we can't quite articulate, don't seem likely candidates for -y suffixation, like *fortress* or *rampage*. It isn't that they are long words, or even ganglier phrases, or that they are redundantly adjectival; perhaps they are used so infrequently that we can't quite conceive circumstances that require an adjective form of the root. Or perhaps we notice, although only intuitively, that suffixation obviates simile and metaphor: like *a fortress* or *on a rampage* are already accepted forms that **fortressy** and **rampagey** replace, some would say for no good reason.

But that misses the fun of such forms, the fun of saying something (or hearing it) in a novel way. While by no means all of the -ness, -age, and -y forms registered in the glossary deserve an appreciative gasp or a round of applause, many of them are eminently clever and the sort of word anyone would be lucky to say or write. I am delighted by the suffixed phrases, like **out-of-the-loopy** and **stiff upper-lippy,** and especially **stay iny,** which Buffy uses to explain, not why she doesn't want

---

[12] *The potential for -y to create a cumbersome form is not new to slayer slang; it has been with us as long as we've had the suffix and has often been realized in actual words—consider forms such as girl-guidey, mentioned in OED2 sv* **guide.**

to leave the house, but why she doesn't want to reveal something publicly: *in here* is clipped from *in the closet*, as opposed to *out* from *out of the closet*, and context enriches the pathos and the humor of the form, because Buffy says it to Tara, Willow's out lesbian partner.

As is sometimes the case with *-age*, slayer slang *-y* affixes to a root with a meaning shifted slightly from what speech habits dictate, a less, if not the least, likely root to take the suffix in any case, though the slayer slang forms do not constitute what we call a semantic shift, the historical development of a new sense from an old one: all of the senses in question are available in standard English. Yet **stay iny** exhibits a tendency for slayer slang to reach for an oblique sense, and so does one of the earliest of slayer slang *-y* forms: in the episode *When She Was Bad* (15 September 1997), Giles insists to Buffy, "Punishing yourself like this is pointless," and Buffy replies, "It's entirely pointy." *Point* in this sense is a noun and, according to the rules, there's no reason it can't become an adjective by taking the *-y* suffix. Yet we tend to reserve *-y* for concrete nouns, like *point* 'end of a stake', as in Mr. *Pointy*, Buffy's mascot stake, the far from stuffed bedside companion of her late adolescence; so to suffix an abstract sense of *point* surprises and delights. Still, we have to question why it does: a day can be *breezy* as well as sunny, but one can have a *breezy* attitude, even on a calm day. The answer is probably a matter of history: some oblique senses have taken *-y* and the form has survived, even prospered; some have not or perhaps have not even been attempted, so strike us as bent even though parallel forms in the general lexicon seem straight enough.

At other times, obliqueness moves in the other direction, not from the concrete to the abstract but from the metaphorical to the concrete: it wouldn't be very polite, but if you called a small-statured person *shrimpy*, those listening would understand what you meant; they don't, however, expect you to use **shrimpy** to describe something, like a stomach, as the OED puts it, "full of" shrimp. As with certain *-age* forms, some *-y* forms in slayer slang do more than, in standard English, a well-regulated word should. The most impressive example is **crayon-breaky**, which Xander uses at the climactic moment in Season Six to describe a Willow who used to break crayons when they were children.

As with -*ness* and -*age*, slayer slang's use of -*y* is unusual, even in American slang, because it bends rules that even most nonce-forms obey to the letter; but one must remember that -*y* suffixation has generated new words throughout the history of English and, as Eble notes, is also productive in American slang. Like -*age*, -*y* is a durably popular slang suffix, and many recent forms with -*y* very likely owe little to slayer slang. In the teen magazine *Twist* (November 2001, p.8/2), we are asked to look at "[t]he vintage-y slip dress" that Gabrielle Union wore to the premiere of the film *Original Sin*; Maile Misajon remarks of the "sixties go-go" outfit in which *Teen Vogue* (Fall 2001, p. 47) dressed her, "This trend feels too costumey to me"; the satirical "newspaper" *The Onion* (24 September 2002) suggests that President "Bush should take up t'ai chi. He'd be a lot more relaxed and not so invady," that is, not of your personal space, but geopolitically; and Tad Friend writes in *The New Yorker* (11 November 2002) that "[Richard Wiseman's] science-y hypothesis that Germans and women like simple jokes because their frontal lobes are relatively puny went nowhere. Like a setup without a punch line." *The Onion* and *The New Yorker* are not periodicals one generally searches for slang, but that makes their use of -*y* all the more interesting. I said at the beginning of this paragraph that slayer slang had influenced these uses "little," but that little is undeniable: -*y* suffixation (and -*age* suffixation) has received a boost from the prominent, hyperactive tendencies of slayer slang. Suffixation that, in the first instance, serves the interests of a narrow speech community, in fact may influence speech practices (or, at least, the acceptability of speech habits) in English generally.

Shifty Slang

On 27 September 1997, dinner in my lap and not much to do, I surfed through the channels until I heard "Love makes you do the wacky," and I was, by virtue of that functional shift of *wacky* from its accustomed role as adjective to the novel one of noun, hooked on *Buffy* from that day forward, from one Monday to the next (or Tuesday, later on), jonesing for more slayer slang, forced by gaps in the season and the summer-long hiatus to compile a glossary or suffer withdrawal. Functional shifts constitute a significant proportion of slayer slang (perhaps as many as 48 items, depending on what counts as a shift, are included in the glossary), and a number of items introduced via that process parallel the **wacky** that caught my wandering attention six years ago.[13] As with the suffixes, shifts from adjective to noun are redundant (by saying "Love makes you wacky," Buffy would have conveyed essentially the same point), and so annoy the linguistic status quo; they are also expressive, because they propose the thingness of an affective state, and doing so makes the adjective palpable, as when personification fleshes out metaphor.

Slayer slang includes many nouns that have become adjectives (see n14), a shift quite frequent in English, indeed, the process by which many of our adjectives historically have been formed. Slayer slang itself demonstrates the tendency, first in the extension of nouns to nouns used attributively, and then in the shift to adjective (**Slayer** is an excellent example). But the shift from adjective to noun is much less frequent in English generally and, unlike the suffixes -age and -y or vogue prefixes like über-, is not particularly characteristic of American slang. Slayer slang usually deploys the definite article (or, in the case of **happy**, the indefinite article) to emphasize that shift's unlikelihood.

Shifts from noun to verb are no more surprising nowadays than shifts from noun to adjective. As noted in the previous chapter, though, they are an important element of slayer slang, partly because, with few exceptions, the forms recorded in the glossary shift, not common nouns,

---

[13] For easy reference, here are the forms included in the glossary: alone, Carrie, crazy, creepy, cryptic, David Lynch, Dawson's Creek, 007, Felicity, funny, genius, good, grim, happy, kung fu, Lifetime TV, mad, mad-on, moral, nasty, postal, somber, special forces, Stepford, suspicious, unfun, Village People, Waco, weird, Wild Bunch, and Willy Loman. It is important to note that these forms are not all precisely parallel to **wacky**. Several shift in reverse, from noun to adjective, especially in verb phrases that involve going all something (**kung fu** or **Wild Bunch**, for instance), but not exclusively (**genius**); **Stepford** is not quite a reversal, since the place-name is already used attributively in the film title from which it is taken. Others are more subtly different: while most adjectives nouned in slayer slang take the definite article (the **wacky**, the **funny**), **happy** conspicuously takes the indefinite article; **alone** and **somber** are unarticled, though the latter is preceded by a pronoun (your **somber**). Shifts from noun to verb receive separate treatment below.

but proper names, usually the names of fictional characters, and reflect Buffy's tendency to trade on pop-cultural references; also, as a matter of semantics, they help the Buffyverse to cohere, because such terms are only comprehensible from a common frame of reference, since there isn't really a meaning in the name that can shift along with the function.[14] Some have suggested that, in order for such shifts to work, a general nominal sense must develop from the name in the minds of those using the verbed name, so that the verb can derive its meaning from that intermediary (and probably unrealized) form. There are a few semantic shifts from proper names to common nouns that would enable a subsequent functional shift: **Carrie** (in sense 1), **Exorcist twist**, **Full Monty**, **Gene and Roger**, **Houdini** (interestingly, the example the Clarks use to discuss the issue in their article), and **William Burroughs**. **Scooby Gang** and **Mod Squad**, while not generalized, are reapplied to new referents that resemble the originals in critical aspects. None of these forms, though, is subsequently verbed.

By far the most significant functional shift in slayer slang, however, is that of **much** from adverb to adjective. As adverb, *much* can mean 'to a great degree', as in "No one can be much happier than I," or 'frequently, often', as in "I don't watch television much." We have long accepted short, interrogative sentences composed of VERB + *much* in colloquial English: if you trip on the sidewalk, your sarcastic companion may ask, "Walk much?" The glossary includes a few examples of this well-established use from the Buffyverse, as a contrastive index against which we can measure the novelty of the shifted form. Even these VERB + *much* constructions strain against the idiom somewhat, however: "Smell of booze much?"; "Over-identify much?"; "Procrastinate much?"; "Invade personal space much?"; "Antagonize much?"; "Hey, respect the narrative flow much?" On hearing some of the longer antecedent phrases, we realize that the pattern we have come to accept is really SIMPLE PRESENT TENSE VERB + *much* + INTERROGATIVE. As usual, even when following an

---

[14] *Slayer slang admits only a few shifts from noun to verb, as follows:* **Andy Sipowicz**, **Clark Kent**, **guinea pig**, **Jimmy Hoffa**, **Keyser Soze**, **Psych 101**, **Sherlock**, **Scully**, *and* **single-white-female**. **Bronzing** *is formed on the hypothetical verb* *Bronze, which, were it recorded, must have shifted from* **Bronze** *in sense* 1.

established pattern of speech, slayer slang resists the rules. And it isn't that slayer slang observes the spirit of the rule rather than the letter; quite to the contrary, it adheres rigorously to the rule, so rigorously that the rule's inadequacy, from a conservative point of view, is unexpectedly exposed.[15]

A page from basic eighth-grade grammar reminds us that adverbs can modify adjectives, as well as verbs—"I feel much better," we say, or "That won't do much good." Technically, then, there should be nothing wrong with much modifying adjectives, but, as with the application of certain suffixes, as soon as we allow it, we realize that our expectations of how much, or any adverb, actually can be used, are much more precise than we had realized. Again, insisting on the letter of the law is a sort of rebellion, as when, having been grounded, but then told to take out the trash after dinner, we say to our parents, "I'm sorry, I can't. Didn't you tell me that I'm not to leave the house? Oh, I see: I can leave the house to do something for YOU but not because I want to. What if a speeding car is about to run over one of the neighborhood children? Should I leave the house to save him, or should I call you for permission first?"

Interrogative sentences of the form ADJECTIVE + much simply sound wrong to anyone who expects to hear standard English. Among other things, we are wary of the semantics of much in these syntactic situations, because the sentences themselves never offer any context, and the much in question usually fuses the two definitions given above: Megan Howard, in her glossary of Buffy terms for *Entertainment Weekly* (1999), attempts to define the whole sentence "Pathetic much?" pragmatically (and inaccurately), as "Feeling sorry for yourself?"; but this merely side-steps the problem of defining much in the sentence, as either 'to a great degree' ("Are you totally pathetic?") or 'often' ("Are you always this pathetic?"), or both.

But word order also bothers the orthodox speaker: in declarative sentences, much precedes the adjective it modifies, and it does so too in the

---

[15] I have often wondered since Buffy's self-sacrifice in Season Five, whether her headstone epitaph, "She Saved the World. A Lot," was quite apt; perhaps it should have read "Save the World Much?" instead.

most likely interrogative sentence ("That didn't do much good"/"Didn't that do much good?"); interrogative sentences in English invert the positions of subjects and verbs ("You are ready for this"/ "Are you ready for this?"), but not other words in other positions. The fact explains why "Walk much?" is immediately more acceptable than "Gross much?" as adverbs generally follow the verbs they modify—the "natural order" is preserved in VERB + much sentences, but not in ADJECTIVE + much sentences.

Also, contemporary English tends to collocate much + COMPARATIVE ADJECTIVE: we can say "I don't like skim milk or powdered milk, but powdered milk is much grosser/more gross than skim"; we are not likely to say either "Powdered milk is much gross" or "Powdered milk is gross much." Again, as a matter of fundamental English grammar, there isn't anything wrong with the latter sentences, but they remind us that a definition isn't necessarily a synonym: we can say "Powdered milk is often/usually gross" and "Powdered milk is gross to a great degree," but we do not accept the simple replacement of much for either of the terms by which it is defined—grammar is sometimes subject to lexical meaning, or perhaps it's better to say that grammar and lexical meaning cooperate in idiom, and interrogative ADJECTIVE + much is, if nothing else, unidiomatic.

Though first introduced, as far as we can tell, in the film *Heathers* (1989), Buffy experiments with the ADJECTIVE + much as early as the 1992 film; present in the television series from the second episode (10 March 1997) and used frequently in every corner of the Buffyverse, it has become a signature feature of slayer slang: "Morbid much?"; "Insane much?"; "Blind much?"; "Typecast much?"; "God, self-involved much?"—these are all mildly outrageous sentences. Neither parents nor teachers gave anyone permission to speak this way; such innovations, as Whitman said, are the poetry of a moment, and because poetry deliberately sees and says things different from the quotidian way, it always taunts convention, even as it exploits it.

VERB + much is, though colloquial rather than standard American English, fully acceptable, given those terms; ADJECTIVE + much is clearly nonstandard and plays cat-and-mouse with the rules, a slightly more adventurous game than that played by the suffixes *-age* and *-y*, though the confrontation with idiom is similar to theirs. But slayer slang goes farther with much than it does with the suffixes: it has generated several instances of NOUN + much, and since adverbs do not modify nouns, such sentences stand precariously on the brink of unacceptability. True, much has standard adjective senses, one of which corresponds to the first adverbial sense given above—'great in quantity, degree, or extent'; but that sense does not really capture the meaning of much in slayer slang's NOUN + much sentences, which retain a vestige of adverbial meaning, even though it shouldn't apply.

Consider some examples culled from quotations in the glossary: "Crush much?";[16] "...fetish much?..."; "God, tuna much?..."; "Meanwhile, My Best Friend's Wedding/Friends much?"; "Control freak much?"; "Curb much?" Does "God, tuna much?" express a concern that there's a great quantity of tuna, "too much tuna," in somebody's sandwich? Not really. In context, it challenges the very state of affairs, that someone would bring a tuna sandwich to the high school cafeteria at all. It might be expanded to "God, are you a tuna sandwich eater?," which isn't far from "God, do you usually bring tuna sandwiches to school?," which reveals a vestige of adverbial meaning in what, according to the rules, ought to be an adjective. Similarly, "Curb much?" questioned the speaker's boyfriend's talent for parallel parking; it can be expanded to "Do you hit the curb often when you park?" and very clearly means much adverbially, even though curb is unquestionably a noun. It can be argued that much in these cases modifies a verb that is understood, but this seems implausible to me: far too much needs to be understood and, as the preceding examples demonstrate, we can't really put our finger on the supposedly understood verb—several verbs might fill the blank. Even more disturbing, ADJECTIVE + much and NOUN + much sentences are not always inflected as questions (as opposed to their VERB + much counterparts), suggesting that there is no verb assumed ("[Buffy:] 'I'm sorry, okay?' [Dawn:] 'Broken-record much.'").

[16] The title of a feature in Seventeen (Spring/Summer 1998), this example is somewhat problematic: it reads like VERB + much, and crush can be a verb, though by far the more usual form is phrasal, (to) crush on (somebody) rather than to crush (somebody). See Chapter 3, pages 91–92.

In the case of NOUN + much, then, either a rule is broken (adverbs don't modify nouns), or a rule is amended (adverbs can modify nouns), or there is a new part of speech (the adnoun), or the adverb shifts to a new adjective sense. In fact, none of these alternatives quite explains the situation. The special quality of slayer slang *much* has attracted many users outside of the Buffyverse; as a result, *much* has already entered mainstream American slang and, as opposed to most items of slayer slang, is likely here to stay. It is too antagonistic, though, to enter standard American English, which is just as well, since such a development would spoil the fun and rob slayer slang *much* of its very purpose. Slang is a type of linguistic jaywalking: you can stand at the crosswalk and wait for the light to change, but that would be boring, as well as slow, so we'd rather not. Adverbial *much* jaywalks when it modifies adjectives; when it modifies nouns, it's about as extreme as language gets.

Pleasantly shocking as it is, NOUN + much doesn't really break new ground; rather, it imitates slang uses of *so* that are somewhat better established, and by now more readily accepted, than the extreme applications of slayer slang *much*. Only the purest among us flinch when one Gap shopper says to another critically, "That's so Eighties," or enthusiastically, "That's so Seventies." Come to think of it, though, the purest among us probably don't shop at the Gap. Like slayer slang *much*, this intensive *so* modifies nouns. Indeed, *so* is entered in the glossary, partly because it isn't yet entered in dictionaries, partly because it, too, is an item of slayer slang, a point of intersection between the English inside and outside of the Buffyverse. Interestingly, though, and perhaps because the application of *so* to nouns is now commonplace, so less transgressive, the glossary includes only two examples of *so* + NOUN, both of them from 1997, when they may have played a role in the gradual development of NOUN + much.

Mixed Etymologies in Slayer Slang

Etymology is the study of word history, primarily history of the forms of words and secondarily in their meanings, since meaning often changes after a word's form is (more or less) permanently established. In dictionaries, etymologies are usually restricted to identifying the form antecedent to that defined. So Modern English *slay* developed from Middle English *slen*, *slayen*, which in turn developed from Old English *slēan*, and so forth. *Slen/slayen* is *slay*'s etymon; *slay* is *slen/slayen*'s reflex. Generally, we assume a one-to-one correspondence between etymon and reflex, but in the last few decades, linguists have begun to question our etymological assumptions. Any form that combines elements is more problematic: *crayon-breaky* is an amalgamation of *crayon*, which has its history, *break*, which has another, and *-y*, which has yet another history; yet we can say confidently that *crayon-breaky* derives from *crayon n* (in some sense) + *break v* (in some sense) + *-y suff* (in some sense)—just as the glossary does word for word (and sometimes sense by sense).

Sometimes, though, and in slang especially, the forming of new words depends not on straightforward development from an etymon by some paradigm (NOUN + -y, for instance), but also on a broad range of source-words. The new word develops, not as matter of form, but as the product of a network of cultural associations. As Roger W. Wescott has argued, while "[l]inguists in general and etymologists in particular usually assume that vocabulary items in any given language are monogenetic and can be derived from single ancestral items," his own experience "inclines [him] to regard many lexifications as linguistic analogs of dreams," and the term for "the process by which the crucial elements of a dream are generated is 'overdetermination'. Overdetermination means multiple causation or motivation," and "the role of overdetermination in generating and perpetuating lexemes is to assert...that most of our overt language behavior is accompanied by a flurry of covert word-association activity." Connie Eble has noticed the phenomenon particularly in American slang: "Sometimes more than one explanation of the origin of a word is plausible—multiple etymology." I prefer the term "mixed etymology," also Eble's, because "multiple" suggests that we can parse the boundaries among various influences when we can't, but also when the various influences may be influencing one another at the same time that they influence the slayer slang (or any other) form.[17] Here follow several case studies of mixed etymology in slayer slang.

If you are 18, you may not find **sabrina** 'witch' difficult to explain etymologically, as you may have watched *Buffy the Vampire Slayer* on Tuesdays and *Sabrina the Teenage Witch* on Fridays throughout your teen years; a Buffyatric, however, approaches the term from a different frame of reference. Sabrina the Teenage Witch first appeared as an occasional character in *Archie* comics in 1962; she first appeared on television as an animated character in *Archie's TV Laugh Out #1* in 1969; she was the central character in her own series of comic books from 1971. Then, more recently, Melissa Joan Hart portrayed the character in a live-action made-for-television film on the Showtime cable network (1996); ABC premiered a prime-time series, *Sabrina the Teenage Witch*, with the same star, in the same year; the series subsequently moved to the WB Network, the network originally responsible for *BTVS*.

Youth culture has so long been aware of Sabrina as a character, through several media, that the script may owe the genericization of her name to any or many possible sources. The show's writers undoubtedly remember an earlier version of Sabrina, but they could hardly have been unaware of the Sabrina with which they shared a network and with which they continue to share a teen audience. Many friends have asked me, in the progress of this book, whether I have ever interviewed *Buffy* writers to determine the etymologies of slayer slang items like **sabrina**, but I have not done so, simply because, about questions of mixed etymologies, the show's writers can have no better answers than I: simply by

---

[17] *Wescott makes a similar point: "To take a polygenetic view of word origins inevitably involves making at least two other basic but controversial assumptions about etymology. The first of these is that lexical ancestry is relative rather than absolute in nature. This means not only that etymologists should distinguish between what might be called the 'lineal' and the 'collateral' ancestors of any given lexeme but that lineality itself is a gradient rather than a discrete aspect of lexical ancestry. The second is that, because of this derivational relativity, there is a gradual 'fade-out' in the etymological antecedence of any lexeme and that this fade-out effect, in turn, leads inescapably to subjectivity in the assessment of degrees of lexical ancestry. While this subjectivity can be mitigated by active etymological collaboration, it cannot be eliminated by this means but only, at best, converted into 'intersubjectivity'—that is, collective (as opposed to individual) subjectivity."*

virtue of age and culture, none of the show's writers could have been unaware of Sabrina pre-Buffy, nor could they have been so oblivious as to overlook *Sabrina the Teenage Witch*, nor could they say reliably which had been the greater influence on their writing. In other words, the source of a slayer slang term need not be immediate: replacement of **Slayerettes** with **Scooby Gang** reached back to the much earlier television cartoon *Scooby Doo*, though the original series had seen several sequels and had been rerun continuously since it first aired. That *Sabrina* shared the WB Network with *Buffy* is probably significant, though, as the term occurred on the show after *Sabrina the Teenage Witch* jumped networks.

Marti Noxon, who wrote the episode of *BTVS* in which it occurred, may have reinvented **manimal**, a fairly obvious blend; but the term had been used before and, as a canonical term in Faith's philosophy, opposed to another pop-cultural reference, it probably refers simultaneously to several previous uses. While nervously moving objects around his desk during his first night as host of NBC's *The Tonight Show* (25 May 1992), Jay Leno turned his coffee mug to reveal *manimal* written on the side, generally hidden from the camera's view. The event might have lodged in Noxon's unconscious until it emerged in her script; or its presence on the mug might indicate the term's currency, otherwise unrecorded at the time. Leno isn't the only self-proclaimed *manimal*, though, and a quick troll through websites called up by a search for *manimal* yields, among many other things, several home pages devoted to those whose nicknames are, apparently, *Manimal*, for instance, that of Richard "Manimal" Brant (www.users.aol.com/rockpage1/rocko.html). Leno and others may have taken their nickname from Hasbro, Inc.'s action figures called *Manimals*, or from the short-lived television series *Manimal*, which lasted from 30 September 1983 to 31 December 1983, on NBC. Both are phenomena of which Noxon was likely aware, if not consciously, at least in the back of her mind.

Edge Girl is an even more vexing item, a product of so many current senses of *girl* that it boggles the mind. It *girl* is notably absent from the dictionary record. The term was introduced by Elinor Glyn's novel "*It*" (1927). The *Historical Dictionary of American Slang* provides examples of it 'sex appeal' to 1992, but none for the phrase. In fact, the phrase is currently very popular. In a review of Clarence Badger's film, It, recently released on videocassette, Glenn Kenny writes in *Premiere* that "This 1927 spoof, which chronicles [Clara] Bow's adventures while trying to live up to the Glyn ethos, permanently fixed the star in the public's mind as, yes, the 'It' girl.... Filling out the series [of films re-released on video] is a documentary, *Clara Bow: Discovering the 'It' Girl*, narrated by would-be inheritor Courtney Love" (September 1999, p. 101/4). The cover of *Entertainment Weekly* (June 26/July 2 1999) announces the "It List: 100 Most Creative People in Entertainment" and features a photograph of the actress, Heather Graham, with the caption, "And the It Girl Heather Graham." Gerri Hershey describes Missy Elliott thus: "It is only 6:00 p.m., but she has been going full-tilt Missy since 6 a.m., owing to the burdens of being hip-hop's It Girl" (*Rolling Stone* [Jul 8–22, 1999]: p. 55/1). Actress Chloe Sevigny is "[n]o longer the 16-year-old 'It girl' and raver I met at NASA seven years ago," writes Walter Cessna (*Raygun* [July 1999]: p. 37). Ray Pride praises "...Guinevere, Audrey Wells' neatly directed take on the way we look at the other person when we're in love, starring this year's 'It' girl, Canadian-born Sarah Polley" (*Filmmaker* [Summer 1999]: p. 10). And Michael Angeli proposes that "[e]very year the Great Western University of Hotties admits a new class of 'It' girls" (*Movieline* [December/January 2000]: p. 74). It, as a clipping from It girl, is not foreign to the Buffyverse: a brief article in the official magazine (Spring 1999, p. 14/4) heralding the imminent appearance of Buffy action figures is titled "'It' Figures," a characteristically clever phrasal pun, but one no less obviously aware of the antecedent, given the quotations marks around It.

But **Edge Girl** may be more than usually susceptible to mixed etymology, especially as multiple origins develop into a self-reinforcing etymological network. For instance, *Riot Grrls* are an alternative contemporary version of *It girls*, not those with classic sex appeal, but those who are wild, independent, and edgy, as appropriate to their urban place and millennial time; the phrase, like many others in our common vocabulary, is formed by analogy with It girl. **Edge Girl** arrives on a scene already populated by both It girls and Riot Grrls, and it's impossible to know which of these, or which other parallel forms, individually or collectively, wrote **Edge Girl** into the script. An aspect of American culture, *Riot Grrls* and **Edge Girls** are at least as affiliated with each other as either with *It girls*. Though writing on a completely different topic, Tom Frank incidentally observes the similarity:

> Not only were the majority of the Planners female and a good number of them British, but I appeared to be the lone square in an auditorium of high-budget hipsters. They had arrived at the Westin in white synthetic T-shirts stretched tightly over black brassieres, in those oblong spectacles favored by European intellectuals, in hair that had been bleached, bobbed, and barretted after the Riot Grrl style.... No one actually came right out and complained that Planning's newfound popularity in the American hinterland meant that it had lost its edge or sold out to the Man, but the feeling was difficult to miss.

The show is explicitly aware of the connections among "girl power" (see **girl powery**), Riot Grrls, **Edge Girl**s, and the show's young women characters: as Willow remarks in the episode Living Conditions (12 October 1999), "Exactly. I mean, did we not put the 'grr' in 'Grrl'?" Others have also noted these connections: "What is Girl (or, correctly, Grrrl) Power all about?" asks Eleanor Bailey (*The Independent* [London] 1996, p. 3).

Girl power, though yet unrecorded in dictionaries, permeated mass culture when the Spice Girls, an internationally popular British, all-girl, short-lived pop group claimed that it was what they were all about. As early as 18 October 1996, the *Scottish Daily Record* quoted a representative of Virgin Records asserting that, in the Spice Girls, "Girl power is seeing off the boy bands." Bailey writes that "Cultural phenomena are like haircuts. They used to last for years, but now experts recommend that you get a new one every six weeks. The latest in the phenomenon line is Girl Power. Personified by the Spice Girls, and vilified by the over-40s, girl power is the babeish answer to the Loaded Lad: girls going wild, showing their knickers and going on drinking sprees, on behalf of women and record companies everywhere."

As is often the case, the British use of the term differs from the American, which has less to do with knickers and drinking and more to do with the authority of young women over their own lives and in the world. And Buffy appears to represent such a young woman to her fans.

According to Debbie Stoller, writing in the pseudo-political magazine *George*, "Buffy the Vampire Slayer, played with uncommon vitality by Sarah Michelle Gellar, represents real girl power, the kind that can kung-fu the undead back into oblivion" (1998, p. 110). *Girl power* is just what qualified Gellar to appear in the collection of *George's* set of brief articles on "The 20 Most Fascinating Women in Politics: Women Who Rule." Buffy and Gellar both are praised as role models for young women because they exhibit *girl power*: Joyce Millman, television critic for the online magazine *Salon*, is quoted by Annabelle Villanueva in *Cinescape* (January/February 1999, p. 39) as saying that she "was also quite taken with Buffy's self-confidence and physical strength—you don't see that very often in television portrayals of teenage girls." Articles on BTVS and Gellar have more than once appeared between the covers of the magazine *Teen Girl Power*. BTVS-inspired novels acknowledge the connection between *girl power* and Buffy's role: "'Hey,' Buffy joined in, 'Just because they've put up their No Chicks Allowed sign doesn't mean we have to agree.' Willow nodded. 'Girl power.'" (Craig Shaw Gardner, *Return to Chaos* [1998], p. 103); and "Ethan raised his brows. 'For heaven's sake, you're just loaded with aggro now, aren't you. Slayer Spice. Girl power. Good Lord, why is the world still extant at all with a hothead like you as the Chosen One?'" (Christopher Golden and Nancy Holder, *Sons of Entropy* [1999], p. 127). The show, too, has made the connection. In the episode *Something Blue* (30 November 1999), Spike resolves an argument with Buffy in the same terms: "[Spike:] 'I may not be able to protect you.' [Buffy:] 'You think you have to protect me?' [Spike:] 'Oh, not with the girl power bit.'" In other words, **girl powery** is not an adventitious form, and *girl power* has survived longer than those who first noted the phenomenon expected.

The impetus for **Edge Girl**, then, may have been quite specific, or it may have been very general, for everyday parallel forms abound, as well, though -girl and -guy aren't registered as combining forms in major dictionaries: *fall guy*, *family guy*, *wise guy* (in two senses), *party girl*, and *society girl* are familiar words that come to mind. BTVS frequently introduces new items combined with -girl and -guy, including **Destructo-Girl**, **Net Girl**, *Tact Guy*, and *Amish Guy*, while the wider lexicon of slayer slang, including forms that have appeared in novels and on websites, offers up *Action Girl*, blood-sucking actor guy, computer girl, cricket guy, *Cryptic Guy*, *Danger Girl*, *Earthgirl*, fang-girl, **Hacker Girl**, Horn Guy, Inactivity Girl, jock guy, metric girl, Mr. Happy Guy, Night Owl's Good Luck Girl, not-sharing-stuff guy, research girl, *Safari Girl*, *Southern Girl*, *Stakegrrrl*, stupid girl, thirsty guy, and *Vacation Girl*.[18] And even these examples, while reinforcing the tendency that forms **Edge Girl**, may have mixed origins, since they belong to the same self-reinforcing system of combining, but may also have been influenced by forms outside of that system: *Stakegrrrl*, a posting board handle, has obvious antecedents; **Net Girl**, while easily re-derived, nonetheless appeared in the chorus to "Virtuality," a song by the rock group Rush, recorded on their album *Test for Echo* (1996): "Net boy, net girl / Send your signal 'round the world / ... Put your message in a modem / And throw it in the Cyber Sea." Needless to say, when the song was written, Net Girls were on the Edge.

Sorting through the alternative origins, as Eble argues, misses the point: **Edge Girl**, and some of the other -girl forms, likely arose from a network of lexical and cultural associations, both specific and general. The show's writers could hardly be unaware (as film buffs) of It girl; nor could they be unaware, as monitors of teen trends, of the late-1990s resurgence of the term; nor could they, as residents of greater Los Angeles, the classic *Edge City* (see *HDAS* sv **Edge City**) have missed the importance of *Edge*, applied to girl, guy, animal, or anything else. Ironically, according to a post on the Bronze (2 June 2001), Sarah Michelle Gellar will appear in a film titled *The It Girl*, though I have been unable to confirm this.

"There is nothing new under the sun," and many aspects of the making of slayer slang, from prefixation, suffixation, and shifting, to everything in between, and even the tendency toward mixed etymologies, seem to confirm the aphorism. While true enough metaphysics,

---

[18] *Readers are reminded that I made many decisions about what would be included in the course of collecting information for the glossary and in compiling and editing it: while I kept most of the -age and -y forms I encountered, I did not do the same for -girl and -guy forms. In part, this was due to a -girl bias, itself a product of cultural forces surrounding Buffy the Vampire Slayer, a show about girl power, if there ever was one. Though I had collected several more -girl forms than I ultimately included in the glossary, I cut them because I had failed to collect parallel -guy forms systematically. In other words, I included some representative and related -girl forms and left it at that. One must accept, however, that the etymological differences between -girl and -guy at the turn of the century are profound.*

Ecclesiastes suggests that the restless should settle down, and that's what bugs: why should we? Slayer slang is for the restless: it proves that we can outsmart ancient wisdom and be just innovative enough within a plethora of constraints to identify ourselves against the mundane, as well as the eternal. If we plan to taunt convention, not to mention mortality, we had better have the necessary words.

References

For a peerless summary of English word-formative processes and their relative importance, see John Algeo and Adele Algeo, *Fifty Years Among the New Words: A Dictionary of Neologisms* (New York: Cambridge University Press, 1991), pp. 3–14. I borrow the selected borrowings, and also the estimates of Latin and French influence on English vocabulary, from Allan Metcalf's *The World in So Many Words* (Boston: Houghton Mifflin, 1999). For a more thorough account of the etymology of *fuck*, see the second edition of *The F-Word*, edited by Jesse Sheidlower (New York: Random House, 1999), pp. xxv–xxxii. John Algeo's comment on the voguishness of certain prefixes is quoted from his article, "The Voguish Uses of Non," published in *American Speech* (Spring/Summer 1971), p. 87. Edna Andrews's analysis of *un-* appears in her article, "A Synchronic Semantic Analysis of *De-* and *Un-* in American English," also in *American Speech* (Autumn 1986), pp. 221–232. One can find Tasha Robinson's *The Onion A–V Club* interview with Joss Whedon in *The Tenacity of the Cockroach: Conversations with Entertainment's Most Enduring Outsiders*, edited by Stephen Thompson and others (New York: Three Rivers Press, 2002), pp. 368–377; the quotation is on p. 396. For further commentary on combining forms, see Adrienne Lehrer's "Scapes, Holics, and Thons: The Semantics of English Combining Forms," in *American Speech* (Spring 1998), pp. 3–28. Mencken's observation on *-dom* can be found in *The American Language* (New York: Knopf, 1936), p. 303. Alan R. Slotkin's "Adjectival *-less* and *-free*: A Case of Shifting Institutional Currency," published in *American Speech* (Spring 1990), pp. 33–49, sets the context for my discussion of *-free* here. Hostility to *-ness* is recorded, even beyond what I have quoted here, in Theodore Williams, "On the '-Ness' Peril," *American Speech* (Winter 1965), pp. 279–286. Burchfield's comment is from his edition of *The New Fowler's Modern English Usage* (New York: Oxford University Press, 1996), p. 520. Connie C. Eble's comments on *-age*, as well as those on *-y*, appear in *Slang & Sociability: In-Group Language among College Students* (Chapel Hill, NC: University of North Carolina Press, 1996), p. 33. Wilson Follett's comments on semantic inflation (for further on which, see Chapter 1) figure in *Modern English Usage. A Guide* (New York: Hill & Wang, 1966), pp. 221–222; Erik Wensberg's revision of Follett, with the same title and from the same publisher, appeared in 1998. Semantic aspects of shifts are treated thoroughly in Eve V. Clark and Herbert H. Clark, "When Nouns Surface as Verbs," *Language* 55 (1979), pp. 767–811. Roger W. Wescott is quoted from "Lexical Polygenesis: Words as Resultants of Multiple Linguistic Pressures," Fifth *LACUS* Forum (Columbia, SC: Hornbeam Press), pp. 81–92; Eble's views on multiple and mixed etymologies can be found in *Slang & Sociability*, p. 46. Tom Frank is quoted at length from his article "Brand You: Better Selling through Anthropology," *Harper's* (July 1999), pp. 74–79; the quotation runs from pp. 75/2–76/1. As in the previous chapter, examples of particular words, when not provided with references, are taken from the glossary.

CHAPTER 3

Studying the Micro-histories
of Words

When dictionaries not dedicated specifically to recording new words enter a word or sense of a word for the first time, it has very likely been around as long as the person who looks it up. Even a dictionary as comprehensive as the *Oxford English Dictionary* (henceforth OED) offers little insight into the early lives of words, as entries include evidence of use usually at 50-year intervals: even if the OED accurately identifies the first known written use of a word (as it does usually, but not infallibly), at least the next 25 years of the word's history is obscure, and those are the very years in which most words assert themselves and gain wider acceptance among English speakers. With all of its commendable detail, the OED nonetheless records only the macro-histories of words.

Dictionaries record a word once it is established within the vocabulary, but they rarely explain when, where, how, or why it appeared in the first place or how, from what must have been a single person's initial utterance, it achieves general use (though, of course, we don't expect them to). Linguists refer to this as The Actuation Problem: new words, new parts of words, sound changes, and developments in syntax have to start somewhere, somehow; but when they do, usually our backs are turned; by the time we turn around they are adolescents, and unless we can recover a record, we've missed their infancies. Slayer slang is interesting partly because it includes items whose origin and early development we can describe fairly reliably. While slayer slang won't solve The Actuation Problem, studying the micro-histories of words in slayer slang is an opportunity to gain insight into actuation.

Words are used for occasional purposes all of the time, well beyond our estimating; and, in the ferment of linguistic activity, those words are often recreated by speakers unaware that the words they make had ever been used previously. Certainly, the nonce-word raises issues of actuation: for instance, what motivated use of the term, and why was it chosen from among what may have been several plausible alternatives? Perhaps a speaker perceived a lexical gap or wanted to express herself with particular style. This is fundamental actuation, of the type we might call A1. But actuation is a problem broader than nonce-creation, or even recreation. All new words, new senses of words, and new syntactic patterns are nonce-forms until they are used again. Anyone who drives a car or makes an Internet connection over a telephone modem knows what it means to throw a spark or dial an access number, but not actually start the engine or make the connection. The Actuation Problem extends to making the connection between a nonce-form and its intrusion into the language, or at least into broader awareness within the relevant speech community (or communities), actuation of a type we might call A2.

Actuation much?

Slayer slang's **much** serves as an excellent case study in many aspects of actuation. It is possible, of course, that a slang sense of much related to that in slayer slang had been hanging in SoCal for some time before it first appeared in a text, but evidence of that has yet to arise. So much's inception (A1) may well have been in the film Heathers (1989), as mentioned before. Characters in the film ask, "God, Veronica, drool much?," an everyday example of colloquial VERB + much, and "Jealous much?," an example of ADJECTIVE + much that anticipates Buffy's innovative emphasis. The actuation here is not of much per se, because no new sense of much is required to collocate with adjectives; rather, ADJECTIVE + much represents the actuation of a syntactic pattern in which adverbial much is implicated. Its motivation is difficult to pin down, but seems to be entirely a matter of style, of speaking individually and rebelliously along the lines discussed in Chapter 1.

Conventional wisdom insists that effective actuation of a word or other linguistic practice requires a certain (undetermined) level of repetition, probably not on the part of the original speaker alone, but by other speakers in various contexts. But it is worth considering a special advantage of film in the age of videos and DVDs and television in the age of syndication: we view our favorite films and television shows over and over again; thus, novel terms or sounds or sentence patterns we might otherwise hear and forget are repeated in our presence as frequently as we like, though in exactly the same context and by exactly the same speaker as each time before, without development of any kind. The circumstance does not change the terms of actuation broadly: if a term never leaves the television screen (or, perhaps more precisely, the speakers), it won't end up in general use; yet invariant repetition would seem to increase the chances that an eccentric term, easily passed over or forgotten, ends up memorable to many auditors and at least one speaker, who ignites use of the term by using it around others to whom it is already subliminally familiar. Many, many American English speakers have seen *Heathers* repeatedly; since its release, the film has attracted a cult following, and its most enthusiastic fans often quote it in conversation. Buffy exhibits the same potential, but exponentially, as terms and patterns of speech develop from episode to episode and then are repeated endlessly in reruns, homemade videotapes, and gradually released DVDs in a way unimaginable; as the effect of hit-and-miss television viewing, this inundation more or less permanently inscribes slayer slang into the mental lexicon.

Inception (A1) and repetition are two of several processes necessary to thorough actuation (A2); they are followed closely by experiment and imitation, two closely related processes (all experiment is, in some sense, imitation, but the relationship is not reciprocal), of which the glossary gives considerable evidence in the case of **much**. Whedon's "Excuse much—rude or anything?" and "Smell of booze much?" are both VERB + much constructions and seem unremarkable, but they are actually subtle, if not awfully successful, experiments in how far a speaker can stretch the syntactic convention. When we say sentences like *Walk much?* we shorten *Do you walk much?*; *Do you* is understood by both

speaker and auditor. At first glance, Whedon's sentences seem well-be-
haved, but they aren't really: *Do you excuse much is not what he has in
mind; if anything is understood, it must be a pronoun, yet it isn't the me
we usually assume, but you, as in the very colloquial declaration Excuse
you! And what is the result? Excuse (you) much, which makes a lot less
immediate sense than Walk much?, not least because the question in
question is "... rude or anything?" rather than the phrase involving much.
"Smell of booze much?" is a question, at least, but it certainly doesn't
shorten Do you smell of booze much? because Buffy knows that Pike smells;
atypically, the new sentence type isn't a shortening at all and once again
isn't really a question, but declaration posing as one.[1]

While it's difficult to imagine that, as a rising screenwriter, Whedon
hadn't registered repeated innovative use of much in Heathers, his experiments with much in the 1992 film may have resulted in ADJECTIVE +
much independently, as a result not of imitation, but out of his experiments with VERB + much in the film. In any event, by the show's second
episode, which aired on the same night as the first (10 March 1997), he
had smoothed out his approach to much and arrived at the adjective
collocation. That episode's "Morbid much?" led to "Pathetic much?"
(22 September 1997), "Having issues much?" (8 December 1997), and
"Over-identify much?" (28 April 1998), all in scripts by different writers; either they were all imitating Heathers, or they were imitating Whedon
imitating Heathers, or they were imitating Whedon after his own idiom
had settled, regardless of Heathers. But imitation doesn't exclude experiment, and writers hadn't given up the notion that something innovative
could be accomplished with VERB + much. They were right: having issues
and over-identify aren't the verbs that typically appear with much in the
colloquial paradigm; they are phrasal or multi-syllabic or contemporary,

---

[1] Increasingly, much constructions have lost their interrogative intonation. I include "Obsess
much," from a conversation I overheard on 26 November 2001, in the glossary to illustrate just
this tendency: the speaker did not intone a question mark in this case, because she meant 'You
obsess too much', not 'Do you obsess often?'; so even the most acceptable type of collocation
with much has developed in a marginally unacceptable direction, since those who object to
uptalking in American English (intoning a declarative sentence as though it were a question)
would likely object to its obverse as well. But it is worth noting that much questions have been
intended by their speakers as much declarations from very early in the form's history; it was
only a matter of time until intonation caught up with the speaker's mood.

where *walk* is not. The show continues to explore the possibilities of VERB + *much* in recent episodes, for example, in *Doublemeat Palace* (29 January 2002), in which Willow objects to Anya, a chronic interrupter, "Hey, respect the narrative flow much?," another instance in which, though the intonation is nominally interrogative, the speaker really makes an observation.

In those early episodes, Whedon and his colleagues, by means of experiment and imitation, tested the pliability of *much* and the syntactical patterns in which it occurs; as anyone involved in the actuation of a slang item must, they looked for something they could bend, and *much* proved very pliable linguistic material. Unless I have missed something, though, they did not experiment enough to arrive at NOUN + *much*, the first certifiable instance of which is the rather outrageous "Meanwhile, *My Best Friend's Wedding/Friends* much?" from *Mademoiselle* (December 1998) mentioned in the previous chapters. The inception of NOUN + *much* is an important event, as it leads to the actuation both of a new sense of *much* and a new sentence pattern in which *much* can occur; thus, it is also an excellent example of the interaction between lexical and syntactical actuation. But NOUN + *much* undoubtedly experiments with *much* because other experiments, especially those on Buffy and, by then, related media, were in the public domain; those experiments and an urge to imitate them bent *much* far more than one would have guessed possible from the standard set by *Walk much?* and similar colloquial sentences. In other words, ADJECTIVE + *much*, in A2, paved the way for NOUN + *much* in A1, which recursively entered the *much* system, and now reinforces mutually with the rest of *much* the ADJECTIVE + *much* A2 from which it sprang.

The emergence of NOUN + *much* was at once bold and hesitant. An article in the "Guys Issue" of *Seventeen* magazine (Spring/Summer 1998) was accompanied by the headline "Crush much?" and the lack of context is misleading. When it functions as a verb, *crush* tends to appear in phrases, usually with *on*: "Take these four revealing quizzes to find out what type of a dude is most likely to crush on you" (YM Special Love [Issue], 1999, p. 35); "The guy I was crushing on was a major skateboarder, so I was convinced that he would be into skater chicks" (Twist Special, 1999, p. 83); "Buffy Crushes on Parker Abrams" (Nancy Holder and others, *The Watcher's Guide*, Volume 2, 2000, p. 127); or it appears as a participle, as on the cover of *Twist* (May 1999): "Stop Crushing[,] Start Dating!" But simple *crush* does sometimes manifest itself as a verb: "She [Buffy] uses the nearest guy as a shield. This is Parker, who is soulful, very sweet, and smart. Buffy crushes, and her friends egg her on" (Holder and others, *The Watcher's Guide*, Volume 2, 2000, p. 199). Carole Braden, Senior Features Editor at *Seventeen* in 1998, probably wrote the headline and she assures me that she took "Crush much?" as VERB + *much*; while acknowledging that *crush on* is the more frequent verbal form, she remembers that *Crush much?* was heard alongside other VERB + *much* constructions in the editorial offices of *Seventeen* at that time.[2]

"Crush much?," then, is not the first recorded instance of NOUN + *much*; it is, however, the first instance that might be interpreted as NOUN + *much*, and misperception can play as important a role in linguistic development as any other human factor. The *Mademoiselle* citation surely does not derive exclusively from the *Seventeen* example, though, given the intra-consciousness and inter-textuality of magazines for young women edited in New York, influence cannot be dismissed. Still, one notes that "fetish much" appears on the Bronze (2 December 1998) too soon after the *Mademoiselle* citation to feel its influence; and if the poster who devised that collocation was more than 18 years old and not American (a distinct possibility), then the earlier citation from *Seventeen* would prove irrelevant to that instance of NOUN + *much*, too. So NOUN + *much* would seem to have undergone a polygenesis, originating in a number of instances, for different reasons, at about the same time.

[2] I asked Carole about the headline because I was afraid that I might have been responsible for it. We are old friends, and on 10 January 1988, after the American Dialect Society's annual meeting, held that year in New York, we caught up over drinks in a Midtown bar. By then I was in thrall to slayer slang, about which I spoke at the next ADS meeting, and we discussed the *much* phenomenon at some length. It occurred to me later, when I registered the implications of the headline's date, that I might have influenced the vocabulary I was studying. Thankfully, I did not, though, of course, I'd have been very pleased had "Crush much?" been an instance of NOUN + *much*; this fortunately imagined scenario explains why I have never announced my interest in slayer slang while lurking on the Bronze and Bronze: Beta, and why I have never notified the show's writers of my interests, either. I am interested in slayer slang as natural language; the only exception to my rule might be **slayer slang** itself, since I made that up.

NOUN + much extends previous experiments with much to the extreme, and it is interesting that, while certainly affected by the example set by *BTVS*, all of the early instances of that form and the resultant syntactic pattern recorded here occur far away from the Buffyverse. If *Jawbreaker*, which was released in 1998, has "Tuna much?," then NOUN + much must have been incipient at about the time that (or before) ADJECTIVE + much received its Buffy boost, regardless of the evidence from *Seventeen*, *Mademoiselle*, and the Bronze. In other words, while slayer slang very likely influenced experiments with *much*, it did not set parameters: Kateland Goldsborough and Stephanie Manzella, both of whom contributed NOUN + much forms to the glossary, were not Buffyfans— neither had seen even a single episode of Buffy when they uttered the statements recorded here. In other words, there is a very complex interaction of repetition, experiment, imitation, and extension evident in the development of NOUN + much in which Buffy plays an essential, but not a sufficient, role; the most remarkable feature of the pattern's progress is that finally, on 24 October 2000, Dawn would say of Buffy's too-frequent apologies, "Broken record much," the first instance of NOUN + much was offered on the show. The development of *much* had come full circle: the show, originally the imitator, became the imitated, but ended up imitating forms that had imitated it.

When we hear a word or sentence pattern, it undergoes scrutiny, whether we're conscious of it or not: we judge its acceptability according to a certain set of standards; the standards vary according to the vocabulary against which the newer item is measured. In the case of *much*, collocations with verbs in brief questions have long been acceptable in colloquial English; collocations with adjectives have not. At first, those saying or listening to ADJECTIVE + much constructions approved of them as slang because such sentences do not pass our acceptability judgments: in other words, acceptability as slang depends on a certain degree of unacceptability with regard to a standard. After a while, though, ADJECTIVE + much had been repeated often enough that it lost at least some of its original unacceptability. Without offense to the perpetually hip Garry Trudeau, when sentences like "Off message much?" appeared in *Doonesbury* (7 October 1999), the once rebellious *much* had begun to conform, to enter the consciousness, perhaps even the verbal repertoire, of the statusful. And it doesn't help the street cred of ADJECTIVE + much that NOUN + much is clearly so much more effectively rebellious against traditional English grammar and conventional meanings of much, of course, but also against the increasingly acceptable ADJECTIVE + much; comparatively, after those more radical collocations began to appear, *Pathetic much?* just doesn't seem so tough. Even NOUN + much faces gradual acceptability: Stephanie Manzella doesn't seem to have missed a beat when asking her boyfriend, Tim Redding, who was having trouble parallel parking, "Curb much?" While NOUN + much consigns ADJECTIVE + much to acceptability, frequent repetition of both ADJECTIVE and NOUN + much gradually may push the latter into colloquial Eng̣ish usage as well.

Actuation of a lexical item or syntactic pattern cannot be accomplished fully by its use in a single register of English; that is, had ADJECTIVE + much only occurred in episodes of Buffy, the syntactic pattern would have been actuated in the narrowest possible sense (A1). But that pattern migrated from the show into other television shows, some on the same network, some not; into fiction, though, admittedly, fiction based on the show; onto the Bronze; then into an internationally syndicated comic strip. If NOUN + much was influenced by ADJECTIVE + much, and if we take a general rebellious *much* back to *Heathers*, as we probably should, then *much* also appeared in feature films and glossy, major-market magazines. Besides reaching out from the show in several directions, *much* also gained prestige over time, as the citation from *Doonesbury* suggests, though it also ended up in the most prestigious register of all, that of everyday use by people unconcerned with its Buffy associations.

It's natural to wonder how long, after its inception, a word or syntactic pattern takes to establish itself. Slayer slang *much* moves remarkably fast. If we take *Heathers* as the starting point, only a decade had passed before ADJECTIVE + much had extended to registers beyond the Buffy scripts; if we take Meadow's "God, self-involved much?" from *The Sopranos* (28 March 1998) as the first 1990s use of ADJECTIVE + much outside of the Buffyverse, it took only a year for Buffy to both influence and reflect the language of American teens. NOUN + much first formed and began its own dissemination within the same decade. Just as a glossary in the official *Buffy* magazine (Winter 1998) noted *much* as a key term in slayer slang (and pinned it to Cordelia's verbal style), NOUN + much appeared in *Mademoiselle* and the film *Jawbreaker*. If NOUN + much received any boost from Buffy's ADJECTIVE + much, that extra impetus was immediate; though, of course, it may have originated in imitation of and experiment with pre-Buffy ADJECTIVE + much. For ADJECTIVE + much, from cultish Buffy to prestigious *Doonesbury* is a journey of only two-and-a-half years. It took only four years or so for NOUN + much to progress from clever journalese into everyday speech.

Recently, Allan Metcalf, in *Predicting New Words: The Secrets of Their Success* (2002), has proposed a scale for predicting the success of new words; we might, by extension, see the scale as applying to syntactic practices like those surrounding much as well. After explaining the circumstances of many new words, some successful and many not, Metcalf outlines what he calls the FUDGE factors:

> Frequency of use
> Unobtrusiveness
> Diversity of users and situations
> Generation of other forms and meanings
> Endurance of the concept.

Given the micro-history of much, we might ask whether Metcalf's scale suggests something about its American English future.

Certainly, much has the makings of a successful new word or, at least, a new sense of a word, and its new collocational patterns may end up successful as well. As Metcalf puts it, "When first coined, a word has a Frequency of 0, and 0 it remains as long as only one person uses it"; in other words, we assign a 0 frequency to items that have achieved A1. But, "[if] level 0 of Frequency is like a struck match, flame ready to flicker and go out, Level 1 is like applying that match to a fuse, where a word can smolder, waiting for an opportunity to explode to Level 2." It is difficult to gauge the frequency of much compared to other words, though we can rest assured that it has at least attained Metcalf's Level 1, since it clearly exceeds the frequency of some 0 words Metcalf mentions, like hyprijimp and whoopdujour. One must remember, though, that the glossary accounts only for the tip of the much iceberg: I cannot have recorded all of the instances of much uttered on television, in films, in print, or in conversation over the last six years, so we must assume that the glossary merely represents, rather than circumscribes, the *much* phenomenon in American English. *Much* is used with reasonable frequency; it is probably a Level 2 form, regardless of collocational pattern.

But on its way from nonce-use to general use, from slayer slang to general American English, a word must also be unobtrusive. As Metcalf puts it, "In plain English, you don't notice it. A successful new word [or syntactic pattern] flies under the radar. It camouflages itself to give the appearance of something we've known all along." In other words, it evades our acceptability judgments, perhaps by blipping across our linguistic screens, yet invites no reprisal. And in this regard, *much* is marked for success, as it is already a core element of English vocabulary; a wholly familiar word, the sort of word that could smuggle an alien syntactic pattern into American English. Given VERB + *much* and the textbook grammatical constraints applied to adverbs, ADJECTIVE + *much*, though surprising, doesn't violate any but vaguely idiomatic rules, and if, even with raised eyebrows, we allow it to fly by, NOUN + *much* is, of course, more hostile, but having allowed ADJECTIVE + *much* to pass, we find it difficult to refuse NOUN + *much*, exactly the lapse in linguistic defense on which purists would filibuster, though usage always manages cloture in the end.

The level of diversity a word or sentence pattern must achieve on the path to full actuation is unclear, but slayer slang *much* starts in films, proceeds to more films, then into network television scripts, then into pulp novels, mass-market magazines, at least one posting board, more films, cable television scripts (not the same thing as network scripts, from a sociolinguistic point of view), more novels, more magazines, internationally syndicated comics, websites, conversation, and then back to network television and posting board activity. Because the Buffyverse comprises many of the venues enumerated, we might view *much* as falling short of Metcalf's prescription that a successful new word (or syntactic pattern) should find "a Diversity of users in a Diversity of situations," yet slayer slang *much* is certainly applied with greater diversity than most of the unsuccessful words Metcalf exposes in his book.

Slayer slang *much* does not generate many new forms, however. Though the overall system of *much* includes VERB + *much*, clearly the progenitor of all other forms, and while ADJECTIVE + much may have influenced NOUN + much, much itself does not generate new forms, except for the quasi-adverbial sense that collocates with nouns. Of course, these developments count, but one must admit that *much* generates many fewer forms than, say, **Slayer** or the suffixes *-age* and *-y*.[3] And again, when it comes to endurance of the underlying concept, the prospects of *much* are difficult to estimate: its underlying concept is mainly a matter of style, a way of dismissing the question or state of affairs to which the *much* construction is a retort. Either style will not ensure the entry of *much* into general American English, or Metcalf has underestimated style as a category of endurance. But, in any event, Metcalf's scale helpfully characterizes the actuation of slayer slang *much*, and, in turn, the behavior of slayer slang *much* endorses the validity of Metcalf's scale.[4] What does it mean for a word or syntactic pattern to be "successful"? *Much* is certainly one of the most successful items of slayer slang, all the more successful because it has entered general American English slang; it may enter general American English, too, on the terms Metcalf provides, but when it does, it necessarily will have lost its slanginess, thus trading one type of success for another.

---

[3] The ubiquitous *much* may, however, have influenced *muchly*, recorded twice in the process of compiling the glossary, first from the episode Life Serial (23 October 2001), "Well, I appreciate it. Muchly," and later from the Bronze: Beta (30 July 2002), "You rock muchly, twin-let."

[4] Michiko Kakutani, in a review of Metcalf's book in The New York Times (17 January 2003, p. B50), takes the scale to task. "'Predicting New Words,'" she writes, "seems highly cursory in the extreme. It pays little attention to the role that popular culture has played in promoting new words and phrases: no discussion of words from movies [...] and scant discussion of computer slang [by which she may mean jargon] and teenage talk as well." But "the problem is that [...] Mr. Metcalf is himself confusing grammatical mistakes with innovation: just one of the stumbles in this book that makes it a lot less persuasive than it might have been." As commentary on slayer slang *much* should make clear, there is no way to separate "teenage talk" from "grammatical mistakes," for just the reason Sledd proposes, as quoted in Chapter 1. Metcalf is right to bring innovation and error to a point of intersection; if he failed to do so with regard to "teenage talk," perhaps this book, among other studies, will supply what Kakutani (and perhaps only Kakutani) sees as a deficiency.

Buffy: What's in a Name?

The answer is, "A lot more than you would expect." The name Buffy carries baggage in American English—it's a cheerleader name, with all of the mildly derisive (and unfair) associations that come with being pretty and popular in American high school life. As a name, it had a special value for Whedon. Nikki Stafford writes in the second edition of *Bite Me!* (2002), that "The basic premise," both for the film and the television show, "was a cheerleader who realizes she is destined to be a vampire slayer when a mysterious man tells her of her vocation. The script mixed comedy with drama, and while the title was a humorous juxtaposition of the words Buffy and *vampire slayer*, it was meant to be tongue-in-cheek, not an excuse for turning the film an all-out comedy." In order to determine whether *BTVS* has improved the name's reputation and boosted its popularity, we'll have to wait and see how many parents, Buffyfans or not, name their future daughters Buffy.

Though the name Buffy has been around for a while, it has been reactuated by the show because it now carries with it quite different associations; those deriving from the character's profession and personal qualities. As a result, it is worth considering Buffy in terms of Metcalf's scale. First of all, Buffy has never been used with the frequency it is now; it is used so frequently that I chose not to illustrate use of the name much in the glossary's entry for **Buffy**, since one encounters it in quotations supporting most of the other entries. Even though the shortened form of the show's title represents a sense of the word different from the character's name, it takes exactly the same form, plus italics. So between character and show, the name has inundated American speech: most people don't watch Buffy, but most people know that there is such a show, focused on a character of the same name. In addition, the name is repeated in many compounds and other words developed from it, but more on this below. Second, like much, Buffy is already established in American speech, and while some words developed from it are hardly unobtrusive, the name itself is, and fully satisfies, the U in FUDGE.

When it comes to diversity of use, no item of slayer slang can beat Buffy. It has appeared in every imaginable medium, receiving much more attention than other slayer slang from newspapers and magazines, for instance, and much more occasional use on television beyond the Buffyverse, not to mention everyday conversation—how many times has someone uttered, "Did you watch Buffy last night?" Even I, with my profound faith in slayer slang's importance to current American English, was surprised to find Buffy in the title and repeatedly in the text of a working paper issued by the Center for Strategic and International Studies. My mother dislikes fantasy of any kind: even though she wouldn't recognize the word, it gives her the *wiggins*, and she has no interest in *stakings* or *manimals*, not to mention *Ewanage* (she might indulge in *Newmanage*); for her, nothing about the Buffyverse is *pointy*. Nonetheless, she knows that I am writing a Buffy book; she says things like, "So how's the Buffy book coming?" From television series, to Sarah Vowell's *The Partly Cloudy Patriot*, to the Center for Strategic and International Studies, to Dark Horse Comics, to Wilcox and Lavery's *Fighting the Forces*, to *Rolling Stone*, to *Femmes Fatales: The Luscious Ladies of Horror*, to my mom: THAT's diversity of use.

And no other item of slayer slang generates (or influences) more forms than **Buffy**. It shifts from name of character to name of show and to several other specific senses; it is clipped and shifted from noun to adjective (**Buff**), clipped and suffixed (for instance, **Buffdom, Buffkin,** and **Buffster**), retained and suffixed (**Buffyatric, Buffycentric, Buffyholic,** and **Buffyness,** among several others), prefixed (as in **crybuffy, FrankenBuffy,** and **überBuffy**), compounded (notably in **Buffy Paradigm** and **Buffy Syndrome**), and figures in blends at a rate higher than any other slayer slang form (for example, in **Buffinator, Buffivor, Buffyverse,** and **Spuffy**). In other words, **Buffy** is, all by itself, a study in American English word-formation, yielding more or less 50 forms, depending on what you count—more if you include all developed senses of derived forms, less if you don't.

Buffy, as a name, is already a feature of standard American English; it is unlikely, however that many of the forms it generates will ever achieve that dignity—**Buffybot** and **Buffypedia** are confined to the **Buffyverse**. That last word, however, is well-attested in a variety of registers and has become essentially a standard term for the 'world of all things related to Buffy or Buffy', a concept for which there is no other word. Users have proposed alternatives. Since the Buffyverse was created by Joss Whedon, some fans have called it the *Jossverse*, as when a participant on the Bronze wrote, "[T]hings don't always have to be complicated, even in the Jossverse" (2 June 2001). Even less tenable is *Jossyverse*: clearly formed, not on *Jossverse*, but on *Buffyverse*, it is not parallel to other NAME + -*verse* forms, due to the misplaced -*y*-; but its very creation underscores *Buffyverse*'s status, because *Jossyverse* is a slang alternative to a term already occupying the lexical gap opened in American English by the existence of the *Buffyverse*. *Jossverse* and *Jossyverse* imitate *Buffyverse*, whose attraction motivates the actuation (A1) of those terms; but the proposal of those terms, the experimentation with them, and their ultimate rejection as alternatives to *Buffyverse* are together a factor in the thorough actuation (A2) of the more successful term.[5]

Unexpectedly, **Buffy** has generated other standard terms. The "dripping" script used in the show's title sequence and in many official print venues is known as **Buffied typeface,** the only term applied to that font, parallel to *Times New Roman* and *Baskerville Old Face.* Even more surprising is Anthony Cordesman's decision to characterize our current national security woes in terms of a **Buffy Paradigm** and a **Buffy Syndrome** (29 September 2001). Cordesman was introduced to Buffy by Buffyholics in his family, watched an episode or two, perceived analogies between the show and America's approach to threats of biological warfare, and developed **Buffy** into compounds that expressed his views on security. In each of these cases, a term was created to fill a perceived lexical gap. *Buffied typeface* was probably inevitable, given the "dripping" script's absolute association with the show. Cordesman's terms are apt, given his reading of Buffy: he coined them for thematic reasons, that is, to map the region in which the show's themes overlap with the themes of his security perspective.[6] Aptness, however, is only one linguistic as-

---

[5] **Buffyverse***'s attraction is so potent that it generates not only alternatives to itself, but other parallel forms, like that introduced on the Bronze: Beta (29 July 2002): "[S]o while she's heard Buffy complain about Spike, it's very likely that even in the Dawnverse versions of Seasons 2–4, she never has first-hand seen Spike the Big Bad in full swing." The meaning of Dawnverse is not parallel to that of Buffyverse, however; rather than referring to the 'world of all things pertaining to Dawn', it describes Dawn's manufactured memory of her life in the Summers household before her incarnation.*

[6] *The* American Heritage Dictionary of the English Language, *Fourth Edition (2000), defines paradigm n in sense 3 as "A set of assumptions, concepts, values, and practices that*

pect of Cordesman's choices: **Buffy Paradigm** and **Buffy Syndrome** are POWERFUL terms, not because of their relevance to Cordesman's argument, but because slayer slang **Buffy** is so thoroughly developed and so incessantly repeated by speakers and writers of American English, young and old.

constitutes a way of viewing reality for the community that shares them"; Cordesman is, in fact, very precise about aspects of the **Buffy Paradigm** that amount to such a "set of assumptions, concepts, values, and practices," as he asks us to extend the "community that shares them" from Buffy, Giles, and the Scooby Gang to cover the United States. Cordesman writes:

> While uncertainty is the dominating motif, the "Buffy Paradigm" has the following additional characteristics:
>
> • What expertise there is consists largely of bad or uncertain advice and old, flawed, and confusing technical data.
>
> • The importance of any given threat changes constantly, past threat behavior does not predict future behavior, and methods of delivery keep changing.
>
> • Arcane knowledge is always inadequate and fails to predict, detect, and properly characterize the threat.
>
> • The more certain and deterministic an expert is at the start, the more wrong they [sic] turn out to be in practice.
>
> • The scenarios are unpredictable and have very unclear motivation. Any effort to predict threat motivation and behavior in detail before the event does at least as much [sic].
>
> • Risk taking is not rationale [sic] or subject to predictable constraints and the motive behind escalation is erratic at best.
>
> • It is never clear whether the threat is internal, from an individual, or from an outside organisation [sic].
>
> • The attackers have no firm or predictable alliances, cooperate in nearly random ways, and can suddenly change method of attack and willingness to take risks.
>
> • All efforts at planning a coherent strategy collapse in the face of tactical necessity and the need to deal with unexpected facts on the ground.
>
> • The balance between external defense, homeland defense, and response changes constantly.
>
> • No success, not [sic] matter how important at the time, ever eliminates the risk of future problems.

Besides the ways in which the view of reality projected by these comments elucidates the definition given in the glossary, taken together they constitute an interesting interpretation of the Buffyverse, one with which many regular viewers of the show might disagree. I suspect that, were Cordesman to post his views on the Bronze: Beta, he would encounter lively debate about the validity of his conclusions as they apply, not to national security, in which he is the expert, but to slaying, about which Betarers have considerable accumulated wisdom.

One should note that **Buffy** had been assigned to the typeface only two years from the show's first episode, and that national security experts were caught up in the **Buffy** wave merely four years into its re-actuation. (I still find it marvelous that members of Joint Chiefs of Staff, who, one hopes, are too busy to watch television, nonetheless know about Buffy, both show and term, via Cordesman's paper.) David Foster Wallace, in a valuable and delightfully eccentric article published in *Harper's* (2001), claims that linguists have issued "five basic edicts": " 1—Language changes constantly; 2—Change is normal; 3—Spoken language is the language; 4—Correctness rests upon usage; 5—All usage is relative." Foster Wallace responds to these edicts with a series of intelligent questions, two of which are particularly relevant here:

> 1. OK, but how much and how fast?
> 2. Same thing. Is Heraclitean flux as normal or desirable as gradual change? Do some changes actually serve the language's overall pizzazz better than others? And how many people have to deviate from how many conventions before we say the language has actually changed? Fifty percent? Ten percent?

Studying the micro-histories of some slayer slang terms helps to answer Foster Wallace's questions.

In answer to the first question, slayer slang suggests that language changes relatively fast, as well as constantly. Consider the time line for **Buffy**: assuming that the glossary records ALL developed forms and senses of the word, and that is by no means a safe assumption, a new term or sense of a term developed from **Buffy** has appeared, on average, every month since the first episode aired. How much does it change? The answer depends on prejudice, I'm afraid. From one perspective, certainly the perspective of this book and most professional linguists, everything in the glossary represents change. Granted, some changes seem minor. No single *-age* suffixation resounds like the horns at Jericho: those who celebrate innovation in language have to admit that the foundations of American English hardly tremble at such a form; those who fear that innovation may cause the walls of our language to tumble down can rest easy.

Yet even if one disallows each new suffixed form in itself as change worth noticing, it appears, just from the evidence of the glossary, that the relative intensity of suffixation changes from time to time, both within a special vocabulary and, as special and general vocabulary intersect, outside of it, as well. If one is reasonably open-minded, one might consider changes in the speech of millions of Americans as changes in American speech. In cases like *much*, though, evidence suggests that use, or at least awareness, has attained Foster Wallace's lowest speculative threshold of 10% of Americans; whether they like it or not, even those unwilling to countenance change must admit that *much* represents change enough. Many of the forms recorded in the glossary illustrate change (A1) initiated by a single television show, and though, as I suggested in Chapter 1, Buffy is an especially influential show, and though, in order to promote thorough actuation of any term (A2), Buffy and even the Buffyverse are insufficient, Buffy concretely and significantly stimulates change in American English. Imagine all of the possible non-Buffy loci of change in all American language media and the actual change thus implied—it boggles the mind.

Is such change flux or gradual change? Let me reinterpret the question as I think Foster Wallace means it: is such change MERELY FLUX or is it gradual change TOWARD PERMANENT INCLUSION IN AMERICAN ENGLISH VOCABULARY? Even if I impose this revised question on Foster Wallace unfairly, many would certainly ask the question as amended. That flux within a language is as normal as gradual change seems obvious upon consideration of slayer slang; indeed, flux may be the predominant category of change since, just as obviously, much change illustrated by the glossary is not permanent—not when measured by the persistence of a particular item. My own bias about the desirability of flux is probably clear by now: it seems to me that any change is desirable if it serves a purpose. If a word fills a lexical gap, it serves a purpose; if a word or syntactic pattern expresses a particular speaker's sense of verbal style, it serves a purpose, too. Such ephemeral purposes, along with their ephemeral effects, are completely justified. Anyway, the assumption that flux and gradual change toward some "end" operate separately from each other is naïve, as study of *much* and Buffy prove. When we look around us, do we see too much fruit or too many flowers? How many flowers does it take to seed the land for a new generation of flowering plants? Would we prefer that nature worked more efficiently, that each and every seed produced a plant, that there were, thus, not only fewer seeds in the world, but fewer flowers as well? Of course, language is not a natural system, but that wouldn't seem to invalidate the analogy: like nature, language is an opportunistic system, and the volume of potential is partly what determines the results.

But we are not finished measuring Buffy according to Metcalf's scale. The final factor in a new word's success is the endurance of the underlying concept. Mutant Enemy won't produce any new episodes of the show, but that won't be the end, either of *BTVS* or the term Buffy: syndication and DVDs will ensure public awareness of both for some time to come, and, as a result, we can expect the term to generate even more forms, most of them "merely" elements of language flux, some of them, perhaps, durable items of American English vocabulary, and, one suspects, the more terms that spring from Buffy and the more widely those terms are disseminated among registers of American English, the more likely that a few slayer slang terms, perhaps formed on Buffy, or perhaps not, will survive the pressures of constant fluctuation and emerge as features of general American slang or general American English.

Lexical Gaps, Loose Idioms, and Folk Etymologies

The appearance of a concept for which we have no name, or the sudden perception that such a concept needs a word to cover it, motivates the actuation (A1) of a new term or new sense of an old term; the endurance of the concept will help to firmly establish the new term or new sense (A2). This explanation is intuitively appealing, perhaps because it is a conservative maxim (if taken as a justification for new words, it limits opportunity), and it is certainly true in many cases; yet conventional wisdom may overestimate the extent to which lexical gaps matter. Slayer slang provides many examples of words that fill lexical gaps: naturally, if you create a profession like that of *vampire slayer*, you will need jargon to describe it, hence **Chosen One**, **Hellmouth**, and **Watcher**; words within a specialized domain, like **Buffy**, can supply lexical needs well outside that domain, as just described; and within the Buffyverse, where speakers are often focused on unconventional things, the sorts of things for which mainstream vocabulary would have no words, new terms (**Spuffy**, for instance) are borne on necessity.

But the very idea of "lexical gap" is notoriously problematic: ostensibly, there is a difference between being happy and getting a **happy**; to argue that **happy** is unnecessary because one could say "I would be happy if..." may miss the distinction between a general state of happiness and a happy moment; an item of happiness tabulated on the balance sheet of a life in which moments laden with other emotions will also contribute to the bottom line. Perhaps winning the game of life requires that one collect more *happies* than *grims*. Often, American English allows us to express ourselves adequately with phrases rather than words; it is unclear whether we can claim a lexical gap if a phrasal alternative exists, though an unlexicalized phrase would seem a square peg to the lexical gap's round hole.

If study of slayer slang exposes anything, it's the potency of style, relative to lexical gaps, in the creation of new words, new senses of words, and new syntactic patterns. As argued in Chapter 1, the fetish of suffixation, while it sometimes produces forms whose meanings are as subtly distinct from such established alternatives as **happy n** from *happy adj*, just as often yields forms without a fillip of lexical meaning different from standard alternatives—**drinkage**, in terms of lexical semantics, does not mean anything other than *drinking*. Yet not all meaning is lexical, and the style expressed in **drinkage**, even though it might not appeal to a language maven any more than a particular cuff or neckline would appeal to Joan Rivers, is style nonetheless. If people with unnaturally colored hair like to hang together, and if they know they'd be more likely to enjoy the company of someone with unnaturally colored hair, because hair color sometimes stands for other shared interests, then why shouldn't citizens of the Buffyverse affiliate by means of a suffix or two? No matter how you value such an affiliation, it undoubtedly motivates the actuation of words and the morphological and syntactic practices that accompany them. And style, it must be remembered, is not merely group-think but, in many contexts, an assertion of individuality as well.

Willow's **Slayerettes** fills a lexical gap, because mythologically and historically, slayers work alone. Why, then, does Xander coin **Scooby Gang**? As suggested earlier, each term carries unintended negative associations—one term is no better than the other in that respect. **Scooby Gang** is cooler because of its pop-cultural associations, and slang is cooler than conventional American English: cool is one of slang's *raisons d'être*. Apparently, some jargon is cooler than others; some jargon verges on slang. **Scooby Gang** does not arise from perceived lexical necessity, but from the perceived unstylishness of its already established alternative. **Dust**, **stake**, and **vamp** are also alternatives developed for reasons of style, perhaps exactly the purpose of the slangy substratum of second-order jargon. Similarly, why can't Buffy, in the show's first episode, say, "That place just frightens me," or at least, "That place just gives me the creeps," hardly standard American English, but acceptably colloquial; or, she could say, "That place just creeps me (out)," a form parallel to all of the other phrasal clippings included in the glossary, or "That place just wigs me (out)"? Why does she invent a new word for the occasion? She says, "That place just gives me the *wiggins*," and once again style actuates a new term, accompanied by the necessary syntactic effects.

Wiggins tells us more about actuation than at first appears. In their early stages, words have to settle into idiom; most of the time, they simply insert themselves into the "natural" idioms of the language to which they belong. **Wiggins** is problematic because the terminal -s makes it look like a plural, but it doesn't behave like one: apparently, you can't say "That scary movie gave me a lot of (or several, or too many) wiggins." Even Whedon seems confused about whether **wiggins** is singular but formed as a plural (so that *gave me a wiggins* would be functionally, but not structurally, parallel to *gave me a fright*) or is a plural without a complementary singular (so that *gave me the wiggins* would be in every way parallel to *gave me the creeps* or, as British English–speaking Keith Topping would have it in his book *Slayer* [2000], *gave me the willies*).[7] Less than a year after Buffy's initial example, Xander would say, in Innocence

---

[7] *The supposed singular *wiggin is probably not an etymological form. Yet wiggin 'needing drugs' is attested in Kuhn, Swartzwelder, and Wilson's Buzzed (1998), and it is not impossible that the wiggins is or are agitation, nervousness, "the shakes" like that or those associated with*

(20 January 1998), "I'm having a thought. And now I'm having a plan. And now I'm having a wiggins." One understands the source of the confusion: if the elements of Xander's list satisfy the style book rule about parallelism of elements within a list, A thought and A plan entail A *wiggins*; but similar logic would not lead us to say that some gave us *a creep* or *a willie*. In their novel, *Halloween Rain* (1998), Christopher Golden and Nancy Holder try out "If this thing is giving you guys a wiggins, I'll just put it aside until we're through," and 43 pages later, write that "One was dressed like a clown, and that one gave her the wiggins worst of all." Perhaps **wiggins** ought to be defined as having two senses, one accommodating each of the directions in which writers take it; but each phrase one could substitute for it is idiomatically fixed, and the form of **wiggins** begs for the same status. It seems likely not that **wiggins** is polysemous, but that it can't find its idiomatic niche.

When modifying **wiggins**, writers invariably prefer *a*, though, because it conforms better to conventions of American English syntax: "And, okay, Mom plus dating could at some point equal sex, and that's a giant economy size wiggins," says Buffy in Christopher Golden's *Sins of the Father* (1999), but not "and that's the giant economy size wiggins"; "You found out that Willow was in kind of an unconventional relationship, and it gave you a momentary wiggins," she says in *New Moon Rising* (2 May 2000), but not "and it gave you the momentary wiggins," but, interestingly, also not "and it momentarily gave you the wiggins." Writers can attempt to avoid the problem by structuring sentences differently: "Oh, major wiggins!," cries Buffy in Dan Brereton's graphic novel, *The Dust Waltz* (1998). But that only avoids the problem of *a* versus *the*; it heightens the idiomatic instability of **wiggins** by proposing yet another way of using the word.

---

withdrawal from a drug. Those who attempt to explain **wiggins**, however, associate it with **wig** and related forms, and given the heavy use of **wig** v and **wigged** adj in slayer slang, and the presence of less frequent **wiggage** n and **wigout** n, the suggestion makes sense. For instance, the glossary of slayer slang in the Winter 1998 issue of the official magazine defines **wiggins** as "the creeps" and then asserts that it is a "form of wigged-out." More likely, of course, **wiggins** forms on **wig**, rather than undergoes the complicated series of clippings and suffixings required by the magazine glossary's explanation. A participant on the Bronze accidentally located the likely derivation: "I hate things that float. They give me the wiggings."

Hellmouth exhibits a similar instability. Citational evidence does not clarify whether Sunnydale is *on the* Hellmouth, or *in the* Hellmouth, or *atop the* Hellmouth, or *on top of the* Hellmouth, or *over the* Hellmouth: of course, some of the alternatives are not mutually exclusive, as *atop* is quaint *on top of*, and in order to be *on* the Hellmouth, Sunnydale must also be *over* it. The show, when it indicates Sunnydale's position relative to the Hellmouth, employs *on*, as far as my evidence shows, without exception. Some of the novels introduce the idiom *in the* Hellmouth, however, and the confusion is unfortunate, as readers may conjure up unintended spatial relations: after all, it's not true, as an article in *Teen* (January 2000) asserts, that "Buffy's grown up a lot since she started hangin' in the Hellmouth," as she hangs in the Bronze, which, like the rest of Sunnydale, is on the Hellmouth; because Buffy and the Gang do sometimes descend into the Hellmouth to slay something, it is worth maintaining the distinction. Sometimes both *on* and *in* occur with Hellmouth in the same novel. Golden and Holder, in *Blooded* (1998), write "It was almost enough to make you forget you lived in the Hellmouth"; somewhat more than 100 pages later, Buffy says, "'Given the fact that we live on the Hellmouth, and that Willow has been acting more like you than yourself....'"

The substitution of *in* for *on* is no surprise, given that both prepositions are mildly unstable in English: as the *Oxford English Dictionary* remarks in its entry for **in**, "The simple relation-words nearest in sense to *in* are *at* and *on*, with which *in* sometimes has common ground, e.g. 'in or at Oxford', 'in or on a street', [etc.]"; and though it defines sense I.1.a of **on** as we expect, "Above and in contact with, above and supported by; upon," it admits several contexts under sense III.28 in which *on* substitutes "where 'in' would normally occur in standard use," and, in the CD-ROM version, quotations appended from the Additions Series (1993) further illustrate the tendency to speak of someone as living *on* the second floor of a building, when we mean that she lives *at* or *within* that floor. Nonetheless, the variety of prepositions accompanying **Hellmouth** in slayer slang represents idiomatic instability present mostly, though not absolutely, early in a word's history.

Both **Hellmouth** and **wiggins** demonstrate the nascent problems of idiom that attend some newly created forms—they illustrate a problem of actuation. Idiomatic instability may inhibit the movement of a term from A1 to A2. This doesn't always happen: when we examined **much** earlier in this chapter, what one might take for instability looked more like experiment, a process that promotes rather than inhibits thorough actuation; but with **much** the issue was precisely what **much** itself could do (or get away with), not the fussier and less exciting question of with what it could combine. **Wiggins** is my favorite item of slayer slang, but it hasn't caught on outside of the Buffyverse, and it probably never will, in spite of its natural attractions and position in the system of items built on **wig**, which ought to give it a big boost. **Hellmouth** will persist as long as there's a slayer in Sunnydale, whether its idiom settles or not. The distance between **Hellmouth** and **wiggins** is the long road from first-order jargon to slang, and while slang is undoubtedly more flexible and fun, jargon has its advantages.

Before we leave the subtleties of actuation, we must consider a rare species of it, indeed, one of a kind within the Buffyverse: we might call it "retroactive actuation." While *smooch*, as the slang synonym for both 'kiss' and 'to kiss', has long resided in the American slang lexicon, BTVS appears to have introduced the form *smoochies*, as in dialogue between Xander and Buffy in *Bad Eggs* (12 January 1998), "'Apparently Buffy has decided that what's wrong with the English language is all those pesky words. You. Angel. Big. Smoochies.' 'Shut. Up.'" "The Kiss and Tell Report" (YM Special Love [Issue] 1999, pp. 18–20) and "Guys Confess Their Most Shocking Smooches" (*Twist* Special 1999, p. 17), which fairly represent use of the term in the teen press, repeatedly use *smooch* n, *smooches* n pl, *smooch* adj, and *smooching* vbl adj, but *smoochies* is nowhere to be found.

Participants on the Bronze and Bronze: Beta have often spelled the term *smootchies* or *smoootchies*, instead, as in "Antiseptic *SMOOTCHIES* to my below par friend" (13 October 1999). While there is plenty of bad spelling on the posting boards, participants may also understand a rationale for variant spellings in this case, as suggested in this comment by frequent and long-term contributor Xanderella: "I didn't invent the *smoootch*. I didn't even put the 't' in it [...] In discussing proper smooch/smooch form, I think with tiggy long ago and far away, I theorized that a 'smoootch' without the 't' was sort of like a kiss without, well, you know. And that it was just missing something. It's perfectly nice, fine and all that jazz, but perhaps missing some of the passion" (30 July 2002).

The question, of course, is HOW long ago and far away did tiggy and Xanderella have their exchange over variant spellings of *smoochies* to represent various types of kisses? It was almost certainly after *smoochies* had already appeared on the board; the appropriateness of one spelling over another, given the speaker's intention, was never in question until some Bronzers wrote variants of *smoochies* into their posts. We have no reason to believe that the originators of those forms operated from motives as clever as those Xanderella ultimately proposed. And unless Nancy Holder and company knew of the supposedly distinct meanings behind the spellings, we would have trouble applying Xanderella's criteria to this from *The Watcher's Guide, Volume 2* (2000): "In 'Lovers' Walk' she and Xander betray Oz and Cordelia by having illicit smoochies together."

Nevertheless, *smootchies* and *smoootchies* still appear regularly on the Bronze: Beta. Now that Xanderella has published his or her theory for all Betarers to see, perhaps those spellings have actuated into new words: *smoochies* refers to a friendly buss on the cheek, as implied by "Well, then, you are a sweetie! *smoochies*" (26 June 1999), while *smootchies* are french kisses about which hygiene might be a concern (hence "Antiseptic *SMOOTCHIES*" in the earlier quotation), and *smoootchies*, by virtue of its extra *o*, is a particularly long and passionate kiss with plenty of *t*. Curiously, and counter-intuitively, what were once probably mere misspellings have been retroactively actuated (A1), if users take Xanderella's folk etymology seriously; as Bronzers and Betarers move into other posting board and e-mail situations, they may even elevate the new terms from A1 to A2.

Every word has its micro-history. The glossary attempts, entry by entry, to tell their stories. Some words have short lives, and, as a consequence, their biographies are concise: the life of **non-mathy** is epitomized in a single quotation. The life history of **much**, on the other hand, takes many twists and turns: far from mundane, it is in an adventurous and compelling story, of which the glossary recounts perhaps only the first volume. The micro-history of **Buffy** is a veritable saga. But the individual histories of items in slayer slang accumulate, both into a cultural history of the Buffyverse and a general description of the language that undergirds the culture; the linguistic description of slayer slang in turn illustrates some fundamental linguistic processes, like actuation, as they manifest themselves in current American English.

References

Allan Metcalf's *Predicting New Words: The Secrets of Their Success* (Boston: Houghton Mifflin, 2002), besides being informative and insightful, is a good read. The quotation about Whedon's choice of Buffy as his Slayer's name comes from Nikki Stafford's revised and much expanded *Bite Me! An Unofficial Guide to the World of Buffy the Vampire Slayer* (Toronto: ECW Press, 2002, pp. 2–4). The full text of Anthony H. Cordesman's "Biological Warfare and the 'Buffy Paradigm'" (Center for Strategic and International Studies, 29 September 2001) can be found at *www.csis.org*. David Foster Wallace's "Tense Present: Democracy, English, and the Wars over Usage," appeared in *Harper's* (April 2001, pp. 39–58). The tenuous connection between slayer slang **wiggins** and the related drug term arises from the glossary in *Buzzed: The Straight Facts about the Most Used and Abused Drugs from Alcohol to Ecstasy*, by Cynthia Kuhn, Scott Swartzelder, Wilkie Wilson, and others (New York: Norton, 1998, p. 303). As with previous chapters, quotations illustrating particular words, and precise references, can be found in the glossary.

CHAPTER 4
Ephemeral Language

I grew up in a family ruled by an English professor who expected us to speak and write with impeccable grammar and elevated vocabulary. Our models were the literature that I went on to study in graduate school and that I teach today; if we had any questions, we could turn to a dozen dictionaries, including the *Oxford English Dictionary*. Whenever we lapsed, we were reminded that standard English comprised more words than we were likely to use and that recourse to low language betrayed an unbecoming emptiness of mind. Experience and study, though, have taught me not only to accept, but to admire ephemeral and other supposedly low forms of English. My conversion began some time ago, but my work on slayer slang has certainly accelerated a change of attitude and intensified my pleasure in all of the language always around me.

By endorsing ephemeral language, I do not mean to depreciate the language of Geoffrey Chaucer or W. E. B. DuBois, of William Shakespeare or Phillis Wheatley. I spend most of my time thinking about it, and I am not above mouthing a medieval roundelay as I drive to work. But whatever one thinks of learned language, of its aesthetic gloss or Latinate precision, one must admit that most people speak most of the time, and in most venues, language unapproved by teachers and books, and one must admit, too, that they have done so throughout history. The language used among family and friends has represented a sort of freedom to serf and slave, has allowed millennia of adolescents throughout human history to rebel against constituted authority, and has enabled one lover to groom another with terms of endearment.

More people currently use a nonstandard construction like ADJECTIVE + much than have ever used some terms one finds in dictionaries (*concatenate, neonate, ululate*). More enjoy Ned Flanders's verbal antics on *The Simpsons* (*okelly dokelley, absotively posilutely*) than appreciate the venerable majesty of *multifarious*. Ephemeral English is the living language, whether or not scholars, teachers, and grouchy language mavens approve; the language in which folks construct their everyday lives, the language of emotion, of work and play. By contrast, much of the standard vocabulary, rather than living, merely survives.

To prefer whimsy over majesty is a personal and legitimate choice. Speakers of American English make choices that reflect their language preferences every day. They have a right to such choices. They better grasp what they intend to say and the audience to whom they will say it than any language maven or reference book. Standard American English, a sort of lingua franca, has its uses, and those who hope to achieve certain social and economic ends must use it well, but they need not use it on all or even most occasions. Living American English, with its ephemeral vocabulary and populist grammar, is more democratic in terms of both access and effects than most American institutions, though some who champion standard American English are uncomfortable with that fact.

Most American culture is wonderfully superfluous, and the language that expresses our experience of it is often wildly creative and relatively short-lived; but words thus created are no less important because they are the linguistic products of living in a particular place, at a particular time, doing particular things, the various threads from which our individual, not to mention our cultural, experience is mostly woven. To travel among ephemeral American English and the conversational grammar that accompanies it is simply to participate broadly and deeply in American culture, here and now. The words and linguistic habits one picks up along the way are souvenirs of any one person's American journey.

The Teleological Fallacy

Many find it difficult to live in the moment, let alone respect language of the moment. Some believe that older words are somehow better words. In the Renaissance, when English began to adopt many neo-Latin words and to form highfalutin words from Latin roots and affixes, some commentators on the language rejected such innovations, partly because they were unnecessary, partly because they seemed foolish, and partly because Anglo-Saxon vocabulary was supposedly plain and muscular. Anglo-Saxon English was preferable even to English derived from French, when Anglo-Saxon offered an alternative to a Frenchified synonym, though the word adapted from French might have persisted in English vocabulary for hundreds of years. What does it mean to claim, as Iceland does, that it is the oldest continuous democracy in the world? Wouldn't it be enough to be a real democracy at any time? Is an older democracy, effective or not, any better than a relatively new one? From a nationalist perspective, yes; from a current political perspective, no. Those who favor old words over new ones expect the language to consolidate into its hypothetically best state; fads may come and go, but words and other language practices of value stick around until the end, until the language is "what we want it to be." In other words, they propose, a language has a τελος, a finished state, toward which change within the language tends.

For those susceptible to the Teleological Fallacy, ephemeral language has little or no value. Consider some of the views expressed in Mark Halpern's recent article, "The End of Linguistics." Halpern argues, correctly, "that language is merely an aspect of human behavior, not an independent entity—that it has no nature, no destiny, no desires, no 'genius', no yearning to be free." The desires, genius, and yearning all belong, not to the language, but to those who speak it. Thus change in language follows human impulses, and language gives "every sign of being an artifact rather than an organic growth. Certainly languages, or at least aspects of them, exhibit changes over time—but then, so do the Dow Jones Industrial Average, the barometer, and the Oregon coastline, none of which we characterize as living or growing." Halpern, it would seem, does not subscribe to the Teleological Fallacy.

Yet he does: "[T]he most impressive changes observed in any language—loss of inflected forms, of moods and of tenses—are in the direction of simplification and economy, not of the enlargement, elaboration, and proliferation we call growth." Eventually, Halpern imagines, when we reach the optimal point of simplification and economy, there will be no change. Well, no change but pernicious change, one supposes. While *Tuna much?* and *Curb much?* assert economy, they aren't simple, and conservative users of American English find the economy jarring, to say the least. And don't all of those extra words developed in the Buffyverse count as change, or is generative application of the various word-formative processes discussed in Chapter 2 somehow beside the point? It is convenient in the course of an argument that American English changes little to insist that speakers of a language move it toward simplicity (of course, it cannot take a direction, but only be given one), but abundant evidence suggests otherwise.

"By far the most common kind of change we make in our language today," Halpern acknowledges, "is an addition to its vocabulary, made for the entirely innocent reason that a new creature has been observed in Eden, and Adam is called on to perform again his onomastic function. There may be occasional objections to the particular token Adam chooses, but no one objects in principle to the coining of new words for new things." Such "innovations," Halpern decides, are "unexceptionable and linguistically trivial." One might, though, object to the coining of a new word for an old thing, since even new words for new things are "linguistically trivial." Perhaps **drinkage** adds little to American English by itself, but what if we dismiss that and other -*age* or -*y* suffixed words and miss an increasing tendency toward their use, if not in American English at large, but at least in some registers of it? Is the more or less sudden use of **much** as an adverb able to modify nouns, or in a new adjectival sense, linguistically trivial? Perhaps, if its use represents only a semantic shift; certainly not, if it constitutes a functional shift. And whether it represents a semantic shift or a functional shift, slayer slang **much** enables certain syntactic patterns otherwise unknown to humankind. In other words, change seems trivial when you ignore it because you think it's trivial.

In Halpern's view, some change is trivial but nonetheless undesirable, and, from his description of what he calls "semantic inflation," pretty much all of slayer slang would deserve this double-edged criticism: "Semantic inflation is the response of the hurried or unimaginative to the facts that figures of speech, like all artifacts, wear out and lose effectiveness over time; that countless voices are competing for public attention, making it necessary, apparently, to scream if one would be heard; and that the substance of what we have to say is often a stale cake that needs tarting up with the most garish possible frosting."[1] Trivial, hurried, unimaginative, garish—Halpern is not afraid to judge others' language; indeed, the point of his article is just that

> someone is going to make decisions on usage—there is no such thing as a moratorium in language usage any more than in politics. We cannot defer usage decisions while waiting for linguists or anyone else to perform further research; we cannot invent for ourselves a language and a set of rules for using it. We can only choose among authorities, and only among those we know of. And if the authorities on usage are not to be the best writers of the recent past and present, and the critics and teachers with whom we study them, who are they to be? Television personalities? Rock stars? Gangbangers? Funeral directors? Gossip columnists? Telemarketing consultants? Or perhaps just Sir Echo, telling us soothingly that whatever we say is fine, just fine?

Speakers of slayer slang, or general American slang or colloquial American English influenced by slayer slang? Of course not. We should turn instead to Mark Halpern and others of his kind—we should not imagine that we are using language well unless we submit to some authority.

As Halpern says, "[W]e should see an end to the use of the 'living, growing language' fallacy as an excuse for misuse of language—

---

[1] Halpern's article, later published in The American Scholar, appeared originally in The Vocabula Review, each issue of which opens with the aphorism, "A society is generally as lax as its language." Could we not say instead, "A society is generally as free as its members are free to use language according to their preferences"? Or we might say, "An animal is as canine as its genus." In order to believe the original, we must start from the assumption that laxity (or is it laxness?) is a bad thing. But I suppose that we could be permissive, that we could be generous about one another's language use without society or the language going to the dogs.

meaning not the solecisms that allegedly trouble schoolteachers, but that truly dangerous abuse, the building of prejudices into the language so as to shut down criticism before it can even raise its voice." But many prejudices are built into Halpern's view of language, not least that language has a desirable end (though not, I would agree, a natural one); those prejudices do not stifle criticism, nor do they deter innovation, for, mercifully, few of us pay any attention to them. For Halpern, American English is a smaller language than it really is; as far as he is concerned, the larger language and those who live large in it don't count because they do not acknowledge that "impressive" change has already been accomplished, trivial change is, well, trivial, and we are close to having achieved the "end" of American English, whether or not we face the imminent end of linguistics.[2]

Lest anyone think that I have used Halpern unfairly, or that his argument is made of straw, allow me a critical comment on Allan Metcalf's *Predicting New Words*, a book I very much admire, but which depends on a version of the Teleological Fallacy. The book's subtitle is *The Secrets of Their Success*, and the book's bias is to measure "success" in terms of a word's longevity and its entry into mainstream American English. Imagine a cocktail party to which all of the adverbs are invited. Parent adverbs naturally compare notes about their offspring, but Mr. and Mrs. Much are having difficulty explaining **much**. Has she joined a cult called the Buffyverse? Rumor has it that she's come out as an adjective; or perhaps

---

[2] Readers have probably already guessed that I count Halpern among the grouchy language mavens mentioned earlier. The views of linguists haven't silenced him much, since he has published several articles on the general theme of "The End of Linguistics," which itself, as mentioned in the previous note, has been not only published, but reprinted. Clearly, I read these articles and I learn from them: I never object to hearing others' views on language, and I agree that the exercise of authority plays a role in usage and even language change. Halpern objects so much to linguists, however, that he ignores what they've learned from intensive study of language. Thus, I don't think that linguists shut down the Halperns of this world; rather, the Halperns hope to shut down professional linguists because they question the bases on which language mavens assert authority. Perhaps, in some areas of life, we must accept authority; I never do this without questioning, though. I think there's a big difference between running a red light and semantic inflation, and I may observe authority in one instance and not the other. If there's meat to Halpern's thinking, take it with a grain of salt, whether you are a gangbanger, a Betarer, or a schoolteacher.

she's just hanging around with the wrong sort—you know, nouns. And of all items of slayer slang, as argued in Chapter 3, **much** has the best chance of meeting Metcalf's standard of success! "Thank goodness I have given birth to standard terms," **Buffy** must muse, "otherwise, how could I live down **Buffivor**?" The Wigs, one imagines, simply avoid social engagements until **wiggins** settles on an idiomatic identity. I guess that the opposite of a successful new word is an unsuccessful one, but I'm not sure that there's any such thing. Why don't we allow those who utter new words to decide what counts as success? If a word is made for the moment, for a particular act of communication or as a matter of style, it can be perfectly successful on the terms intended—perhaps it needs no other justification than the speaker's satisfaction.[3]

If the artifact of American English is nearly complete, why should we fiddle with it; especially, why should we allow people with no aesthetic sense to fiddle with it? Such questions admit various answers: first, teleology (at least for language) is a fallacy; second, the *hoi polloi* can fiddle with it because it's theirs as much as it's anyone else's; and third, *De gustibus non est disputandum*—there's no disputing taste, for taste is relative to a lot of things. As I have suggested throughout this book, necessity as a process that leads us toward a hypothetical end is no more important to language development and change than style, or social affiliation, or the attraction of one form to another (as when **unlife** follows **undead**, or **Slayerness** follows **Buffyness**). If language isn't an organic whole, then it coheres, or makes sense, on terms that we construct. We expect a certain level of consistency, but sometimes a law allows exceptions, and sometimes the exception proves the rule; sometimes we agree that a crime has been committed, but we also agree that there were

---

[3] Metcalf would undoubtedly agree with me: as originator and annual moderator of the American Dialect Society's "Word of the Year" elections, a Contributing Editor to the Barnhart Dictionary Companion: A Quarterly Journal of New Words, co-author (with David K. Barnhart) of America in So Many Words (which introduces American "words of the year" from Colonial times to the present), and author of The World in So Many Words (which illustrates the extent to which American English has borrowed words from languages from across the globe), no one is more enthusiastic about whatever new American English has to offer; success is a reasonable metaphor, given the subject of his book. Nonetheless, Metcalf's metaphorical choices demonstrate just how easily one can back into the Teleological Fallacy.

mitigating factors, that folks are sometimes justified in doing what we don't approve of. American culture still possesses a healthy inclination toward dissent, at least in language use, of the kind endorsed by Whitman and Sledd.

When you rise in the morning and set off to work or school, you don't plan to jaywalk; you come to a light, you don't want to wait, and you make your own way. But maybe, contrary to what Halpern supposes, innovation in language isn't dangerous, or change impressive, or the speech of one time, place, and situation trivial, just because it isn't part of the artifact that someone conceives, or because it doesn't tend toward an end. It is mistaken, surely, to think that value inheres only in the ancient, the stable, the approved, the teleological. And if teens today find the surrounding world **wiggy** rather than **creepy** (and who can blame them?), then it can give them the **wiggins** rather than the **creeps**, regardless of whether or not their lexical preferences contribute to semantic inflation. Language is not a natural organism, fair enough, but beauty is in the eye of the beholder, and each of us satisfies his or her own taste, and the ephemeral often serves us very well: I have never seen a superfluous daisy; I have never eaten a trivial pear; and I have relished many words and linguistic practices of the here and now.

Ephemera and the Record of English

Scholars must record and study ephemeral language because no comprehensive history of American English is possible without accounting for it. We have lost most ephemeral and "low" language of earlier periods in the history of English; still, we write about Middle English, for instance, as though we know the linguistic context sufficiently to explain the language, yet we know neither how most people of the period spoke nor how their speech affected the literate language we study. Every once in a while, for example, in Chaucer's *The Canterbury Tales*, or *The Second Shepherd's Pageant*, or Dan Michel of Northgate's *Ayenbite of Inwit*, we encounter representations of pithy, everyday English. But most texts written in Middle English are lost to time and most wouldn't have included much colloquial language, anyway: books of religious instruction and courtly romances would tell us next to nothing about how peasants spoke to one another over their ale. Though I know some who would say that the speech of common people, as opposed to that of the powerful and learned, is historically unimportant, I cannot accept a judgment that seems to me elitist, inhumane, and a handy excuse for knowing less.

Thus our picture of the past is distorted by ignorance. And we shouldn't assume that all we've missed is ephemeral language. Because, within any period, language is a system responsive to influences within and from without, the language of all was probably to some degree affected by all of the language. The poet's choice of elevated diction partly depends on what it avoids, the language folks speak; or, in some instances (the poetry of John Skelton and the Scottish "makar" William Dunbar, who provided for us the first written evidence of the F-word, comes to mind), the relationship between poetic diction and common speech is unusually tight. How we wish we knew more about what role the "low" words such poets apparently introduced into English played in the speech and lives of English speakers before the poets caught on! So, while ephemeral language NEEDS no historical justification, it has one, nonetheless.

Anyway, without a comprehensive understanding of the language over time, how do we know what is ephemeral and what is not? How do we correctly assess the dynamics of language change? Elliptical *with* is a familiar item of colloquial American English, from sea to shining sea: *I'm going to the mall, do you want to go with?* one friend asks another; in New York City, if you want cream in your coffee, you had better ask for *coffee with.* Surprisingly, Middle English also had elliptical *with,* as evidence cited in the *Middle English Dictionary* proves. But the idiom apparently disappears from the fifteenth to the eighteenth century—unless it is captured in the current revision, you won't find evidence of it in the *Oxford English Dictionary* (henceforth OED) during that 300-year stretch. Of course, folks may have stopped using elliptical *with* around 1450 and then reinvented it centuries later: it happens. Yet one suspects that elliptical *with* survived in colloquial speech that simply eluded printed texts and documents examined in the course of compiling the OED. While hardly of earth-shattering significance, it would be good to know, be-cause if we were lucky enough to have a comprehensive record of Early Modern English, the complete and true history of elliptical *with*, among many, many similar items in the English language, would contribute to it. The more information about English, ephemeral or otherwise, we have at hand, the better we can understand it.

Today, the boundaries between literate language and ephemeral lan-guage are more fluid; the influence of the latter on the former is more likely. Even if one or another scholar prefers the language of standard dictionaries to the language of everyday American living, it takes a cer-tain arrogance to assume that studying what one prefers leads finally to the truth about American English, or any other language. The study of ephemeral American English takes an open mind, patience, and wide-ranging interests: one must explore traditional sources of words and grammatical patterns, like books and magazines; but one must look at out-of-the-way magazines, like *Toyfare* and *Cinefantastique*, as well as *Seventeen* and *Newsweek*, not to mention television, movies, websites, chat rooms, posting boards, and billboards—American English wherever it occurs. Of course, slayer slang is one of the many sites of current inno-vation in American English worth watching.

Ephemeral language plays a much larger role in the history of English than many assume. If you turn in the *Oxford English Dictionary, Second Edition*, to the beginning of the letter F and examine the entries through *fac-*, you'll discover a remarkable proportion of words with apparently short lives. The range includes 210 entries, 26 of which are cross-refer-ences, leaving 184 entries with definitions and quotations. Of those 184, 46 entries include only a few quotations taken from within 50 years (and often, only a single quotation), suggesting that, as far as we know, the word entered occurred at least once and at most very rarely, and then only for a short period. In addition, 30 complex entries include at least one sense that satisfies the same criteria. So 76 entries or subentries, 41% of the bona fide entries in the alphabetical range, record ephemeral English. Some of these words, like *fabaceous* 'like a bean', survive only in early dictionaries; others, like *factionate v* 'to form factions', which filled a lexical gap, apparently just didn't appeal to many writers or speakers, however useful they might have proved; still others, like Shakespeare's "I will carie no Crotchets: Ile Re you, Ile Fa you; do you note me?," where *Fa* refers metaphorically to the fourth note of the octave, are poetic flights of fancy unlikely outside of their contexts; and, finally, some are slang, like *facty* 'full of facts', used three times within a decade in the *Pall Mall Gazette*.

Of course, we cannot be sure that all apparently ephemeral words and senses of words found in this alphabetical range of the *OED2* are REALLY ephemeral: we may not have examined all of the relevant sources of such words, and some may have lived, for the most part, far away from print, so that we have exhausted the record yet misunderstood their currency in speech. And we can be quite sure that the *OED2* does not include ALL items of ephemeral English: James Murray and the other editors of the *OED* were frequently criticized for including as much colloquial English from colloquial sources as they did, and even a dictionary as massive as the *OED* faces constraints of space and cannot include all of the English words ever uttered. But we are grateful for what we have, and the present challenge is to record as much ephemeral language as we can, so that future estimates of twentieth- and twenty-first-century English take into account much more evidence than possible for accounts of previous periods. Fascinated with the apparent novelty of slayer slang, one might think that oblique -y suffixation, as described in Chapter 2, originated in 1997. It didn't, though, as *facty*, quite similar to slayer slang's **pointy**, proves. Is the history of oblique -y suffixation continuous in English? Does it rise in rebellion against stuffy English periodically? Is the frequency of such suffixation greater now, as a result of slayer slang, than ever before? We can't answer such questions confidently, given the record of ephemeral English up to the present. It would be valuable to expand the record of English so that, in the future, such questions are answered easily and accurately.

Living Language in the Moment

Language, as Halpern argues, is not a natural force, but something we create; notably, we have been creating it for a long time, which explains why we inevitably consider it historically. When we have questions about the state of the language, we take a backward glance and we try to understand current American English in terms of continuity and change. Nothing could be more natural or more appropriate, as long as we are not mired in the past, as long as our sense of value in language is not dominated by canons handed down to us by those indulging certain prejudices about language and its use. That Shakespeare used *Fa* in a way apparently neither anticipated nor imitated by anyone else is important from a literary perspective, but is it of any particular linguistic importance? Is it more important, in mapping the historical contours of the English language than, say, the occasional use of **Spuffy** on the Bronze: Beta? If millions of speakers and writers have used *concatenate* since it first appeared in English (the OED's first quotation is dated 1598), is their use of a Latinate, literary word over centuries more important to a history of English than the explosion of use among millions of speakers and writers of pop-cultural **Scooby Gang** over a very short period? The answer is "No," unless one lives in the past or commits the Teleological Fallacy.

Anyway, the value of ephemeral American English exceeds its role in the history of the whole language. Slayer phenomena have had a considerable impact on current American culture, and slayer slang, the verbal manifestation of those phenomena (in fact, one of those phenomena), has contributed fundamentally to that impact. Though none of us knows all of the culture that surrounds us, knowing American culture of our time fully requires knowing about *Buffy the Vampire Slayer* and slayer slang. It is a strange sort of self-loathing, it seems to me, for a culture to deny its own value, looking backward and forward, but without much appreciation for its own time and place, for what it says and how it's said, and for the pleasure that cultural moment brings. If our language is an artifact, an aspect of human behavior, and the product of human impulse, dismissing ephemeral American English means devaluing the artifact, our behavior, and our impulses. The ephemeral, we need reminding, isn't merely something we observe, but where we live; awareness of the living language and, even better, using it, means more living. Study of slayer slang has certainly expanded the volume of my own living somewhat, and, as a result I feel, like Chaucer's Wife of Bath, that I have had my world as in my time.

My father's rules for American English reflected the still common attitude that one must prefer EITHER standard American English OR ephemeral and "low" American English, when we really should admire (and perhaps even use) BOTH the standard AND the ephemeral aspects of our language, and through language, revel democratically in American culture's inevitable pluralism. We could take ourselves seriously and enjoy ourselves, as though they were the same thing.

References

Mark Halpern's "The End of Linguistics" first appeared in *The Vocabula Review* (July 2001), conveniently available online at www.vocabula.com; it later appeared in *The American Scholar* (Winter 2001, pp. 13–26). Teleological metaphors abound in Allan Metcalf's *Predicting New Words: The Secrets of Their Success* (Boston: Houghton Mifflin, 2002), without detracting from its overall excellence. With David K. Barnhart, Metcalf also wrote *America in So Many Words* (Boston: Houghton Mifflin, 1997) and wrote *The World in So Many Words* (Boston: Houghton Mifflin, 1999) solo—these two books are filled with brief articles about individual words and make the best possible subway or bedtime reading on language. For more on the functions and history of elliptical *with*, see my article "Elliptical *with*," in *American Speech* (Summer 1997, pp. 220–224). Those interested in the relationship of Standard English to other varieties should read two books not specifically cited here: Richard W. Bailey's *Images of English: A Cultural History of the Language* (Ann Arbor, MI: University of Michigan Press, 1991) and James Milroy and Lesley Milroy's *Authority in Language: Investigating Standard English*. This chapter reprints almost all of my brief article, "Ephemeral Language," originally published in the journal *American Speech* (Winter 2000, pp. 382–384).

Glossary

Guide to the Glossary

Those using the glossary may find the following notes a helpful guide to judging the value of material presented there including both subtly embedded information that one might initially overlook, and unavoidable faults inherent to recording ephemeral televised and Web-based language.

Entries and subentries: Selection of words has been, of necessity, partial and somewhat arbitrary. No two viewers or readers will find the same words particularly representative or interesting. Originally, I tried to include all of the words and derived forms of words that might be either, but the glossary I had compiled by October 2002 was nearly 100 pages longer in typescript than the one presented here, and finally I realized that I could not include entries for all of the words I had collected. When deciding what material to cut, I first turned to superfluous quotations supporting words entered here, but approximately three dozen entries were cut as well. Many of the words omitted are discussed in the preceding chapters; some are not. But I must admit that, four years into collecting quotations, I might have chosen different material, especially from the early episodes: for instance, I did not realize early on how many combinations with *guy* would appear in the show or in novels based on the show, so I did not begin to record them until it was too late to provide a continuous record of such forms. For whatever reason, I have very likely, intentionally or unintentionally, omitted someone's favorite item of slayer slang. Anyone interested in these omissions, whether whole entries or quotations, is welcome to contact the author for more information.

Though I am unusually attentive to "new" words, my attention lapses just like everyone else's; every time I watch an episode again or reread a novel based on the television show, I encounter terms I might have included, and in the process of revising this glossary, I have frequently added terms or evidence for terms that I had overlooked previously; but if I have missed forms and then incorporated them on reviewing or rereading, I have to admit that I may have missed still more, even at this late date.

While I have pursued slayer slang diligently and fairly comprehensively over the last few years, there are unavoidable gaps in the corpus of works from which I have taken words and quotations illustrating them: I have read many, but not all, novels based on the television show; I have read many, but not all, of the articles in the mainstream press about the show; I have looked at many, but not all, of the websites devoted in some sense to the television show; and I have searched through several days of posting board transcripts (totaling several thousands of pages), but the Bronze and Bronze: Beta are lively sites for slayer slang on every day of the year, not just on the days I lurked there, looking for innovative language. I have read widely in newspapers and magazines over the last few years, in order to catch slayer slang as it migrated from the show into mainstream media, but I have doubtless missed many instances. But no search by one person through all media will be complete, given the number of sources to consult. In other words, there are many, many items of slayer slang that I simply have not encountered and, given the ephemeral nature of some of the media I have consulted, never will. The glossary is merely a snapshot of American slang as represented by language in the Buffyverse; to be complete and accurate, one would need to shoot a movie of American slang continuously from 1997 to 2002.

I have focused especially on very productive terms (**Buffy** and **Slayer**, for instance) and on terms within the scope of slayer slang's formative patterns (those terms suffixed with -*age*, -*y*, and -*ness*, for instance, or terms that shift the grammatical function of a film/TV character name or title). I have also included some terms (**bad, bail, creep, hang, so,** and **-thing,** for instance) that slayer slang has borrowed, some from recorded and some from unrecorded American slang. I am claiming neither that these terms are unique to the show, nor that general use derives from the show; rather, these terms are an aspect of slayer slang grafted from current language, but recorded in a glossary or dictionary for the first time here, or at least more fully here than anywhere previously. Indeed, many items in the glossary (for instance, **damage** and **much**) first appeared elsewhere, perhaps only once, and are given new currency or significantly emphasized in slayer slang.

Entry forms: Many forms in the glossary were collected directly from broadcast or videotaped episodes of *Buffy the Vampire Slayer*. Usually, notes taken during the original broadcasts were supplemented and corrected later from videotapes of the same episodes. But collecting forms and citations from the show has been almost exclusively an aural enterprise, with this result: I have devised the registered forms and regularized spellings as I have thought fit, without recourse to original scripts or published transcripts of them. For instance, I have no evidence that the authors of scripts in question hyphenated words formed on -free, but have introduced the hyphens myself, better to reflect the status of -free as a combining form.

Part of speech: Often an item's grammatical function (noun, adjective, verb, etc.) is presented in italics immediately after the entry-form. Subentries are marked with their own part of speech labels. When part of speech varies for different senses of an entry, the label is provided sense by sense, not after the entry-form.

Forms and etymologies: Like most slang, the vocabulary itemized here is coined much less often than derived, and an item's fundamental etymology, or those of its parts, are usually available in standard, unabridged dictionaries. I include superficial etymologies after the last appropriate sense within each entry, essentially analyses of the recorded forms into constituent parts, with cross-references to dictionaries that have already treated the form, or the form's immediate precursor.

Among these dictionaries, the *American Heritage Dictionary of the English Language, Fourth Edition*, edited by Joseph P. Pickett and others (Boston: Houghton Mifflin, 2000; henceforth AHD4) serves as the dictionary of record, primarily because it treats suffixes particularly well: the suffix is frequently the most significant element of an item in this vocabulary; the element that transforms standard American English into slang. But AHD4 is also an appropriate dictionary of first resort because

Buffy is, in the first instance, American literature, this book is foremost, though not exclusively, a study of American slang, and *AHD4* is a dictionary of American English. *AHD4* records many slang senses of otherwise standard words, but I have also consulted several other dictionaries, listed here with the abbreviations that represent them in the glossary. Unless otherwise noted, specific senses cited in etymologies refer to senses of the word given in *AHD4*.

HDAS   *Historical Dictionary of American Slang*, edited by J. E. Lighter (New York: Random House, 1994–), two volumes to date, covering the range A–O;

DAS3   *Dictionary of American Slang, Third Edition*, edited by Robert L. Chapman, with Barbara Ann Kipfer (New York: HarperCollins, 1998);

NTC   *NTC's Dictionary of American Slang and Colloquial Expressions*, edited by Richard A. Spears (Lincolnwood, IL: NTC, 1994);

ODNW   *Oxford Dictionary of New Words*, edited by Sara Tulloch (New York: Oxford University Press, 1991);

ODFN   *A Dictionary of First Names*, edited by Patrick Hanks and Flavia Hodges (New York: Oxford University Press, 1996).

When an item as used in the show appears in any of these dictionaries, or when any of the dictionaries records the item's superficial etymon, the appropriate abbreviations are included in the form section.

If only one dictionary is listed, then only one included the form or the form's etymon; otherwise, all dictionaries consulted that include the item are listed in the form section. Much of the slang recorded here is already in the air, though unrecorded in most dictionaries, so indicating how many major dictionaries include the item suggests something about currency and longevity, though what, exactly, is sometimes difficult to tell. Also, dictionaries that record slang do not all belong to the same register: that a term is recorded in *HDAS* but neither in *AHD4* nor *NTC* suggests that the form is either historical (thus, like **five-by-five**, rejuvenated in the show) or relatively inconspicuous (again, **five-by-five** is a good example); a term recorded as slang in *AHD4*, but absent from the slang dictionaries, must be used so frequently and generally that specialized dictionaries are no longer sure that the item is slang at all; a term recorded in *DAS3* and *NTC* but not in *HDAS* may be more current (and also more ephemeral) than items recorded in general dictionaries. All such comparative statements are conjectural, of course, unless one has collected more evidence than the dictionaries in question combined (unlikely, in most cases, in this study); but such conjecture is interesting, and the evidence underlying it should be available to anyone pursuing the significance of a particular term.

References to dictionaries in these form sections are organized some-what like mathematical statements: parenthetical references are subordinate to those which precede them. When unlabeled, forms and their senses have been adopted from *AHD4*. When a term or constituent part of a term cannot be found in *AHD4*, then HDAS, as the most inclusive alternative and the one most likely to articulate precise senses and sub-senses, becomes the dictionary of record.

Of course, sometimes the item in question cannot be found anywhere, usually because the etymon (the title of a film, the name of a character in a film, etc.) would not generally be entered in a dictionary. In such cases, the etymology is my own. But just because an item is not recorded in any currently published dictionaries does not mean that it is unique to slayer slang: terms like **-thing** and **so**, while not registered in dictionaries in the senses recorded here, have nonetheless been current for a decade or more—such terms are important to slayer slang, but merely reflect otherwise widespread, current usage.

In many cases, words entered pose interesting formal, etymological, or grammatical problems that require extended discussion, which I attempt in the chapters that precede the glossary.

Definitions: Many of the terms included here are more or less self-explanatory; thus, definitions are brief, often synonymic. When a word is used in several senses, each sense is provided with its own definition. Generally, definitions observe the Principle of Substitutability: the word or phrase supplied as a gloss can substitute for the entry-form in a sentence. There are exceptions to this, of course, as when a word is used as a name or component in a name.

Illustrative quotations: Given constraints of length, I have included as much evidence as I thought useful, for one purpose or another. Presumably ephemeral terms sometimes lead rather intense lives and can be found in use from month to month during a particular period, so I have included more quotations than an editor of a historical dictionary would be inclined to. The glossary attempts not only to illustrate the usage of the terms entered in it, but to provide, where appropriate, the "micro-histories" of those words, the manners in which they are used, and change between when they were first introduced and then subsequently developed. Thus, I have attempted to include all derivative forms (including possessives and plurals) when evidence is available, since even simple development shouldn't be taken for granted, and since forms introduced in the show are frequently developed in other venues, thus showing the use others (authors, journalists, posting board participants, and other folk) make of what appears in the show. I have also attempted to represent accurately the variety of syntactical situations in which entered terms occur; so even though the word as it appears from one quotation to another might not be defined differently, quotations illustrate the intersection of semantics and syntax as fully as space has allowed. Especially, though, I have tried to cast a wide net: that a term appears in the show is one thing, that it appears in a book about the show is another, and that a term appears in mainstream magazines, in graphic novels, on a posting board, or in any other medium, is yet another. The cultural value of these terms can only be gauged accurately if we locate the various registers in which they occur.

Each citation has several parts. **Dates** are important to this study and are given first. Citations from episodes of BTVS include the year, month, and date on which the episode first aired. Magazines and newspapers are given as specific dates as possible, sometimes year, month, and date, but sometimes only year and month, or even year and season, as appropriate. Copyright dates are included for books. Under any given sense, citations are arranged in date order: year by year, citations from episodes are listed first; citations with relatively specific dates in each year follow in date order; books with only a copyright year are listed last.

Although most BTVS scripts are now available on the Web, and some are available in book form, viewers do not read scripts or transcripts as they watch the show: their experience is wholly aural, and thus even original scripts have limited textual authority. In this respect, the glossary is different from dictionaries, which rely almost exclusively on printed texts. In some cases, citations from episodes of BTVS or other television shows given according to air-date here will be recorded differently than in dictionaries, for when dictionaries have access to published scripts, the date of an episode will precede that given here, because the script was written before the episode aired. When it comes to language from the television show, I have been more interested in what people have heard than what authors wrote, because what people have heard has influenced American English. In cases where what was heard and what was written differ, what was heard took priority. So one may find the forms registered here somewhat inconsistent with other published versions of the evidence; I do not consider my choices of form any more authoritative than these others, except in those cases where the other versions are simply mistakes (see, for example, **vague up**).

Authors and titles of works cited appear according to the following rules: citations from episodes always include both the writer's name (or writers' names) and the episode title (e.g., 1997 Mar 10 Whedon *Welcome to the Hellmouth*). Those from periodicals include publication date followed by the author's surname and periodical title (e.g., 1999 Oct 1 Howard *Entertainment Weekly* 49/2). Complete URLs for websites are included in glossary entries. Citations from the official BTVS posting boards, The Bronze and Bronze: Beta, are signified by the posting board's name, not the URL. I have long debated how to refer to quotations from the posting boards. Because handles are not actual names, and because handles can change and single participants can use more than one name (I remember one instance when a participant pretended to be a VIP from the show), I have decided to refer merely to the board and not to the poster; but I do this reluctantly, as I greatly admire the role Bronzers and Betarers have played in the development of slayer slang, and I am grateful to have lurked among them to collect material for the glossary. Because the boards have a strong, continuous group identity (discussed in quotations included here), I hope that my choice will not offend anyone.

Page numbers for citations are indicated immediately after the author's name or the title, as appropriate. The number given locates the page on which the entry-form appears, not necessarily the beginning or ending of a quotation. Sometimes, works are published in columns; these are provided after the page number (e.g., 45/2). Page numbers for comic books and graphic novels are editorially contrived: I have counted pages, without exception, from the first page inside the cover, including front matter, title pages, advertisements, and back matter, in order to avoid confusion; all page references from these sources are enclosed in brackets.

I have attempted to record **quotations** as I have found them. Of course, I have transcribed quotations from the shows in my own spelling and punctuation; but users will notice that printed and Internet sources do not always adopt my form, nor do they spell or punctuate correctly, nor even make much sense out of a context too extensive to quote here—the conversational nature of posting boards means that I have too often had less defining context than desirable. Some confusing aspects of quotations, those so close to being clear that such aspects might appear to be my transcriptional mistakes, are marked with *sic*: otherwise, readers should assume that "mistakes," if they choose to think of them as such, are in the original.

Bracketed initials at the ends of quotations from episodes and novels indicate the speaker. Certain speakers tend to say certain types of things, and productivity depends in part on the association of certain speech habits with certain characters or "types" of people. In those cases where I have recorded dialogue, the speakers are bracketed prior to their quoted speech, rather than afterward. Regular character names are abbreviated to their initials (B = Buffy, W = Willow, C = Cordelia, X = Xander, G = Giles, O = Oz, D = Dawn, A = Angel, F = Faith, R = Riley, S = Spike), but less familiar characters' names are spelled out.

Cross-references: There are relatively few of them, marked in small capitals at the ends of entries. Cross-references usually indicate a semantic relationship, but there aren't many of note in this vocabulary; rather, items cluster around formative tendencies, but there are so many items associated with principal tendencies that cross-references would quickly become repetitive and cumbersome. Users interested in formative questions should turn to Chapter 2, where notes collect items related by formative tendencies (groups similarly prefixed are not listed in notes, however, because they can be located alphabetically in the glossary).

Slayer Slang

activeness n Propensity to do (illicit) things
1999 Jan 12 Espenson *Gingerbread* "Makes me glad my mother doesn't know about my extracurricular activities...or my curricular activities...or the fact of my activeness in general." [W] [*active adj* in sense 3.a + *-ness suff*][1]

afterness n Residual effects
1999 Nov 2 Forbes *Beer Bad* "I'm suffering the afterness of a bad night of badness." [B] [*after prep* in sense 4 + *-ness suff*]

agreeage n Shared opinion
2002 Jul 27 Bronze: Beta "Agreeage on 'The Simpsons'...should've left the air five years ago." [*agree vi* in sense 2 + *-age suff* in sense 4.b]

AIMage n Communication by AOL Instant Messenger
1999 Oct 13 The Bronze "[G]uilty if nil AIMage to you...but I am multitasking and have so much on at the homestead." 1999 Oct 13 The Bronze "No worry on the no AIM age...I have been busy anyways." [*AOL* Instant Messenger + *-age suff* in sense 1.a]

AIMness n Having access to AOL Instant Messenger
2000 Sep 1 The Bronze "I noticed elsewhere that you were bemoaning the lack of AIMness." [*AOL* Instant Messenger + *-ness suff*]

almost really adv Not quite genuinely
1998 Feb 10 Noxon *Bewitched, Bothered, and Bewildered* "I'm glad that you guys are getting along, almost really." [B] [*almost adv* + *really adv* in sense 2]

---

[1] Unless otherwise noted, specific senses cited in etymologies refer to senses of the word given in AHD4.

alone n Solitariness
2002 May 8 DeKnight *Spiral* "I'm just looking to curl up with a quiet alone tonight." [X] [fr. *alone* adj in sense 1]

Andy Sipowicz v Interrogate aggressively, perhaps with physical violence
1999 Golden *Sins of the Father* 160 "'Why don't you lie down for a few minutes while I Andy Sipowicz our little mind-leech here.'" [B] [fr. *Andy Sipowicz* 'name of a character on the television series *NYPD Blue*']

Angely adj Involving Angel
2000 Feb 22 Petrie *This Year's Girl* "How did you handle the Angely parts?" [W] [*Angel* 'vampire with a soul whom Buffy loves' + -y[1] suff in sense 1]

angsty adj Depressing, anxiety-evoking
2002 Sep 13 *Entertainment Weekly* 65/1 "'We're going to get Buffy back to a lighter, less angsty place,' says exec producer Marti Noxon." [*angst*[1] n + -y[1] suff in sense 1]

appearage n Visible presence
2002 Jul 23 Bronze: Beta "Yes, Riley appearage does sort of distract from Buffy's actions in As You Were." [*appear* vi in sense 1 + -*age* suff in sense 4.b]

ash-free adj Lacking ashes
2000 Holder *The Evil That Men Do* 312 "'Hear that, Mabel? They are ash-free.'" [B] [*ash*[1] n in sense 1 + -*free*, fr. *free* adj in senses 4.a & 4.b]

avoidy adj Evasive
2001 Oct 2 Fury *Bargaining* 2 "[Xander:] 'What went into you back there, Will?' [Willow:] 'It doesn't matter anyway.' [Xander:] 'Do not get all avoidy on me.' [Willow:] 'I'm not avoidy...I...just...we have bigger problems. Demons.' [Xander:] 'Demons. Ah, well, there's something you don't see everyday. Unless you're us.' [Willow:] 'Yeah, and now we're lost, so c...What's that?' [Xander:] 'See? Avoidy.'" [*avoid* vt in sense 2 + -y[1] suff in sense 1]

bad 1: n   Mistake
1995 *Clueless* "Oops! My bad."   1998 Golden and Holder *Blooded* 93
"'Now here I am, what you've been waiting for, and all I'm going to do
is break your hearts…. Oops, my bad. I meant stake your hearts, of
course.'" [B]   1999 Fall *Twist* Special 22 "'The most irritating thing
people do is […]' [title] […] 'Say, "My bad!" when they a make a mistake.'"   1999 Nov 23 *Angel* (WB Network) "She killed him! Oops, my
bad. It's just dust I forgot to sweep under the rug." [C]   1999 Golden and
Holder *Sons of Entropy* 161 "'My bad,' Buffy murmured."   2000 Gilman
and Sherman *Deep Water* 136 "'Sorry, my bad.'" [B]   2000 Sep 1 The
Bronze "Did I miss you? My bad!"   2000 Holder *The Evil That Men Do*
23 "'My bad. I should have paid better attention.'" [B]   2002 Apr 30
Greenberg *Entropy* "No. It's my bad. I'm the one that got caught taking
stuff." [D]   2002 Jul 28 Bronze: Beta "My bad for not being able to
hang."   [fr. *bad*[1] *adj* in sense 15]

bad guyness   n   State of being morally corrupt
2001 Odom *Revenant* 295 "'Greed,' Buffy said, 'is one of the seven deadly
sins. That's kind of a criteria for bad guyness.'"   [*bad adj* in sense 2 + *guy*
n in sense 1 + -*ness suff*]

badness   n   Evil
2000 Nov Watson *Pale Reflections* [83] "Guess those goth girls stole the
museum's pendant to unleash major badness." [B]   [*bad adj* in sense 2 +
-*ness suff*]

bail   v   Leave, quit
1992 Whedon *Buffy the Vampire Slayer* "[Girl:] 'I gotta bail—you coming?'"   1997 Mar 10 Whedon *Welcome to the Hellmouth* "Buffy, we bail
now, right?" [X]   1997 Mar 31 Des Hotel and Batali *Never Kill a Boy
on the First Date* "Then I can bail? I can go to the Bronze and find Owen?"
[B]   1998 Oct 20 Noxon *All Men Are Beasts* "Okay, you know that
thing where you bail in the middle of an upsetting conversation?" [O]
1999 Odom *Unnatural Selection* 160 "'Let's bail.' He passed Xander,
heading for the door to the outer office." [Hutch]   2000 May 2 Noxon
New Moon Rising "Some stuff came up and Oz pretty much bailed
overnight." [B]   2000 Gallagher *Prime Evil* 182 "'And maybe if Anya
and the others know they've been duped, they'll bail.'" [B]   2000

Bring It On "I go out on a limb for you, and you just bail?" 2001 Odom
Revenant 381 "'Good. Then when you're ready, we'll bail.'" [X] 2001
Daugherty *Reading the Vampire Slayer* 157 "Buffy tells Giles about her
father and how he 'bailed' on the family to run off with his secretary."
2002 Odom *Crossings* 106 "Most of the audience had chosen to bail and
headed for the exits singly or in small groups." [HDAS; DAS3 sv *bail out*;
bail out in sense 2 sv *bail²* v; NTC sv *bail (out)*]

beefstick   n   Male HOTTIE
2000 Feb 22 Petrie *This Year's Girl* "I wake up to find out this blonde
chick isn't even dating the guy she was nuts about before. She's moved
on—to the first college beefstick she meets." [F]   [*beefcake* n in sense 2
+ *stick* n]

Be kind—rewind   *catchphr*   Repeat (what was just said)
1998 Nov 24 Vebber *Lovers' Walk* "Be kind—rewind." [B]   [*be* v in sense
5.d + *kind adj* in sense 1 + *rewind* v in sense 2; fr. a request to customers
sometimes attached to rental videocassettes]

Beta   1:   n   Second incarnation of the BRONZE posting board
2002 Jul 29 Bronze: Beta "I never went to the old bronze, I've only been
posting a year now…or december will be a year. I agree with them
because they feel strongly about this and the original bronze was a great
place. Similar to here in many ways but compleatly different. That's why
I always refer to this place as the 'Beta' and not the bronze. All that
and…'Beta' is just easier to type."
  2:   n attrib   Pertaining to the BRONZE: BETA
2002 Jul 30 Bronze: Beta "It'll be stale but once Beta drunk you'll never
know the difference."   2002 Jul 30 Bronze: Beta "My very first Beta
smootch to you, dear."   [(BRONZE:) BETA sv BRONZE]

Betarer   n   Participant on the Bronze: Beta posting board
2002 Jul 29 Bronze: Beta "Whether you consider yourself a Bronzer (as
I do, but I'm sure others would disagree) or a Batarer [sic], I personally
haven't experienced an online community like this." [BETA + -r- + -er¹
suff in sense 1.d]

bezoar 1.a: n Rotten person (with pun on *bad egg*); poster who does not follow posting board rules or observe posting board etiquette
1999 Apr 29 The Bronze "But why waste time on a bezoar?" 1999 Apr 29 The Bronze "Does he think he's funny? That he even has any talent at writing or whatever? What a bezoar! How eeeevil!" 1999 May 13 The Bronze "What is it about these stupid bezoars that put in their Email addresses?" 1999 Jun 27 *http://www.angelfire.com/in/btvsjade/ newbie.html* "**Bezoar** A poster who comes to the Bronze with the sole purpose of upsetting other posters by posting rude or obscene posts. From the episode *Bad Eggs*." 2000 Sep 1 The Bronze "Take my advice and treat me as you would a bezoar." 2001 Jun 2 The Bronze "Newbies, cant live with em......bezoars, could live withough [sic] em." 2001 Jun 2 The Bronze "I seem to be dumber than a bezoar tonight." 2002 Jul 29 Bronze: Beta "And yes it;s [sic] true, as soon as you don't show yourself to be a bezoar or absolute a hole then people in this community are more than willing to chat."
   1.b: n An element in names
1999 Jun 26 The Bronze "Hello. Again. Me here. Yeah. Little Bezoar want someone to talk to." 2001 Jun 2 The Bronze "Scourge the Bezoar Annihilator"
   2.a: n *attrib* Of or pertaining to bezoars or their offensiveness
1999 Jun 26 The Bronze "Me is back! Me swear! Cross me little bitty Bezoar heart." 2001 Jun 2 The Bronze "I'm sure that's why no one was there, to avoid the Bezoar droppings." 2002 Jul 29 Bronze: Beta "I figure it's anyone who can manage to get through the bezoar attacks, flame wars, controversial arguments, petty bickering, not-so-petty bickering, and all the assorted events that go on here in cyberspace without losing their sense of humor or their perspective."
   2. b: n *attrib* [fr. sense 1.b] Of or pertaining to one named Bezoar
1999 Jun 26 The Bronze "I smell Bezoar control." See 1999 Jun 26 The Bronze under 2.a
   3: *adj* Offensive
1999 May 13 The Bronze "On your bezoar e-mail rhetorical (?) question. Not bright?" [fr. *Bezoar*, a monster that appears in the episode titled *Bad Eggs* (see Golden and Holder *Watcher's Guide* 1 [1998, 157]); cf. *bezoar* n

'indigestible mass of fibrous material found in the stomachs or intestines of many animals, once considered an antidote for poisons']

　—**bezoar-speak**　n　Language of an impolite poster

1999 Apr 29 The Bronze "Sometimes I archive the strange bezoar-speak to use it on them later." [Bezoar + -*speak* suff]

　—**jerk-bezoar**　n　Rotten person (with pun on *bad egg*)

1999 Apr 29 The Bronze "Yeah, I got to go back and see what the hell this guy posted. Seems to have caused some upset like any self-respecting jerk-bezoar normally does." [jerk¹ n in sense 5 (also *HDAS* in sense 1.a; *DAS3* in sense 4; *NTC*) + Bezoar]

big　n　Big deal

1998 Oct 20 Noxon *All Men Are Beasts* "No big, you can count on me." [X]　1998 Golden and Holder *Blooded* 103 "'What's the big?' Cordelia demanded, as he stubbornly stayed on the porch."　1999 Oct 12 Noxon *Living Conditions* "It's no big." [B]　1999 Nov 30 Forbes *Something Blue* "See? Lite [beer]. No big." [W]　1999 Nov 30 Forbes *Something Blue* "I don't see the big." [W]　1999 Golden and Holder *Sons of Entropy* 13 "'One Slayer dies, another one is called. No big.'" [B]　2000 Sept 27 Noxon *Buffy vs. Dracula* "It's no big. Just have to balance the elements." [W]　2000 Passarella *Ghoul Trouble* 27 "'No big,' Xander said. 'You can ace any topic.'"　2001 May 8 Kirshner *Tough Love* "No, I just, I know I can't know what you went through, but I...it's no big." [W]　[fr. *biggie* n in sense 2 (also *HDAS* in sense 2 & *DAS3* in sense 2) or *big deal* n in sense 1 (also *HDAS* in sense 1, *DAS3* in sense 1, & *NTC* in sense 1); see also *HDAS big* n in sense 1]

bitca　1.a:　n　Bitch

1997 Sep 15 Whedon *When She Was Bad* "[Willow:] 'I mean, why else would she be acting like such a b-i-t-c-h?' [Giles:] 'Willow, I think we're all a little old to be spelling things out.' [Xander:] 'A bitca?'"　1998 Dec 2 The Bronze "[D]evil's bitca and drinking buddy, but she's MY buffkin." [Fax1's signature]　1998 Dec 2 The Bronze "Fax1's drinking buddy and buffkin (5'4") but he's my bitca." [Devil's signature]　1999 Jun 26 The Bronze "If I want to spell it Stripe, instead of Stipe, I'll spell it Stripe, not Stipe, bitca."　1999 Jun 26 The Bronze "Love's Bitca" [signature]　1999 Jun 27 http://www.angelfire.com/in/btvsjade/newbie.html "**Bitca** The polite way of saying bitch [on the posting board in question]. From *When She Was Bad."* 1999 Jun 29 http://home.earthlink.net/ ~leathrjacket/ stima_Faq.html "Bitca: essentially a more family friendly version of b-i-t-c-h, taken from 'When She Was Bad.'" 2000 Sep 1 The Bronze "Dirty Socks says: **socKs** 'Well there's Papa Socks, Ma Socks, Brother Socks and Satan's Bitca Socks (my little sister).'" 2000 Sep 1 The Bronze "I really am not trying to come across as a bitca here." 2002 Jul 27 Bronze: Beta "Hey! Just got through watchin' 'Bring It On' myself…you mean Lindsey Sloane, 'Big Red the Bitca'? I never knew her and S[arah] M[ichelle] G[ellar] were friends."

    1.b: n An element in names
2002 Jul 23 Bronze: Beta "Bitca"   [bitch n in sense 2.a + -a]

    2: *adj* Bitchy
1999 Oct 13 The Bronze "Okay, as i missed out on hearing about Buffy and Angel earlier, i have some questions to ask…Who was introduced (eg. that bitca person Kate…)?"

    3: *vi* Complain
2000 Sep 1 The Bronze "Basically they all bitca about each other for half an hour until there's noone left."   [bitch vi]   See RIDDICHIO

    —**bitcalet** n Diminutive bitch (term of endearment)
2002 Jul 30 Bronze: Beta "Hey bitcalet! :-) Haven't seen you here in aaaages."   [BITCA + -*let* suff]

    —**über-bitca** 1: n Superbitch
2000 Sep 1 The Bronze "Okay, an example of the suckworthiness of my uber-bitca. Her office clerk…is out sick until 9/18. So she cancelled [sic] my vacation time of 9/13–15."

    2: *adj* Super-bitchy
2000 Sep 1 The Bronze "Not computer problems, uber-bitca boss problems."   [German *über-* *pref* in sense 'super' + BITCA]   See ÜBERBUFFY sv BUFFY and other entries under ÜBER-

bite-fest n Extreme amount of killing by biting
2000 Oct 3 Fury *Real Me* "Judging by the bite-fest, I'd say it was more than one vampire." [B]   [bite vt in sense 2.a + -*fest* suff, fr. *fest* n]   See SLAYERFEST, SUCKFEST, and VIDFEST

bitey *adj* Bound to bite

1997 Nov 3 Whedon *Lie to Me* "We usually call them the nasty, pointy, bitey ones." [X]   1999 Mar Watson *The Remaining Sunlight* [22] "Besides, isn't there a big bitey guy you should be worrying about?"   [fr. *bite* vt in sense 2.a + *-y*[1] *suff* in sense 1]

blood-coughage n Coughing up blood

1999 May 13 The Bronze "I'm slowly getting better. No more blood-coughage but voice getting sexier raspier." [*blood* n in sense 1.a + *cough* vt + *-age* suff in sense 4.b]

blood-free *adj* Clean of blood

1999 Oct 13 The Bronze "I went back and the fridge appeared to be blood-free." [*blood* n in sense 1.a + *-free* suff, fr. *free* adj in senses 4.a & 4.b]

booksville Accounting

2001 Feb 12 Greenberg *Older and Far Away* "Stuck in doing the booksville." [Anya]   [*books* n pl in sense 3.b + *-ville* suff]

bookwormy *adj* Like an inveterate reader

1997 Mar 31 Des Hotel and Batali *Never Kill a Boy on the First Date* "But you don't seem bookwormy, the type to lock yourself in a dark room with a lot of musty old books." [Owen]   [*bookworm* n in sense 1 + *-y*[1] suff in sense 2.a]

brainwashy 1: *adj* Associated with being brainwashed

2000 Feb 22 Petrie *This Year's Girl* "I'm looking for brainwashy chips in your head." [*brainwash* vt + *-y*[1] suff in sense 1]

   2: *adj* Engaged in mind control

2000 Feb 22 Petrie *This Year's Girl* "But the Initiative has a whole branch of brainwashy, behavior modification guys." [B]   [*brainwash* vt + *-y*[2] suff in sense 2.a]

breakage n Breakdown

1999 May 13 The Bronze "May not be able to post for a couple of days due to computer breakage." [fr. *break down* in sense 4 sv *break* v + *-age* suff in sense 4.b]

break and enterish *adj* Suitable for crime

1999 Mar 16 Petrie *Enemies* "I'll go home and stock up on weapons, slip into something a little more break and enterish." [B] 1999 Oct 1 Howard *Entertainment Weekly* 48/2 "**break-and-enterish** Comfortable slay wear." [sv *breaking and entering* n + *-ish* suff in sense 2.a]

Bronze 1: n A club in fictional Sunnydale, California

1997 Mar 10 Whedon *Welcome to the Hellmouth* "The Bronze—it's the only club worth going to around here." [C] 1997 Nov 3 Whedon *Lie to Me* "Aw, you just need cheering up, and I know just the thing—crazed dance party at the Bronze." [X] 1998 Golden and Holder *Child of the Hunt* 12 "He didn't have to hang with someone as young as she was—even though she was very mature for her age—she often passed at the Bronze for much older—and she was grateful beyond words that he did." 1998 Gardner *Return to Chaos* 22 "There was no argument that couldn't be solved by a good half hour of necking out by the Bronze's back stairs." 1999 Oct 1 *Entertainment Weekly* 34/3 "A slutty Buffy, whose Angel-provoking bump and grind with Xander at the Bronze is at once fascinating and icky." 1999 Massie *Power of Persuasion* 19 "'He wants to make the empty banquet room into a dance floor so his place can compete with the Bronze.'" [X] 1999 Golden and Holder *Immortal* 14 "The Bronze stank with the odor of wet wool laced with coffee." 1999 Mar Watson *The Remaining Sunlight* [10] "'You've never been in the Bronze's toilets, huh?'" [X] 1999 Iyer *Official Yearbook* 20/1 "[A]fter a close call with a stake at the Bronze, Buffy quickly became the freak of the week." 2000 Topping *Slayer* 27 "Buffy's red miniskirt and knee-length leather boots are smashing, but the two skirts she considers wearing to the Bronze make her look, she believes, like either a slut or a Jehovah's Witness." 2000 Dokey *Here Be Monsters* 3 "They were still back there, just the way she'd known they would be. Two guys. The ones she'd spotted for the first time in the alley behind the Bronze." 2001 Jul Golden and Sniegoski *Food Chain* 34 "'Giles and I are going to have a little meeting of the minds that will end with me at the Bronze tonight, come hell or high water.'" [B] 2001 Dec Andrews *Starburst* 22 "When Buffy enters the Bronze, Sunnydale's only nightclub, she finds a horde of vampires methodically chomping their way through the bright young things of town." 2001 Odom *Revenant* 10 "Oz and Dingoes Ate My Baby were playing at the Bronze tonight." 2001 Kaveney *Reading the Vampire Slayer* 22 "She has to be prompted by Willow to kill a vampire in the Bronze." 2002 Feb 26 Petrie *As You Were* "Blow it off! Dawnie and I are headed out to the Bronze." [W] 2002 Sep 13 Robischon *Entertainment Weekly* 158/2 "You'll also get to wander around The Bronze and other familiar locales, vanquishing vamps with stakes, reaper blades, crossbows, rakes, shovels and baseball bats." 2002 Navarro *Tempted Champions* 25 "In the end Celina parked it a couple of blocks away from a nightclub for the younger set called the Bronze and left it there." 2002 DeKelb-Rittenhouse *Fighting the Forces* 146 "In a scene rife with sexual tension, [Spike] stalks Buffy as she dances with her friends at The Bronze." [fr. bronze n in indefinite sense]

   2: n *attrib*   Pertaining to The Bronze
1999 Gallagher *Obsidian Fate* 62 "'So—you like history, too. Maybe we could, uh—go to that Bronze place to talk some time.'" [Dem]   2001 Odom *Revenant* 228 "A young Asian guy worked the counter, hair slicked back and wearing a Bronze tee shirt." [fr. sense 1]

   3.a: n   Official *Buffy the Vampire Slayer* posting board
1999 Jun 26 The Bronze "I think I am so pathetically addicted to the Bronze it isn't even funny—I was watching a movie, really enjoying it, and then started thinking of going back to the Bronze." 2002 Jul 29 Bronze: Beta "I've found that most of the posters with whom I've developed close online friendships are those who have been on the Bronze a relatively short time." 2002 Zweerink and Gatson *Fighting the Forces* 240 "Finally, both Ms. Calendar's successful merging of the techno with the pagan as well as her use of the Internet for specifically community purposes […] were the most reflective of The Bronze's use of a new tool to do what is arguably the most traditional of human work." [fr. sense 1]

   3.b: n   A component of a URL

   3.c: n   An element in names
2000 Sep 1 The Bronze "Bronzeboy"

   4: n *attrib*   Pertaining to the Bronze posting board
1998 Dec 2 The Bronze "Bronze Welcome Wagon says:…"   1999 Jun 26 The Bronze "Never, never let the Bronze clock shame you."   1999 Oct 13

The Bronze "[L]et's hear a great big bronze shout out for ['F]ly by [N]ight[']!" 2001 Jun 2 The Bronze "We know tiggy is a Bronze hottie. She denies it, but this just adds to her hottiness." 2001 Jun 2 The Bronze "I'll give $100 bronze bucks to anyone who can describe that worse than I just did." 2002 Jul 29 Bronze: Beta "What makes a Bronze veteran? Interesting question, one which I of course feel compelled to answer because I've been here since the finale of season six and, therefore, am an expert on all things Bronze." 2002 Jul 30 Bronze: Beta "There are at least two truisms of Bronze lore." [fr. sense 3.a]

    5: vi Participate on the posting board
1999 Oct 13 The Bronze "And alas now I must vanish, for the boss returneth directly, and he doest not like his staff who Bronzeth." [fr. sense 2]

    —**Bronzability** *adj* Freedom to stay on the Bronze
1999 Oct 13 The Bronze "But you didn't answer the most important question: will you have Bronzability?" 1999 Oct 13 The Bronze "As a matter of fact, I'm there now, so yes, I'll have Bronze-ability (neat word!) Until I get caught spending too much time here." [BRONZE + -*ability* suff]

    —**Bronze: Beta** 1.a n Second incarnation of the BRONZE posting board
2002 Jul 23 Bronze: Beta "Satine jumps up off her couch spins and pirouet's out the door of the Bronze: beta." 2002 Jul 28 Bronze: Beta "I cannot remember his exact words, but little bam bam once described the Bronze (and I think it should apply to the Bronze Beta) as a field upon which posters may engage in a battle of wits with language and logic as our weapons."

    1.b n An element in a URL
[BRONZE + : + *beta* n in sense 2]

    —**Bronzed** *adj* Assilimated into the Bronze posting board community
1999 Oct 13 The Bronze "I'm a Bronzed Aussie myself!" [fr. sense 2]

    —**Bronzer** or **Bronzers** 1: n Participants on the Bronze posting board
1998 Dec 2 The Bronze "[S]everal of you may have [...] noticed [by] my little advertisements that I am putting together a page of Bronzers' links." 1999 Jun 26 The Bronze "If I could fit into a Buddy Lee costume to scare

all the Bronzers on the board last year, I'm sure you could get into a Mini-Me get up." 1999 Oct 13 The Bronze "Bronzers are what make this all possible!" 2000 Sep 1 The Bronze "Or were you just inspired by the fact that the majority of Bronzers have made it through the year without killing a bezoar?" 2001 Jun 2 The Bronze "It's more than a Posting Board, it's a second home to all of us Bronzers." 2002 Jul 25 Bronze: Beta "Using the correct terminology, acknowledging the attempted rape, allows us (the whomever kind of us, be it you, me, Buffy, Spike, M[utant] E[nemy], any ol' Bronzer) to start to deal with the situation." 2002 Jul 29 Bronze: Beta "Perhaps I am completely wrong on this and the posters I haven't been able to engage in conversation are just trying to add another Bronzer to their posting family." 2002 Zweerink and Gatson *Fighting the Forces* 239 "In this chapter, we delve into some of the nonvirtual realities of some people's use of Internet technology and the mass media product *Buffy the Vampire Slayer* to form a community based in a textually mediated format, that exists simultaneously on- and off-line, namely, the devotees of the official *Buffy* Web site, otherwise known as The Bronze and Bronzers." 2002 Zweerink and Gatson *Fighting the Forces* 243 "Jan is not the only Bronzer who complained about these new group boundaries."

2: *n attrib* Pertaining to those who participate on the Bronze posting board

1999 May 13 The Bronze "And hellos to all the others out their [sic] in bronzer land." 2001 Jun 2 The Bronze "I'm announcing the PBA's Bronzer Bash." 2002 Jul 30 Bronze: Beta "And not here if your contribution to the discussion is an endless series of drive-by posts calling joss a liar or citing some article that makes the same sloppy one-sided arguments, and then slamming the Bronzer community here as a whole." 2002 Zweerink and Gatson *Fighting the Forces* 246 "On July 27, 2000, the committee released the survey results and issued a call for a 'Bronzer Liaison' position." [BRONZE + -er[1] suff in sense 1.d + -s[1] suff]

—**Bronzerdom** n World of the BRONZE or BRONZE: BETA
2002 Jul 28 Bronze: Beta "Passionate, thoughtful, and fierce debate are staples of the Bronzerdom." [BRONZER + -dom suff]

—**Bronzey** adj Of The Bronze
2000 Sep 1 The Bronze "Good night my Bronzey friends!" 2000 Sep 1

The Bronze "So don't be angry, it just bronzy fun." [BRONZE + -y[1] suff in sense 1]

   —**Bronzing** 1.a: vi Partying at the Bronze in Sunnydale, California 1998 Golden and Holder *Blooded* 103 "'So she's Bronzing with Oz,' Cordelia shrugged. 'Maybe she's gone shopping with Buffy.'"

   1.b: vt Partying at the Bronze in Sunnydale, California 1999 Massie *Power of Persuasion* 57 "'Bronzing it tomorrow night?' Oz asked."

   2: n Activity of partying at The Bronze 1999 Gilman and Sherman *Visitors* 71 "'Listen, I think I've got a line on a job. Money for Bronzin,' here I come!'" [X]

   3: n Participation on the Bronze or Bronze: Beta posting boards 2000 Sep 1 The Bronze "Bronzing next week will be really small [']cause...exam week!" 2001 Jun 2 The Bronze "However, I don't want to ruin anyone's Bronzing for them." 2002 Jul 24 Bronze: Beta "Been lurkin' for the last couple of days for no apparent reason. Miss daytime Bronzing." 2002 Jul 28 Bronze: Beta "Just Bronzin' at the moment." 2002 Jul 31 Bronze: Beta "And now, back to your regularly scheduled Bronzing."

   4: n *attrib* Pertaining to participation on the Bronze or Bronze: Beta posting boards 2002 Jul 25 Bronze: Beta "No way will I be able to do the Bronzing thing at my new job." [BRONZE + *AHD3* -ing[1] suff in sense 1.a]

   —**unBronzian** n Inappropriate to the posting board named The Bronze 2001 Jun 2 The Bronze "The board depends on the random dropping of tags within posts. It's a system of symbolic beauty apparently lost on some people. Look at 'em. Perusing the tag-shelves. Undressing the tags with their eyeballs, all ogle, no dropping. It's not just annoying. It's unBronzian." [un-[1] *pref* in sense 2 + BRONZE + -ian *suff* in sense 1]

broody *adj* Melancholy
2000 Sep 26 Noxon *Buffy vs Dracula* "They're both broody immortals." [R] 2002 Navarro *Tempted Champions* 120 "'It's not like he ever says anything, you know. Just stalks around being all tall and dark and broody.'" [S] [*brood* vi in sense 3.a + -y[1] suff in sense 1]

Buffy   1.a: n   First name of Buffy Summers, the Vampire SLAYER
1992 Whedon *Buffy the Vampire Slayer* "[Pike:] 'What's your name?'
[Buffy:] 'Buffy.'" [For more examples, see quotations throughout the
glossary.]   1997 Mar 17 Reston *The Witch* "Miss Buffy and friends are
sneaking around stealing bits of my hair." [Amy]   2001 Sayer *Reading the
Vampire Slayer* 117 "It's odd that Buffy & Co rarely inhabit spaces typical
of their age-group."   2001 Playden *Reading the Vampire Slayer* 132 "An-
gel-Adam, returned from Hell, is also Angel-Christ, on an equal footing
to Buffy-Christ, whose death and return to life is emphasized in the
same episode by her mother being told of it."   2001 West *Reading the
Vampire Slayer* 183 "It is illuminating at this point to compare the TV
'Buffy' with the 'Buffy' from the feature film that preceded the show."
2001 Saxey *Reading the Vampire Slayer* 200 "Buffy-as-Slayer and her problems are often an exaggerated parallel of the concerns of Buffy-as-teen-
ager."   2001 Shuttleworth *Reading the Vampire Slayer* 229 "Buffy qua
Buffy attempts a normal high-school life by running for Homecoming
Queen."   2001 Shuttleworth *Reading the Vampire Slayer* 230 "Most im-
pressively, Gellar can take on board the entire body language of another
person, whether as the Buffybot in 'Intervention' (5.18) or as Faith-in-
Buffy's body in 'Who Are You?' (4.16), without veering into gross parody.
(Eliza Dushku is almost as impressive as Buffy-in-Faith, but more of her
screen time is conflict of one kind or another rather than character work.)"
   1.b: n   The television show; the BUFFYVERSE
1999 Oct Watson *Buffy the Vampire Slayer* 14 [Dark Horse Comics] [29]
"My daughter and I are hooked on Buffy."   2001 Aug Epstein *Out* 50/1
"'She's a very generous actress who is 100% there in a scene,' says Amber
Benson, who plays [Alyson] Hannigan's on-screen girlfriend, Tara. 'I met
her long before Buffy, and the first thing I remember thinking was that
she had a great laugh.'"   2001 West *Reading the Vampire Slayer* 167 "This
notion, that one's fate is decided at birth and is inescapable, was ex-
plored throughout Japanese martial arts cinema and, as we shall see, it is
ever present in Buffy too."   2002 Jul 25 Bronze: Beta "I hardly doubt
Buffy's target audience is 8 year old girls." [*Buffy the Vampire Slayer*]
   1.c: n   Conflict at the heart of any episode of the television show
2000 Holder *Watcher's Guide* 2 112 "In Whedon parlance this is 'the
Buffy' of any given episode: the pain a character must endure—or cause—
in order to learn the next lesson on the hero's journey."

1.d: n   An element in names

1999 Apr 29 The Bronze "Lady of Buffdom"   1999 May 13 The Bronze "BuffFrog...BuffyBrazil...Closet Buffyholic...VaBuffyFan"   1999 Jun 26 The Bronze "Buffy Sheridan"   1999 Jun 26 The Bronze "FilmBuff"   1999 Oct 13 The Bronze "Buffyenta"   1999 Oct 13 The Bronze "UkBuffyfan"

1.e: n   An element in a URL

2001 Jun 2 The Bronze "Buffyguide.com"   2002 Wilcox and Lavery *Fighting the Forces* xxiii "Official Buffy publications, like the two volumes of *The Watcher's Guide*, not to mention numerous Web sites (e.g., Buffyguide.com) devote significant space both to series continuity and to popular culture references and allusions."

1.f: n   California girl cheerleader

2000 *Bring It On* "'Can we beat these Buffys down so I can go home?'"

2.a: n *attrib*   Pertaining to Buffy

1997 Dec 25–Jan 8 Hedegaard *Rolling Stone* 180/1 "'It's a Buffy thing,' [Sarah Michelle Gellar] says, remarkably. 'Buffy colors and stuff!'"   1999 Gallagher *Obsidian Fate* 121 "'Really?' Giles grinned. 'Captivated by the Buffy charm, is he?'"   2000 Gilman and Sherman *Deep Water* 80 "Angel frowned, concentrating his senses on Ariel instead of the familiar Buffy-rant."   2001 Feb 20 Espenson *I Was Made to Love You* "'My fun-time Buffy party-night involved watching a robot throw Spike through a window.'" [B]   2002 Jul 25 Bronze: Beta "What kind of Buffy dreams does everyone else have?"   2002 Jul 25 Bronze: Beta "She battled herself for much of the season, she's only now learning to consolodate (sp?) Herself as slayer-buffy & huffy buffy."   2002 Wilcox and Lavery *Fighting the Forces* xxii "[...] Charisma Carpenter as Cordelia Chase, rich, bitchy Buffy adversary who eventually becomes a Scooby."

2.b: n *attrib*   Pertaining to the television show or the BUFFYVERSE

1999 Jun 26 The Bronze "[T]he LOSERs around at this hour are seldom wrapped in hardcore Buffy topics. [D]ifferent vibe."   1999 Oct Watson *Buffy the Vampire Slayer* 14 [Dark Horse Comics] [29] "If there were ever a Buffy cartoon by those WB *Batman* guys, I would think that it would look a little like issue eight." [letter to the editor]   2001 Shuttleworth *Reading the Vampire Slayer* 232 "In his early appearances in Buffy Season One, Angel is positively playful, more like a vastly attenuated Angelus."   2002 Jul 25 Bronze: Beta "Does anyone know where I can find the buffy

AIM icon?" 2002 Jul 27 Bronze: Beta "I don't buy Buffy stuff. But my girlfriend bought me a Buffy Lunch Box." 2002 Vowell *The Partly Cloudy Patriot* 112 "Doug the Buffy writer, talking about Giles says, 'He'll be disdainful of these young Americans for not knowing this stuff.'" 2002 Wilcox and Lavery *Fighting the Forces* xxiii "Official Buffy publications like the two volumes of *The Watcher's Guide* [...] devote significant space both to series continuity and to popular culture references and allusions." [from sense 1.b]

—**Buff** *adj* Pertaining to BUFFY or *Buffy the Vampire Slayer*
2001 Nov 12 buffysearch.com "**Buffy is the Slayer** 2000 Loads of Buff stuff. Including spells, Multimedia, A-Z Buffy, Pictures, Biographies and much much much much much more." 2001 Playden *Reading the Vampire Slayer* 122 "She is a constructed woman, a kind of 'cyborg,' 'a creature of social reality as well as science fiction': constructed within the terms of the series, as the means for a male élite, the Council, to get their dangerous work done; constructed by the entertainment industry as soft SM porn; disguised as adventure story to legitimize scenes of violence against women; and constructed within media capitalism to provide image-branding and related merchandising opportunities, whether as tie-in 'Buff-stuff' or generic halter-neck tops for eleven-year-old girls." [fr. BUFF(Y) in sense 2]

—**Buffdom** *n* The world of Buffy, the Vampire Slayer
1999 Oct 1 *Entertainment Weekly* 37/3 "Bergstrom plans to move our Lady of Buff-dom 'away from the real cutesy clothing.'" [BUFF(Y) + -dom suff in sense 2.a] See BUFFYVERSE and SLAYERDOM

—**Buffied (typeface)** *n* Typeface adapted from the television show's logo, with distinctive "dripping" script
1999 Dec 3 Stewart *Entertainment Weekly* 18/3 "The Buffied typeface is based on the WB show's creepy, dripping logo, and can be downloaded for free." 1999 Dec 3 Stewart *Entertainment Weekly* 18/3 "At FontFace.com, Buffied is among the more popular of the hundreds of typefaces." [fr. *Buffy v, fr. BUFF(Y) + -ed² suff + typeface n in sense 2]

—**Buffinator** 1: *n* BUFFY
1999 Oct 12 Noxon *Living Conditions* "That's because he got hit by the Buffinator."

2: n One who criticizes Buffy

1999 May 13 The Bronze "[B]ut I am glad that you will not be the Buffinator anymore." [BUFF(Y) + terminator n in sense 1, most immediately fr. the title character of the film, *The Terminator* (1984), dir. James Cameron]

—**Buffivor** n Game in which posting board participants vote their least favorite character on Buffy *the Vampire Slayer* out of The Bronze

2000 Sep 1 The Bronze "**Hey kids, Its that time again.** *Are you ready again for the nations fastest and probably soon to be overdone game sensation…* Well welcome to **BUFFIVOR Rules** The game is a cross between Survivor and Big Brother… Each day you will have an opportunity to vote a character out of the Bronze." [BUFF(Y) + Survivor 'name of a reality-based television show on the CBS Television Network (from 2000), in which contestants compete to be the last remaining in the contest', fr. *survive* vi in sense 2]

—**buffkin** 1.a: n Sweetheart

1998 Dec 2 The Bronze "What my buffkin said." 1998 Dec 2 The Bronze "Fax 1's drinking buddy and buffkin (5' 4") but he's my bitca" [signature] 1999 Apr 29 The Bronze "'Nite Mircalla—Great to see my fav Buffkin."

1.b: n An element in names

1999 Oct 13 The Bronze "Honorary Buffkin" [signature] [BUFF(Y) + -kin suff]

—**Buffman** n Male fan of the television show

1999 Oct 13 The Bronze "Member #36 of 'The Buffman is a hottie club'— when do I get to see his picture?" [BUFF(Y) + -man n in sense 3]

—**Buffmyster** n Buffy, the character

2001 Jun 2 The Bronze "Whedon, you are a creative genuis [sic]…looking forward to seeing you bring the Buffmyster back." [BUFF(Y) + -myster, fr. -meister suff]

—**Buffster** 1.a: n Buffy, the character

1998 Oct 6 Noxon *Dead Man's Party* "It's great to have the Buffster back." [X] 1999 Sept 25 Weeks *TV Guide* 21 "From what we've seen [of the spinoff television show, *Angel*], we agree, even if the hunky 244-year-old had to leave the Buffster brokenhearted to get his own spooky show."

1999 Oct 13 The Bronze "No, I don't think she wants to distance herself from the Buffster, nor do I think she should try." 1999 Nov Brick *Toyfare* 60 "Featuring the lovely Sarah Michelle Gellar as our favorite stake slinger, the Buffster's all dolled up for the prom, just like in the episode "Prophecy Girl." 1999 Official *Yearbook* 12/2 "He does his best to keep the Buffster on the slaying straight and narrow." 2000 Apr *Sky Magazine* 86/1 "It's a normal day in Sunnydale, and there are bloodsuckers in need of skewering, but the Buffster isn't her usual wise-cracking self." 2000 Holder *The Evil That Men Do* 27 "He slammed his locker shut and galumphed along the hallowed halls of Sunnydale High, searching for the Buffster." 2001 Jun 2 The Bronze "I reckon that Dawn should be a slayer alongside the Buffster when she turns 16."

    1.b: n Term of address for BUFFY
2000 Sept 27 Noxon *Buffy vs. Dracula* "'Cause she didn't want to worry us, right Buffster?" [X] 2000 Navarro *Paleo* 131 "'Hey, Buffster, did you hear that Oz's band manager says she can find a place for all of us?'" [X]

    2: n *Buffy the Vampire Slayer*, the show
1999 Jun 26 The Bronze "Last nights ep of the Buffster was fab." [BUFF(Y) + -*ster* suff in sense 1]

    —**buffter** n Fan of *Buffy the Vampire Slayer*
2001 Jun 2 The Bronze "Hey buffters! Speculation about next series and spoiler so…" [BUFF(Y) + -*ter* suff]

    —**Buffyatric** n Older fan of *Buffy the Vampire Slayer*
1999 Apr 29 The Bronze "[T]emporarily clean-living Buffyatric." 1999 May 13 The Bronze "Buffyatric Wannabe" [signature] 1999 May 13 The Bronze "lexiconically-challenged Buffyatric" [signature] [BUFFY + geri-atric n]

    —**Buffybot** 1a: n Robot made to resemble Buffy
2001 Jun 2 The Bronze "There was a scene where Xander knocked over the Buffybot in the basement." 2001 Oct 2 Fury *Bargaining* 2 "It's just—we're missing a Buffybot." [Anya] 2001 Nov Spelling *Xposé* 33/2 "The Buffybot tricked the baddies for only so long." 2001 Kaveney *Reading the Vampire Slayer* 25 "When Buffy poses as the Buffybot to find out whether Spike has betrayed her, she sees him stripped of his attitudes and bravado." 2002 Jul 27 Bronze: Beta "I like Dawn. A number of times since she first appeared, I've had great sympathy for her. Her en-

counter with the just resurrected Buffy on top of the scaffolding, climbing in bed and curling up with the recharging Buffy-bot, etc."

    1.b: n Name of the robot made to resemble Buffy

2001 Sep 7 Jensen *Entertainment Weekly* 61/1 "That isn't Buffy after all, it's her android counterpart, Buffybot, which in the drama's two-hour season premiere [...] attempts to substitute for its presently deceased doppelgänger." 2001 Oct 2 Noxon *Bargaining* 1 "I brought that soldering wire you wanted for Buffybot's tune-up." [X] 2001 Oct 2 Noxon *Bargaining* 1 "You know, Buffybot, maybe you should let the machine, uh, the other machine answer the phone from now on." [W] 2002 Jul 30 Bronze: Beta "You may be right that Buffy did think, 'Katrina—who's Katrina—Spike—Buffybot—Katrina—Warren!' But the flashback had nothing to do with Spike."

    2: n *attrib* Pertaining to the Buffybot

2001 Sep 7 Jensen *Entertainment Weekly* 61/2 "'I hear that I will be on the show in some form this year,' says Sarah Michelle Gellar during a break in shooting, a prosthesis of wiry Buffybot entrails visible under her demon-shredded blouse." [BUFFY + *robot* n in sense 1]

    —**Buffycentric** *adj* Focused from the perspective of the BUFFYVERSE

2002 Jul 29 Bronze: Beta "I thought maybe the board could use a break from the topic as it seemed to be diverging from a Buffy-centric arena." [BUFFY + *-centric* suff in sense 3] See SCOOBY-CENTRIC sv SCOOBY GANG

    —**Buffyfan** 1.a: n Fan of Buffy *the Vampire Slayer*

2001 Jun 2 The Bronze "My absolute fave is Eliza, but she aint established much outside of us buffyfans."

    1.b: n An element in names

2001 Jun 2 The Bronze "Yeah, buffyfan it's true." [BUFFY + *fan*² n]

    —**Buffyholic** 1.a: n Person who is addicted to Buffy and/or *Buffy the Vampire Slayer*

1999 Fall *Buffy the Vampire Slayer* 8 "I'm not afraid to admit that I'm a Buffy-holic!" [letter to the editor]

    1.b: n As an element in names

2000 Sep 1 The Bronze "Closet Buffyholic" [BUFFY + *-holic*, ult. fr. *alcoholic* n]

    —**Buffyholism** n Addiction to Buffy and/or *Buffy the Vampire Slayer*

1999 May 13 The Bronze "Buffyholism" [signature] [BUFFY + *alcoholism*]

—**Buffy-ish** *adj* In the manner of *Buffy the Vampire Slayer*, the television show

1999 Oct 1 *Entertainment Weekly* 22/2 "These reach as far back as the 1915 silent-movie serial *Les Vampires*, a clutch of blood-soaked adventures strikingly Buffy-ish in their tales of vampire hunting as both a noble calling and a down-and-dirty day (and night) job." [BUFFY + -ish suff in sense 2.a]

—**Buffy-ism** *n* Word or phrase typical of Buffy or of *BTVS*

1998 Sep 10 http://www.geocities.com/bdrink.txt "[Drink when...] Buffy utters a 'Buffy-ism.' *(This DOES NOT include CBSs (Cute Buffy Sayings) like: 'Goodbye Stakes, Hello flying fatalities!' CBSs require 2 sips." [BUFFY in sense 1 + -ism suff in sense 2]

—**Buffyland** *n* The BUFFYVERSE

2000 Gilman and Sherman [iii] "Josepha would like to dedicate this book to: Joss, the Buffy cast, and Lisa the Longsuffering for allowing us another trip into Buffyland." [BUFFY + *land* n in sense 7]

—**Buffyless** 1.a: *adj* Lacking Buffy

2002 Money *Fighting the Forces* 101 "In 'The Wish,' the episode following 'Lover's Walk,' vengeance demon Anyanka (disguised as Anya, a new Sunnydale High student) grants selfish Cordelia an alternate reality of a Buffyless Sunnydale and ritually effects the transformation by presenting Cordelia with her amulet of power." 2002 Jul 31 Bronze: Beta "Season 6 was rather Buffyless."

1.b: *adj* Without the television show

1999 Oct Watson *Buffy the Vampire Slayer* 14 [Dark Horse Comics] [29] "We are now in a Buffy-less time in Germany." [BUFFY + -*less* suff in sense 1]

—**Buffyly** *adv* In Buffy's quippy manner

1999 Apr Conroy *Us* 70/2 "Asked recently whether she was working too hard, [Sarah Michelle Gellar] responded Buffy-ly, 'I can sleep when I'm dead.'" [BUFFY + -*ly*[1] suff in sense 1]

—**Buffymobile** *n* Car

2002 Jul 23 Bronze: Beta "Got to go do some errands in my red buffy mobile[.] It's really just a normal car, but I like that name." [BUFFY + *automobile* n]

—**Buffyness**   1 :   n   The television show
1999 Oct 13 The Bronze "I'm a Bronzed Aussie myself! …from the South…the part where Buffy-ness is delayed considerably!"

2: n Involvement in all things related to Buffy or the television show
2000 Sept 1 The Bronze "Adventures in Buffyness" [link included in a message] [BUFFY + -ness suff] See SLAYERNESS

—**Buffy Paradigm** n View of biological warfare based on a comparison with BTVS
2001 Sept 29 Cordesman *Biological Warfare and the "Buffy Paradigm"* 3 "I am going to suggest that you think about biological warfare in terms of a TV show called 'Buffy the Vampire Slayer,' that you think about the world of biological weapons in terms of the 'Buffy Paradigm,' and that you think about many of the problems in the proposed solutions as part of the 'Buffy Syndrome.'" 2001 Sept 29 Cordesman *Biological Warfare and the "Buffy Paradigm"* 5 "One way of illustrating the validity of the 'Buffy paradigm' is to examine the range of possible scenarios and the obvious uncertainties they create." [BUFFY + *paradigm* n in sense 3]

—**BuffyPedia** n Encyclopedia of the BUFFYVERSE
2001 Nov 12 buffysearch.com "**BuffyPedia** The Ultimate Encyclopedia of all things Buffy and Angel." [site name] [BUFFY + *encyclopedia*]

—**Buffyspeak** n English as spoken by Buffy and her colleagues
1999 Oct 13 The Bronze "I'm still chuckling over David's use of Buffyspeak." 2002 Overbey and Preston-Matto *Fighting the Forces* 76 "She is neither a solitary Speaker nor a solitary Slayer, and this (as we will see) is what makes Buffy-combat, and Buffy-speak, efficacious." 2002 Edwards *Fighting the Forces* 91 "She not only looks different but also sounds different, so different, in fact, that she does not understand 'Buffy-speak.'" [BUFFY + -speak suff] See SLAYER SLANG sv SLAYER

—**Buffy Syndrome** n Chronically undesirable set of behaviors supposedly illustrated in BTVS
2001 Sept 29 Cordesman *Biological Warfare and the "Buffy Paradigm"* 5 "If this is the 'Buffy paradigm,' the 'Buffy syndrome' is different. The characters in Buffy constantly try to create unrealistic plans and models, and live in a world where they never really face the level of uncertainty they must deal with. They do not live in a world of total denial, but they do seek predictability and certainly to a degree that never corresponds to

the problems they face. In short, they behave as if they could create and live with the kind of strategy and doctrine that is typically developed by the US joint chiefs [sic], could develop and implement an NSC decision memorandum, or solve their problems with the equivalent of a Quadrennial Defense Review." [BUFFY + *syndrome* n in senses 2.a & 2.b]

—**Buffytime** n Time taken in the television show's context
1999 June 26 The Bronze "[R]emember, in Buffytime, she will have had the entire summer to get over Angel somewhat." [BUFFY + *time* n in sense]

—**Buffyverse** 1 : n Fictional world of which BUFFY is the center
1999 May 13 The Bronze "And they have the 'grown up' outlook on things, which in the Buffyverse, is a great weakness for most." 1999 May 13 The Bronze "[G]eez, I have an alternate Buffyverse brewing." 1999 Jun 27 angelfire.com/in/btvsjade/newbie.html "**Buffyverse** The Joss Whedon created universe that Buffy the Vampire Slayer takes place in." 1999 Sep DeCandido *American Libraries* 44 "[H]ere is a rundown of the dramatis personae in the Buffyverse." 2000 Dec 1 The Bronze "The main answer to your question is that vampire populations in the Buffyverse don't go out of control for a number of reasons." 2000 Holder *Watcher's Guide* 2 v "This book contains more information on both levels of the Buffyverse." 2001 Jun 2 The Bronze "[T]he first rule in the Buffyverse is 'death doesn't have to be a permanent thing.'" 2001 Sep 7 Jensen *Entertainment Weekly* 65/2 "She plans to rule the Buffyverse by one simple edict." 2001 Nov 12 buffysearch.com "**Buffy & Angel: Forbidden Lovers** Site about all things in the Buffyverse. A place where one can get info on BTVS and Angel at one stop." 2001 Kaveney *Reading the Vampire Slayer* 7 "He bequeaths to Cordelia the blinding headaches that go with the visions and his role as Angel's link to The Powers That Be, the Buffyverse's rather shadowy equivalent of Providence." 2002 Jul 29 Bronze: Beta "[O]ne can imagine [Tara] and Willow going through such a process of dealing with Willow's personal issues and magic dependence...but, this being the Buffyverse, they didn't get the chance." 2002 Busse *Fighting the Forces* 207 "Generating their own versions of the Buffyverse, these fans use fiction to emotionally respond to the show."

2 : n *attrib* Pertaining to the Buffyverse
2001 Shuttleworth *Reading the Vampire Slayer* 226 "'Fool for Love' (5.7)

reveals both this and the delightful if heavy-handed truth about his human existence as 'William the Bloody,' putting his frequent incompetence as an evildoer into perspective and once again emphasizing that the reality of Buffyverse identity is more complicated than Buffy's specious reassurance to Willow in 'Doppelgangland' that a vampire's personality 'has nothing to do with the person it was.'" 2002 Jul 25 Bronze: Beta "I think he believes that the writers are not facing Buffyverse reality." 2002 Jul 26 Bronze: Beta "I'm hoping the writers are able to make it interesting and believable (in a Buffyverse sense) to see what he [Spike] does with the soul." [BUFFY + universe n in sense 3]

—**Cave-Buffy** n Prehistoric SLAYER
2001 Kaveney *Reading the Vampire Slayer* 252 "The apartment is perfect, except for the vengeful fetchingly monosyllabic Cave-Buffy." [*caveman* n in sense 1 + BUFFY]

—**crybuffy** n Crybaby (referring to Buffy)
1999 *Angel* (WB) "I'm not a sniveling, whiny little crybuffy." [C] [*crybaby* + *buffy*, fr. BUFFY]

—**Franken-Buffy** n Monster in the guise of Buffy
2000 Nov Watson *Pale Reflections* [58] "The Buffy we've been seeing isn't the real Buffy, but some kind of Franken-Buffy." [W] [*Frankenstein* n + BUFFY]

—**Spuff** n Romantic relationship between Spike and Buffy
2002 Jul 25 Bronze: Beta "I do not get the Spuff, either." [SPUFFY]

—**Spuffy** 1: n Romantic relationship between Spike and Buffy
2002 Jul 25 Bronze: Beta "My name is wolfguard and I'm an anti-Spuffy (the relationship, not the fans of the relationship)." 2002 Jul 26 Bronze: Beta "I liked Spike but didn't love Spuffy."
2: n Those who favor a romantic relationship between Spike and Buffy
2002 Jul 25 Bronze: Beta "Spuffies are a passionate breed. They stand up to be counted. They sound off to the roll call. They buy Spike plushies. It's said that one Spuffy is equal to three 'regular' fans."
3: n attrib [fr. sense 1]
2002 Jul 26 Bronze: Beta "I was not posting to you as a Spuffy fan." [Spike + BUFFY]

—**Spuffyness** n Condition of desiring a romantic relationship between Spike and Buffy

2002 Jul 25 Bronze: Beta "Ooohh, 'Intervention'—yes, I also love that episode […] What a wonderful blend of comedy and romance-angst—that's really the episode that solidified my Spike-love and Spuffy-ness." [SPUFFY + -ness suff]

　—**Team Buff**　n　Buffy and the SCOOBY GANG
2002 Overbey and Preston-Matto *Fighting the Forces* 79 "Willow's spells of protection and detection, discovery and subjugation, allow Team Buff to operate effectively on the Forces of Darkness."　[*team* n in sense 2 + BUFF(Y)]　See TEAM SLAYER sv SLAYER

　—**überBuffy**　1:　n　Buffy who exceeds herself
2000 Holder *Watcher's Guide* 2 8 "In 'Primeval' and 'Restless,' the primal source of the Slayer is tapped, and Buffy becomes imbued......with that primal force. She becomes, according to the script, 'ÜberBuffy.'"

　2:　n attrib　Pertaining to the ÜBERBUFFY
2001 Wall and Zryd *Reading the Vampire Slayer* 57 "Yet there are things he cannot understand: muttering 'Interesting,' he is dissassembled by the uberBuffy gestalt."　[German *über-* pref in sense 'super' + BUFFY]　See ÜBERBITCA sv BITCA, ÜBERACHIEVER and other ÜBER- forms

bug　vi　Bother
2000 Oct 3 Fury *Real Me* "And that's what bugs...she gets to be a kid." [B]　[HDAS *bug* v in sense 9.a, fr. HDAS *bug* (out) v in sense 3, or fr. *bug* vt in sense 1.a & 1.b]

buttonpalooza　n　Festival of buttons
2002 Jan 29 Espenson *Doublemeat Palace* "There are so many buttons, it's, like, buttonpalooza." [B]　[*button* n in sense 1.a + *lollapalooza* (also HDAS in sense 1 & NTC in sense 1, most immediately from the rock concert Lollapalooza, organized annually, 1990–1998)]

capade　n　Adventure, challenge, contest
1998 Nov 3 Greenwalt *Homecoming* "[Cordelia:] 'After all that we've been through tonight, this whole who-gets-to-be-Queen capade seems pretty...' [Buffy:] 'Damn important.' [Cordelia:] 'Oh yeah!'"　[*escapade* n]

carbon-dated　adj　Very out of date
1997 Mar 10 Whedon *Welcome to the Hellmouth* "[Buffy:] 'Deal with that

outfit for a moment.' [Giles:] 'It's dated?' [Buffy:] 'It's carbon-dated.'"
1999 Oct 1 Howard *Entertainment Weekly* 48/2 "**carbon dated** Beyond
passé." [fr. *carbondating* v + -ed² suff]

cardboardy *adj* Tastes like cardboard
1998 Jan 12 Noxon *Bad Eggs* "Mmm, cardboardy [of a breakfast bar]."
[X] [*cardboard* n + -y¹ suff in sense 2.a]

Carrie 1: *n* Supernaturally vengeful stunt
1999 May 11 Noxon *The Prom* "I've got to stop a crazy from pulling a
Carrie at the prom." [B] 1999 Oct 1 Howard *Entertainment Weekly* 48/3
"**(a) carrie** Psycho prom moment in spirit of '76 horror flick."
    2: *adj* Supernaturally vengeful
2000 Garton *Resurrecting Ravana* 112 "'She was the one who went all
Carrie.'" [B] [fr. *Carrie* 'name of a character in a horror movie of the
same name (1975), dir. Brian de Palma']

cartoony *adj* Unrealistic, fanciful
2002 May 21 Fury *The Grave* "I was gonna walk you off the cliff and
hand you an anvil, but it seemed kinda cartoony." [X] [fr. *cartoon* n in
sense 3 + -y² suff in sense 2.a]

checky *adj* Made of checked fabric
2000 Topping *Slayer* 130 "**It's a Designer Label!:** Willow's orange sweater,
Buffy's grey pants and Xander's red shirt and checky strides." [check n in
sense 12.c + -y¹ suff in sense 1]

chickeny *adj* Purportedly chicken
2002 Jan 29 Espenson *Doublemeat Palace* "The beefy layer is definitely
people! Probably not the chickeny part! But who knows? Who knows?!"
[B] 2002 Jul 28 Bronze: Beta "The Doublemeat Medley is people! ...
The meat layer is definitely people! Probably not the chickeny part. But
who knows? Who! Knows!" [chicken n in sense 1.c + -y¹ suff in sense 2.a]

childhood trauma *n* Problem
1997 Mar 10 Whedon *Welcome to the Hellmouth* "God, what is your childhood trauma?" [C] 1998 Winter *Buffy the Vampire Slayer* 50/2 "**childhood trauma:** [...] n. problem—as in 'What's your childhood trauma?'"
[*childhood* n in sense 1 + *trauma* n in sense 2; fr. the psychoanalytic

principle that later emotional problems descend from emotional pain experienced in childhood]

Chosen One 1.a: n Alternative title for the current SLAYER
1992 Whedon *Buffy the Vampire Slayer* "You want me to go to the grave-yard with you because I'm the Chosen One, and there are vampires?" [B] 1997 Golden and Holder *Halloween Rain* 6 "Buffy the Chosen One, the Slayer, the complete moron, went home to concentrate on eating all the frozen yogurt in the house." 1998 Golden and Holder *Child of the Hunt* 22 "Even now, her mom was trying desperately to cling to the idea that Buffy had done something that had made her the Chosen One." 1998 Gardner *Return to Chaos* 14 "If her daughter was destined to be the Chosen One, Joyce wanted to be included, too." 1998 Golden and Holder *Blooded* 18 "As for the Chosen One, Buffy was quaking with fear." 1999 May 13 The Bronze "Disability must be another fear for a Slayer—to still be alive and the Chosen One, but be unable to fight back." 1999 Massie *Power of Persuasion* 66 "Buffy let out a breath and wondered, once more, why she was the Chosen One. Why she was responsible for stopping evil." 1999 Golden *Sins of the Father* 20 "' But you're the Chosen One, not me.'" [Pike] 1999 Gallagher *Obsidian Fate* 23 "Apparently, her mother didn't want to spoil a perfectly good morning discussing her dangerous duties as the Chosen One either." 2000 Apr *Sky Magazine* 86/1 "The reason for Buffy's bizarre behaviour? It all started when a high school lame-o persuaded her to smoke a spliff. The Chosen One is throwing a serious whitey." 2000 Dokey *Here Be Monsters* 21 "In her job as the Chosen One, the Slayer, Buffy had seen some pretty horrific things in her young life." 2000 Passarella *Ghoul Trouble* 15 "As the vampire Slayer, the Chosen One, she recovered faster than an ordinary person." 2000 Holder *Watcher's Guide* 2 3 "As we learned in seasons one and two, the Slayer is the Chosen One, who will fight the forces of darkness." 2000 Topping *Slayer* 14 "'Killing time' takes on a whole new meaning at Hemery High when Buffy (a blonde-brained cheerleader) is told by the mysterious Merrick that she is the Chosen One—the Vampire Slayer." 2001 Jun 2 The Bronze "FRAY is a limited-series comic book (eight issues) about a Slayer 500 years in the future who doesn't know she's the Chosen One." 2001 Jul Golden *Food Chain* [8] "Fortunately, Sunnydale has some help

with the big evils. Buffy Summers. The Slayer. The Chosen One." 2001
Odom *Revenant* 3 "She was the Slayer, the girl born to be the Chosen
One." 2001 Wall and Zryd *Reading the Vampire Slayer* 71 "At once the
title seems tinged with values of supervision and hierarchy—as if the
Slayer, the Chosen One, were little more than a resentful worker on the
assembly line." 2002 Sep 13 Robischon *Entertainment Weekly* 158/3
"When the Chosen One loses a fight, she doesn't simply die." 2002
Odom *Crossings* 38 "'I'm lookin' for the Chosen One.'" 2002 Siemann
Fighting the Forces 123 "With the acceptance of the responsibilities of the
Chosen One and her growing romantic attachment to Angel, the vam-
pire with a soul, her priorities begin to shift."

   1.b: n Term of address for Buffy, as the Slayer "'Beg me for your life,
Chosen One.'" [Helen]

   1.c: n Any of a number of those called to be Slayers
1997 Mar 10 Whedon *Welcome to the Hellmouth* "Into each generation, a
Slayer is born. One girl, in all the world, a Chosen One." [G] 1999 Oct
1 Tucker *Entertainment Weekly* 22/1 "Sure, Buffy is Earth's current Chosen One—the latest in a centuries-long line of demon slayers (all female, we may add)." 1999 Golden and Holder *Ghost Roads* 140 "'We are
Chosen Ones. We were handed a sacred obligation.'" [Maria Regina]
1999 *Official Yearbook* 8/1 "Even for a Chosen One, Buffy is pretty choice."
2002 West *Reading the Vampire Slayer* 169 "The very notion that the Slayers are the Chosen Ones is indicative of the predetermined role that fate
has given them."

   1.d: n Someone like the Slayer, but outside the Buffyverse
1999 Nov 11 *Charmed* (WB Network) "He's known as the Chosen One."
1999 Nov 11 *Charmed* (WB Network) "So, you're witches, and I'm the
Chosen One."

   1.e: n Those destined to be exceptional
2001 Dec Andrews 20 "The Chosen Ones" [title]

   1f: n As an element in names
1999 Jun 26 The Bronze "The Chosen One"

   2: n attrib "'Okay, she's been through some pretty rough stuff thanks
to the whole Chosen One business.'" [B] [*chosen* adj in sense 1 + *one* n
in sense 9]

Christian Baleage n Lust for Christian Bale
2001 Jun 2 The Bronze "And about American Psycho (rented for the Christian Bale-age. *drool*)." [*Christian Bale* 'name of an actor' + *-age suff* in sense 1.a]

Clark Kent v Disguise
1999 Dec 12 Whedon *Hush* "We have a gig that would inevitably cause any girl living to think we are cool upon cool, yet we must Clark Kent our way through the dating scene and never use this unfair advantage." [R] [fr. *Clark Kent* 'name of Superman's alter ego']

clearage n Removal of sediment or obstructions
2000 Sep 1 The Bronze "The first trout is backpedalling from the pond clearage decision." 2000 Sep 1 The Bronze "Horrifying, newfan, that cryptic comment about pond clearage." [*clear vt* in sense 2 + *-age suff* in sense 4.a]

clueage n Clues, evidence
1999 Nov 23 Espenson *Pangs* "How 'bout that ceremonial knife, huh? Pretty juicy piece of clueage, don't you think?" [B] [*clue* n + *-age suff* in sense 1.a]

collegey adj Related to college
1999 Nov 2 Forbes *Beer Bad* "I'm finally an essential part of your collegey life—no more looking down on the townie." [X] [*college* n in sense 1.a + *-y¹ suff* in sense 1]

commandery adj Like someone in charge
2000 Feb 15 Noxon *Goodbye, Iowa* "Very commandery." [B] [*commander* n in sense 1 + *-y¹ suff* in sense 2.a]

coolness 1: n Acceptableness
2000 Sep 1 The Bronze "Coolness. I'll send you an e[-mail] as soon as it's uploaded."
   2: n A hip attitude
2000 Holder *Watcher's Guide* 2 152 "Striving for coolness, Principal Snyder refers to John Travolta's character on the TV series *Welcome Back, Kotter*." 2002 Jul 30 Bronze: Beta "It is you who is definitely way to [sic] cool for me. I can't compare to your coolness."

3: n attrib   Of or pertaining to being cool

2000 Holder *Watcher's Guide* 2 126 "Not only did she jeopardize her coolness factor by publicly dating Xander, but she had to suffer humiliation at the hands of her 'friends' [...] when she caught him cheating on her." [*cool* adj in sense 6.b (also HDAS *cool* adj in sense 3.a & DAS3 *cool* adj in sense 10) + -*ness* suff]

Cordette 1:   n   Popular friends of Cordelia Chase who are not among the SCOOBY GANG or SLAYERETTES

1998 Golden and Holder *Blooded* 130 "Cordelia stopped short, looked left, right, must have decided that none of the Cordettes could possibly witness her speaking to one of the untouchables, and rushed over to Buffy." 1999 *Angel* (WB) "I think she's one of Cordelia's group. People called them the Cordettes, bunch of girls from wealthy families; they ruled the high school, decided what was in, who was popular; it was like the Soviet secret police if they cared about shoes." [A]   2000 Topping *Slayer* 124 "**Cast:** [...] Kristen Winnicki (Cordette)"   2000 Holder *Watcher's Guide* 2 64 "And Harmony, one of her Cordettes, completely humiliates her by suggesting she has just 'the stallion' for Cordelia." 2002 Money *Fighting the Forces* 103 "When she returns to school in 'The Wish,' even her Cordettes ridicule her for being rejected by a boy with no score on the popularity scale."

2:   n attrib   Pertaining to those friends

1998 Golden and Holder *Blooded* 29 "She was flanked by two of her Cordette wanna-bes, who stood just so, smirked just so, and were just...not." 1999 Massie *Power of Persuasion* 53 "Nothing like showing off the goods. The Cordette-types would love that." [ODFN Cordelia + -*ette* suff in senses 2 & 3]   See SLAYERETTE sv SLAYER

couply adj   Engaged in activities typical of romantic couples

1998 Oct 13 Greenwalt *Faith, Hope, and Trick* "Maybe we shouldn't be too couply around Buffy." [W]   [*couple* n in sense 3.a + -*y*¹ suff in sense 2.a]

crack whore–free adj   Lacking crack whores (or those for whom "crack whore" is a nickname)

1999 May 13 The Bronze "This board is been [sic] crack whore-free long enough." [*crack* n in sense 9 (also HDAS *crack* n in sense 10 & DAS3

crack n in sense 12) + *whore* in sense 3 + *-free,* fr. *free adj* in senses 4.a &
4.b]

crayon-breaky   1.a: *adj*   Clumsy, insecure
2002 May 21 Fury *The Grave* "Yeah, I love you: I love crayon-breaky
Willow and I love scary, veiny Willow." [X]
   1.b: An element in names
2002 Jul 30 Bronze: Beta "CrayonBreaky"   [*crayon* n in sense 1 + *break* vt
in sense 2.a + -*y*² *suff* in sense 1]

crazy   n   Insanity, foolishness
1999 Mar 17 Petrie *Enemies* "Stop with the crazy; go talk to Angel." [W]
2000 May 9 Petrie *The Yoko Factor* "[Buffy:] 'Riley, have I ever given you
reason to feel you couldn't trust me?' [Riley:] 'No.' [Buffy:] 'Then why
with the crazy?' [Riley:] 'Because I'm so in love with you I can't think
straight.'"   [fr. *crazy adj* in sense 2.c]

creep   v   Make uncomfortable or frighten
1997 Oct 13 Greenwalt *Reptile Boy* "Those frat guys creep me." [X]   1999
Golden and Holder *Out of the Madhouse* 102 "Willow sat in the school
library, feeling a bit creeped."   [*HDAS* sv *creep* (out) (also *DAS3*)]

creepy   n   Unsettling situation
1997 May 19 Whedon *Out of Mind, Out of Sight* "How much the creepy
is it that this Marcie's been at this for months?" [C]   1999 Oct 1 Howard
Entertainment Weekly 48/3 "**(the) creepy** Frightening."   [fr. *creepy adj* in
sense 1]

cryptic   n   Obscurity, obliqueness
1999 May 11 Noxon *The Prom* "Angel, drop the cryptic." [B]   2001 Oct
2 Fury *Bargaining* 2 "Giles isn't around. You can dump the cryptic." [X]
1999 Oct 1 Howard *Entertainment Weekly* "**(the) cryptic** Manner of speaking without imparting imformation."   [fr. *cryptic adj* in sense 1]

cuddle-monkey   n   Male lover
1998 Feb 10 Noxon *Bewitched, Bothered, and Bewildered* "Every woman in
Sunnydale wants to make me her cuddle-monkey." [X]   [*cuddle* v +
monkey n in sense 2, by analogy fr. *HDAS* (also *DAS3* and *NTC*) sv *cuddle
bunny* 'affectionate, passionate, or sexually attractive young woman']

cuddlesome *adj* Suitable for cuddling
1998 Nov 3 Greenwalt *Homecoming* "A private limo. It is pretty... cuddlesome." [W]   2000 Topping *Slayer* 133 "A sick Buffy in her fluffy bed socks is so cuddlesome, you want to hug her till she pops."   [*cuddle* v + -*some*¹ suff]   See DOLLSOME and FREAKSOME

damage n Problem
1992 Whedon *Buffy the Vampire Slayer* "My trust fund's in the graveyard? What's your damage?" [B]   1997 Golden and Holder *Halloween Rain* 5 "'What's your *damage*, Buffy?' Aphrodesia yelled, as John scrabbled away from Buffy."   1998 Oct Brereton *The Dust Waltz* [36] "Brrr. What's her damage?"   2001 *Jay and Silent Bob Strike Back* "What is your damage, little boy? You got a sick and twisted world perspective."   [*damage* n in sense 1]

dateville n Romantic liaison
1997 Oct 6 Kiene and Reinkemeyer *Inca Mummy Girl* "And we enter dateville. Romance. Flowers." [B]   1999 Oct 1 Howard *Entertainment Weekly* 48/3 "**dateville** Early stage of a relationship, between Big Fun Group Town and Romantic Twosome Burg."   [*date* n in sense 7.a + -*ville* suff]

David Lynch *adj* Nonlinear
2002 Feb 5 DeKnight *Dead Things* "[Anya:] 'Its presence in our dimension causes a sort of temporal disturbance.' [Buffy:] 'So that's why time went all David Lynch.'"   [fr. *David Lynch* 'name of American television and film director']

Dawson's Creek *adj* Cheesy
1999 Golden and Holder *Out of the Madhouse* 120 "'I mean, I don't want to sound all *Dawson's Creek*, but maybe I'm just lashing out at you when it's other things that are bothering me.'" [X]   [fr. *Dawson's Creek* 'title of a dramatic television show on the WB network']

deal v Handle, manage
1998 Jan 20 Whedon *Innocence* "But even if she was, we'd deal." [A] 1998 May 19 Whedon *Becoming, Part 2* "Don't worry, I can deal." [B] 1998 Oct 6 Noxon *Dead Man's Party* "There was nothing anyone could

do. I just had to deal on my own." 1998 Dec 8 Noxon *The Wish* "How do you deal?" [X]   1999 Nov 16 Petrie *The Initiative* "[Xander:] 'How's Will doing with the…' [Buffy:] 'With the black hole of despair she's lived in since Oz left? She's dealing. I'm helping. It's hard.'"   1999 Golden and Holder *Ghost Roads* 228 "'That breach was a big honkin' deal, and she dealt.'" [X]   1999 Gilman and Sherman *Visitors* 31 "Not that she really remembered days like that anymore, but… Oh well. Deal, move on."   1999 Odom *Unnatural Selection* 84 "'Hey, we'll deal later.'" [O] 2000 Sep 1 The Bronze "[T]his semester's gonna be tougher than I thought. But I'll deal."   2000 Holder *The Evil That Men Do* 56 "'I'm sorry he brought up Kendra,' Angel continued. 'It's okay,' [Buffy] said tightly. 'I've dealt.'"   2001 Nov 6 Whedon *Once More, with Feeling* "You can't tell the ones you love; / You know they couldn't deal." [S]   2001 Nov Golden *Food Chain* 62 "But three days a month, we can deal." [O] 2001 Odom *Revenant* 5 "Angel nodded. 'Okay. I can deal.'"   2002 Feb 26 Petrie *As You Were* "Your turn up front. I'll deal back here; you take the customers." [Fast food manager]   2002 Apr 30 Greenberg *Entropy* "You want to tell 'em so badly, go ahead. Know why? I tried to kill my friends, my sister, last week. Guess how much they hate me. Zero. Zero much. So I'm thinking, sleeping with you—they'll deal." [B]   2002 Odom *Crossings* 46 "[Buffy:] 'Stopping the Craulathar demon will be up to us.' [Willow:] 'If he's not already finished doing what he's going to do.' [Buffy:] 'If he has […] then we can still deal.'"   2002 Navarro *Tempted Champions* 142 "[D'Hoffryn:] 'You will die like a bug.' […] [Anya:] 'I can deal.'" [fr. *deal* (with); sv *deal*[1] vi in sense 3]

demony *adj*   Characterized by evil supernatural beings
2001 Dec 3 *Angel* (WB) "I suppose we don't know what this other dimension is like, except fortressy and demony." [A]   2002 Jul 25 Bronze: Beta "You are talking about fish, right? Not the phallic demony snakelike thing?"   2002 Sep 13 *Entertainment Weekly* 65/2 "[T]he school is still conveniently located on the Hellmouth, ensuring 'there's going to be some demony action,' says [Marti] Noxon."   2002 Odom *Crossings* 29 "'I meant it could be really bad that the smell of all this fresh blood might attract—you know, demony things.'" [W]   [*demon* n in sense 1 + -*y*[1] suff in sense 1]

—non-vengeance demon-y *adj* Unlike a vengeance demon
2002 Jul 24 Bronze: Beta "Your wish is my command, in a non-vengeance demon-y way." [non- *pref* + *vengeance* demon 'demon devoted to avenging the wrongs suffered by women at the hands of men, when they wish for revenge' + DEMONY]

depressedy *adj* Representing low spirits or dejection
1999 Dec 14 Whedon *Hush* [quoted in 2000 Holder *WG2* 222] "Her room is wicca-y and also painted black and depressed-y." [*depressed adj* in sense 1 + -y[1] *suff* in sense 1]

destiny-free *adj* Uninfluenced by destiny
1998 May 12 Whedon *Becoming, Part 1* "I don't have a destiny. I'm destiny-free." [B] 1999 Sep Golden and Brereton *The Origin* [6] "Destiny Free" [chapter title] [*destiny n* in sense 4 + -free, fr. free *adj* in sense 4.a & 4.b]

Destructo Girl *n* 1: Girl dedicated to destruction of something or someone
1997 Mar 25 Greenwalt *Teacher's Pet* "Destructo-Girl, that's me." [B]
    2: As an element in names
1998 Dec 2 The Bronze "Destructo Girl's Super Natural" [signature] 1999 Jun 26 The Bronze "Destructo Girl" [*destruct vt* + -o + *girl n* in sense 2]
See EDGE GIRL and NET GIRL

developmenty *adj* Pertaining to character development
2001 Jun 2 The Bronze "I agree with the villain—Glory, lack of developmenty stuff. I think she had potential for huge villainy, but all we really saw was some brain sucking and lots of whingeing." [*development n* in sense 1 + -y[1] *suff* in sense 3]

Dewage *n* Quantity of the soft drink, Mountain Dew
1999 Jun 26 The Bronze "[under the heading, 'What L.O.S.E.R.s Use to Stay Awake'] Maximum Dewage and sheer determination." 1999 Oct 13 The Bronze "I remember when there wasn't LOSERs…just us babbling on and on about Buffy and trying to get Ty to leave but then he wouldn't and Alex's Mtn. Dewage and wow…." [fr. Mountain *Dew*, a registered trademark of the Pepsi-Cola Company + -*age suff* in sense 1.b]

diddy n Sex
1998 Oct 20 Noxon *All Men Are Beasts* "Do you ever catch kids doing the diddy out here?" [F] [perh. fr. *diddle²* v in sense 2.a (also *HDAS* in sense 1 & *NTC* in sense 2)]

diggy adj Characterizing digging or other construction work
2000 Jan 25 Espenson *A New Man* "[Buffy:] 'Oh, right—very manly—not at all Village People.' [Anya:] 'So much sexier than his last job. I'm imagining having sex with him right now. Ooh, look at him.' [Willow:] 'Very…diggy.'" [*dig* vt in sense 1 + *-y¹* suff in sense 1]

discipliny adj Characterized by discipline
2001 May 8 Kirshner *Tough Love* "C'mon, you can bring Dawn. It'll be fun. Good, educational-type fun, in a discipliny sort of way." [W] [*discipline* n in sense 3.c + *y¹* suff in sense 1]

Disco Dave n Boy or man who looks as though he is from the 1970s
1998 Oct 13 Greenwalt *Faith, Hope, and Trick* "Check out Slut-o-rama and her Disco Dave." [C] 2000 Holder *Watcher's Guide* 2 145 "She is distracted by one of the dancers, whose extroverted personality looks doomed to meet with an untimely end by a vamp-face (AKA 'Slut-o-rama and Disco Dave' in Cordy-speak)." [*disco* n in sense 2.b + *Dave* in sense 'any guy', by analogy with *Tom, Dick, and Harry*]

do a William Burroughs on v phr Shoot to death
2000 May 2 Noxon *New Moon Rising* "Stay back, or I'll do a William Burroughs on your leader here." [B] [*do* vt in sense 1.a + *a²* indef art in sense 1 + *William S. Burroughs* 'name of an American author (1914–1997)']

dollsome adj Extremely attractive
1999 Sep 22 King *Some Assembly Required* "Ms. Calendar is reasonably dollsome, especially for someone in your age bracket." [X] [fr. *doll* n in sense 3.a (also *HDAS* in sense 3.b, *DAS3* in senses 1 & 4, & *NTC* in sense 1) + *some¹* suff] See CUDDLESOME and FREAKSOME

007 adj Debonair, in a stereotypically British manner
1999 May 11 Noxon *The Prom* "I bet you'd look way 007 in a tux." [C]

1999 May 13 The Bronze "You would look way 007 in a tux." [signature] 1999 Oct 1 Howard *Entertainment Weekly* 49/4 "**way 007** Sartorially James Bond (e.g., Wesley in a tux)." [fr. 007 'operational pseudonym of Ian Fleming's fictional British spy, James Bond', spoken as "double O seven"]

double-shiftiness n (Sudden) Assignment of a double shift 2002 Jan 29 Espenson *Doublemeat Palace* "[Manny:] 'Buffy! […] You're working a double shift.' [Buffy:] 'What happened? Why the double-shiftiness?'" [*double shift* n (fr. *double* adj in sense 1 + *shift* n in sense 2.b) + -i- + -*ness* suff; in context, perhaps punning on *shifti-* and *shifty* adj in sense 1 or 2]

downage n Lower body parts 2000 Sep 1 The Bronze "And I got a pic[ture] of your downage. Impressive." [*down* adv in sense 1.a + -*age* suff in sense 1.a]

Dracy adj Associated with Dracula 2000 Sep 26 Noxon *Buffy vs Dracula* "At least you weren't making time with the Dracy babes, like Giles here." [R] [*Dracula* 'name of vampire in Bram Stoker's eponymous novel' + -y[1] suff in sense 1]

drastic distraction reduction n Increased attention 1998 Nov 3 Greenwalt *Homecoming* "[Scott:] 'Before we were going out, you seemed so full of life, like a force of nature. Now you just seem distracted all the time.' [Buffy:] 'I'm getting better, honest. In fact, from here on, you're going to see a drastic distraction reduction. Drastic distraction reduction…try saying that ten times fast.'" [*drastic* adj in senses 1 & 2 + *distraction* n in sense 1 + *reduction* n in sense 3 (fr. sense 5.a)]

drinkage n Drinking 2001 Jun 2 The Bronze "There is some major drinkage going on here this evening luv." [*drink* vi in sense 2 + -*age* suff in sense 4.a]

driveyness n State of driving 1998 Nov 10 Espenson *Band Candy* "I told my mom I wanted to be treated like a grown-up and, voila, driveyness." [R] [*drive* v in sense 3 + -y[2] suff in sense 1 + -*ness* suff]

droppage 1: n Omission, loss
2000 Sep 1 The Bronze "Ooh. Tag droppage." 2000 Sep 1 The Bronze "Oh, double tag droppage, is there a prize for that?" 2001 Jun 2 The Bronze "Oh, and nice tag-droppage—you're almost on a par with me there." 2001 Jun 2 The Bronze "gratuitous siggy [i.e., signature] droppage" [fr. *drop* vt in sense 12 + *-age* suff in sense 4.b] See TAGGAGE
    2: n Falling, because released from a grip
2001 Nov 9 Tracey Thompson [conversation] "A little phone droppage never hurt me." [*drop* vt in sense 1 + *-age* suff in sense 4.a]

dump-o-gram n Statement that a romantic relationship is over
1998 Nov 17 Petrie *Revelations* "[Willow:] 'A boyfriend? Why wouldn't she tell us?' [Cordelia:] 'Excuse me? When your last steady killed half the class and then your rebound guy sends you a dump-o-gram? It makes a girl shy.'" 1999 Oct 1 Howard *Entertainment Weekly* 48/3 "**dump-o-gram** Kiss-off." [*dump* v in sense 3.b (also *HDAS* dump v in sense 2.a & *DAS*3 in sense 9) + -o- + *-gram* suff in sense 2] See SLAYER-O-METER, SLUT-O-RAMA, and SUPPORT-O-GAL

dust 1: vt Kill a vampire
1997 Golden and Holder *Halloween Rain* 114 "'Yeah, well, he's the same vampire she dusted for unauthorized snacking not five minutes later.'" [X] 1997 Cusick *The Harvest* 116 "'So [...] I dust anyone sporting this look, and no Harvest.'" [B] 1998 Winter *Buffy the Vampire Slayer* 50 "**dust:** [...] v. [B] to eliminate vampires using a stake." 1998 Golden and Holder *Blooded* 108 "Already, one of the dead jocks had been dusted." 1999 Spring *Buffy the Vampire Slayer* 41 "One wooden stake dusts vamps as well as the next." 1999 Oct 1 *Entertainment Weekly* 34/3 "**Historic moments**...Spike becomes boss bloodsucker after dusting the Annoying (Anointed) One." 1999 Oct 1 Howard *Entertainment Weekly* 48/3 "**dust** Stake a vampire; form that demon takes at death." 1999 Golden *Sins of the Father* 51 "'Giles,' Buffy screamed, even as the other vamp was dusted." 1999 Golden and Holder *Immortal* 25 "She whipped her arm down to dust the dude." 2000 Holder *The Evil That Men Do* 133 "[B]ut a vampire was just a vampire, after all, and she hadn't been exaggerating too much about how many she'd dusted." 2000 Dokey *Here Be Monsters* 51 "Not that it had taken that long to come up with their plan of attack,

which was pretty straightforward: 1. Locate twin vamps. 2. Dust 'em. 3. Call it a night and head for home." 2000 Gilman and Sherman *Deep Water* 117 "'Being undead limits the kind of damage that can be inflicted on a vampire. Short of dusting one—'" [G] 2000 Passarella *Ghoul Trouble* 42 "'I saw them dust a vampire,' Rave said." 2000 Holder *Watcher's Guide* 2 157 "Buffy invites Angel in and prepares to dust Spike." 2001 Kaveney *Reading the Vampire Slayer* 13 "Indeed, one shocking piece of trickery is the introduction of Jesse along with the others as if he were important and not the first to be turned and then dusted (staked through the heart and turned to dust)." 2001 Kaveney *Reading the Vampire Slayer* 238 "Darla attacks Buffy with guns and Angel dusts her." 2002 Jul 28 Bronze: Beta "She'd passed up at least one opportunity to dust Angelus." 2002 Jul 30 Bronze: Beta "The only reason he wasn't dusted in S[eason] 4 was because he couldn't attack people directly." 2002 Jul 31 Bronze: Beta "Buffy dusts two vamps in opening sequence." 2002 Navarro *Tempted Champions* 39 "'She dusted them, man. Like that.'" 2002 Dechert *Fighting the Forces* 321 "As Xander dusts a troublesome vamp at The Bronze, an enraptured Buffy watches."

    2: *vi* Disintegrate when STAKED

2001 Odom *Revenant* 103 "Reaching nearly max gross-out potential, because it was one thing for vampires to dust after they were dead and another for a still-warm and bleeding body to be so up close and personal, Xander shoved the dead man from him."

    3: *vt* Kill, as though killing a vampire

1997 Golden and Holder *Halloween Rain* 54 "'I'm glad you told me the assistant manager shut the basement door. Otherwise I might assume there was some major plot to dust me. I think we'll be okay now,' Buffy replied hopefully."

    4: *vt* Break

1999 *Official Yearbook* 10/2 "In the end, Buffy was forced to send her love to the netherworld and dust her own heart in the process." [fr. dust *n* in sense 1 and *HDAS* dust *v* in sense 1.d (also *DAS3* in sense 3 and *NTC* in sense 3); on the show, when vampires are STAKED, they turn to dust]

    —**dusted** *adj* Slayed

1999 Oct 13 The Bronze "[I]n the words of the dusted vamp, 'this is starting to SUCK.'" 1999 Massie *Power of Persuasion* 46 "'You tried Friday night and look what it got you. A coupla dusted companions.'" [Barb] 2000 May 31 Udovitch *Rolling Stone* 66/4 "In fact, though rarely does an episode pass when at least one vampire doesn't get dusted [...] Buffy is the most realistic show on the air." [DUST + -*ed*² *suff*]

—**dusting**   1: n   Episode of vampire killing

1999 Oct 1 *Entertainment Weekly* 47/2 "While the visual effects (such as the dusting of vampires) are left to computer-graphics house Digital Magic, Minkus can take credit for the show's demonic paraphernalia." 1999 Golden and Holder *Immortal* 17 "'It's just one dusting. It'll be over like that.'" [B]   2000 Holder *The Evil That Men Do* 325 "The sound of a dusting vibrated around her."   2002 Jul 31 Bronze: Beta "More time spent on sex than opening dustings, but throw in Xander with the axe and stake, and it's about equal time."

   2: n   Activity of killing, as though killing a vampire

2001 Playden *Reading the Vampire Slayer* 121 "My invitation, therefore, is to come on patrol with a select group of Slayers, to join Buffy, the Scoobies, and feminist thinkers, and to help in doing the dusting." [DUST + -*ing*¹ *suff*]

—**dustized**   *adj*   Turned into dust

2000 Navarro *Paleo* 248 "'So I think it's safe to assume that the T. Rex bodies we left in the alley by the Bronze and in the museum are also dustized?'" [B]   [dust n in sense 2 + -*ize suff* in sense 4 + -*ed*² *suff*]

—**Dustville**   n   Place where DUSTED vampires go

2002 May 14 Noxon *Villains* "He's just as bad as any vampire you sent to Dustville." [X]   [fr. DUST in sense 1 + -*ville suff*]

—**dusty**   *adj*   Dead by means of STAKING

2002 Jul 28 Bronze: Beta "Without a spoken desire to do good, followed by actions of the same, he's dusty boy." [DUST + -*y*¹ *suff* in sense 1]

eaty   *adj*   Appropriate to be eaten

1999 Watson *The Remaining Sunlight* [60] "For groceries, Cordy. Y'know, eaty stuff?" [*eat vt* in sense 1.a + -*y*¹ *suff* in sense 1]

Edge Girl   n   Girl whose values or behavior place her on the margin of mainstream culture

1998 Nov 3 Greenwalt *Homecoming* "[Faith:] 'I mean, you really got some quality rage going. Really gives you an edge.' [Buffy:] 'Edge Girl, just what I always wanted to be.'" [fr. *on the edge* sv *edge* n; cf. *HDAS Edge City*; perh. by analogy fr. *DAS3* It girl; see *HDAS* It in sense 6.b]

eeuch *vt* Disparage, with a guttural sound
2001 Nov 13 Kirshner *Tabula Rasa* "Did you just eeuch my name?" [B] [fr. *eeuch interj*]

elsewhere *n* Other place
1997 Mar 10 Whedon *Welcome to the Hellmouth* "Don't you have an elsewhere to be?" [C] [fr. *elsewhere adv*]

Ewanage *n* Exposure to (conversation, writing about) Ewan McGregor
1999 May 13 The Bronze "We're never around when the other needs major Ewan-age." [fr. the name of film actor *Ewan McGregor* + *-age suff* in sense 1.a]

Exorcist twist *n* 360 turn of the head
1997 Mar 25 Greenwalt *Teacher's Pet* "No, I'm not saying she craned her neck; we're talking full-on Exorcist twist." [B]   1999 Oct 1 Howard *Entertainment Weekly* 48/4 "**full-on exorcist twist** Ability to turn one's head 360 degrees, à la praying mantises or Linda Blair." [fr. The Exorcist 'title of a film dir. William Friedkin (1973)' + *twist* n in sense 2]

fangy *adj* Possessed of fangs, vampiric
1997 Golden and Holder *Halloween Rain* 39 "She wondered if all the really cool fangy people there knew the Slayer was in their midst." 1999 Nov 16 Petrie *The Initiative* "I hate being obvious, all fangy and 'eeer'— it takes the mystery out." [S]   2000 Oct 17 Kirshner *Out of My Mind* "'Now, I agree that Marat wasn't a real martyr, but the death in the tub, the neck wound, all that blood—it's just a little more fangy than knifey.'" [B] [*fang* n in sense 3 + *-y*[1] suff in sense 1]

Felicity *adj* Short
2000 Apr 25 Forbes *Where the Wild Things Are* "There's ghosts and shaking and people going all Felicity with their hair." [X] [fr. *Felicity* 'name of character on WB dramatic series of the same name, who notably returned in the second season with much shorter hair than in the first']

fester-free *adj* Unagitated
1999 Feb 16 Noxon *Consequences* "Good, because I've been letting things fester and I don't like it. I want to be fester-free." [W]   1999 Oct 1 Howard *Entertainment Weekly* 48/3 "**fester-free** State of being relieved of silent seething." [fr. *fester* v in sense 4.b + -*free*, fr. *free* adj in sense 4.a & 4.b]

fevery *adj* Afflicted with fever
2002 Jul 30 Bronze: Beta "You just feeling yucky or fevery as well?" [*fever* n in sense 1.a + -*y*[1] suff in sense 1]

fighty *adj* Violent
2002 Jul 23 Bronze: Beta "Having dispatched Warren, Willow searches for Jonothan and Andrew. Buffy and the others try to stop her. Big fighty fight in the Magic Box." [*fight* vi in sense 1.a + -*y*[1] suff in sense 1]

five-by-five 1: *adj* Satisfied, good
1998 Oct 13 Greenwalt *Faith, Hope, and Trick* "Hey, as long as you don't go scratchin' at me or humpin' my leg, we're five-by-five, ya' know?" [F]   1998 Oct 13 Greenwalt *Faith, Hope, and Trick* "I'm five-by-five here, B, living entirely large, actually wondering about your problem." [F]   1998 Nov 17 Petrie *Revelations* "[Buffy:] 'How are you?' [Faith:] 'Five-by-five.' [Buffy:] 'I'll interpret that as good.'"   1998 Dec 2 The Bronze "Hopes to one day be 5 x 5 with Faith" [signature]   1998 Winter *Buffy the Vampire Slayer* 50 "**five by five:** [...] adj. [Faith] still friends or allies after a misunderstanding or a bout of personal friction; cool."   1999 Oct 1 Howard *Entertainment Weekly* 48/3 "**five by five** Feeling no pain; aviation radio term favored by Faith."   2000 Feb 29 Whedon *Who Are You* "[Joyce:] 'Are you sure you're okay?' [Buffy/Faith:] 'Five by five.'"   2000 May 2 *Angel* (WB) "Five by five, right Faith?" [A]   2000 Holder *Watcher's Guide* 2 180 "Faith has developed the habit of calling Buffy 'B,' begun in 'Faith, Hope & Trick,' and her habit of saying 'five by five' was established then, too."
    2: *n* [fr. sense 1] As a name
2001 Shuttleworth *Reading the Vampire Slayer* 224 "The extent to which she is living out a role she has assigned to herself is finally revealed by her breakdown during the climactic fight with Angel, in 'Five by Five'

(A [i.e., *Angel*] 1.18)." [*HDAS* in sense 2.b, w/one quot fr. 1983; five n in sense 1 + *by prep* in sense 11.b + *five n* in sense 1; i.e. a *square*, so synonymous *square 'O. K.', fr. *DAS3 square* v in sense 6]

—**5 by 5ness** n Satisfaction
2000 Sep 1 The Bronze "Greetings and wishes of 5 by 5ness to everyone." [FIVE BY FIVE + *-ness* suff]

flake *vi* Behave oddly, badly or irresponsibly
1997 Jun 2 Whedon *Prophecy Girl* "You don't understand. I'm not mad. He totally flaked on me." 1997 Oct 27 Ellsworth *Halloween* "It's like, he thinks that being in a band gives him an obligation to flake." [C] 2000 Sep 1 The Bronze "Okay, off to tutor…or shop, depending on if my tutee's mom flakes again." [sv *flake (out) phr* v in senses 2 & 3 sv *flake*[1] n; *HDAS* in sense 3]

flingage n Sudden love affair; party or night out; binge [?]
2000 Sep 1 The Bronze "Have missed Timtam flingage." [*fling* n in senses 2 and 4 + *-age* suff in sense 1.a]

foot putting downer n Disciplinarian
2001 May 8 Kirshner *Tough Love* "You can be the foot putting downer." [B] [*foot* n in sense 1 + *putting* sv *put* vt in sense 1 + *down adv* in sense 1.a + *-er*[1] suff in sense 1.a; reanalyzed fr. *put (one's) foot down* sv *put*—idioms]

fortressy *adj* Resembling a military stronghold
2001 Dec 3 *Angel* (WB) "I suppose we don't know what this other dimension is like, except fortressy and demony." [A] [*fortress* n + *-y*[1] suff in sense 1]

foulness n Unpleasant odor
1998 May 5 Fury and Hampton *Go Fish* "[Gage:] 'Aw, dude, what is that foulness?' [Buffy:] 'There's just something about the smell of chlorine on a guy.'" [*foul adj* in sense 2 + *-ness* suff]

fray-adjacent *adj* Near combat
1999 Jan 26 Vebber *The Zeppo* "Maybe you shouldn't be leaping into the fray like that. Maybe you should be…fray-adjacent." [B] 1999 Oct 1

Howard *Entertainment Weekly* 48/3 "**fray adjacent** In the vicinity of the thick of things." [*fray*¹ n in sense 1 + *adjacent adv* in sense 1]

freak 1.a: vi Lose control, flip out
1995 *Clueless* "[Cher:] 'How do you like California?' [Ty:] 'Man, I'm freakin.'" 1998 Edwards *Buffy X-Posed* 129/2 "Angel freaks and furiously leaves." 1998 Nov 10 The Bronze "When Joyce said that she didn't want Buffy driving just so that she could limit her movements I don't know why Buffy didn't just freak" 1999 Mar 21 http://www2.uicedu/~ahufan1/btvs/wns quoting original material cut from 1998 Dec 8 Noxon *The Wish* "Oh, you know, my mom freaks if I'm late." [B] 1999 Nov 6 Noxon *Wild at Heart* "I don't want to be the kind of girl who freaks every time her boyfriend notices somebody else." [W] 1999 Golden and Holder *Immortal* 139 "'Hey Buffy,' Xander said gently. 'I know you're scared, but don't freak.'" 1999 Golden and Holder *Ghost Roads* 281 "Xander was, in a word, freaking." 2000 May 2 Noxon *New Moon Rising* "Are you freaked?" [W] 2000 Gilman and Sherman *Deep Water* 148 "You're freaking, Will." [X] 2000 Navarro *Paleo* 150 "Devon winced. 'Drop out? Man, my parents would entirely freak.'" 2001 Jun 2 The Bronze "Freak not." 2001 Odom *Revenant* 139 "'Do you know how many girls you can take out on a date, have this kind of thing happen to you, and have them not totally freak on you?'" [X]
    1.b: vt Make (one) lose control
1999 Golden and Holder *Ghost Roads* 30 "When Angel got all vampy, it freaked him something fierce."
    1.c: vi Go crazy (expletive)
2001 Jun 2 The Bronze "Ive got one of the Buffy choccie bars, but i want to get another one before i eat it! *freak*...i second that any on fully clothed pics leave my hands!" [*freak* v in sense 3 (also *HDAS* in sense 3.a & *NTC* in sense 1)]
    —**defreak** Calm down
2001 May 8 Kirshner *Tough Love* "[Buffy:] 'I'm more than stressed out—I'm freaked out.' [Willow:] 'Well, maybe you need a break, to defreak.'" [*de-* pref in sense 1 + FREAK]
    —**freaking-meter** n Index of agitation
2001 Oct 23 Fury and Espenson *Life Serial* "On the freaking-meter I'd

say she was at a 6." [Warren]   [FREAK in sense 1.a + -ing² suff in sense 1.a + meter³ n in sense 1]

freaked *adj* Upset, frightened
1997 Jun 2 Whedon *Prophecy Girl* "Calm may work for Locutus of Borg here, but I'm freaked and I intend to stay that way." 1998 Golden and Holder *Child of the Hunt* 111 "Cordelia, looking freaked, ran past Buffy and stopped at Angel." 1999 Mar 16 Petrie *Enemies* "I was freaked; I needed somebody." [F] 1999 Golden and Holder *Sons of Entropy* 57 "Willow was a bit freaked by hearing the ghost woman's voice." 2000 May 9 Petrie *The Yoko Factor* "I knew Buffy was freaked." [W] 2000 Gallagher *Prime Evil* 68 "'You have been acting on the near side of freaked.'" [X] 2001 Odom *Revenant* 125 "'No way am I getting into my interest in witchcraft at this point. Jia Li's already freaked.'" [W] 2002 Apr 30 Greenberg *Entropy* "She's O.K. A little freaked." [W] 2002 Navarro *Tempted Champions* 14 "'Why don't you take Anya home?' [Buffy] suggested. 'She looks a little freaked.'" [FREAK + -ed² suff (also HDAS in sense 3, DAS3 freak in sense 6, & NTC freaked [out])]
   —**power-freaked** *adj* Extremely upset
1997 Nov 17 Noxon and Gordon *What's My Line, Part 1* "And Angel was power-freaked by that ring." [B] 1999 Oct 1 Howard *Entertainment Weekly* 49/2 "**power freaked** Exponentially scared; see also (The) Wig." [*power* n in sense 8 + FREAKED]

freaksome *adj* Strange
1998 Jan 27 Des Hotel and Batali *Phases* "It's not every day you find out you're a werewolf: that's fairly freaksome." [O] 1999 Oct 1 Howard *Entertainment Weekly* 48/3 "**freaksome** Worrisome." [fr. freak¹ adj + -some¹ suff] See CUDDLESOME and DOLLSOME

freaky-deaky *adj* Weird
1998 Oct 20 Noxon *All Men Are Beasts* "[Buffy:] 'Oh boy, Faith and her nutty books.' [Giles:] 'Exploring Demon Dimensions and History of Acathla.' [Buffy:] 'Yeah, and she still listens to heavy metal. Freaky-deaky.'" 1998 Winter *Buffy the Vampire Slayer* 50 "**freaky deaky:** [...] adj. [B] odd or ironic; funky." 1999 Golden *Sins of the Father* 50 "Giles might have been acting freaky-deaky lately, but he was her Watcher, and her friend be-

sides." 1999 Golden and Holder *Sons of Entropy* 72 "Ethan Rayne, on the other hand, was out trying to figure out where Buffy's mom was, and that was as freaky-deaky as anything else that had happened in the last couple of weeks." [*freaky adj* in sense 1 + *deaky*, a nonsense reduplication]

frowny *adj* Disapproving
2000 Navarro *Paleo* 146 "'What,' [Buffy] asked, as [Giles] folded his arms. 'Why do you have that frowny face. Frowny faces aren't good. Especially on you.'" [*frown n* + -*y*¹ *suff* in sense 1]

Full Monty *n* Nakedness
1998 Oct 20 Noxon *Beauty and the Beasts* "I can handle the Oz Full Monty."
[X] [fr. The Full Monty 'title of a film (1997), dir. Peter Cattaneo']

fun *n* (in phrase *the fun*) Fun, amusement or entertainment
1999 Apr 29 The Bronze "Have the big fun folks." 2001 Nov 6 Whedon *Once More, with Feeling* "You're, like, a good demon? Bringing the fun in?" [D] [*fun n* in sense 2] See UNFUN

funny *n* Humor
1998 May 12 Whedon *Becoming, Part 1* "Relax, Will, I was making with the funny." [B] 1998 Dec 15 Whedon *Amends* "[Angel:] 'I'm sorry to bother you.' [Giles:] 'Sorry. Coming from you, that phrase strikes me as rather funny. Sorry to bother me.' [Angel:] 'I need your help.' [Giles:] 'And the funny keeps on coming.'" 1999 Jan 12 St. John and Espenson *Gingerbread* "No one else is seeing the funny here?" [X] 1999 May 13 The Bronze "Yes, you guys were certainly making with the funny this morning." 2002 Jul 30 Bronze: Beta "Steve DeKnight was vile? Why, because he attempted to make with the funny." 2002 Aug 1 *The Daily Show with Jon Stewart* "You show up with your game-face on, you still deliver the funny." [fr. *funny adj* in sense 1.b]

geek *adj* Unstylish, awkward
1998 Nov 10 Espenson *Band Candy* "What was I thinking when I bought that geek machine?" [Joyce] 1999 Oct 1 Howard *Entertainment Weekly* 48/4 "**geek machine** Joyce Summers' totally uncool Jeep." [fr. *geek n* in sense 1.a (also *HDAS* in sense 1, *DAS3*, & *NTC* in sense 1)]

geek-dance free *adj* Without awkward dance moves
1999 Gilman and Sherman *Visitors* 143 "'No geek dancing whatsoever tonight. I shall be totally geek-dance free. I will limit myself to the moves you have personally preapproved.'" [X] [fr. *geek* n in sense 1.a (also *HDAS* in sense 1 & NTC in sense 1) + *dance* n in sense 1 + *-free* suff, fr. *free adj* in senses 4.a & 4.b]

geeker 1: *adj* Computer inspired
1997 Dec 8 Greenwalt and Whedon *Ted* "That's the sound she makes when she's speechless with geeker joy." [X] 1999 Golden and Holder *Immortal* 40 "'Willow could make a computer model. That would elicit squeals of geeker joy.'" [B] 1999 Oct 1 Howard *Entertainment Weekly* 48/4 "**geeker joy** Effusive feeling nerdy Willow gets when she's happy."
    2: n Narrowly expert, focused person
1999 Oct 13 The Bronze "Can we tell that there is at least one lawgeeker on the PBP Committee?"
    3: n attrib Pertaining to geeks
1999 Jun 26 The Bronze "I need help from any computer geeker type person who knows." [*geek* n in sense 1.b (also *HDAS* in sense 1.b, *DAS3* in sense 4, & NTC in sense 2 + *-er* suff[1] in sense 2.b)]

geekiness n Condition of being awkward or socially inept
2002 Jul 25 Bronze: Beta "[E]mbrace your geekiness...it works for many of the people here." [*geeky adj* sv *geek* n + *-ness* suff]

Gene and Roger n Criticism
1997 Sep 22 King *Some Assembly Required* "If you don't mind a little Gene and Roger..." [X] 1999 Oct 1 Howard *Entertainment Weekly* 48/4 "**gene and roger** Unsolicited criticism such as that given by movie critics Siskel and Ebert." [*Gene Siskel and Roger Ebert* 'names of newspaper and television film critics who worked as a team on television']

genius *adj* Clever, ingenious
1997 Oct 27 Ellsworth *Halloween* "Don't want to blow my own horn, but—it's genius." [Ethan] 1998 Apr 28 Noxon *I Only Have Eyes for You* "I mean, whose genius idea was that?" [C] 1999 Mar 12 *Entertainment Weekly* 56/2 "Not even the *Love Boat* had casting this genius." 1999 Oct 18 *New Yorker* 256 "That keepsies call was genius, but did you have to

throw in the stock options?" 2001 *National Lampoon's Van Wilder* "Bikini fly judges for a fundraiser? That's pretty genius." [fr. *genius* n in sense 1.a, or perhaps *ingenious adj* in sense 1]

get gone *v phr* Go away, leave
1997 Oct 27 Ellsworth *Halloween* "Get gone." [B] 1998 Jan 19 Noxon *Surprise* "Maybe I should get gone, too." [B] 1998 Nov 17 Petrie *Revelations* "Ronnie...deadbeat, Steve...klepto, Kenny...drummer—eventually I had to face up to my destiny as a loser magnet. Now it's strictly get some and get gone. You can't trust guys." [F] 1999 Jun 26 The Bronze "Bronzers Who Can't Get Gone/The BWCGG is a club for all bronzers who feel that they just can't leave the posting board." 2000 Fiona Apple *Get Gone* "How many times do I have to say / To get away—get gone." [*get* vi in sense 5 + *gone* v in sense 1]

girl-powery *adj* Like one involved in the girl-power movement
1998 Oct Brereton *The Dust Waltz* [33] "I don't know, I think she's kind of 'girl-powery.'" [*girl-power* 'girls' ability to confront the world with strength of purpose and character, and to change the worlds in which they live', fr. *girl* n in sense 2 + *power* n in sense 3 + *-y¹ suff* in sense 1]

girly girl *n* A girl without supposed masculine abilities
1998 Jan 27 Des Hotel and Batali *Phases* "Don't forget, you're supposed to be a meek little girly girl, like the rest of us." [W] 1998 Nov Brody *In Style* 290 "It's the ultimate ode to femininity, much appreciated by a self-proclaimed 'girly girl' who was born in Las Vegas and named after a perfume." 2001 Dec 6 Udovitch *Rolling Stone* 88/3 "'You seem like you're kind of a girl's girl. Would you say that's true?' [Britney Spears:] 'For sure I'm a girly-girl. I try to tell J [i.e., Justin Timberlake] I like basketball and stuff like that, and he says, "No, you're a girly-girl. Trust me."' [...] OK. But I didn't mean girly-girl. I meant you're a girl who likes girls.'" [*girlie adj* + *girl* n in sense 2]

gladness *adj* Good
1998 Jan 27 Des Hotel and Batali *Phases* "[Oz:] 'Is everybody okay? Did anyone get bitten or scratched?' [Willow:] 'No, we're fine.' [Oz:] 'Gladness.'" [*glad adj* in sense 1 + *-ness suff*]

glib-free adj Serious

1999 Jan 19 Fury *Helpless* "Since it is part of your training, I would appreciate your glib-free attention." [G]   1999 Jan 12 Espenson *Gingerbread* "Buffy, I'm aware of your distaste for studying vibratory stones, but as it's part of your training, I'd appreciate your glib-free attention." [G]   [*glib* adj in sense 2 + *-free* suff, fr. *free* adj in senses 4.a & 4.b]

glowery adj With a stern or angry glance

1999 Nov 23 Espenson *Pangs* "So, this is Angel. He's large and glowery, isn't he?" [Anya]   [*glower* vi + *-y*[1] suff in sense 1]

going outness n Partying away from home

2000 Sep 1 The Bronze "[S]low board…must be Friday night going out-ness (if that's a word)."   [*go out* v phr sv *go* v (in sense 3) + *-ness* suff]

good n Beneficial

2000 Holder *Watcher's Guide 2* 38 "Riley listens in agony as his Commando comrades on patrol engage the enemy—demons—over and over again, with results so very often not of the good."   [fr. *good* adj in sense 1]

griefy adj Stimulated by bereavement

2002 May 21 Petrie *Two to Go* "Back there, she was out of her head, running on griefy magics." [X]   [*grief* n in sense 1 + *-y*[1] suff in sense 1]

grim n Seriousness

1999 Jan 12 St. John and Espenson *Gingerbread* "What's with the grim?" [X]   1999 Oct 1 Howard *Entertainment Weekly* 48/4 "**(the) grim** Sullen faces; also Tragedy Masks."   [fr. *grim* adj in sense 2]

groiny adj Sexual

1999 Nov 23 *Angel* (WB Network) "They suffer, they fight, that's business as usual. They get groiny with one another, the world as we know it falls apart." [C]   1999 Dec 3 Tucker *Entertainment Weekly* 80/1 "Angel briefly regained his soul and, in the words of Cordelia, 'got groiny' with Buffy."   [*groin* n in sense 1 + *-y*[1] suff in sense 1]

Guiltapalooza n Excessive guilt

1998 Dec 8 Noxon *The Wish* "Look, you wanna do Guiltapalooza, fine,

but I'm done with that." [X]   1999 Oct 1 *Entertainment Weekly* 38/4
"Will's guiltapalooza over betraying Oz with Xander...offer[s an] el-
egant examination of those tandem minefields, intimacy and trust." 1999
Oct 1 Howard *Entertainment Weekly* 48/4 **"guiltapalooza** Excessive-
remorse festival." [guilt n in sense 3.b + lollapalooza n (also HDAS in
sense 1 & NTC in sense 1), most immediately fr. the rock concert
Lollapalooza, organized annually 1990–1998]

guinea pig   vi   Serve as a subject in an experiment
2002 May 8 DeKnight *Spiral* "Someone had to guinea pig and wear the
suit." [Warren]   [fr. *guinea pig* n in sense 2]

Hacker Girl   n   A girl who uses computers illegally to obtain private or
restricted information
1999 Gilman and Sherman *Visitors* 93 "'Okay, so there's a job for Hacker
Girl, too.'" [W]   [*hacker*[1] n in sense 1 + *girl* n in sense 2]   See NET GIRL

hackery   adj   Associated with gaining illegal access to computer networks and systems
2002 Overbey and Preston-Matto *Fighting the Forces* 79 "[Willow] knows,
and she finds—but no one quite knows how. Some secret, hacker-y thing,
no doubt."   [*hacker* n in sense 2 + *-y*[1] suff in sense 1]

hang   v   Spend time
1995 *Clueless* "Yeah, come here. Hang with us." 1997 Mar 17 Reston *The
Witch* "There's a bitter streak, but Amy's nice. We used to hang in junior
high." [W]   1999 Jan 12 Espenson *Gingerbread* "If you're gonna hang
with them, expect badness." [C]   1999 Oct 12 Noxon *Living Conditions*
"I just figured I'd hang here, you know, until my roommate goes to
class." 1999 Golden and Holder *Out of the Madhouse* 5 "'We'll still hang
with the G-man,' Xander said quickly." 2000 Gallagher *Doomsday Deck*
56 "He turned her down to hang with Cordelia." 2000 Passarella *Ghoul
Trouble* 108 "'Reasonable assumption,' Oz said. 'Not many other places
to hang.'"   2001 Oct 2 Noxon *Bargaining* 1 "We don't really have to
hang, if you're bored." [D]   2001 Jul Golden *Food Chain* [5] "And you're
wondering why I hang with him and his crew, huh?" 2001 Nov 27
Noxon *Wrecked* "Then go home. God, I thought we were hanging." [W]

2002 May 21 Fury *The Grave* "I know you're about to do something apocalyptically evil and stupid, and, hey, I still want to hang." [X] 2002 Jul 28 Bronze: Beta "My bad for not being able to hang." 2002 Odom *Crossings* 17 "Xander charged across the aisle, thinking the whole time that he ought to be looking out for his own neck the way most of the rest of the people in the theater were doing. But he couldn't. He'd been hanging with the Slayer too long for that." [*hang* v in sense 15.b (also *HDAS* in sense 3.b; see also *DAS3 hang out* v phr)]

happy 1 : n Moment of pleasure
1997 Nov 3 Whedon *Lie To Me* "If Angel's doing something wrong, I want to know—'cause it gives me a happy." [X] 1998 Nov 17 Petrie *Revelations* "For what? For Angel to go psycho again the next time you give him a happy?" [X] 1998 Dec 2 The Bronze "Hockey season gives me a really big happy, too." 1999 May 13 The Bronze "Just be optimistic. It'll give you a happy. Trust me." 1999 Jun 26 The Bronze "Ryan Phillippe nekkid, I'm going to have a happy!" 1999 Golden and Holder *Immortal* 53 "'Does that give you some kind of whacked-out happy?'" [B] 1999 Golden and Holder *Ghost Roads* 188 "'I just had a thought. A happy.'" [X] 2000 Gilman and Sherman *Deep Water* 43 "'Angel says the local undead community doesn't have a happy on about it.'" [B] 2001 Jun 2 The Bronze "Willow was like = = 'You couldn't have figured that out in 10th grade!' LOL gave me a happy—after all these seasons without even a shred of W/X'ness." 2002 Feb 26 Petrie *As You Were* "[Willow:] 'But if I did call, she wouldn't hang up on me.' [Dawn:] 'That's progress.' [Willow:] 'Hence the happy.'"
  2 : n Good wishes
2000 Sep 1 The Bronze "Good Night and Weekend happies for little bam bam!" 2000 Sep 1 The Bronze "Thanks [...] to [...] DreamLurker, Lovely Poet [...] and Monique, for their bold, centered and occasionally underlined birthday happies." 2002 Jul 26 Bronze: Beta "Birthday happies, superrmk." [fr. *happy* adj in sense 2]

hards n Harsh or resentful feelings
1999 Golden and Holder *Out of the Madhouse* 119 "'You want to find a new lead guitar player, that's cool with me. No hards, all right?'" [O] [*hard feelings* n, fr. *hard* adj in sense 7.b + *feeling* n in sense 5.b + *-s¹* suff]

haunty *adj* Scary

1999 *Angel* (WB) "Back off, polygrip! You think you're bad? All mean and haunty?" [C]   [*haunt vt* in sense 1 + -*y*¹ *suff* in sense 1]

heart-of-darknessy *adj* Depressing

2000 May 23 Whedon *Restless* "[Xander:] 'I'm putting in a preemptive bid for *Apocalypse Now*.' [Willow:] 'Did you get anything less heart-of-darknessy?'"   [fr. *Heart of Darkness* 'title of a novel (1902) by Joseph Conrad' + *y*¹ *suff* in sense 1]

Hellmouth (or hellmouth)   1.a: *n*   Opening into Hell on which Sunnydale, California sits

1997 Mar 10 Whedon *Welcome to the Hellmouth* [episode title]   1997 Mar 17 Reston *The Witch* "That is the thrill of living on the Hellmouth." [G]   1998 Nov Ventura *Psychology Today* 59/3 "Drugs, alcohol and gangs are conspicuously absent from Buffy's high school, but it's clear that these are Hell Mouth's vomitus."   1998 Edwards *Buffy X-Posed* 65 "[Joss Whedon:] 'I came up with this idea that her new high school was built on an area called Boca del Inferno [sic], which roughly translates into Hellmouth.'"   1998 Golden and Holder *Child of the Hunt* 33 "For once it actually looks like we live in the Hellmouth outside, and you're grinning."   1998 Golden and Holder *Child of the Hunt* 208 "'The old we-live-on-the-Hellmouth excuse is handy, but sometimes it just isn't enough, you know?'" [X]   1998 Gardner *Return to Chaos* 9 "Buffy sighed, 'Oh, well. Just another night in the Hellmouth.'"   1998 Golden and Holder *Blooded* 17 "It was almost enough to make you forget you lived in the Hellmouth."   1998 Golden and Holder *Blooded* 131 "'Given the fact that we live on the Hellmouth, and that Willow has been acting more like you than herself...'" [B]   1999 May 11 Noxon *The Prom* "Once again, the Hellmouth puts the 'special' in special occasion." [O]   1999 May 13 The Bronze "Faith is a harrowing threat, especially when you include factors like being on the hellmouth and working for an invincible soon to be demon."   1999 Summer Stokes *Buffy the Vampire Slayer* 36 "Perched atop the Hellmouth, Harry Groener likes what he sees."   1999 Golden *Sins of the Father* 5 "Sunnydale had been built over what its original Spanish settlers called *Boca del Infierno*: the Hellmouth."   1999 *Official Yearbook* 14/2 "[W]hy else would they give up top of the line colleges for a little-known school in a place also known as the Hellmouth." 1999 Gardner *Return to Chaos* 26 "It came with living on top of the Hellmouth." 1999 Gilman and Sherman *Visitors* 53 "[Buffy:] 'Why does that phrase suddenly give me a bad case of Uh-Oh?' [Cordelia:] 'Because we live on the Hellmouth?'" 1999 Massie *Power of Persuasion* 124 "'We are here at the Hellmouth to stop supernatural evil from overrunning the world.'" [B] 1999 Golden and Holder *Ghost Roads* 10 "Sunnydale sits on the Hellmouth, and it both attracts and disgorges various and sundry manifestations of the dark forces of evil." [G] 2000 Jan Sullivan *Teen* 59 "It's clear Buffy's grown up a lot since she started hangin' in the Hellmouth." 2000 May 11 Udovitch *Rolling Stone* 62/4 "If the Hell mouth were opened, the world as we know it would come to an end, and demons would rule the earth." 2000 Gallagher *Doomsday Deck* 15 "Even though he tackled whatever the Hellmouth threw at him, courage couldn't offset his strictly human status in his own mind." 2000 Dokey *Here Be Monsters* 1 "In the darkness, in the town that sat atop the Hellmouth, a teenage girl was running for her life." 2000 Garton *Resurrecting Ravana* 9 "In Sunnydale, on the Hellmouth—an entryway for the undead and other supernatural creatures—that usually meant something very bad was going on." 2000 Garton *Resurrecting Ravana* 24 "Life went on...even at the Hellmouth." 2000 Passarella *Ghoul Trouble* 49 "Solitaire soon discovered that Sunnydale, sitting atop the Hellmouth, had its own sewers and an extensive system of utility tunnels." 2000 Passarella *Ghoul Trouble* 88 "'We're on the Hellmouth,' Willow said." 2000 Topping *Slayer* iv "'I think I need help,' I said, and they came like bats out of the Hellmouth." 2000 Holder *Watcher's Guide* 2 53 "While Buffy and the others battle monsters crawling out of the Hellmouth, it is up to Xander to stop the dead guys from killing them all." 2001 Feb 20 Espenson *I Was Made to Love You* "'Buffy, y'ever think maybe the reason you haven't found a great relationship on the Hellmouth is that it's a hellmouth?'" [X] 2001 Jun 2 The Bronze "There is now a severe lack of Slayer on the Hellmouth." 2001 Oct 2 Fury *Bargaining* 2 "Nowhere like the Hellmouth for a party!" [Demon] 2001 Jul Golden and Sniegoski *Food Chain* [50] "[Oz:] 'Are toys supposed to be alive?' [Buffy:] 'One would think not, but y'know... Hellmouth.'" 2001 Odom *Revenant* 3 "She knew a lot about vampires, and she was still learning about demons and other things that hunted, haunted, and otherwise lurked around the Hellmouth that Sunnydale had been built on." 2001 Kaveney *Reading the Vampire Slayer* 4 "A teenager in 1990s California, she is called on the death of her predecessor, to cull vampires and combat a variety of supernatural evils that congregate at the Hellmouth at Sunnydale." 2001 Wall and Zryd *Reading the Vampire Slayer* 64 "By the third season of Buffy, however, references to the special nature of Sunnydale (a suburb situated over the Hellmouth) creep into the show more and more." 2001 Kaveney *Reading the Vampire Slayer* 237 "Buffy saves Willow and Xander from the girlish vampire Darla and monstrous Luke, who are gathering food for the Master, who is trapped in the Hellmouth." 2002 May 21 Fury *The Grave* "Man, they've really tightened security out here lately—one too many squatters from the Hellmouth." [X] 2002 Odom *Crossings* 16 "Playing the hero went against all his natural instincts, but years of spending time at Buffy's side fighting the worst the Hellmouth had to offer up had changed him." 2002 Navarro *Tempted Champions* 16 "Buffy wanted to think as positive as anyone else, but doing that around here could get you killed. After all: this *was* the Hellmouth." 2002 Vowell *The Partly Cloudy Patriot* 109 "Her high school was built on top of a vortex of evil, the Hellmouth." 2002 Williams *Fighting the Forces* 64 "Given that the series foregrounds the parallels between adolescence as hell and life on the Hellmouth, it is unsurprising that conflicts between mother and daughter appear frequently on *Buffy*."

1.b: n Any such opening

1997 May 5 Whedon *Nightmares* "Hellmouth: center of mystical convergence, supernatural monsters—been there." [X] 1997 Oct 13 Greenwalt *Reptile Boy* "Who needs a social life when they've got their very own Hellmouth?" [B] 1997 Cusick *The Harvest* 146 "'Hey, that's a plan,' Xander was agreeable. ''Cause a lot of schools aren't on Hellmouths.'" 1998 Apr 28 Noxon *I Only Have Eyes for You* "I'm doing everything I can, but you people have to realize [...] that we are on a Hellmouth. Sooner or later, people are going to figure that out." [Principal Snyder] 1999 April Conroy *Us* 70 "Gellar's Buffy, an 18-year-old chosen to battle the supernatural villains spewing from the 'hellmouth' over which her high school is built, is fearless, fast, funny and buff." 1999 Sep 25 Weeks *TV Guide* 21 "Series creator Joss Whedon says locating *Angel* in L.A. was only natural: 'Unlike Sunnydale, L.A. isn't a hellmouth, but we're convinced everything that comes out of a hellmouth comes directly to L.A.'" 1999 Oct 1 *Entertainment Weekly* 33/1 "[H]e wastes no time acquainting our reluctant slayer with the uncoincidental reason she ended up in this 'one-Starbucks town' (its proximity to Hellmouth)." 1999 Golden and Holder *Ghost Roads* 169 "Must have a hellmouth or something. Or a breach." [B]   2000 May 11 Udovitch *Rolling Stone* 62/4 "Sunnydale is the center of an extra-heaping helping of evil, because it is situated on a Hell mouth. If the Hell mouth were opened, the world as we know it would come to an end." 2000 Sep 1 The Bronze "For those places that don't have hellmouths, sure, vampires can go there" 2000 Holder *Watcher's Guide* 2 20 "Season One revealed that Sunnydale is a town situated two hours on the freeway from Los Angeles. It sits on a hellmouth, which is a portal to the demon dimensions." 2002 Navarro *Tempted Champions* 25 "She'd heard it rumored that a Hellmouth was here."

   1.c: *n* An element in names
2001 Nov 12 buffysearch.com "**The Hellmouth**" [site name]   [*hell* n in sense 2 + *mouth* n in sense 7]

   2: *n* Something evil, like a hellmouth; misery, torture
2000 Sep 1 The Bronze "I actually still have my original AOHellmouth acct." 2002 Jul 30 Bronze: Beta "Escape Rerun HELLmouth by reading a new Buffy tale each week this summer at Buffy's European Summer Adventure." [fr. HELLMOUTH in sense 1.a, fr. *hell* n in sense 3.a + *mouth* n in sense 7]

   3: *n attrib* Of or by the Hellmouth
1998 Oct 6 Noxon *Dead Man's Party* "Welcome to the Hellmouth petting zoo." 1999 Oct 1 *Entertainment Weekly* 33/1 "**Introduces** [...] Buffy's season 1 bête noir, the Hellmouth-trapped Master." 1999 Gallagher *Obsidian Fate* 52 "'Unless—some weird Hellmouth thingie, you know—got to him?'" [W] 1999 Golden and Holder *Out of the Madhouse* 315 "'Okay, someone has to stay behind on Hellmouth duty, and that would be Giles.'" [B]   2000 Gilman and Sherman *Deep Water* 14 "'Two shapechangers for the price of one. What is this, the Hellmouth Zoo?'" [X]   2000 Garton *Resurrecting Ravana* 123 "'They're all under the same umbrella, and in the same Hellmouth town, of course.'" [B]   2000 Navarro *Paleo* 92 "She supposed it could be one of those dragon thingies,

but real-world endangered wasn't Hellmouth style."   2000 Holder *Watcher's Guide* 2 156 "Cordelia points out that non-Hellmouth options are a good thing."

4: n Hell (expletive)

1999 Apr 29 The Bronze "I know in advance that there's no way in hellmouth I'll figure out those *Matrix* codes without some serious help." 1999 Apr 29 The Bronze "Hey, I was born in L.A....so, what in the Hellmouth am I doing in Seattle???"   1999 May 13 The Bronze "Where the hellmouth is Whirlwind? She owes me $13.54 for cookies."   1999 Jun 29 http://home.earthlink.net/~leathrjacket/stima_Faq.html "Hellmouth: Often used instead of just Hell, i.e. 'Where in the Hellmouth is so-and-so?"   1999 Oct 13 The Bronze "Adulating Sycophant...ack how the hellmouth do you spell and say that!"   2001 Jun 2 The Bronze "To Hellmouth with topics—let's talk about MY obsession."   [fr. HELLMOUTH in sense 1.a, fr. *hell* n in sense 8 (also *HDAS* sv *the hell* in sense 1 & *DAS3* adv phr in sense 2 + *mouth* in sense 7]

—**hellmouthish** *adj* Demoniacal

1999 May 13 The Bronze "[H]ow about a version of Fran[ken]steins [sic] monster as her boyfriend? That would make someone powerful enough to help her, be 'well-built' and hellmouthish all at the same time."   [fr. HELLMOUTH in sense 1.a + -ish suff in sense 2.a]

Hellsville n Hell
2001 Nov 6 Whedon *Once More, with Feeling* "I can't kill you, you take me to Hellsville in her place." [B]   [Hell n in sense 2 + -s- + -ville suff]

hit a major backspace v phr Lose ground, esp. in popularity or social position
1997 Mar 31 Des Hotel and Batali *Never Kill a Boy on the First Date* "Doesn't Owen realize he's hitting a major backspace by hanging out with that loser?" [C]   1998 Winter *Buffy the Vampire Slayer* 50 "**hitting a major backspace:** [...] v. [C] losing points in popularity status." [hit v in sense 3 + -ing[1] suff in sense 1 + a[2] indef art in sense 1 + major adj in sense 2 + backspace n]

hotness n Sexual attractiveness
2001 Nov 10 Whedon *Once More, with Feeling* "[Willow:] 'Those guys

are checking you out.' [Tara:] 'What?' [Willow:] 'The hotness of you, doofus.'" [*hot* adj in sense 7 + -*ness* suff]

hottie 1: n Attractive guy or girl
1997 Mar 10 Whedon *Welcome to the Hellmouth* "'That's right, I saw her—pretty much a hottie.'" [X] 1997 Golden and Holder *Halloween Rain* 5 "'Way psycho,' John replied. 'She's a hotty, though.'" 1998 Winter *Buffy the Vampire Slayer* 50 "**hottie:** [...] n. [B] attractive female or male—including vampires." 1998 Golden and Holder *Blooded* 182 "The hotties gave each other a 'let's-go-for-it' look." 1999 Feb 16 AOL's Entertainment Asylum (Posting Board) "Angel is such a hottie." 1999 April *Us* "Who's Sexy Now: Sarah Michelle Gellar & the Rest of Hollywood's New Hotties." [cover headline] 1999 May 13 The Bronze "I'm working on being a shallow abusive jerk so I can date the hotties too." 1999 Jun 26 The Bronze "Do I look like Kevin Costner??? He's a major hottie." 1999 Summer *Buffy the Vampire Slayer* 55 "For one brief shining moment, lonely-guy Jesse hooked up with a bona fide hottie." 1999 Official *Yearbook* 8/1 "It was slim pickens with the hotties." 2001 Jul Golden *Food Chain* [11] "[Buffy:] 'But I got to spend some time with Sandy and she's—' [Xander:] 'A smokin' hotty.'" 1999 Golden *Sins of the Father* 4 "'Let's face it, Joyce is a young, unattached woman, and not half a hottie for a woman of her age'" [X] 2000 Sep 1 The Bronze "Wanttoknow leaves with 1 construction 'hottie' to assist her with constructing her ideal relaxation site." [stage direction in posting board role-playing] 2000 Dec/Jan *Movieline* 74 "Every year the Great Western University of Hotties admits a new class of 'It' girls." 2001 Jun 2 The Bronze "James Marsters is a Hottie#23" [in a signature] 2002 Feb 4 *Angel* (WB Network) "But ask him to mack on hotties and he wigs." [C] 2002 Feb 26 Petrie *As You Were* "I'm not advertising this to the missus, but you're still a hottie." [B] 2002 Jul 26 Bronze: Beta "I have seen your picture and you are a hottie."

2: n Attractiveness
1998 Jan 20 Whedon *Innocence* "Can't spend the rest of your life waiting for Xander to smell the hottie." [B] [fr. HOTTIE 1]

3: n attrib Pertaining to hotties
1999 Oct 1 Tucker *Entertainment Weekly* 23/1 "We also get stories of

friendships tested to the breaking point, as well as relationship between a hottie mortal slayer and soulfully soulless vampire." 1999 Oct 1 Fretts *Entertainment Weekly* 60/4 "Even dramas are raiding *Melrose's* hottie closet for comic—and ratings—relief." 1999 Oct 13 The Bronze "Buffman is a Hottie Club Members…You all have E[-mail]." 2000 Sep 1 The Bronze "[I]n shorts…is that a hottie moment?" 2001 Jun 2 The Bronze "That's it! You in all of your hottie Goddess goodness." 2002 Jul 30 Bronze: Beta "[C]ongrats on the Hottie Poll."

   4: *adj* Attractive
2002 Jul 23 Bronze: Beta "How's the hottie boyfriend?" [*HDAS* 1991–; *DAS*3; fr. *hot adj* in sense 7 + -(t)*ie sv* -y³ *suff* in sense 2]
   —**hottiness** n Attractiveness
2001 Jun 2 The Bronze "But on the ACTUAL issue of my hottiness heres a averaged out picture of me." [HOTTIE + *-ness suff*]

Houdini n Disappearing act
2001 Oct 30 DeKnight *All the Way* "Dawn and her little friend pulled a Houdini." [S] [Harry Houdini 'name of a famous illusionist and escape artist']

huntery *adj* Like someone hunting game
2000 Dec 19 Noxon *Into the Woods* "Hey, don't do anything huntery." [X] [*hunter* n in sense 1 + -y¹ *suff* in sense 2.a]

inner moppet n Inner child, innocent aspect of one's personality
1997 Sep 15 Whedon *When She Was Bad* "Whatever is causing the Joan Collins 'tude, deal with it. Embrace the pain, spank your inner moppet, whatever, but get over it." [C] [*ODNW* inner child n (fr. *inner adj* in sense 3 + *child* n in sense 1) + *moppet* n] See INNER SLAYER sv SLAYER

Jimmy Hoffa vi Disappear
1997 Golden and Holder *Halloween Rain* 58 "'And the vampires who hit on Xander and me have Jimmy Hoffa'd, so maybe we can actually hang out and enjoy the rest of the masquerade.'" [W] [fr. Jimmy Hoffa 'nickname of James Riddle Hoffa (1913–1975?), U.S. labor leader, presumably abducted and murdered by organized crime, whose body has never been found']

Jossage n   Mass of information about Joss Whedon
2001 May 30 www.Buffyguide.com "Jossage Update, Goodie Bag on Hold"
[main page headline]   [*Joss* Whedon + -*age* suff in sense 1.a]

judgy *adj*   Critical
2001 Nov 27 Noxon *Wrecked* "Willow's a grownup. Maybe she doesn't
need to be monitored. She's going through something, but we're not
her. I mean, maybe she has reasons for acting this way. And, so what if
she crossed a line? You know, we all do stuff—stupid stuff. But then we
learn, and we learn, and we don't do it again. Oh, so, who are we to be
all judgy?" [B]   [*judge* vi in sense 1 + -*y*[1] suff in sense 1]

Keyser Soze   *vt*   Definitively manipulate, outmaneuver
1997 May 5 Batali and Des Hotel *The Puppet Show* "Does anyone feel like
we've been Keyser Sozed?" [X]   1999 Oct 1 Howard *Entertainment Weekly*
49/1 "**kcyser sozed** Duped by an actual bad guy into believing in a
villain that doesn't exist; reference to imaginary character in the film *The
Usual Suspects*."   [fr. *Keyser Soze* 'name of the character in the film, *The
Usual Suspects*, dir. Bryan Singer (1995)']

kick   *adj*   Terrific
1999 May 11 Noxon *The Prom* "Well, at least now we've all got someone
to go with.... More importantly, I've got the kick dress." [B]   [*HDAS* kick
ass *vbl phr* in sense 2.b sv kick *v* or fr. *kicking adj* (also *DAS3* sv kickin')]

kickage n   Episode of kicking or beating
1999 May 13 The Bronze "I was quite disappointed Sunday night. No
arse kickage of the X-Files kind."   [kick *v* in sense 1 + -*age* suff in sense
1.a]

kicking the gear shift   *v phr*   Having sexual relations (in a car)
1998 Oct 20 Noxon *All Men Are Beasts* "Bet you and Scott have been up
here kicking the gear shift." [F]   [kick *vt* in sense 1 + -*ing*[1] suff in sense
1 + the[1] def art in sense 2 + *gear shift*]

kissage n   Episode of kissing
1998 Jan 20 Whedon *Innocence* "It's like, freeze frame. Willow kissage—
but I'm not gonna kiss you." [O]   1999 Mar 21 http://members.tripod

.com/~b_t_v_s/index.shtml "Buffy will get a new boyfriend called 'Scott' and they will have major 'kissage' as will Willow and Oz, all taking place in school."   2000 Holder *The Evil That Men Do* 170 "'Will,' Buffy said, wounded. 'What's wrong.' 'Oh, nothing. Just that you have plenty of time to give Angel kissage and not nearly enough to look for my boyfriend.'" 2000 Holder *Watcher's Guide* 2 52 "It's all still there—the bickering, the kissage—except that the Slayer is missing." [kiss n in sense 1 + *-age suff* in sense 4.b]

kitteny *adj*   Like a kitten
2000 Oct 24 Petrie *All in the Family* "[Riley:] 'You sure this isn't just your way of trying to make me feel less cute and weak and kittenish?' [Buffy:] 'Kitteny.'"   [kitten n + y¹ suff in sense 2.a]

knifey *adj*   Associated with knives
2000 Oct 17 Kirshner *Out of My Mind* "'Now, I agree that Marat wasn't a real martyr, but the death in the tub, the neck wound, all that blood— it's just a little more fangy than knifey.'" [B]   [knife n in sense 1 + y¹ suff in sense 1]

kung fu *adj*   Crazy, ballistic (as though a martial arts hero)
2001 Oct 30 DeKnight *All the Way* "Don't make me go kung fu, man!" [Vampire Boy]   [fr. ADH4 kung fu n]

Lifetime TV *adj*   Overly dramatic
2000 Garton *Resurrecting Ravana* 43 "'Friday, Mom,' Buffy said. 'Not that long ago, so don't go all Lifetime TV on me.'"   [fr. *Lifetime TV* 'name of a cable television network that specializes in dramatic shows about women and their relationships']

linkage *n*   Links to websites
2000 Sep 1 The Bronze "Thanks for the linkage too."   [link n in sense 7 + *-age suff* in sense 1.a]

lizardy *adj*   Reptilian
2001 Nov 13 Kirshner *Tabula Rasa* "So what have we got? What kind of oogly-booglies? Lizardy types, or zombies, or vampires, or what?" [D] [lizard n in sense 1 + -y¹ suff in sense 1]

love whammy n Love spell
1998 Feb 10 Noxon *Bewitched, Bothered, and Bewildered* "Amy's into witch-craft and I was hurtin,' I guess, so I made her put the love whammy on Cordelia." [X] [*love* n in sense 2 + *whammy* n]

lunchable 1: *adj* Yummy
1997 Oct 6 Kiene and Reinkemeyer *Inca Mummy Girl* "There's mine. Sven. Isn't he lunchable? Mine's definitely the best." [C] [*lunch* vi + -*able* suff in sense 1]
   2: n Victim, to a vampire
2001 Oct 30 DeKnight *All the Way* "So, whaddya think? Lunchables? Or should we go all the way and turn them [into vampires]?" [Vampire Boy] [*lunch* vi + -*able* suff in sense 1 + -*s*[1] suff] See SPOOKABLES

lurkage 1.a: n Observing activity on a posting board without posting
1999 Jun 26 The Bronze "…lurkage ensues…" [stage direction in posting board role-playing] 2000 Sep 1 The Bronze "*much lurkage* [stage direction in posting board role-playing] 2001 Jun 2 The Bronze "Ok I'm on my lunch break but certain people have called me out of whup/lurkage." 2002 Jul 25 Bronze: Beta "Thoin, who's had a long, trying day, shuffles in from the Lurkage and looks around." [stage direction in posting board role-playing] 2002 Jul 30 Bronze: Beta "Welcome from lurkage."
   1.b: n An element in names
2001 Jun 2 The Bronze "Irene from Lurkage"
   2: n attrib Pertaining to lurking
2000 Sep 1 The Bronze "lurkage mode engaged" [stage direction in posting board role-playing] [fr. *lurk* v 'observe activity on a posting board without posting', fr. *lurk* vi in sense 3 + -*age* suff in sense 1.a]

machoness n Self-conscious masculinity
2001 Oct 2 Fury *Bargaining 2* "So what brings you so early here—machoness?" [W] [*macho* adj in sense + -*ness* suff]

mad n Episode of anger
2000 Gallagher *Doomsday Deck* 64 "Buffy was ready to swear Xander was an alien from another planet if that's what he wanted to believe. What-

ever it takes to get him out of this major mad." [fr. *mad adj* in sense 1]
See MAD-ON

mad-on n Episode of anger
2001 Jul Golden and Sniegoski *Food Chain* [64] "We all know when
your mom comes around, she's gonna have a serious mad-on, and I'm
gonna have to deal with it." [B] 2001 Odom *Revenant* 258 "It wasn't a
true berserker mad-on, but it overpowered the part of him that was so
scared." 2002 May 14 Noxon *Villains* "That's why you had a mad-on
for the Slayer." [W] [fr. *mad adj* in sense 1 + *on adv* in sense 2]

manimal n Sexually aggressive man or boy; man who 'behaves like an
animal'
1998 Nov 3 Noxon *All Men Are Beasts* "Every guy, from Manimal right
on down to Mr. I-Loved-*The English Patient*, has beast in him." [F] [*man
n* in sense 1 + *animal* in sense 3]
   —**humanimal** n A name
1999 Oct 13 The Bronze "Humanimal" [fr. *human n* in sense 2 + *animal*
in sense 3]

manness n Particularly masculine nature
1999 Nov 2 Forbes *Beer Bad* "I'm tired of you men and your...manness."
[W] [*n* in sense 1 + *-ness suff*]

matchy adj Coordinated in color or pattern
2000 Oct 10 Espenson *The Replacement* "That's not me. For one thing,
he's too clean and his socks are all matchy." [X] [*match vi* + *-y¹ suff* in
sense 1]

mathiness n Condition characterized by mathematics
2002 Jul 28 Bronze: Beta "'How many times is the phrase "I know"
intoned in the middle of the Bill Withers classic "Ain't No Sunshine"?'
Well, it's fourteen at a time, and I think he does it twice, doesn't he? Or
does he? Maybe I should stick with fourteen here. Say, you're verging on
mathiness here! Careful!" [*math n* + *-y¹ suff* in sense 1 + *-ness suff*]

meetage n Rendezvous
2000 Sep 1 The Bronze "Countdown to Mia meet-age huh?" 2002

Jul 31 Bronze: Beta "My hotmail addy is above, so we can hopefully work out some meetage details." [*meet* v in sense 1 + *-age* suff in sense 4.b]

melty *adj* Characterized by melting
2001 Oct 23 Fury and Espenson *Life Serial* "You need to see Giles...I'd start by IDing those demons...the whole melty thing ought to narrow it down." [X] [*melt* vi in sense 1 + *-y*[1] suff in sense 1]

messed *adj* Confused, frustrated
1997 Nov 17 Noxon and Gordon *What's My Line, Part 1* "I just get messed sometimes." [B] 1999 Oct 1 Howard *Entertainment Weekly* 49/1 "**messed** Out of sorts." 2001 Oct 23 Fury and Espenson *Life Serial* "There's this thing: someone's doing stuff to me, messing up my life, except that it was pretty messed already." [B] [*HDAS messed* (up) in sense 1 (cf. *DAS3 mess up* v phr in senses 1 & 2 and *NTC mess up* in sense 1)]

metaphory *adj* Full of metaphor
2000 Oct 24 Petrie *All in the Family* "[Monk:] 'My journey is done.' [Buffy:] 'Don't get metaphory on me.'" [*metaphor* n in sense 1 + *y*[1] suff in sense 1]

Miata-free *adj* Without a Miata automobile
1999 Oct 13 *The Bronze* "Yes, I'm Miata-free. How are you?" [*Miata*, an automobile brand name + *-free* suff, fr. *free* adj in sense 4.a & 4.b]

militant *adj* WILD BUNCH
1999 Oct 13 *The Bronze* "I just broke up with my boyfriend of 2 yrs yesterday, and still was in stitches while watching Buffy go militant on her Roommate, (what's with the army guys??? New Plot is REALLY thi[c]kening, because when Oz spotted that chick—other werewolf?—the army guys looked like they were moving in pretty close to that chick." [fr. *militant* adj in sense 1]

missage *n* Missing
1997 Sep 29 Whedon and Greenwalt *School Hard* "It's Angel missage." [W] 1999 Jun 28 http://www.gate.net/~woof/message3.htm "Angel Missage" [site title] [fr. *miss* v in sense 8 + *-age* suff in sense 3]

Mod Squad n Slayerettes, Scooby Gang
1999 Golden and Holder *Immortal* 40 "'Anyway, the Mod Squad's gonna track down the grave-robbing angle.'" [B]

mootville *adj* [*moot adj* in sense 2.b + *-ville suff*] Irrelevant
1997 Nov 17 Noxon and Gordon *What's My Line, Part 1* "It's all mootville for me." [B] [fr. *Mod Squad* 'name of the group of juvenile detectives on the television show of the same name (on ABC, 1968–1973), or in the film of the same name (1999, dir. Scott Silver); ult. fr. *mod adj* in sense 2 + *squad n* in sense 3]

moral n Sense of right and wrong
2002 Jul 28 Bronze: Beta "You're coming from the moral." [fr. *moral adj* in sense 1]

moveage n Moving
2000 Sep 1 The Bronze "You're our moveage knight in shining armor, riding in on a white hor-…pickup truck." [*move v* in sense 5 + *-age suff* in sense 4.a]

move-free *adj* Without any attempt to engage romantically
1998 Nov 3 Noxon *All Men Are Beasts* "[Pete:] 'Well, I guess you didn't think about that when you put the moves on Debbie.' [Oz:] 'We talked, yeah, but it was move-free.'" 1999 Oct 1 Howard *Entertainment Weekly* 49/1 "**move free** A chaste date lacking hanky-panky." [*move n* in sense 4 (also NTC sv *move* [*on someone*]) + *-free suff*, fr. *free adj* in sense 4.a & 4.b]

Mr. I-Loved-The English Patient n Apparently sensitive and thoughtful man or boy
1998 Nov 3 Noxon *All Men Are Beasts* "Every guy, from Manimal right on down to Mr. I -Loved-The English Patient, has beast in him." [F] [*Mr.* in sense 1 + *I pron* + *love vt* in sense 5 + *The English Patient*, fr. the novel by Michael Ondaatje (1992) or the film adapted from it (1996, dir. Anthony Minghella)]

much *adj* Often, a lot, intensively
1992 Whedon *Buffy the Vampire Slayer* "Excuse much—rude or any-

thing?" 1992 Whedon *Buffy the Vampire Slayer* "Smell of booze much."
1997 Mar 10 Whedon *The Harvest* "[Buffy:] 'How did he die?' [Cordelia:]
'I don't know.' [Buffy:] 'Well, are there any marks?' [Cordelia:] 'Morbid
much? I didn't ask.'" 1997 Sep 22 King *Some Assembly Required* "Pathetic
much?" [C] 1997 Dec 8 Greenwalt and Whedon *Ted* "Having issues
much?" [X] 1997 Golden and Holder *Halloween Rain* 3 "Pathetic much?"
1997 Golden and Holder *Halloween Rain* 5 "'Insane much? Are you, like,
asylum bound, or what?'" [Aphrodesia] 1997 Golden and Holder *Halloween Rain* 149 "'Blind much?' [Buffy] asked." 1998 Apr 28 Noxon *I
Only Have Eyes for You* "Over-identify much?" [C] 1998 Spr/Sum *The
Seventeen Guys Issue* 24 "Crush much?" [headline] 1998 Nov 5 *The
Bronze* "Typecast much?" 1998 Dec *Mademoiselle* 69 "Q: My ex-fiancé is
getting married in two weeks. Now I realize I still love him. Should I tell
him? [...] A: Meanwhile, *My Best Friend's Wedding/Friends* much?" 1998
Dec 2 *The Bronze* "Liddie pauses for a moment from her last minute
studying for finals[.] [P]rocrastinate much?" 1998 Dec 2 *The Bronze*
"Keep forgetting to post to ya...no worries, and in case you forget, my
constant obsessing over Jeremy Piven in a kilt traditional Scottish style
(fetish much?) should be a pretty good reminder." 1998 Winter *Buffy
the Vampire Slayer* 50 "**much** [...] adj. [Cordelia] great in degree—often
used as a put-down, as in 'Pathetic much?' or 'Overidentify much?'"
1998 *Jawbreaker* "[Courtney:] 'God, tuna much? [...] We never, ever eat
at lunch period, do you understand me? If for some damned good reason we ever did, we would never, ever eat out of a brown paper bag. I
don't care if there's a four-star fucking culinary masterpiece in there.'"
1998 Golden and Holder *Child of the Hunt* 101 "'I'd like you to check out
the mutilations first, if you don't mind.' 'Morbid much?' Cordelia asked."
1998 Cover *Night of the Living Rerun* 134 "'Invade personal space much?'"
[C] 1999 Mar 16 AOL's Entertainment Asylum (Posting Board) "[D]on't
you think it's silly for people to go into a Buffy room and say they hate
it? Antagonize much?" 1998 Mar 28 *The Sopranos* (HBO) "[Anthony,
Jr.:] 'Probably I can't go to that dance now either.' [Meadow:] 'God, self-
involved much?'" 1999 May 13 *The Bronze* "Um, Bezoar much?" 1999
May 13 *The Bronze* "Overposting much?" 1999 Jun 26 *The Bronze* "Hi
there—sarky ['sarcastic'] much?" 1999 Oct 1 Howard *Entertainment
Weekly* 49/2 "**pathetic much** Feeling sorry for yourself?" 1999 Gilman

and Sherman *Visitors* 25 "'Gee, defensive much? I mean, you go around killing things, why shouldn't things come around trying to kill you?'" [C]   1999 Massie *Power of Persuasion* 108 "From her hiding place Buffy wondered, 'So he'd rather find trouble than be dragged out of his office for no reason? A fine example of maturity to the pupils of Sunnydale High much?'"   1999 Gallagher *Obsidian Fate* 71 "'Eeew. Gross much!' Sienna wrinkled her nose."   1999 Oct 7 *Doonesbury* "Off message much?" 2000 Mar 30 *Popular* (WB Network) "Jealous much, fast-food Hagatha?" 2000 Apr 26 [Website forum dedicated to the iMac] "How's that for a real life test, ol' Billy boy!!!!!!! Feel like eating crow much??!!!"   2000 Sep 1 The Bronze "OTT [Off The Topic] much?"   2000 Sep 1 The Bronze "I read a story about evil Gnomes once, don't remember which, but I do remember that it gave me nitemares for ages…and I have been scared of them ever since! I know, Pathetic much?"   2000 Oct 24 Petrie *All in the Family* "[Buffy:] 'I'm sorry, okay?' [Dawn:] 'Broken-record much.'"   2000 Nov 23 Kateland Goldsborough [private conversation] "Control freak much?"   2000 Passarella *Ghoul Trouble* 97 "'Pathetic much?' Cordelia said."   2001 Feb 29 Stephanie Manzella [private conversation] "Curb much?" [i.e., 'Do you park often?']   2001 Apr 17 *Angel* (WB Network) "Awkward much?" [C]   2001 Jun 2 The Bronze "Confusing much?" 2001 Nov 26 [Unknown student, private conversation] "Obsess much." 2002 Jan 29 Espenson *Doublemeat Palace* "Hey, respect the narrative flow much?" [W]   2002 Jul 25 Bronze: Beta "Oh, and I personally *hated* that, 'give that b.itch [sic] what she deserves line, cause, bait & switch much?'" 2002 Jul 25 Bronze: Beta "Excuse me, but double-standard much? You can't have it both ways just because you like or don't like someone." 2002 Jul 26 Bronze: Beta "'I'm an Aussie, so I basically rock'?? *snicker* Egotistic much? Not that I dis-like aussies, I'm just wondering if I should start saying 'I'm a Californian, so I basically rock.'"   2002 Jul 26 Bronze: Beta "Deja vu much."   [fr. *much adj* in sense 1 & *much adv* in senses 1 & 3]

muchly *adv* Tremendously
2001 Oct 23 Fury and Espenson *Life Serial* "Well, I appreciate it. Muchly." 2002 Jul 30 Bronze Beta "You rock muchly, twin-let!"   [*much adj* + -ly² *suff* in sense 3]

murdery *adj* Lethally dangerous
2001 Nov 13 Kirshner *Tabula Rasa* "Hey, take it easy, guy. OK, no one's hurt, right? And none of us look all passiony murdery, so we're probably safe here." [B]   [*murder* n in sense 1 + -*y*¹ *suff* in sense 1]

nasty *n* Extreme badness
1999 Golden *Sins of the Father* 198 "'Giles called my mom earlier, so you already know he's back and alive [...] but the nasty is still happening.'" [B]   2000 Oct 24 Petrie *All in the Family* "'That's a new kind of nasty.'" [X]   [fr. *nasty* adj in senses 1.b & 2]

neat-freakishness *n* State of being obsessively clean or orderly
2001 Odom *Revenant* 3 "'All this neat-freakishness is really creeping me out.'" [B]   2001 Odom *Revenant* 293 "That intrigued Willow, because the Black Wind gang members didn't really strike her as totally dedicated to neat-freakishness." [*neat freak* n (fr. *neat* adj in sense 1 + *freak* n in sense 4.c) + -*ish suff* in senses 2.a & 2.b + *ness suff*]

necklacey *adj* Characterized by possession of a necklace
2001 Jun Fassbender and Pascoe *Buffy the Vampire Slayer* 34 [Dark Horse Comics] [23] "'It's not like people just show up in Sunnydale—with creepy, buggy, necklace-y things—and aren't involved in the buggy badness.'" [W]   [*necklace* n in sense 1 + -*y*¹ *suff* in sense 1]

Net Girl *n* Girl proficient at using the Internet
1997 Nov 3 Whedon *Lie to Me* "[Angel:] 'I want you to track someone down. On the Net.' [Willow:] 'Oh, great! I'm so the Net girl.'"   1999 Jun 26 The Bronze "She [Willow] would be devastated if she couldn't retain knowledge, if she were unable to learn new things, if she became 'stupid girl' instead of 'net girl' and 'research girl.'"   1999 Fall Williams *Buffy the Vampire Slayer* 18 "Net girl Willow is a perfect example of today's independent witch."   [*DAS3* (fr. *Internet* n) + *girl* n in sense 2]   See HACKER GIRL

non-mathy *adj* Mathematically challenged
2002 Jul 29 Bronze: Beta "You're right, though, it is an excellent book, even for non-mathy types."   [*non- pref* + *math* n + -*y*¹ *suff* in sense 1]

Old Ones 1.a: n Prehistoric demons, including vampires
1997 Mar 10 Whedon *The Harvest* "What remains of the Old Ones are vestiges—certain magics, certain creatures." [G] 1997 Cusick *The Harvest* 66 "'...The world will belong to the Old Ones...,' Luke recited." 1999 Oct Brereton *The Dust Waltz* [45] "Because it's the perfect time to attempt a revivication of the old ones." 2000 Topping *Slayer* 30 "The vampires refer to themselves as 'the Old Ones.'" 2000 Holder *Watcher's Guide* 2 20 "The negative energy attracts demons, vampires, and other denizens of evil, some of whom have made concerted efforts to open the Hellmouth and overrun the human population with the Old Ones and their descendants." 2001 Tonkin *Reading the Vampire Slayer* 50 "'This is definitely So Cal,' as Joss Whedon wrote: forever the land of uprooted incomers, which in the case of Buffy include Celtic vampires, who might once have fed in Anne Rice's New Orleans, and the ancient, malignant 'Old Ones' blown in from H. P. Lovecraft's *New England*."
      1.b: n An element in names
2000 Sep 1 The Bronze "Old One" 2000 Sep 1 The Bronze "And Oldest One will snicker up his sleeve at you, which he does anyway, so I guess it's not important." [*Old Ones* 'prehistoric demons', fr. *old* adj in sense 7 + *ones* n, fr. *one* adj in sense 4]

ooginess n Sick feeling
1998 Mar 3 Des Hotel and Batali *Killed by Death* "[Buffy:] 'I feel all oogy.' [Xander:] 'Increased ooginess—that's a danger signal.'" [reanalyzed fr. *uglies* n pl sv *ugly* adj (see also HDAS *ooky* 'icky' + *-ness* suff)]

oogly-booglies n SPOOKABLES
2001 Nov 13 Kirshner *Tabula Rasa* "[Dawn:] 'So what have we got? What kind of oogly-booglies? Lizardy types, or zombies, or vampires, or what?' [Giles:] 'There are no oogly-booglies, Dawn.'" [reanalyzed fr. *uglies* n pl sv *ugly* adj (see also HDAS *ooky* 'icky') + *bogey* in sense 1, with reduplication of *-ly*]

otherwhere adv Elsewhere
1998 Nov 10 Espenson *Band Candy* "Also, I think she wanted me otherwhere." [B] 1999 Oct 1 Howard *Entertainment Weekly* 49/2 "**otherwhere** Elsewhere; also Someplace That's Away." 2000 Garton

Resurrecting Ravana 75 "Oz cleared his throat. 'Download otherwhere?'"
[fr. *other* adj in sense 3 + *where* n in sense 1]

out-of-the-loopy *adj* Unincluded
2000 Jan 25 Espenson *A New Man* "He's feeling all neglected and out-of-the-loopy." [W] [*out of the loop* sv *loop* + *-y*[1] suff in sense 1]

overshare 1: *v* Share generously or in excess
1997 Oct 27 Ellsworth *Halloween* "If you haven't noticed, he's not exactly one to overshare." [B]
   2: *n* Excessive piece of information
2000 *Bring It On* "'I didn't need to hear that   that's an overshare.'"
[*over-* pref in sense 4 + *share* vt in sense 3]

pants-free *adj* Naked
1999 Oct 13 The Bronze "Member of the Society For A Pants Free Bronze"
[signature] [*pant* n in sense 1 + *-free*, fr. *free* adj in sense 4.a & 4.b]

passiony *adj* Dangerously angry
2001 Nov 13 Kirshner *Tabula Rasa* "Hey, take it easy, guy. OK, no one's hurt, right? And none of us look all passiony murdery, so we're probably safe here." [B] [*passion* n in sense 4 + *-y*[1] suff in sense 1, with a vestige of *crime of passion* (see BLD *passion*)]

patheticness *n* Susceptibility to humorous scorn
2002 Feb 26 Petrie *As You Were* "I'm sure my incredible patheticness softened the blow for you." [B] [*pathetic* adj in sense 2 + *-ness* suff]

pluggage *n* Promotion, advocacy
1998 Dec 2 The Bronze "Pluggage!" [section heading]   [fr. *plug* vt in sense 4 + *-age* suff in sense 1.a]

pointy *n* Meaningful, purposeful
1997 Sep 15 Whedon *When She Was Bad* "[Giles:] 'Punishing yourself like this is pointless.' [Buffy:] 'It's entirely pointy.'"   1998 Golden and Holder *Watcher's Guide* 1 [back cover] "Exclusive Interviews. Totally Pointy Profiles. Behind-the-Scenes Info, and Other Buff-stuff About the Hit Show."
1998 Gardner *Return to Chaos* [advertisement among backmatter] "**The Watcher's Guide**: The totally pointy guide for the Ultimate Fan!"   1999

Oct 1 Howard *Entertainment Weekly* 49/2 "**pointy** Worthwhile—in response to something being described as pointless." [pointless in sense 1 + -y¹ suff in sense 1]

pokey *adj* Given to poking
2000 Oct 24 Petrie *All in the Family* "You find yourself a good anger management class, and I'll slam this pokey wood stick through your heart." [B]   2002 Mar 12 Gutierrez *Normal Again* "Its pokey stinger carries an antidote to its own poison." [W]   [*poke vt* in sense 2 + *y¹ suff* in sense 1]

poofage *n* Exit, disappearance
2000 Sep 1 The Bronze "Sorry for the unannounced poofage earlier." 2001 Jun 2 The Bronze "*hockey game poofage*" [role-playing stage direction]   2002 Jul 29 Bronze: Beta "[T]here is thunderstorm inspired *poofage* coming." [*poof vi* 'exit from a posting board, as a stage direction in board role-playing, fr. *poof interj* + *-age suff* in sense 4.b]

postage *n* Messages on a posting board
1999 May 13 The Bronze "Or do I mean, 'God, Whedon not!' in that I missed Joss postage earlier today."   1999 Oct 13 The Bronze "If you scroll on, I think, the last board, there is Joss postage."   2000 Sep 1 The Bronze "It's been a little slow, but lots of the usual interesting postage." 2002 Jul 30 Bronze: Beta "Thanks again for the postage. It always makes me feel sane when I read you."   [*post¹ vt* in sense 3 + *-age suff* in sense 4.b]
　　—**repostage** *n* Messages posted again
2002 Jul 28 Bronze: Beta "Thanks for the repostage. I don't know if I'll bet any money on what I said, though." [*re- pref* in sense 1 + POSTAGE]

postal *n* Insanity
1998 Nov 17 Petrie *Revelations* "Just seeing the two of you kissing after everything that happened, I leaned toward the postal, but I trust you." [X]   [fr. *go postal sv postal adj*]

posty *adj* Characteristic of posting a message on a Web-based posting board
2002 Jul 30 Bronze: Beta "I'll try the posty thing over on the UPN some-

time this week." 2002 Jul 30 Bronze: Beta "[H]ey there, posty boy! *smooootch*" 2002 Jul 31 Bronze: Beta "I am not nearly scrolled, but I think I saw you were very posty last night!!" [*post*¹ vt in sense 3 + -*y*¹ suff in sense 1]

poundage n Beating
2002 Jul 31 Bronze: Beta "'Life Serial'—no sex, demon Slayage at construction sight [sic] multiple-Mummy Hand Slayage (the customer complains about it being dead), Jonathan poundage." [*pound*² vt in sense 1 + -*age* suff in sense 4.a]

pre-posy *adj* At a stage in a relationship before flowers appropriately would be sent
1998 Oct 20 Noxon *All Men Are Beasts* "[Scott:] 'Well, we're not up to flowers. Are we? Up to flowers? Did I miss flowers?' [Buffy:] 'No, we're pre-posy, definitely.'" [*pre-* pref in sense 1.a + *posy* n in sense 1]

Psych 101 vt Analyze in a (too) basic way
2000 Oct 24 Petrie *All in the Family* "Don't Psych 101 me." [B] [fr. *Psychology 101* 'name (actual or metaphorical) for an introductory Psychology course', fr. *psychology* n in sense 1 + *101* 'of an introductory nature']

punctury *adj* Appearing punctured
2000 Sept 27 Noxon *Buffy vs. Dracula* "Two deep, punctury scratches." [W] [fr. *puncture* n in sense 1 + *y*¹ suff in sense 1]

punnage n Word-play
2002 Jul 26 Bronze: Beta "Well, since you broke out with the punnage… I was going to ask if Oregon was well-done or extra crispy." [*pun* vi + -*age* suff in sense 4.a]

put me in jail *v phr* Disapprove if you like
1997 Dec 8 Greenwalt and Whedon *Ted* "Yeah, I kicked my ball in, put me in jail, but he totally wigged." [B] [*put* vt in sense 1 + *me* pron in sense 1 + *in* prep in sense 1.b + *jail* n in sense 1]

quotage n Mass of quotations
1999 Jun 26 The Bronze "[under the heading, 'What L.O.S.E.R.s Use to

Stay Awake'] "MMM, Dru quotage & slumber parties are my secret to staying up late." 2000 Sep 1 The Bronze "im never invited to parties. (red dwarf quotage for all outthere) [sic]." 2001 Jun 2 The Bronze "Got some quotage, includes a little about my baby James." 2001 Kaveney *Reading the Vampire Slayer* viii "The episode guides Buffyguide.com […] and the Screening Room, Home of the Angelguide […] are excellent sources of quotage and pop culture references." [quote n in sense 4 + *-age* suff in sense 1.a]

rampagey *adj* Bent on mayhem
2000 Feb 8 Fury *The I in Team* "Why are they here? Sacrifices, treasures, or are they just getting rampagey?" [B] [*rampage* n + *-y*[1] suff in sense 1]

ranty *adj* Violently argumentative
2002 Jul 29 Bronze: Beta "I remember one particularly ranty night spending hours on board planning how one could use a stopwatch to parallel events and devising a chart to represent it all." [*rant* vi + *-y*[1] suff in sense 1]

researchy *adj* Prone to do research
2002 May 7 DeKnight *Seeing Red* "I'm guessing she's not feeling real researchy right now." [B] [*research* vi + *-y*[1] suff in sense 1]

revealy *adj* Characterized by making apparent
2000 Oct 10 Espenson *The Replacement* "Figure out a spell—something revealy." [X] [*reveal*[1] vt in sense 2 + *-y*[1] suff in sense 1]

riddichio *adj* Absurd
1998 Golden and Holder *Child of the Hunt* 28 "'Well that's just riddichio,' Xander said." [rid(d)iculous adj + *-hio*, supposed parallel to *radicchio*]
See BITCA

rinsey *adj* Capable of conditioning the hair
1997 Sep 29 Whedon and Greenwalt *School Hard* "I spent half my allowance on that cream rinse and it's neither creamy nor rinsey." [B] 2002 Jul 30 Bronze: Beta "When other fans complain she's whining, I think 'Of course she is. Her cream rinse is neither creamy nor rinsey and she has to save the world. Again.'" [*rinse* n in sense 3 + *-y*[1] suff in sense 1]

roby *adj* Characterized by wearing a robe
2000 Oct 10 Espenson *The Replacement* "You mean, a great, tall, roby thing, like that one?" [S] [*robe* n in sense 1 + *-y*¹ *suff* in sense 1]

round robin n Telephone calls by a group intended to mislead those called about the callers' whereabouts
1998 Jan 20 Whedon *Innocence* "Better do round robin… It's where everybody calls everybody else's mom and tells them they're staying at everybody's house." [W] 1998 Winter *Buffy the Vampire Slayer* 50 "**round robin:** […] n. [B] group process of phoning individual members' parents to say each is staying at another's house for an alibi, especially when used in vampire slaying." [fr. *round robin* in sense 1]

rumble-free *adj* Without a fight to attend
1999 Golden and Holder *Immortal* 17 "[Oz:] 'Is there a rumble?' [Buffy:] 'We're rumble-free.'" [*rumble* n in sense 4.b + *free, fr. free adj* in senses 4.a & 4.b]

rumbly *adj* Upset
2001 Nov 27 Noxon *Wrecked* "My tummy's feeling kind of rumbly." [W] [*rumble* vi in sense 2 + *-y*¹ *suff* in sense 1]

rushy *adj* Precipitate
2001 Oct 2 Noxon *Bargaining* 1 "Then why the sudden rushy rush?" [X] [*rush* n in sense + *-y*¹ *suff* in sense 1]

sabrina n Witch
1997 Mar 17 Reston *Witch* "She's our sabrina." [B] 1998 Winter *Buffy the Vampire Slayer* 50 "**Sabrina:** […] n. [B] witch." 1999 Oct 1 Howard *Entertainment Weekly* 49/3 "**sabrina** Teenage witch." 1999 Golden and Holder *Out of the Madhouse* 201 "[Oz:] 'Do you think you can learn to bind me?' […] [Willow:] 'I could work on it.' […] [Oz:] 'My Sabrina.' [Willow:] 'I'm not a witch.'" 2002 May 21 Petrie *Two to Go* "Yeah, what if the Slayer's dead already? We're just supposed to sit around and wait for Sabrina to disembowel us?" [Andrew] [fr. *Sabrina* 'name of a comic, cartoon, and television character, most recently in the WB network television show, *Sabrina the Teenage Witch,* ult. fr. ODFN *Sabrina*]

sadness n Humiliation
2002 May 21 Petrie *Two to Go* "You're looking for implants? You are sadness personified." [Jonathon] [*sad* n in sense 'pathetic', perh. fr. *DAS3 sad adj* in sense 'inferior; botched or bungled' or *DAS3 sad* sack n in sense 'awkward, unfortunate, maladjusted person' + *-ness* suff]

samey adj In a manner similar to another
2002 Jul 29 Bronze: Beta "Beths [sic] new album [...] A bit 'samey' didn't you think?" [*same* adv + *-y*[1] suff in sense 2.a]

Sanity Fair n A fictional magazine about normalcy
1999 Feb 23 Whedon *Doppelgangland* "I know Faith isn't exactly on the cover of Sanity Fair, but she's had it rough." [B] 1999 Oct 1 Howard *Entertainment Weekly* 49/3 "**sanity fair** A magazine Faith will not be gracing the cover of." [*sanity* n in senses 1 & 2 + *fair*[2] n in sense 1, adapted fr. *Vanity Fair* 'name of a magazine', fr. *Vanity Fair*]

saveage n Rescue
1998 Jan 20 Whedon *Innocence* "Thus freeing us up for world saveage." [B] 1999 Gilman and Sherman *Visitors* 3 "Enough world-saveage for one night." [*save*[1] vt in sense 1.a + *-age* suff in sense 4.a]

Scareapalooza n Festival of fright
1997 Oct 27 Ellsworth *Halloween* "Halloween quiet? I figured it would have been a big ole vamp Scareapalooza." [X] [*scare* vt + *lollapalooza* (also *HDAS* in sense 1 & *NTC* in sense 1), most immediately fr. the rock concert Lollapalooza, organized annually 1990–1998]

Scooby Gang 1.a: n Those who assist the Slayer
1997 Nov 17 Gordon and Noxon *What's My Line, Part 1* "You wanna be a member of the Scooby Gang, you gotta be willing to be inconvenienced now and then." [X] 1998 Dec 2 The Bronze "Maybe all the foreshadowing is just to throw us off, and she is destined to learn to love again, to truly become one of the scooby gang, and little flowers will spring up behind her whenever she walks." 1998 Golden and Holder *Blooded* 9 "But once the research was done, she'd already served her purpose in the little cadre of Friends of Buffy that Xander affectionately referred to as the Scooby Gang." 1999 May 13 The Bronze "[I]t would give enought

[sic] time to kill at least pone [sic] of the Scooby gang." 1999 Aug Richardson *Xposé* 16 "As Snyder becomes a nerdy young geek, so he becomes a temporary member of Buffy's 'Scooby Gang.'" 1999 Aug *Xposé* 25 [letter to the editor] "I am extremely grateful for the picture of our beloved Scooby Gang." 1999 Sep DeCandido *American Libraries* 44 "Buffy's buds (called affectionately the Slayerettes or the Scooby Gang) include the never-cool Xander; his best friend, the brilliant and fashion-impaired Willow." 1999 Oct 1 *Entertainment Weekly* 34/3 **"Historic moments** Miss Calendar and Cordy join the Scooby Gang." 1999 Oct 1 Howard *Entertainment Weekly* 49/3 **"scooby gang** Buffy and her slaying pals; reference to '70s TV cartoon *Scooby Doo*; also Undead Playgroup; Slayerettes." 1999 Oct 13 The Bronze "'Shall we assemble the Scooby Gang?'" [signature] 1999 Oct Watson *Buffy the Vampire Slayer* 14 [Dark Horse Comics] [29] "The panels with the 'Scooby Gang' at the movie theatre on page eight were great." 1999 Iyer *Official Yearbook* 20/1 "She fills the role of the Scooby Gang's Daphne pretty well." 1999 Golden and Holder *Immortal* 205 "To put it bluntly, the Scooby Gang were going about their regular lives, on hold until Buffy needed them." 1999 Golden and Holder *Out of the Madhouse* 9 "'So what do we do? List the Slayerettes Club or Scooby Gang or whatever under our activities in the yearbook and go back to the real world?'" [C] 2000 Sep 1 The Bronze "[A] strange sense of deja vu unsettled our wacky scooby gang all summer long." 2000 Nov Watson *Pale Reflections* [5] "As the town prepares for a huge outdoor festival and parade, Buffy, Angel, and the Scooby Gang must get to the heart of Sunnydale's Bad Blood problem." 2000 Dokey *Here Be Monsters* 23 "As a result, the Scooby Gang was sort of on hiatus." 2000 Topping *Slayer* 20 "Given that the entire population of the USA will, according to recent statistics, be clinically obese by the year 2032, how likely is it that a group of high school misfits like the Scooby Gang would all be slim to the point of anorexia?" 2000 Holder *Watcher's Guide* 2 32 "Buffy realizes that that's what they did to Spike—who has sought asylum with the Scooby Gang." 2001 Jun 2 The Bronze "I'm assuming she's learned/inherited some of Buffy's strength and, along with the Scooby Gang, will carry on as Buffy would want, to honor Buffy's memory." 2001 Jul Petrie *Food Chain* [67] "Yeah, you're talking to the Scooby Gang here. Normal for us has more than the usual loop-

holes." [O] 2001 Aug Epstein *Out* 48/1 "In fall 1999 the 'Scooby Gang' (their self-given nickname because of their tendency to be those 'meddling kids' who ruin the bad guy's day) arrived at college." 2001 Nov 12 buffysearch.com "Season 6 is waiting there for you. [T]he Scooby Gang need you." 2001 Nov Spelling *Xposé* 33/2 "As the episode ended, it did so with the Scooby Gang realizing what they've done." 2001 Dec Andrews *Starburst* 23/1 "[T]he Scooby gang are desperately trying to protect the town by using a robot Buffy." 2001 Kaveney *Reading the Vampire Slayer* 5 "These emotional structures have more in common with soap opera relationships than with most genre series—an original core of characters, which eventually becomes known as the Scooby gang, in homage to the cartoon series *Scooby Doo* which also features a group of young adventurers who fight what often appears to be supernatural evil, but is almost always rationalized away." 2002 Sep 13 Robischon *Entertainment Weekly* 158/3 "Gamers who don't know the Scooby Gang from Shaggy may find *Slayer* less exciting." 2002 Edwards *Fighting the Forces* 91 "The road to acceptance begins when Buffy, in front of Giles and the Scooby Gang, thanks Kendra for saving her life during an assassin's attack at school." See SLAYERETTES

    1.b: n An element in a URL
2001 Jun 2 The Bronze "ScoobyGang.com" 2001 Nov 12 buffysearch.com "scoobygang.net"

    1.c: n An element in names
2001 Jun 2 The Bronze "Scooby Gangster"

    2: n *attrib* By or associated with Buffy's friends
2001 Jun 2 The Bronze "I know Joss doesn't want to go with the alternative universe Buffy and I also don't see a scooby gang resurrection either." [fr. *Scooby Doo* 'name of the canine hero in the cartoon television series *Scooby Doo* (originally aired 1969–1986), in which the dog and his friends are sleuths of the supernatural' + *gang*[1] n in sense 3]

    —**Scoobies** n The circle of Buffy's associates
2000 Sep 1 The Bronze "Since the vamps and demons also seem to enjoy summer vacation, I'll say the Scoobies spent plenty of time decompressing and relaxing." 2000 Oct 3 Fury *Real Me* "'They're gonna be a little while longer doing the detective thing—best non-Scoobies like you and

me stay out of their way.'" [Amber] 2000 Holder *Watcher's Guide* 2 48 "Together they take on Sunday and her gang, with all the Scoobies arriving just in time to watch Buffy mop up the mess." 2001 Jun 2 The Bronze "If dawn was slated to die I could of [sic] seen the ending a little differently: Buffy/Glory fighting and Buffy losing miserably, while the other Scoobies are captured." 2001 Nov 10 Whedon *Once More, with Feeling* "You're the cutest of the Scoobies/With your lips as red as rubies/And your firm but supple, tight embrace." [X] 2001 Dec Andrews *Starburst* 24/1 "He'd walked the whole path from prime threat, to loser, to neutered loser, to unwelcome hanger-on who betrays the Scoobies and thus alienates the only people who had been willing to tolerate him." 2001 Sayer *Reading the Vampire Slayer* 108 "The Scoobies' fluidity, and therefore their strength is highlighted when, though he has been absent since the middle of Season Four, in the middle of Season Five, Xander remembers Oz as another man who'd get his jokes." 2002 Jul 30 Bronze: Beta "Standing around the merry-go-round, but far away are the scoobies." 2002 Dechert *Fighting the Forces* 218 "One factor that ties the Scooby Gang together is a shared love of popular music, and in this, the Scoobies are no different than typical teens." [*Scooby* 'member of the SCOOBY GANG' + -s[1] suff] See SLAYERETTES

—**Scoobs** n The circle of Buffy's associates
2000 Holder *Watcher's Guide* 2 133 "She discovers the level of contempt the Scoobs hold her in." 2002 Jul 30 Bronze: Beta "No selfish motive there to be good in order to attract Buffy. Just a guilty conscience that he [Spike] wasn't able to protect Dawn and Buffy on that tower, and the determination to keep Dawn safe, despite being bored to tears with no immediate threat apparent cause Buffy was not there to do so herself and the Scoobs had left Dawn in his charge." [SCOOBIES] See SLAYERETTES

—**Scooby** 1: n Member of the SCOOBY GANG
2001 Kaveney *Reading the Vampire Slayer* 8 "Spike's subsequent status as a quasi-Scooby and as Buffy's suitor could thus be explained without the assumption that he is necessarily engaged in any process of redemption." 2002 Feb Fassbender and Pascoe *Buffy the Vampire Slayer* 42 [Dark Horse Comics] [6] "'Just because I can't cast spells or do a good job with research, I'm suddenly a second-class Scooby.'" [X] 2002 Jul

30 Bronze: Beta "When one Scooby (you know the real Scoobies, the big 4 of hand, heart, mind and spirit) would interact with the other, or spy [on] the other, that was shared and concurrent." 2002 Larbalestier *Fighting the Forces* 234 "He wants to be a Scooby."

2: n attrib Of or pertaining to the SCOOBY GANG
2000 Oct 3 Fury *Real Me* "You're completely one of the gang now… maybe I can talk to the rest of the group and we can do something, some kind of Scooby intiation." [W] 2000 Holder *Watcher's Guide* 2 60 "In 'New Moon Rising' Tara has been invited to sit in on a Scooby meeting." 2001 Jun 2 The Bronze "Perhaps the new scooby crew could all sport hats of various styles." 2001 Oct 2 Noxon *Bargaining* 1 "[Dawn:] 'What's tonight?' [Tara:] 'Oh, just a Scooby meeting.'" 2002 May 7 DeKnight *Seeing Red* "I don't think he's really in the Scooby space. Give him some time." [B] 2002 Jul 29 Bronze: Beta "There are quite a few people who do feel they can't cope with the whole Scooby ambience and leave with or without their shields, rather than on them." [fr. SCOOBY (GANG)]

—**Scoobycentric** adj Focused from the perspective of Buffy's friends
2000 Oct 24 Petrie *All in the Family* "Actually, I have a little Scooby-centric deal to deal with first." [B] [SCOOBY (GANG) + -centric suff in sense 3] See BUFFYCENTRIC sv BUFFY

—**Scooby ganger** n A member of the SCOOBY GANG
1999 Oct 1 *Entertainment Weekly* 36/3 "A devoted Will discovers Xander and Cordy kissing—which opens the door for Oz, now a Scooby Ganger." [SCOOBY GANG + -er suff in sense 1.d]

—**Scooby-sense** Faculty by which members of the SCOOBY GANG sense danger
2001 Jul Rich and Clugston-Major *Food Chain* [132] "I don't know, but my Scooby-sense is tingling." [W] [SCOOBY + *sense* n in sense 1.a] See SLAYER SENSE sv SLAYER and SPIDER-SENSE

—**semi-Scooby** n One who resembles a SCOOBY in some character-istics
2002 Wilcox *Fighting the Forces* 6 "[Buffy] accepts help from her enemy the phallically named punk vampire Spike (later a semi-Scooby)." [semi-pref in sense 3 + SCOOBY in sense 2]

scorage n   Points
1999 Gilman and Sherman *Visitors* 72 "[Xander:] 'You mock me.' [Willow:] 'I see target, I take aim, I achieve scorage.'"   [*score* n in sense 2.c + *-age* suff in sense 1.a]

scrollage n   Quick scanning of text on a computer screen
2000 Sep1 The Bronze "~*~ More scrollage~*~"   2000 Sep 1 The Bronze "Forgive the non scrollage but I have drunk a wee bit much tonight and the scrolling would for sure hurt my eyes."   2002 Jul 25 Bronze: Beta "[W]ill attempt scrollage at whup [i.e., work] tomorrow."   2002 Jul 30 Bronze: Beta "For tomorrow's scrollage, as I know you are going beddy-bye now."   [*scroll* vi in sense 1 + *age* suff in sense 1.a]

scrollsville n   Reviewing posting board activity
2002 Jul 23 Bronze: Beta "Hello Bronzers and lurkers, off to scrollsville." [*scroll* vi in sense 1 + *-s-* + *-ville* suff]

Scully 1 : vt   Make (one) exercise skepticism
1997 Apr 7 Kiene and Reinkemeyer *The Pack* "I cannot believe that you of all people are trying to Scully me." [B]   1999 Oct 1 Howard *Entertainment Weekly* 49/3 "(**to**) **scully** Explain paranormal activity with scientific rationale; homage to Dana Scully of *The X-Files*."
   2 : *adj*   Skeptical
1999 Odom *Unnatural Selection* 77 "Willow turned on her. 'You drive stakes through the hearts of vampires on a daily—make that nightly—basis, and you're trying to talk me out of believing in fairies? Don't go Scully on me, Buffy.'"   [fr. Dana Scully, 'name of a principal character in the Fox Network television series *The X-Files*, which first aired 10 September 1993']

secret agency *adj*   Clandestine
2002 Feb 26 Petrie *As You Were* "So, you gonna say good-bye this time, or just split all secret agency like last time?" [D]   [*secret* adj in sense 3 + *agent* n in sense 5 + *-y*[1] suff in sense 2.a]

Sherlock v   Investigate
2002 May 7 DeKnight *Seeing Red* "We should go back. Tara and I could

Sherlock around." [W] [fr. Sherlock Holmes 'name of a fictional private consulting detective featured, from 1887, in many novels and short stories by Arthur Conan Doyle, and in much subsequent fiction and film by various authors']

show v Come
1997 Mar 10 Whedon *Welcome to the Hellmouth* "You should show." [C] 1998 Golden and Holder *Child of the Hunt* 6 "'All I asked was that you show.'" [Joyce] 1999 Golden and Holder *Out of the Madhouse* 202 "'And all we can do to get them to show is insult them?'" [O] 2000 Holder *The Evil That Men Do* 45 "'And I didn't show,' Buffy thought miserably. 'Because I fell asleep at Angel's.'" [*show up* sv *show* v (also *DAS3 show up* v phr)]

shrimpy adj Full of shrimp
2002 Jul 30 Bronze: Beta "A man and a woman are on a date. At the end of the date, the man is feeling pretty attracted to the woman and is hoping she's attracted too. The woman, on the other hand, is feeling slightly nauseated by the smell of the guy's cologne and the shrimp she ate at dinner, and wants nothing more than to get inside, lock the door behind her, and drink a gallon of Pepto-Bismol. [...] The woman has the door unlocked now. Her stomach has never felt worse. [...] 'No, I can't let you in tonight, sorry.' With that she whips around the door and slams it in his face. [...] She then runs to the bathroom to take care of her shrimpy stomach." [*shrimp* n in sense 1 + -*y*¹ suff in sense 1]

sighage n Sighs
2000 Sep 1 The Bronze "And his devotion to Willow, even now that they're no longer together, is something I never get tired of watching. Much sighage there." [*sigh* n + -*age* suff in sense 1.a]

signage n Autograph
1999 Apr 29 The Bronze "You still want Juliet [Landau] signage?" 1999 Apr 29 The Bronze "*LB* or anyone who went to the concert after the James [Marsters] signage: Moriah posted I think earlier today, but she had a different e-addy." [*sign* vt in sense 2 + -*age* suff in sense 4.b]

single entendre 1 : n The obvious
1998 Jan 27 Des Hotel and Batali *Phases* "That's great, Larry, you've really mastered the art of the single entendre." [O]   2000 Feb 29 *Angel* (WB) "[Cordelia:] 'Demons, Demons, Demons. Wow. They put a lot of thought into that title.' [Wesley:] 'It's a demon database. What would you call it?' [Cordelia:] 'I don't know. How 'bout...Demon Database?' [Wesley:] 'Ah. A name rife with single-entendre.'"

   2: adj Transparent, straightforward
2000 Feb 29 *Angel* (WB) "I'm way too single entendre to benefit from therapy." [C] [*single adj* in sense 2.a + double *entendre n* in sense 2]

single-white female v Harass someone by imitating them obsessively
1998 Oct 13 Greenwalt *Faith, Hope, and Trick* "[Joyce:] 'Does anybody else think Faith is creepy?' [Buffy:] 'No, but I'm the one getting single-white-femaled here.'"   1999 Oct 1 Howard *Entertainment Weekly* 49/3 "**single white femaled** Have existence duplicated by an obsessive acquaintance in manner of Jennifer Jason Leigh/Bridget Fonda film." [fr. *Single White Female* 'title of a film dir. Barbet Schroeder (1992)' + -*ed* suff?]

sitch 1.a: n Situation
1992 Whedon *Buffy the Vampire Slayer* "What's the sitch? I'm bored." [B]   1992 Whedon *Buffy the Vampire Slayer* "Buffy, what's your sitch?" 1997 Mar 10 Whedon *Welcome to Hellmouth* "What's the sitch?" [B] 1997 Golden and Holder *Halloween Rain* 38 "'No way. You stay up here. Monitor the sitch.'"   1998 Winter *Buffy the Vampire Slayer* 50 "**sitch:** [...] n. [B] situation."   1998 Gardner *Return to Chaos* 242 "Buffy bopped into the room. She was smiling for a change. Well, that wouldn't last for long. 'Hey, what's the sitch?' she called."   1999 Apr 29 The Bronze "My financial sitch is so lousy right now that I worry that I won't be able to afford a move anytime soon."   1999 May 13 The Bronze "Sorry to hear about the job sitch."   1999 Golden and Holder *Immortal* 112 "'Here's the sitch. We cruised the deadfill for grave-robbers, and we found some.'" [C]   1999 Golden and Holder *Sons of Entropy* 217 "Not unless Buffy and Giles had something up their sleeves back in Sunnydale that they hadn't told anyone about. That would be nice, especially since they didn't know

the sitch." 2000 Jan *Teen* 47/1 "**DOWN TO YOU The stars**: Freddie Prinze, Jr., Julia Stiles, Selma Blair, Shawn Hatosy, Ashton Kutcher **The sitch**: College kids Al and Imogen fall in love, but when mischievous outsiders enter the picture, they find that staying committed is harder than they thought." 2000 Holder *The Evil That Men Do* 193 "'Please, you know the sitch.'" [B] 2000 Garton *Resurrecting Ravana* 113 "'What's the sitch?'" [O] 2000 Sep 1 The Bronze "I have salvaged the sitch somewhat."

    1.b: n Good situation
1992 Whedon *Buffy the Vampire Slayer* "[Girl:] 'Is Jeffrey really spending the night at your house?' [Buffy:] 'That's the plan.' [Girl:] 'Oooh, what a sitch.'" [fr. situation n in sense 2]

skulky *adj* Given to or characterized by lurking in corners
1999 Golden and Holder *Ghost Roads* 150 "[Angel:] 'They might not be our roadies, but they're skulking around the way those guys tend to skulk.' [Oz:] 'They're very skulky.'" [skulk v in sense 1 + y¹ suff in sense 1]

slay 1.a: vi Kill vampires or other demons
1998 Jan 12 Noxon *Bad Eggs* "[Buffy:] 'Dissect it? Why me?' [Xander:] 'Because you're the Slayer.' [Buffy:] 'And I slayed! My work here is done.'" 1998 Golden and Holder *Blooded* 33 "'Suddenly, I'd rather be Slaying,' she muttered to herself." [B] 1999 May 13 The Bronze "They were going to slay!" 2000 Passarella *Ghoul Trouble* 65 "'We've done some amateur slaying on our own, now and then.'" [W] 2000 Holder *Watcher's Guide* 2 159 "Xander and Willow help Buffy slay as a distraction from their broken hearts." 2001 Feb 20 Espenson *I Was Made to Love You* "I could spend less time slaying." [B] 2001 Apr 24 Espenson *Intervention* "I don't know. To slay, to kill—it means being hard on the inside." [B] 2001 Jun 2 The Bronze "if so will SMG somehow come back to slay again?" 2001 Jul Golden *Food Chain* [20] "The one time I listen to Giles' advice **not** to 'Slay first, ask questions later'...that oughta teach me." [B] 2001 Sayer *Reading the Vampire Slayer* 117 "There is one example of Buffy slaying there [...] and one episode when she shops there with her mom." 2001 Playden *Reading the Vampire Slayer* 127 "[T]hey are born Slayers and simultaneously they learn to slay." 2002 Jul 30

Bronze: Beta "He stayed, he slayed, he baby-sat Dawn." 2002 Odom *Crossings* 157 "'I can't stay. I've gotta slay.'" [B]

   1.b: vt Kill vampires or other demons

1997 Dec 8 Greenwalt and Whedon *Ted* "[Buffy:] 'Vampires are creeps.' [Giles:] 'Yes, that's why one slays them.'" 1997 Golden and Holder *Halloween Rain* 86 "'Well,' he said, 'we're just going to have to slay those vampires outside, now aren't we.'" [G] 1998 Winter Boris *Buffy the Vampire Slayer* 54 "The vamps are slayed, the babies are saved—and all in less than five minutes' time." 1998 Golden and Holder *Child of the Hunt* 315 "'Buffy, I command your loyalty,' Hern the Hunter declared. 'Slay my son.'" 1998 Cover *Night of the Living Rerun* 162 "'Slay them!' said Xander/Sarah desperately, turning to Buffy. 'Why don't you slay them?'" 1999 Oct Watson *Buffy the Vampire Slayer* 14 [Dark Horse Comics] [29] "I guess it would be cool seeing my favorite Vampire Slayer slaying Vampires." 1999 Odom *Unnatural Selection* 205 "Buffy hated letting them go, wishing she was able to slay them all now, but there was no way." 2000 Sep 1 The Bronze "Slayed vampires and went to Disneyworld." 2000 Nov Watson *The Remaining Sunlight* [87] "Fun. How do I slay him?' [B] 2000 Holder *The Evil That Men Do* 131 "'I'm the McDonalds of slaying. Over three billion slain.'" [B] 2000 Gilman and Sherman *Deep Water* 74 "'You know I get cranky when I can't slay something.'" [B] 2001 Odom *Revenant* 162 "He and Cordelia Chase had never traveled in the same circles—except when they were out slaying vampires and other demonic beings." 2001 Kaveney *Reading the Vampire Slayer* 34 "And the almost classic encounter at the start of 'The Gift' may prove the last time she actually slays a vampire." 2001 Sayer *Reading the Vampire Slayer* 117 "There is one example of Buffy slaying there [...] and one episode when she shops there with her mom." 2001 Playden *Reading the Vampire Slayer* 127 "[T]hey are born Slayers and simultaneously they learn to slay." 2002 Odom *Crossings* 112 "'How?' Buffy asked [...] 'By slaying the Craulathar demon,' Spike replied." 2002 Jul 30 Bronze: Beta "I almost expected to see Buffy slaying a vamp over at the next crypt." 2002 Jul 31 Bronze: Beta "Warren slays the big demon at the beginning." 2002 Edwards *Fighting the Forces* 87 "In Whedon's world, monsters are often the shy boy next door or the homecoming queen, and the hero who slays them is a girl."

1.c: *v* Defeat something other than vampires, as though one were a Slayer of them

1999 May 13 The Bronze "Hopefully DarkLady will be willing to slay any and all roaches that may invade our room." 2000 Sept 27 Noxon *Buffy vs. Dracula* "Buffy slayed the football." [R] 2001 Playden *Reading the Vampire Slayer* 121 "Over the years, the feminist project has been concerned to slay its own vampires, in the form of ideas that, hundreds of years old, have prowled and fed on society's marginalized communities, especially women." 2002 Mar *Teen People* 89/2 "**BEST BUTT-KICKING FEMALE (LITERALLY AND METAPHORICALLY) Sarah Michelle Gellar** (*Buffy the Vampire Slayer*) (36.596) The kickboxing coed slayed the competition." 2002 Feb Fassbender and Pascoe *Buffy the Vampire Slayer* 42 [Dark Horse Comics] [28] "Slay the Critics" [title of "Letters to the Editor" section]

1.d: *v* An element in names

1999 May 13 The Bronze "If [S]layanna comes in, tell her I said 'hey.'" 1999 Jun 26 The Bronze "slay_me" 2000 Sep 1 The Bronze "BuffyRileySlayTA"

2: *adj* Inclined to kill vampires and demons

1999 Jan/Feb *Cinescape* [cover] "Slay Time: The Complete Guide to Buffy the Vampire Slayer." 1999 Apr 27 Espenson *Earshot* "Scabby demon number two got away. Scabby demon number one—bug check in the slay column." [B] 1999 Jul 13 Whedon *Graduation, Part 2* "My point, however, is, crazy or not, it's pretty much the only plan. Besides, it's Buffy's, and she's slay gal—you know, Little Miss Likes-to-Fight." [C] 2001 Apr 24 Espenson *Intervention* "I was, um, thinking about maybe taking a break or something. Just ease off for a while, not get into full slay mode." [B]

3: *n* Killing

1999 Nov 30 Forbes *Something Blue* "Oh, make a move. Please. I'm dying for a good slay." [B] 2002 Jul 31 Bronze: Beta "'Normal Again'—Sex—no. Slayage—much demon fighting, one Slay. (And some near-Slays—oops…)." [fr. *slay vt* in sense 1]

—**non-slayey** *adj* Other than involving slaying

1999 Nov 23 Espenson *Pangs* "I do want to stop him. I'd just like to find

a non-slayey way to do it." [B] [fr. non- *pref* + SLAY + -(e)y[1] *suff* in sense
1]

——**slayed** *adj* An element in names
2001 Jun 2 The Bronze "Slayed Soul" [SLAY + -ed[2] *suff*]

——**slayground** 1.a: n Name of a BTVS focused website
2000 Sep 1 The Bronze "The slayground rocks!" 2001 Jun 2 The Bronze
"Slayground is full of fun facts to know and tell about Buffy the Vampire
Slayer and spinoff Angel."

1.b: n Component in a website address   1999 Apr 29 The Bronze
"Little Willow's Slayground" [link in signature] [fr. SLAY + *playground* n
in sense 1]

——**slay-heavy** *adj* Filled with vampire killing
1999 Oct 5 Whedon *The Freshman* "I've been busy, you know? It's been a
slay-heavy summer." [B] [SLAY v in sense 1.a + *heavy* adj in sense 3.b]

——**slaying** (and **vampire slaying**) 1.a: n Vocation to kill vampires
and demons
1997 Oct 6 Kiene and Reinkemeyer *Inca Mummy Girl* "Oh, I know this
one: 'Slaying entails certain sacrifices, blah, blah, blahbiddy, blah, I'm so
stuffy, give me a scone.'" [B] 1997 Golden and Holder *Halloween Rain* 9
"Buffy was the Chosen One. Slaying was her job."   1998 Dec 2 The
Bronze "The book is tentatively titled 'Come as You Aren't: Anonymity,
Community, and Vampire Slaying in Cyberspace.'" 1998 Gardner *Return
to Chaos* 50 "'I was hoping Slaying might lead to a career.'" [B] 1998
Golden and Holder *Blooded* 56 "'Because when it comes to this life, to
Slaying, it doesn't feel like just me, Willow Rosenberg, against all this
horrible stuff.'" 1999 Feb 16 Noxon *Consequences* "From now on, anything you have to say about slaying, you say to me." [Wesley] 1999
Gilman and Sherman *Visitors* 16 "How much can you talk about before
you get to the subjects marked Do Not Mention in big red letters? Those
subjects being Slaying, Slaying, and the ever popular Slaying." 2000 Feb
29 Whedon *Who Are You* "Buffy's, like, my best friend, and she's really
special, plus, you know, Slayer, that's a deal, and there's the whole bunch
of us, and we have this group that revolves around the slaying, and I
really want you to meet them and meet Buffy." [W] 2000 Gallagher
Prime Evil 236 "Spellcasting came naturally to her, just like slaying came

naturally to Buffy." 2000 Topping *Slayer* 77 "Buffy is worried that Slaying is interfering with her trigonometry homework." 2000 Holder *Watcher's Guide* 2 46 "In her first public speech about MOO [Mothers Opposed to the Occult], Joyce equates slaying with all the other strange things wrong with Sunnydale." 2001 Apr 24 Espenson *Intervention* "[Buffy:] 'I'm just starting to feel uneasy about stuff.' [Giles:] 'Stuff?' [Buffy:] 'Training. Slaying. All of it.'" [B] 2001 Daugherty *Reading the Vampire Slayer* 159 "Even Buffy, which obviously promotes female strength and power, still avoids open mention of menstruation, except during Buffy's row with her mother in 'Becoming Part 2' (2.22), when a general equation of Slaying and sexuality [...] includes as part of Buffy's list of Joyce's state of denial a mention of having to wash bloodstains out of Buffy's clothes." 2001 West *Reading the Vampire Slayer* 184 '[T]he displays of martial arts are more thoroughly incorporated in to the act of slaying." 2002 Jul 27 Bronze: Beta "If you can make a Slaying show without Buffy, Dawn could be part of a group that serves Buffy's role." 2002 Odom *Crossings* 4 "'Not the slaying,' Buffy said. 'That hasn't gotten any harder.'" 2002 Vowell *The Partly Cloudy Patriot* 111 "Vampire slaying requires an astonishing amount of research."

1.b: n Destruction of vampires and demons
1997 Mar 31 Des Hotel and Batali *Never Kill a Boy on the First Date* "Ninety percent of the vampire-slaying game is waiting." 1997 Golden and Holder *Halloween Rain* 20 "'Attention K-Mart shoppers, no slaying tonight.'" [X] 1998 Oct 13 Greenwalt *Faith, Hope, and Trick* "Slayin' always just makes you hungry and horny." [F] 1998 Tracy *The Girl's Got Bite* 204 "While Xander accidentally killed a vampire in the past [...] most of the slaying has been at the hands of Buffy." 1998 Gardner *Return to Chaos* 7 "He depended on Buffy for most of the slaying." 1998 Cover *Night of the Living Rerun* 146 "Buffy had done a bunch of slaying at a nearby post office." 1999 Fall *Buffy the Vampire Slayer* 29 "She doesn't want to eat or to...do anything else after Slaying." 2000 Garton *Resurrecting Ravana* 265 "'In your hands, Buffy, I have great faith that nothing will [happen to it]. Except, of course, for the slaying of Rakshasa.'" [G] 2000 Holder *Watcher's Guide* 2 87 "They joke about the new Olympic category, 'synchronized slaying.'" 2001 Playden *Reading the Vampire Slayer* 134 "It is this transformative potential—enacted literally by Buffy's day-

time school and college, and her night-time slaying—that is the theologically and philosophically important aspect of Buffy." 2002 Jul 31 Bronze: Beta "I think Slaying got more screen time here." 2002 Odom *Crossings* 62 "'Get us into the way station and let us do a bit of slaying so I can get on with my evening.'" [S] 2002 Edwards *Fighting the Forces* 91 "Kendra begins to accept Buffy's style of slaying, too."

 2: n Episode of destroying vampires or other demons
1998 Nov 17 Petrie *Revelations* "You telegraph punches, leave blind sides open, and, for a school-night slaying, you both take entirely too much time." [Gwendolyn Post] 2000 Garton *Resurrecting Ravana* 101 "There's nothing more dangerous than amateurs crashing a Slaying.'" [B]

 3: n attrib Pertaining to killing vampires
1998 Golden and Holder *Child of the Hunt* 85 "[I]t bugged her a little whenever they put her in the fearless leader position during a non-Slaying event." 1999 Oct 1 *Entertainment Weekly* 33/1 "Xander overhears Giles scolding Buffy about her slaying ambivalence." 1999 Oct Watson *Buffy the Vampire Slayer* 14 [Dark Horse Comics] [2] "Slaying time." [B] 1999 Golden and Holder *Ghost Roads* 77 "'Now I think it's just the whole slaying thing, the whole hero thing, that's got him.'" [C] 1999 *Official Yearbook* 81/3 "Above ground, while Giles critiques Buffy's slaying form as she dusts another vampire, they discover a ring left behind in the ashes." 2000 Dokey *Here Be Monsters* 101 "It wasn't smart to leave your back exposed. Any Slayer, and a whole lot of non-slaying people, knew that." 2000 Topping *Slayer* 74 "When Xander is telling Cordelia not to mention Buffy's Slaying abilities in public, watch the guy in the blue shirt on the right of the screen." 2000 Holder *Watcher's Guide* 2 2 "Buffy thought her slaying days were over, and that she could return to the life of a normal teenager." 2002 Pender *Fighting the Forces* 35 "Feminist critiques of popular culture frequently mobilize a strategy similar to Buffy's slaying technique when they question if any given text is part of the solution, or part of the problem." [SLAY + -ing² suff in sense 1.a]

 —**Slaymaster General** n Slayer
2000 Oct 24 Petrie *All in the Family* "You're not worried about the Slaymaster General, are you big chief?" [X] [SLAY in sense 1.a + Postmaster General]

—**slayworthy** *adj* Excellent

2001 Jun 2 The Bronze "your girl [link]::over two dozen slayworthy sites" [signature]   [SLAY + -*worthy suff in sense 2*]

—**Slay you later** *catch phr* See you later

1999 May 13 The Bronze "Slay you later, I'm having my TEA!"   [SLAY + *you pron in sense 1 + later adv sv late adj in sense 1*]

slayage 1.a: n Killing (vampires or other demons)

1997 May 19 Whedon *Out of Mind, Out of Sight* "It's all part of the glamorous world of vampire slayage."   1997 Oct 27 Ellsworth *Halloween* "I was late due to unscheduled slayage." [B]   1997 Golden and Holder *Halloween Rain* 14 "One in every generation, that was Giles' favorite part of the Big Book of Slayage."   1998 Jan 27 Des Hotel and Batali *Phases* "Sorry I'm late. I had to do some unscheduled slayage in the form of Theresa." [B]   1998 Oct 6 Noxon *Dead Man's Party* "You guys seem down with the slayage, all tricked out with your walkies and everything." [B]   1998 Oct Brereton *The Dust Waltz* [14] "'Xander, just because a person looks extremely frightening, we can't automatically assume they're in need of slayage.'" [B]   1998 Nov 5 The Bronze "There is no profit in slayage."   1998 Golden and Holder *Child of the Hunt* 130 "'As former treasurer of the We Hate Cordelia club, and current Semi-Grand Poobah of World Slayage Incorporated, I open this meeting of We Jolly Four.'" [X]   1998 Golden and Holder *Watcher's Guide* 1 11 "Rule Five: Don't be fooled by a lull in slayage."   1998 Stafford *Bite Me!* 29 "Make Way for Some Serious Slayage" [section title]   1998 Tracy *The Girl's Got Bite* 204 "But in the church, Xander, Cordelia, Giles, and Willow all participate in the slayage."   1999 Oct 1 *Entertainment Weekly* 34/3 "Cordy warns a cranky Buffy, who, still haunted by her death experience, returns from her summer in L.A. with zero interest in slayage, friends, and Angel."   1999 Oct 13 The Bronze "Maybe not consciously, but she is developing a life outside of the slayage."   1999 Odom *Unnatural Selection* 40 "She'd pulled her hair back in case Willow's call resulted in some real Slayage."   1999 Golden and Holder *Immortal* 15 "'Time off from slayage doesn't get any better than this.'" [B]   2000 Holder *The Evil That Men Do* 93 "She changed into more slayage-friendly clothes."   2000 Garton *Resurrecting Ravana* 40 "There had been a lot of excess slayage lately, complete with late hours and little sleep, and she was feeling over-worked." 2000 Holder *Watcher's Guide* 2 10 "Watchers are responsible for training their Slayers in the ways of, well, slayage." 2002 Feb 26 Petrie *As You Were* "I just thought you were busy with the slayage, 'cause of the gross stain." [W] 2002 Jul 30 Bronze: Beta "And Spike was the only person [...] who seemed at all concerned with actually listening to her, and spending time with her that didn't involve her 'getting over it' and getting back to slayage as usual." 2002 Jul 31 Bronze: Beta "The Slayage seems to be an afterthought in many episodes." 2002 Overbey and Preston-Matto *Fighting the Forces* 75 "Buffy is easily able to play with language in this way—it is tied to Slayage." [SLAY + -*age* suff in sense 4.a]

   1.b: n Discussion, scholarly or otherwise, about the BUFFYVERSE 1999 Mar 21 http://members.tripod.com/~SpiffyGalX/sm.htm "Spiffy Gal's Spiffy Slayage" [site title] 1999 Oct 1 *Entertainment Weekly* 32/1 "That said, let the slayage begin!" 2002 Wilcox and Lavery *Fighting the Forces* xxv "The wealth of material inspired the editors to launch an e-journal devoted to Buffy as well: *Slayage: The Online International Journal of Buffy Studies* (http://www.slayage.tv). [transf. metaphorically from SLAYAGE in sense 1.a]

   1.c: n Result of ultimate dispatch of things other than vampires or demons 1999 Mar 21 http://www2.uic.edu/~ahufan1/btvs/wns "Written, Not Scene: After Script Slayage [page title]

   2: n *attrib* Pertaining to killing vampires and demons 1998 Oct Brereton *The Dust Waltz* [18] "Weird. All last month was really slow-going in the slayage department." [B] 1998 Golden and Holder *Blooded* 134 "'Pit stop at my locker for my Slayage stuff.'" [B] 2000 Holder *The Evil That Men Do* 145 "Xander had assumed that once Mrs. Summers knew about Buffy's special calling, she'd let up. Give up trying to treat Buffy like a normal teenage girl and get on board the slayage train." 2000 Dokey *Here Be Monsters* 23 "Buffy thought it had something to do with the Slayage action during the last few days, which was definitely at an all-time low." 2000 Holder *Watcher's Guide* 2 21 "As Season Three begins, Willow, Xander, Oz, and Cordy have assumed the slayage duties." 2001 Odom *Revenant* 35 "The whole slayage thing [...] took up a lot of part-time job hours." [fr. SLAYAGE in sense 1.a]

Slayer (or **Vampire Slayer**) 1.a: n The one girl currently destined to hunt vampires and other demons
1992 Whedon *Buffy the Vampire Slayer* "The only one with the strength or skill to stop their heinous evil is the Slayer." 1997 May 12 Whedon *Nightmares* "So this is the Slayer. You're prettier than the last one." [The Master] 1998 Jan 19 Noxon *Surprise* "While I'm loath to say it, the fact is, the Slayer rarely lives into her mid-twenties." [G] 1998 Oct Doherty *Femmes Fatales* 9/4 "The versatile Sarah Michelle Gellar plays the high-kicking Buffy Sommers [sic], this generation's designated vampire slayer and luscious babe." 1998 Dec Ventura *Psychology Today* 59/2 "Two students, a boy and a girl, are Buffy's allies, but she's the Slayer." 1998 Golden and Holder *Child of the Hunt* 74 "'You really do think I'm a bimbo, don't you? The most air-headed Slayer in all of southern California.'" [B] 1998 Gardner *Return to Chaos* 291 "'Unfortunately, the only job opening I have is for Slayer's friend.'" [B] 1998 Golden and Holder *Blooded* 165 "[A]nother Watcher has been alerted, and readies his young lady for her debut [...] into the terrible world that shall be her secret domain: the world of the Vampire Slayer." 1998 Tracy *The Girl's Got Bite* 48 "He's a vampire, and her duty as the Slayer calls for her to kill him." 1999 Mar Watson *The Remaining Sunlight* [26] "Sunnydale's greatest fighter is a school girl **and** the Slayer." 1999 Jan/Feb Villanueva *Cinescape* 38/1 "She is the Slayer—strong, intuitive, courageous and able to kickbox in strappy leather sandals." 1999 Spring Springer *Buffy the Vampire Slayer* 12/1 "Three novels. Lots of scary monsters. One Slayer. Sound like fun?" 1999 Sep DeCandido *American Libraries* 44 "Giles is the Watcher: the source of training, counterintelligence, and guidance for high-school student Buffy Summers, the one of her generation to be chosen Vampire Slayer." 1999 Gilman and Sherman *Visitors* 2 "One of the few good things about being the Slayer, the one girl in all the world with the strength and skills, yadda yadda yadda, was that it made it a major chore for anyone to creep up on her." 1999 Gallagher *Obsidian Fate* 23 "In the Summers's household, breakfast meant Buffy had survived another night as the Slayer, the world's first and foremost line of defense against the

vampires and miscellaneous demons that staked their claim on Sunnydale at night." 1999 Golden and Holder *Out of the Madhouse* 6 "'So, it's not like you graduate and get your Slayer's diploma?'" [O] 2000 Nov Watson *Pale Reflections* [15] "A toast to a dead Slayer." 2000 Gallagher *Doomsday Deck* 13 "Sunnydale attacks the Slayer. That's a twist." [O] 2000 Garton *Resurrecting Ravana* 2 "The Slayer looked up at the moon in the ink-black sky." 2000 Topping *Slayer* 18 "She had the 'hairy mole' birthmark that identified her as The Slayer removed." 2001 Apr 24 Espenson *Intervention* "'I'm starting to feel like being the Slayer is turning me into stone.'" [B] 2001 Jun 2 The Bronze "About the slayer's power, I guess there is no physical explanation of the strength a slayer posses [sic]." 2001 Aug Epstein *Out* 48/1 "The show, based on Whedon's flop 1992 movie of the same name, centers around the Slayer (Sarah Michelle Gellar), whose job is to protect innocents (i.e., us human folk) from the likes of vampires, demons, and all-around shady characters." 2001 Sep 7 Jensen *Entertainment Weekly* 65/2 "Toodle-oo to Anthony Stewart Head, who plays the Slayer's tweedy British mentor, Giles." 2001 Oct 23 Fury and Espenson *Life Serial* "We took on the Slayer." [Warren] 2001 Nov 10 Whedon *Once More, with Feeling* "She'll get pissed / If I'm missed; / See, my sis / -ter's the Slayer." [D] 2001 Nov 13 Kirshner *Tabula Rasa* "I've taught you all I can about being the Slayer, and your mother taught you what you needed to know about life." [G] 2001 Nov Spelling *Xposé* 33/2 "In it, the Scooby Gang continued to mourn the loss of Buffy Summers [...] the beloved Slayer." 2001 Dec Andrews *Starburst* 22 "But Buffy's mother, Joyce, is as much the little girl lost as her daughter—listening to motivational tapes to help her be a better parent, trying to balance nurturing with discipline, and winning both the audience and the Slayer's respect in the process." 2001 Kaveney *Reading the Vampire Slayer* 23 "The dreams in 'Restless' (4.22), as well as being an opportunity for the First Slayer to punish them for drawing on her power, brings the four central characters of the show face to face with the dilemmas at the heart of their situations." 2001 Kaveney *Reading the Vampire Slayer* 27 "The Prime Slayer tells her that her gift is death, and she chooses to interpret that unselfishly, by dying rather than killing." 2001 Kaveney *Reading the Vampire Slayer* 36 "Is there any significance in the fact that William stays to be seduced and killed by Drusilla instead of hurrying home to look after his mother, whereas the Chinese Slayer he kills dies talking of her mother?" 2001 Playden *Reading the Vampire Slayer* 121 "Judging by standards such as Raymond's and Greer's, Buffy is another degrading sexploitation of the patriarchy, a woman who is objectified as a function—'the Slayer'—and controlled to serve ends which are not her own." 2001 Shuttleworth *Reading the Vampire Slayer* 228 "'The Slayer' is a distinct concept from 'Buffy Anne Summers,' and indeed the meat of the underlying drama lies in her attempts to reconcile the two elements of the series title or to find an accommodation with both." 2002 Feb 5 DeKnight *Dead Things* "We have two problems: the body and the Slayer." [Warren] 2002 Feb 26 Petrie *As You Were* "Finn, how could you recruit the Slayer without filling her in on the objective?" [Sam] 2002 May 7 DeKnight *Seeing Red* "Guys, hello! Slayer here." [B] 2002 May 21 Fury *The Grave* "I'll take anything you can throw at me, if it'll get me what I need to take care of the Slayer, give her what's coming to her." [S] 2002 Jul 29 Bronze: Beta "Well, it will be interesting to see if ME addresses the origins of the slayer in more detail." 2002 Navarro *Tempted Champions* 12 "'Doesn't the current Slayer have to die before you get a new one?'" [Tara] 2002 Wilcox *Fighting the Forces* 5 "Kendra points out that her unidentified culture takes the calling of Slayer very seriously." 2002 Pender *Fighting the Forces* 38 "Buffy's tank tops, high heels, and, most repetitively and insidiously, her cleavage suggest that, Slayer aside, Buffy herself is something of a stumbling block for feminist criticism." 2002 Overbey and Preston-Matto *Fighting the Forces* 75 "Humbled, Xander muses on the Slayer's skills." 2002 Edwards *Fighting the Forces* 90 "Like the classic tragic mulatta figure's, Kendra's quest for legitimacy, to be accepted as this generation's slayer, is denied because of the threat she poses to Buffy's identity as the slayer." 2002 Skwire *Fighting the Forces* 203 "Buffy's task, then, is not only to save Sunnydale as she has done so often before but also to save the group of people in Sunnydale who are, like her, neither children nor adults. She is neither child nor adult. She is 'Slayer.'" See CHOSEN ONE

    1.b: n Term of address for Buffy, as Slayer
1998 Golden and Holder *Child of the Hunt* 315 "'Kill him, Slayer!' the Erl King roared." 1998 Gardner *Return to Chaos* 66 "'When I come back, little miss Slayer, I won't be alone.'" [Gloria] 1998 Golden and Holder

Blooded 131 "'I'm thinking, Miss Slayer, that I left Xander at Willow's last night because he was all so worried about her, and now they're missing.'" [C] 1999 Oct Watson *Buffy the Vampire Slayer* 14 [Dark Horse Comics] [6] "'Let my friend go, Slayer.'" 2000 Oct 10 Espenson *The Replacement* "Oh, Slayer, one of these days." [S] 2000 Holder *The Evil That Men Do* 8 "Slayer, I come. I challenge you." 2001 Oct 23 Fury and Espenson *Life Serial* "C'mon, Slayer, a big fight's just what you need." [S] 2001 Jul Petrie *Food Chain* [78] "I'm doubting it, Slayer." 2002 Feb Fassbender and Pascoe *Buffy the Vampire Slayer* 42 [Dark Horse Comics] [3] "'Look, Slayer, the offer was on the table. You passed, so I went elsewhere.'" [S] 2002 Odom *Crossings* 58 "Spike rolled his eyes. 'Come on, Slayer. The Craulathar demon has gone to all this trouble to secure a mate.'" [S] 2002 Navarro *Tempted Champions* 64 "'You just keep on mocking me, Slayer.'" [S] [fr. sense 1.a]

   1.c: Any of a number of Slayers, historically or currently

1997 Mar 10 Whedon *Welcome to the Hellmouth* "[Giles:] 'Into each generation a Slayer is born, one girl, in all the world, a Chosen One, one born with the...' [Buffy:] '...the strength and skill to hunt the vampires, to stop the spread of evil, blah, blah, blah. I've heard it, okay?'" 1997 Mar 17 Reston *The Witch* "And a cranky slayer is a careless slayer." [B] 1997 Sep 29 Whedon and Greenwalt *School Hard* "You know what I find works real good with Slayers? Killing them." [S] 1997 Golden and Holder *Halloween Rain* 6 "And there had to be something to keep a Slayer busy on Halloween." 1998 Nov 10 Espenson *Band Candy* "You're my slayer. Knock those teeth down his throat!" [G] 1998 Edwards *Buffy X-posed* 75 "Little more than a wink is given to Buffy's past as a Slayer." 1998 Golden and Holder *Child of the Hunt* 209 "'This isn't the first time a Slayer has crossed paths with the Wild Hunt.'" [G] 1998 Gardner *Return to Chaos* 35 "'I never argue with a Slayer,' Xander replied." 1998 Cover *Night of the Living Rerun* 3 "'Other Slayers have kept dream journals.'" [G] 1999 Jan 12 St. John and Espenson *Gingerbread* "This isn't our town any more: it belongs to the monsters and the witches and the slayers." 1999 May 13 The Bronze "She is willing to fight so hard so that the people she loves stay safe, something that previous slayers knew nothing about." 1999 Fall *Buffy the Vampire Slayer* 29 "Now as she lies in a coma (keeping any other Slayers from being activated), maybe only Buffy un-

derstands the torment Faith's soul endured." 1999 *Official Yearbook* 8/1
"Through it all, she's staked her claim as the top Slayer." 1999 Golden
and Holder *Ghost Roads* 53 "'A hungry Slayer is a cranky Slayer,' [Oz]
riposted." 2000 Sept 27 Noxon *Buffy vs. Dracula* "Do you know what a
slayer is?" [B] 2000 Passarella *Ghoul Trouble* 23 "Slayers tended to die
young." 2001 Nov 27 Noxon *Wrecked* "That's what this is about? Doing
a Slayer?" [B] 2001 Odom *Revenant* 3 "Slayers, as a general rule, didn't
die of old age." 2001 Wall and Zryd *Reading the Vampire Slayer* 61 "Kendra
is a by-the-book Slayer whose regimented training by the Watcher's
Council [...] functions as more of a limitation than a strength." 2001
Playden *Reading the Vampire Slayer* 133 "Erishkigal is represented most
obviously by Faith, the Slayer-gone-bad, who figuratively kills Buffy by
taking her body from her." 2002 Mar Espenson *Haunted* [22] "[Wil-
low:] 'So the dream was sent to help you.' [Xander:] 'Wait? By Faith?'
[Buffy:] 'I don't think so. By whoever looks out for slayers, I guess.'"
2002 Jul 29 *Bronze: Beta* "Think watchers are as concerned with watching for Slayers turning as they are in watching for evil[?]" 2002 Navarro
Tempted Champions 12 "'Hey, maybe she's another rogue slayer, like Faith.'"
[W] 2002 *John Carpenter's Vampires: Los Muertos* "'Why do I need to
pose as an archaeologist?' 'The Mexican government has not yet recognized Vampire Slayer as a legitimate occupation.'" 2002 Wilcox *Fighting
the Forces* 4 "Like the king in a patriarchal succession, each Slayer is born
to the position and assumes it only on the death of the preceding Slayer."

   1.d: n One who dominates in some activity
1997 Oct 27 Ellsworth *Halloween* "Look, Buffy, you may be hot stuff when
it comes to demonology or whatever, but when it comes to dating, I'm
the Slayer." [C] 1997 Dec/1998 Jan Hedegaard *Rolling Stone* 180/2 "For
some reason, we don't think she's much of a slayer." 1998 Golden and
Holder *Child of the Hunt* 96 "Cordelia had once told Buffy she, Cordelia,
was the Slayer of dating. But she was also the Slayer of consumer abuse."
2000 Holder *The Evil That Men Do* 298 "'Who died and made you Slayer
slayer.'" [B] 2001 Nov 12 buffysearch.com "**Buffy the Patriarchy Slayer**
Explores feminist themes in BtVS." [site name] 2002 May 21 Petrie *Two
to Go* "[Willow:] 'C'mon, this is a huge deal for me. Six years as a sideman,
now I get to be the Slayer.' [Buffy:] 'A killer isn't a Slayer.'" 2002 Jul 25
Bronze: Beta "Dirty-Minded Bronzer Birds Club [...] no. 8 Sarah Michelle

Gellar (VIP Member)—'Slayer of Talk Show Smut.'" 2002 Wilcox and Lavery *Fighting the Forces* xviii "There is, in fact, a Web site titled "Buffy the Patriarchy Slayer [http://daringivens.home.mindspring.com/btps.html]." [fr. sense 1.a]

1.e: n As an element in names

1999 Apr 29 The Bronze "Shadowslayer" 1999 May 13 The Bronze "The English Slayer" 1999 May 13 The Bronze "Leather slayer" 1999 May 13 The Bronze "Thy Slayer." 1999 May 13 The Bronze "Adam the Canadian Vampire Slayer"

2: n Weapon

1999 May 13 The Bronze "Keeper of: the Louisville-Slayer-Slugger baseball bat Angel used on Faith."

3: n attrib Pertaining to Slayers

1997 Golden and Holder *Halloween Rain* 13 "'For me? I'm an extreme no-show tonight,' Buffy protested. 'It's the Slayer Superbowl.'" 1998 Oct 13 Greenwalt *Faith, Hope, and Trick* "I've tried to march in the Slayer pride parade but..." [Jonathan] 1998 Gardner *Return to Chaos* 29 "Her Slayer radar was working overtime." 1998 Gardner *Return to Chaos* 104 "She remembered with a pang how Kendra, in full Slayer mode, hadn't known how to act around Xander." 1998 Vornholt *Coyote Moon* 17 "It was bad enough that Willow and Xander knew about her Slayer secret and insisted on helping and/or meddling, as the case may be." 1999 Jan 19 Fury *Helpless* "Maybe what we should be looking for is something like Slayer kryptonite." 1999 Oct 1 *Entertainment Weekly* 25/2 "[H]e's been moping the world ever since, shunning other vampires and atoning for his multitudinous sins, even lending a hand to the slayer brigade." 1999 Oct 13 The Bronze "I could see him wanting Slayer blood." 1999 Oct Watson *Buffy the Vampire Slayer* 14 [Dark Horse Comics] [9] "'Are we talking some kind of Slayer kryptonite here?'" 1999 Golden and Holder *Sons of Entropy* 293 "Okay, time for a Slayer assessment of the sitch." 1999 Massie *Power of Persuasion* 22 "Not only was Giles the librarian, he was also her Watcher, the wise soul who was responsible for her Slayer training and education." 1999 Cover *Night of the Living Rerun* 131 "She had an idea. It was risky and broke every Slayer rule in the book, but that had never stopped her before." 1999 Gilman and Sherman *Visitors* 44 "'Great. Back to hitting up Giles for loans, I guess.

They've really got to reorganize, make the Slayer gig come with a paycheck.'" [B]   1999 Odom *Unnatural Selection* 4 "The way Buffy's mom said that let Willow know Buffy was out doing Slayer things."   1999 Gallagher *Obsidian Fate* 77 "Buffy grabbed her jacket and Slayer bag off the back doorknob."   2000 Oct 24 Petrie *All in the Family* "[Dawn:] 'What are you talking about?' [Buffy:] 'Slayer stuff.'"   2000 Holder *The Evil That Men Do* 298 "'Who died and made you Slayer slayer?'" [B]   2000 Nov Watson *Pale Reflections* [41] "[Willow:] 'Buffy, what's the problem?' [Buffy:] 'Nothing! Just—slayer stuff.'"   2000 Dokey *Here Be Monsters* 29 "She knew her Slayer strength and skills would give her a definite edge."   2000 Gilman and Sherman *Deep Water* 71 "'Hello Willy,' [Buffy] said in her most charming voice, giving him the benefit of full Slayer perkiness."   2000 Gallagher *Prime Evil* 5 "Since nothing supernatural registered on her Slayer sonar, Buffy had to conclude that Crystal Gordon was human."   2000 Holder *The Evil That Men Do* 6 "[Joyce:] 'And so you were going to attack me?' 'Not you,' Buffy blurted, then shrugged with a little laugh, 'Just my demons. Slayer in-joke there.'"   2001 Jun 2 The Bronze "But what about this slayer issue?"   2001 Jul Golden *Food Chain* [28] "Buffy, that's just......disgusting and, okay, amazing, but please tell me your aim had more to do with slayer skill than luck." [X]   2001 Oct 2 Fury *Bargaining* 2 "That's how all Slayer/Watcher relationships end." [G]   2001 Odom *Revenant* 16 "Bouncing lightly on her toes, getting her balance, Buffy sprinted toward the vampire, totally locked into Slayer mode."   2001 Sayer *Reading the Vampire Slayer* 102 "For example, re the Boxer Rebellion, we hear Spike's story of his first Slayer kill in 'Fool for Love' (5.7)."   2002 Feb 26 Petrie *As You Were* "And it's not just the Slayer status I'm talking about—it's you." [Sam]   2002 May 21 Petrie *Two to Go* "I get it now: the Slayer thing isn't about violence; it's about power." [W]   2002 Jul 23 Bronze: Beta "All that dealing—with vampires and reality and things that go bump in the night—was Buffy in the Slayer zone."   2002 Jul 28 Bronze: Beta "What I was telling her was that Drusilla has a slayer-like mind going for her and maybe she was a slayer-candidate that wasn't called before Angelus got to her."   2002 Navarro *Tempted Champions* 90 "'It's just a few bumps and thumps, nothing not included in the Slayer Job Description.'" [B]   2002 Helford *Fighting the Forces* 21 "I focus, in particular, on the three

Slayer characters introduced in the present day of the series: Buffy, Kendra, and Faith." 2002 Edwards *Fighting the Forces* 91 "Ironically, Buffy's Slayer-quest is ultimately fulfilled when she is finally able to slay Angelus." 2002 Rose *Fighting the Forces* 141 "Adam is too strong for even Buffy's slayer strength." [fr. sense 1.a]

4: *adj* An element in names
1999 May 13 The Bronze "Slayer Babe" [fr. SLAY + -er¹ suff in sense 1.a; clipped fr. *vampire slayer*]

—**Caveslayer** *n attrib* Prehistoric slayer
2000 Holder *Watcher's Guide* 2 49 "Buffy is so crushed she seeks solace in the campus bar, drowning her sorrows in magickal beer that turns her and her drinking buddies into Cro-Magnon people. However, even Caveslayer Buffy obeys her innate instinct to protect people." [fr. *Caveman* n in sense 1 + SLAYER] See CAVE-BUFFY sv BUFFY

—**inner Slayer** *n* Essential person of a SLAYER, SLAYERNESS
2002 Jul 25 Bronze: Beta "Buffy embraces her inner slayer." 2002 Jul 25 Bronze: Beta "But after six seasons (and six embrace-the-inner-slayer epiphanies?) She probably needs to be consistently confident about herself." [*inner adj* in sense 3 + SLAYER, by analogy with *inner child* 'essential person'] See INNER MOPPET

—**pre-Slayer** *adv* Before the period in which Buffy was the Slayer
2000 Holder *The Evil That Men Do* 96 "Pre-Slayer, it had been just as bad, only without monsters and demons." [pre- pref in sense 1.a + SLAYER]

—**slayerage** 1: *n attrib* Affiliated with slaying or the Slayer
1999 May 11 Noxon *The Prom* [quoted in 2000 Topping *Slayer* 227] "Buffy and Angel share a 'post-Slayerage nap thing.'" [SLAYER + -*age* suff in sense 4.a]

2: *n attrib*
2001 Jun 2 The Bronze "Anyway fellow fans of the undead and slayeridge types I'm off to wallow in my sorrow." [SLAYER + -*age* suff in sense 3]

—**Slayercam** Camera that would film the Slayer while on patrol
2000 Holder *The Evil That Men Do* 148 "'Maybe I should buy her a police scanner. Or I could wear a camera. Slayercam. It's a thought.'" [B] [SLAYER + *camera* n in sense 1]

—**Slayerdom** 1: *n* Buffy's reign as the Slayer
1999 Oct 13 The Bronze "As Cordelia was Anne's alter ego so Cordy is

what Buffy was like before Slayerdom." 2001 Shuttleworth *Reading the Vampire Slayer* 228 "In Buffy's case the process explicitly begins only a little while after physical puberty, with Slayerdom foisted upon her at the age [...] of fifteen." 2002 Navarro *Tempted Champions* 82 "So much of her chance to be a teenager had been stolen by the Slayer's calling, but she seemed to have gotten it together, rallied to find a balance between Slayerdom and college and a possible future." 2002 Mendelsohn *Fighting the Forces* 54 "Buffy's emotional dependence on men exists independently of issues of Slayerdom."

2: *n attrib* [fr. sense 1] Of or relating to Buffy and her activities 2002 Navarro *Tempted Champions* 134 "He'd been doing pretty nicely, [...] he'd had no thoughts of the Slayerdom type at all." [SLAYER + -dom suff in sense 1] See BUFFDOM

—**Slayeresque** *adj* Resembling the SLAYER
2002 Overbey and Preston-Matto *Fighting the Forces* 75 "Buffy is able to play with language in this way—it is tied to Slayage. But it is not a role that just anyone can fill, as Willow discovers when she substitutes for the AWOL Buffy in 'Anne.' 'That's right, big boy,' she entices the vamp, with Slayeresque attitude, 'come and get it.'" [SLAYER in sense 1.a + -esque suff]

—**Slayerette** 1.a: *n* Person who assists Buffy in her role as the Slayer 1997 Mar 17 Reston *The Witch* "You're the Slayer, and we're, like, the Slayerettes." [W] 1998 Golden and Holder *Child of the Hunt* 37 "'I think we may be getting a bit carried away with this whole business of 'Slayerettes.'" [G] 1998 Golden and Holder *Blooded* 13 "She wanted to walk and think and come down off the adrenaline rush of playing Slayerette, which was, like, one of the Slayer's backup singers." 1999 Jul 9 http://www.slayerette.org "A Very Suave, Very Not Pathetic Slayerette Site: A Site Devoted to Buffy the Vampire Slayer's Faithful Sidekicks, the Slayerettes." 1999 Sep DeCandido *American Libraries* 44 "Buffy's buds (called affectionately the Slayerettes or the Scooby Gang) include the never-cool Xander; his best friend, the brilliant and fashion-impaired Willow...." 1999 Golden and Holder *Ghost Roads* 226 "It seemed like a waste of Slayerettes to be back in Sunnydale, and going to school, of all things." 1999 Odom *Unnatural Selection* 68 "All the Slayerettes went on alert at once." 1999 Gallagher *Obsidian Fate* 28 "Cordelia Chase was the only exception to the freaky, weird loser reputation that separated the Slayer and Slayerettes from the mainstream of student society." 2000 May 9 Petrie *The Yoko Factor* "You want to even the odds in the fight, you don't want the Slayerettes marching about." [S] 2000 Holder *The Evil That Men Do* 31 "Looked like he was the only Slayerette available for the job." 2000 Gilman and Sherman *Deep Water* 111 "Angel, unlike the Slayerettes, never underestimated the intelligence that fueled the Watcher." 2000 Gallagher *Prime Evil* 236 "Sudden understanding of Buffy's position when she was fighting vampires and the Slayerettes were trying to help hit Willow with a force greater than Shugra's magick." 2000 Holder *Watcher's Guide* 2 2 "Buffy is also one of the only Slayers ever to have a band of friends help her with her battles [...] The group often refers to itself as the Slayerettes or the Scooby gang." 2001 Dec Andrews *Starburst* 22 "Then we are introduced to Buffy Summers, Joss Whedon's little blonde superhero, and the friends who support her, initially christened the Slayerettes, latterly the Scooby Gang." 2002 Odom *Crossings* 35 "Strangely enough, Buffy and her little pack of Slayerettes had become Spike's reluctant companions." 2002 Williams *Fighting the Forces* 70 "Jenny, however, continues to be a presence in the Slayerettes' lives." See Scooby Gang

   1.b: n Fans of the Slayerettes; Slayerette wannabes
1999 May 13 The Bronze "Good afternoon, fellow Slayerettes." 2001 Nov 12 buffysearch.com "**The Net Slayerette** Everything I can relate that's Buffy. I've got monologues, to essays, to humor." [site name] 2001 Nov 12 buffysearch.com "**a slayerettes best friend** This site has a lot of what you would expect like Cast Bios and Pics and stuff but I have some of the not so normal stuff."

   1.c: n Element in a URL
1999 Jul 9 See previous citation

   1.d: n An element in names
2000 Sep 1 The Bronze "Slayerette 2000" 2001 Jun 2 The Bronze "slayerette 2K"

   2: n attrib Pertaining to Buffy's assistants
1997 Golden and Holder *Halloween Rain* 133 "Xander looked at Willow, who was doing a much better Slayerette job of pounding them than he would have expected, she being, er, a non-guy." 1999 Golden and Holder

Out of the Madhouse 9 "So what do we do? List the Slayerettes Club or Scooby Gang or whatever under our activities in the yearbook and go back to the real world?'" [C]   1999 Gilman and Sherman *Visitors* 33 "'Okay, gang. Time to head for Temporary Slayerette Headquarters.'" [B] 1999 Massie *Power of Persuasion* 73 "'I'll watch them. Slayerette-mode, sharp, vigilant. All that.'" [B]   2000 Gilman and Sherman *Deep Water* 10 "It was, they thought with a silent giggle, the Slayerette creed."   2000 Passarella *Ghoul Trouble* 132 "'The Slayerette flag will be flying at all times.'" [X]   [SLAYER in sense 1.a + -*ette* suff in all senses]

3: n   Assistants, helpers
2000 Topping *Slayer* iv "A special thank-you to my Slayerettes."   [fr. SLAYERETTES]

—**Slayer-eyes** n   Stern, powerful glance
1999 Golden *Sins of the Father* 3 "With a withering glance, Buffy silently challenged Xander to continue with that train of thought. Wisely, he didn't say another word. For at least five seconds. 'Okay, make Slayer-eyes at me, I don't care,' he said, throwing his hands up." [X]   [fr. SLAYER + *eyes* n in sense 5.a; cf. *DAS*3 *make goo-goo eyes* v phr]

—**Slayerfest** n   1: n   Celebration at which vampire slayers are killed
1998 Nov 3 Greenwalt *Homecoming* "Hello, ladies. Welcome to Slayerfest '98. What is a Slayerfest, you ask? Well, as in most of life, there's the hunters and the hunted. Can you guess where you two fall?...Faith, Buffy, have a nice death." [Mr. Trick]   1999 Oct 1 *Entertainment Weekly* 38/3 "Their ensuing battle for the crown gets ugly, though perhaps not as life-threatening as Mr. Trick's come-one-come-all invitation to kill Buffy and Faith: SlayerFest '98."   2000 Topping *Slayer* 167 "Mr. Trick assembles a team of specialists to take part in Slayerfest '98 and rid him of Buffy and Faith."   2001 Odom *Revenant* 143 "[Xander:] 'Another Slayerfest?' 'No,' Giles said. 'This is something else.'"   2001 Tonkin *Reading the Vampire Slayer* 45 "This undead homeboy, come straight outta hell and Compton to organize the 'Slayerfest,' rather labours the obvious when he points out that Buffy's textbook 'white flight' neighbourhood 'is not a haven for the brothers, strictly the Caucasian persuasion in the Dale but you gotta stand up and salute their death rate.'"

2: n *attrib*   Pertaining to Slayerfest '98
2000 Holder *Watcher's Guide* 2 150 "The competition heats up on both

the Homecoming and Slayerfest fronts." [SLAYER + -*fest*, fr. *fest* n]   See
BITE-FEST, SUCKFEST, and VIDFEST

    —**Slayer Handbook** n   Manual of SLAYERHOOD
1997 Nov 24 Noxon *What's My Line, Part* 2 "There's a Slayer Handbook?" [W]   1998 Golden and Holder *Watcher's Guide* 1 11 "Rules of
the Game, or The Slayer Handbook According to Buffy Summers."   1999
Golden and Holder *Child of the Hunt* 242 "'Is that in the Slayer's Handbook, or is it just more proof that I'm all wrong for the job?'" [B]   2000
Holder *Watcher's Guide* 2 4 "We discovered in Season Two that there is a
Slayer's Handbook, and that Buffy has not been given it because Giles
figured she was too unconventional too adhere to it."   2002 Jul 28
Bronze: Beta "Forget Giles' books or the Slayer handbook."   2002 Helford
Fighting the Forces 27 "Nonetheless, the series allows Buffy to retain her
outsider status when we learn that there is an official Slayer's Handbook
that Kendra has memorized and that Giles knows about but has decided
not to share with the anti-intellectual Buffy."   [SLAYER + *handbook* n in
sense 1]

    —**Slayerhood** n   Condition of being SLAYER
2001 Kaveney *Reading the Vampire Slayer* 13 "In each of these episodes,
Buffy has to reaffirm herself and her Slayerhood."   2002 Navarro *Tempted
Champions* 228 "[H]ow many of her dreams had disintegrated because
of her Slayerhood anyway?"   [SLAYER in sense 1.a + -*hood* suff in sense
1.a]

    —**Slayerish** *adj*   Like a Slayer
1999 Gilman and Sherman *Visitors* 110 "'And I get to...stand around
looking Slayerish again.'" [B]   [SLAYER + -*ish* suff in sense 2.a]

    —**Slayerism** n   Condition of being the Slayer
1999 Golden and Holder *Immortal* 32 "'Gave me bruises on my bruises,
even with the whole no-Band-Aid-required bonus of Slayerism.'" [B]
2002 Navarro *Tempted Champions* 82 "A dangerous thing, that solo
Slayerism, especially when facing someone like Catia."   [SLAYER + -*ism*
suff in sense 3.a]

    —**slayerness** n   Quality of being the Slayer
1999 May 4 Fury *Choices* "You can't just define me by my slayerness.
That's something-ism." [B]   2000 Feb 29 Whedon *Who Are You* "''Cause
I could do anything I want, but instead I choose to pout and whine and

feel the burden of slayerness?" [Faith/Buffy]   2001 Shuttleworth *Reading the Vampire Slayer* 229 "Buffy qua Slayer ... experiences the temptation personified by Faith to set herself above the law by virtue of her Slayerness."   2002 Jul 31 Bronze: Beta "But the Buffy I watched for the first 5 years, didn't primarily define herself by her slayerness." [SLAYER + -*ness suff*]   See BUFFYNESS

—**Slayer-o-meter**   n   SLAYER SENSE
2000 Gilman and Sherman *Deep Water* 90 "She'd managed to grab on hour or so of shut-eye after that, thankfully of the undreaming kind, which had helped more, but the Slayer-o-meter was redlining in the foul mood zone." [SLAYER + -*o*- + *meter*³ n in sense 1]   See DUMP-O-GRAM, SLUT-O-RAMA, and SUPPORT-O-GAL

—**Slayerpalooza**   n   Celebration of the Slayer
1999 Spring *Buffy the Vampire Slayer* 17 "Slayerpalooza!" [article title] [SLAYER + *lollapalooza* n (also HDAS in sense 1 & NTC in sense 1]

—**Slayer-patrol**   n   Standing guard against the forces of evil
1998 Golden and Holder *Blooded* 18 "She was busy out on Slayer-patrol last night, keeping the world safe from dead folks." [SLAYER + *patrol* n in sense 1]

—**Slayer practice**   n   Training regimen specific to SLAYERS
1998 Golden and Holder *Blooded* 53 "While Willow continued her search, Giles put Buffy through the hell she called 'Slayer practice': weapons and martial arts training that more often than not left poor Giles with welts and bruises he would be hard pressed to explain if he had a love life." [SLAYER + *practice* n in sense 2.b]

—**Slayer's bag**   n   Receptacle for the Slayer's tools
1997 Golden and Holder *Halloween Rain* 33 "Buffy cocked her head and put her hand on the zipper of her Slayer's bag."   1998 Golden and Holder *Blooded* 2 "Buffy reached into her Slayer's bag and handed Giles a large wooden crucifix and a long, tapered stake."   1999 Golden and Holder *Immortal* 17 "Buffy smiled slightly and picked up her Slayer's bag."   2000 Holder *The Evil That Men Do* 38 "Buffy picked up her Slayer's bag and went down the hall to wash up in the bathroom."   2000 Gallagher *Doomsday Deck* 42 "Buffy reached for the Slayer bag on the floor and pulled out a stake." [SLAYER + -'*s suff* + *bag* n in sense 1.a; see also 1999 Gallagher sv SLAY in sense 3, for *slayer bag*]

—**Slayer sense** n Ability to detect vampires, demons, or other danger
1998 Gardner *Return to Chaos* 23 "Her Slayer sense was on red alert."
1998 Gardner *Return to Chaos* 73 "They might be strange, even infuriating, but her Slayer sense told her they didn't mean her any harm." 1999
Odom *Unnatural Selection* 16 "Her Slayer senses also told her the vampire
on the bulldozer's canopy was leaping down at her back as she turned."
1999 Gallagher *Obsidian Fate* 9 "Her enhanced Slayer senses were attuned to her surroundings, aware of every nuance. A soft rustle in the
grass. A shadow shifting on a crypt. The musty scent of composting
leaves. Nothing triggered the inexplicable sixth sense that warned a Slayer
of imminent danger." 2000 Dokey *Night of the Living Rerun* 24 "As if
on cue, Buffy's slayer senses went on red alert." 2001 Odom *Revenant* 12
"Her Slayer senses flared out, reading her opponents and the terrain
she'd been given to fight on." 2002 Odom *Crossings* 5 "Buffy recognized them as vampires from the way they moved and the tingle her
Slayer senses made." 2002 Navarro *Tempted Champions* 216 "She'd be
the first to admit she'd had to learn to pay better attention to that special
Slayer 'sense' that would let her know when a vampire was sneaking up
on her." [SLAYER + *sense* n in sense 1.a; cf. *Slayer radar* & *Slayer sonar* sv
SLAYER in sense 2.a, 1998 Gardner *Return to Chaos* & 2000 Gallagher
Prime Evil, respectively] See SLAYER-O-METER and SPIDER-SENSE
—**slayer slang** n Informal language coined, developed, or adopted
in *Buffy the Vampire Slayer* in whatever medium; jargon of Buffy and the
SCOOBY GANG
1999 Summer Adams *Verbatim: The Language Quarterly* 1 / 1 "Examination of mainstream and cult magazines, fan book, and websites, however, suggests that slayer slang, far from being ephemeral vocabulary,
steadily intrudes on speech and may be here to stay." 1999 Neufeldt
Dictionaries: Journal of the Dictionary Society of North America 18 "In a
paper, 'Slayer Slang,' presented to the annual meeting of the American
Dialect Society in Los Angeles this year, Michael Adams of Albright College discussed the linguistic creativity of the show." 1999 Johnson *USA
Today* 4D "That's just one example of about 200 'slayer slang' terms and
usages that Buffy writers and fans have invented or re-introduced."
[SLAYER in sense 2 + *slang* n in senses 1 & 2] See BUFFYSPEAK sv BUFFY

—**Slayer's Litany**   n   Passage of lore describing the legend of the Slayer
2000 Navarro *Paleo* 27 "The Slayer's Litany—'*As long as there have been vampires, there has been the Slayer. One girl in all the world*...'—was something that had a tendency to run through her mind with bummer-level regularity." [SLAYER + -'s suff + litany n in sense 2]
   —**Slayersville**   n   An order of danger worthy of the SLAYER
1998 Gardner *Return to Chaos* 98 "'Some of the supernatural stuff they've faced is right up there in Slayersville.'" [X]   [SLAYER + -s- + ville suff]
   —**Slayerverse**   n   The BUFFYVERSE
2002 Jul 23 Bronze: Beta "[T]he other slayers (including Kendra) were automatons, doing their duty with little thought of life outside their violent slayerverse." [SLAYER + universe n in sense 3]
   —**Slayerwise**   adv   Regarding one's role as the Slayer
1999 Golden and Holder *Immortal* 207 "'Well, nothing's happening Slayerwise, so I can devote all of my time to being with you.'" [B]   [SLAYER + -wise suff in sense 2]
   —**Team Slayer**   1:   n   The SLAYERETTES, the SCOOBY GANG
2000 Holder *Watcher's Guide* 2 179 "Buffy and Angel reveal they've been duping Faith just as the rest of Team Slayer arrives."   See TEAM BUFF sv BUFFY
   2:   n attrib   Pertaining to the SLAYER and her SLAYERETTES
2000 Holder *Watcher's Guide* 2 143 "Xander nearly stakes Buffy when she interrupts a Team Slayer staking."   [team n in sense 2 + SLAYER]

sliceage   n   Killing by means of a sharp implement
1998 Mar 3 Des Hotel and Batali *Killed by Death* "[Buffy:] 'Backer was curing the kids—and taking away the Kindestod's food.' [Cordelia:] 'Hence the sliceage.'"   1999 Oct 1 Howard *Entertainment Weekly* 49/3 "**sliceage** Death by slashing." [slice vt in sense 3 + -age suff in sense 4.b]

slippy   adj   slippery
2000 Oct 17 Kirshner *Out of My Mind* "Oops! String was slippy." [Harmony]   [fr. slip v in sense 7 + -y¹ suff in sense 3]

slowage   n   Sluggish transmission of messages
1999 May 13 http://board.buffy.com/bronze/pb.shtml "I knew the board

slowage at work…was a heinous plot!" [*slow adj* in sense 2.b + *-age suff* in sense 3]

Slut-o-rama   n   Girl or woman who looks as though she is both morally loose and from the 1970s
1998 Oct 13 Greenwalt *Faith, Hope, and Trick* "Check out Slut-o-rama and her Disco Dave." [C]   2000 Holder *Watcher's Guide* 2 145 "She is distracted by one of the dancers, whose extroverted personality looks doomed to meet an untimely end by an obvious vamp-face (AKA 'Slut-o-rama and Disco Dave') in Cordy-speak." [*slut n* in sense 1.a + -o- + DAS3 -*rama*]   See DUMP-O-GRAM, SLAYER-O-METER, and SUPPORT-O-GAL

smoochies   1:   n   Kisses
1997 Oct 27 Ellsworth *Halloween* "You know how dispiriting it is for me to even contemplate you grownups having smoochies." [B]   1998 Jan 12 Noxon *Bad Eggs* "[Xander:] 'Apparently Buffy has decided that what's wrong with the English language is all those pesky words. You. Angel. Big. Smoochies.' [Buffy:] 'Shut. Up.'"   1998 Jan 27 Des Hotel and Batali *Phases* "He's great, we have a lot of fun, but I want smoochies." [W]   1998 Winter *Buffy the Vampire Slayer* 51 "**smoochies** […] n. [Willow] kissing, general date stuff."   1998 Golden and Holder *Blooded* 91 "Also, there would be big smoochies during Angel-prowling nights, as Xander so quaintly put it on occasion. Very big smoochies."   1999 Jan 12 St. John and Espenson *Gingerbread* "You are guilty. You got illicit smoochies, gonna have to pay the price." [B]   1999 Golden *Sins of the Father* 13 "Willow turned to Xander with a mischievous grin on her face. 'Like hot-with-the-smoochies Pike.'"   1999 May 13 The Bronze "The VT brat Squad send smoochies & hugs."   1999 Oct 13 The Bronze "Antiseptic *SMOOTCHIES* to my below-par friend."   2000 Passarella *Ghoul Trouble* 18 "Fewer distractions that way…distractions in the form of actual smoochies or thinking about potential smoochies."   2000 Holder *Watcher's Guide* 2 58 "In 'Lovers Walk' she and Xander betray Oz and Cordelia by having illicit smootchies together."
   2:   interj   Kisses
1999 Apr 29 The Bronze "[Ron:] '[To] KrazyKat: *big smoochies*'"   1999 Jun 26 The Bronze "Well, then, you are a sweetie! *smoochies*"   2000 Sep 1 The Bronze "Hello Sugar :) {{{button melting smoochies}}}"

[smooch n (also *DAS3* smooch in sense 2 & NTC in sense 2) + -ies suff]

snoozey *adj* Inclined to nap
2002 Jul 25 Bronze: Beta "[S]omewhat scrolled and now very snoozey."
[snooze vi + -y¹ suff in sense 3]

so *adv* Very much
1995 *Clueless* "Thank you, Josh. I so need lessons from you on how to be cool." 1997 Sep 15 Whedon *When She Was Bad* "Please, I'm so over her." [X] 1997 Nov 3 Whedon *Lie to Me* "Oh, Great! I'm so the Net girl." [W] 1997 Nov 24 Noxon *What's My Line, Part 2* "We so need to get out of here." [X] 1997 Golden and Holder *Halloween Rain* 26 "'So nothing there, Mom,' Buffy said, rolling her eyes." 1997 Golden and Holder *Halloween Rain* 29 "She'd totally been there, had so done that." 1998 Winter *Buffy the Vampire Slayer* 51 "**so:** [...] adv. [W] very much— as in Willow is so the net girl." 1998 Oct 6 Noxon *Dead Man's Party* "I tried to communicate with the spirit world and I *so* wasn't ready for that." [W] 1999 Springer *Official Yearbook* 26/2 "I was *so* not used to this big protruding belly." 2000 Gallagher *Doomsday Deck* 87 "This is so not good." 2001 Aug Epstein *Out* 50/1 "'Obviously, during a couple of the spells, they were *so* fucking,' notes [Alyson] Hannigan." 2001 Oct 16 Petrie and Espenson *Life Serial* "Oh, c'mon, Tara, I am so old enough to do research." [D] 2001 Odom *Revenant* 136 "'I was so toast when you stepped into that little adventure.'" [X] 2002 Jan 13 Robinson *www.theonionavclub.com* 2 "[Joss Whedon:] 'He was my beacon of hope in that whole experience, that he was such a good guy and so got it.'" 2002 Jan 29 Espenson *Doublemeat Palace* "Oh, yeah, practical jokes, not really right for the workplace—I so get that now." [B] 2002 Jul 30 Bronze: Beta "I was thinking of one of the points I read a long time ago about sociopaths it was something like 'Has a need to justify his actions and needs his victim's affirmation' and that included things like respect, love or gratitude. Which is so Spike." 2002 Odom *Crossings* 101 "'Now that I think about it,' Xander told himself as he stood outside Robby Healdton's room in the Intensive Care Unit at the hospital, 'this is so really not a good idea.'" [fr. *so*¹ adv in sense 3]

somber n Grave aspect
2001 Oct 2 Noxon *Bargaining* 1 "So, you got your somber on, Will. Is the urn not up to spec?" [X] [fr. *somber adj* in sense 2.b]

sparkage n Romantic possibility
1998 Jan 19 Noxon *Surprise* "Hey, speaking of wow-potential, there's Oz over there. What are we thinking, any sparkage?" [B] 1999 Oct 1 Howard *Entertainment Weekly* 49/3 "**sparkage** Romantic electricity." [*spark n* in sense 4.a + *-age* suff in sense 3]

special forces *adj* Out of control
1997 Golden and Holder *Halloween Rain* 16 "'Don't invade her personal space or she'll go all, like, special forces on you.'" [fr. *Special Forces pl n*] See WILD BUNCH

spider-sense n Faculty by which one discerns danger or the potential for it
1997 Apr 28 Gable and Swyden *I Robot, You Jane* "I can just tell something's wrong: my spider-sense is tingling." [B] 1999 Oct 1 Howard *Entertainment Weekly* 49/3 "**spider sense** Tingling sensation Buffy gets when something's up in demonsville; reference to Spider-Man's intuition." 1999 Gilman and Sherman *Visitors* 2 "It might have just been the wind— or it could have been her spider-sense kicking in again, warning her of bloodsucking reinforcement on the way." 2000 Dokey *Here Be Monsters* 25 "Way to use your Spidey [from Spiderman's nickname] senses, mom." 2002 Odom *Crossings* 70 "'Okay, that gave my Spidey senses a little jolt.'" [X] [fr. the ability of the comic strip/book character, Spider-Man, to detect potential danger; *spider n* in sense 2 + *sense n* in sense 1.a, by association with a spider's tactile awareness of prey caught in its web] See SLAYER SENSE

spoilage 1: n Information that gives away crucial elements of an unseen television episode
1999 Mar 21 http://members.tripod.com/~SpiffyGalX/sm.htm "Spoilage" [option on site menu] 1999 Mar 21 http://members.tripod.com/ ~SpiffyGalX/sm.htm "Third Season Spiffy Spoilage" [section title] 1999 Mar 21 http://members.tripod.com /~SpiffyGalX/sm.htm "Miscellaneous

Spoilage" [section title]   2002 Jul 24 Bronze: Beta "I'm not up to date yet on what has been posted about yet, so I probably won't be talking too much spoilage for a while."

   2: *n attrib*

1999 Jun 29 http://slayer.simplenet.com/tbcs/gradspoilers.html "Some join in on all the Spoilage discussion at: The Buffy Cross & Stake Spoiler Board." [fr. *spoilage* n in sense 1.a; fr. *spoil* 'disclose item of information that reveals a crucial element of an unseen television episode', fr. *spoiler* n in sense 2) + -*age suff* in sense 1.a]

spoilerage   n   Information that gives away crucial elements of an episode of a television show

2002 Jul 24 Bronze: Beta "Has anyone heard anything about Tim Curry appearing on Buffy? *Potential spoilerosity so highlight (Only in the new character possibility...so, not maaaajor spoilerage." [fr. *spoiler* n in sense 2 + -*age suff* in sense 1.a]

spoiler-free   *adj*   Lacking information that would give away crucial elements of an unseen episode

1999 May 13 The Bronze "I have been spoiler-free now for a whole month."   1999 Oct 13 The Bronze "spoiler-free girl" [signature]   2002 Jul 23 Bronze: Beta "I was a spoiler-free person this year." [spoiler 'item of information that reveals a crucial element of an unseen television episode', fr. *spoiler* n in sense 2 + -*free suff*, fr. *free adj* in senses 4.a & 4.b]

spookables   1:   n   Victims of fear

1998 Golden and Holder *Blooded* 45 "'No. Big male-type person with a huge sword who lived on top of a mountain and let the spookables come to him?'" [B]

   2: n   Ghosts

1999 Golden and Holder *Ghost Roads* 78 "On the front lawn of Sunnydale High, Xander bounced on his heels, looking out into the darkness for spookables."   2000 Holder *The Evil That Men Do* 53 "No vamps tonight; no demons, no spookables, as Xander called them." [fr. *spook* vt in senses 1 & 2 + -*able suff* in sense 1 + -*s¹ suff*]   See LUNCHABLE

stakage   n   Killing by means of a stake

2000 Garton *Resurrecting Ravana* 3 "'I'm gonna draw them outside, and then I wanna see some serious stakage.'" [B]   [*stake* n in sense 1 + -*age* suff in sense 4.a]

stake   1.a: vt   Kill a vampire with a stake
1995 Auerbach *Our Vampires, Ourselves* 36 "[O]nly Clara, the one girl he transforms into a vampire, is sufficiently fledgling to be staked to death." 1997 Oct 13 Greenwalt *Reptile Boy* "Or what it's like to stake vampires while you're having fuzzy feelings towards one." [B]   1997 Golden and Holder *Halloween Rain* 35 "[Buffy:] 'I'm supposed to stake our lives on your word?' [Willow:] 'Pun intended.'"   1997 Golden and Holder *Halloween Rain* 48 "Buffy staked the fang-girl in the heart, and she exploded into blood-scented ashes."   1998 Gardner *Return to Chaos* 229 "'I think a vampire was meant to be staked.'" [B]   1998 Golden and Holder *Blooded* 93 "'Now here I am, what you've been waiting for, and all I'm going to do is break your hearts.' Her face changed then. A sneer—almost cruel—visited her mouth. 'I meant *stake* your hearts, of course.'" [B]   1998 Golden and Holder *Watcher's Guide* 1 11 "Stake all you want, they'll make more."   1998 Tracy *The Girl's Got Bite* 192 "But the shot seen after the rewind is actually the end of the fight when Buffy stakes the vamp with a wooden sign."   1999 Jun 26 The Bronze "Vote for the Cordelia Chase Crew at the Battle of the Sites and/or the Stake me! Awards as the best Charisma site."   1999 Oct 1 *Entertainment Weekly* 33/1 "Willow (a.k.a. Will) sees Buffy stake a vamp."   1999 Oct 13 The Bronze "[M]y first reaction to the roomie was, 'Stake her. That snoring wasn't human.'" 1999 Nov 16 Petrie *The Intiative* "'Bastard! You dumped me, and staked me, and hurt me, and left me.'" [Harmony]   1999 Nov 16 Petrie *The Initiative* "Xander, if I find Spike, I'm staking him, not signaling ships at sea." [B]   1999 Golden *Sins of the Father* 265 "Buffy staked it in midair, then spun out of the way of flying dust."   1999 Golden and Holder *Ghost Roads* 216 "'And sometimes I wonder if I'll have time to do my homework while I'm staking some vamp.'" [B]   1999 Gilman and Sherman *Visitors* 24 "'Cause I'm not going to spend my nights looking over my shoulder for some creepie when I'm supposed to be staking the ghoulies.'" [B]   1999 Odom *Unnatural Selection* 26 "'Or I'll stake you like a butterfly in biology class,' Buffy promised."   1999 Massie *Power of Persuasion* 111 "'When I tried to stake her, there was no blood, no screaming, no writh-

ing in pain or anything!'" [B]   2000 Sept 27 *Angel* (WB) "Prio's nasty: not some big mosquito like you turn to dust whenever you stake it." 2000 Holder *The Evil That Men Do* 65 "'Since it didn't involve staking a bad guy or looking for a good one, I sort of bypassed the direct feed and went for bandwidth.'" [B]   2000 Gilman and Sherman *Deep Water* 15 "'I don't have to stake any elves, do I?'" [B]   2000 Gallagher *Doomsday Deck* 3 "Slayer. As in stake-a-vampire Slayer." [Joyce]   2000 Garton *Resurrecting Ravana* 30 "Willow felt a little better after they'd staked all five of the hellhounds."   2000 Topping *Slayer* 94 "Ford tackles the female, but instead of staking her he lets her go."   2000 Holder *Watcher's Guide* 26 "Unfortunately, while patrolling, Faith accidentally stakes the deputy mayor." 2001 Apr 17 *Angel* (WB Network) "Don't stake me guys, please." [A]   2001 Oct 23 Fury and Espenson *Life Serial* "[Spike:] 'So who's gonna advance me a tiny tabby to get started? C'mon, someone's gotta stake me.' [Buffy:] 'I'll do it. [Pause] What, you thought I was just gonna let that lie there?'"   2001 Dec Andrews *Starburst* 22 "Buffy stakes an unseen vampire with a pool cue, and we see the end of the cue wobble and then slowly swing upwards as the vamp collapses off the screen." 2001 Odom *Revenant* 29 "'You mean alone-time as in patrolling, staking the occasional vampire, and not giving in to a case of raging hormones?'" [B]   2001 Kaveney *Reading the Vampire Slayer* 6 "Angel definitively breaks with his past by staking Darla, his vampire lover and sire."   2001 Daugherty *Reading the Vampire Slayer* 162 "And when Dracula's dust re-assembles, Buffy is there to stake him, again and again."   2001 Kaveney *Reading the Vampire Slayer* 248 "Vamp Willow is sent back and staked." 2002 Mar Espenson *Haunted* [4] "'It means that even when we stake him, he's still out there somewhere.'" [G]   2002 Jul 23 Bronze: Beta "She should have staked him then, staked Angel then, and staked Drusilla then."   2002 Odom *Crossings* 75 "Willow didn't share the same interest that [Tara] had in *Othersyde*, but was willing to watch the show with her when they weren't doing homework, working on a new spell, or helping Buffy cope with the loss of her mom or with staking the latest rash of vampires newly risen from their graves."   2002 Money *Fighting the Forces* 102 "In the melee, Buffy and Oz meet and stake the vampire Willow and Xander, then Buffy is caught by the Master and her neck snapped."

2002 Krzywinska *Fighting the Forces* 183 "He retains his outsider bad-boy appeal yet is unlikely to be staked by Buffy."

1.b: vi Kill a vampire with a stake

1998 Gardner *Return to Chaos* 9 "That was one nice thing about vampires. Since they disintegrated once they were staked, there was no messy cleanup afterward." 1998 Oct Brereton *The Dust Waltz* [18] "'Wanna go look for more of the undead to stake?'" [B] 2000 Sep 1 The Bronze "In true Buffy fashion you will be vamped…hang on a minute, ok, I forgot, you'll just get staked then." 2001 Feb 20 Espenson *I Was Made to Love You* "Oh dear, if looks could stake." [S] 2002 Navarro *Tempted Champions* 76 "Celina simply wasn't there to be staked." 2002 Overbey and Preston-Matto *Fighting the Forces* 76 "While Buffy's romping vernacular suffices for run-of-the-mill vampires, the old quip-and-stake is not the only kind of combative language in Buffy."

1.c: vt Kill something other than a vampire with a stake

1995 Auerbach *Our Vampires, Ourselves* 146 "Cornered with Lucy on a ship to Romania, he stakes Van Helsing."

1.d v An element in names

2000 Sep 1 The Bronze "StakeMe" [fr. *stake* n in sense 1]

—**stake that** v phr Submit to staking

1999 Gallagher *Obsidian Fate* 124 "'Like, stake that, vamp boy!'" [B] [fr. STAKE in sense 1.a + *that* pron in sense 1.a, a blend of indeterminate boundary with *take* vt in sense 21.b]

—**stakey** *adj* Characterized by staking

2002 Jul 25 Bronze: Beta "So basically, I think you're right…except for the stakey/ashtray bit." [STAKE in sense 1.a + -y[1] suff in sense 1]

—**staking** 1.a: n Death by means of a wooden stake

1995 Auerbach *Our Vampires, Ourselves* 128 "Helen's staking by a coven of faceless, chanting monks is the most authentically frightening sequence in the Hammer series." 1998 Golden and Holder *Blooded* 108 "The other two were persistent, and she'd fought them off several times without getting the opening she needed for a staking." 1999 Golden and Holder *Immortal* 23 "[S]he charged the vampire who held Xander in a death grip, fully expecting the staking to be a simple matter." 2000 Holder *The Evil That Men Do* 289 "Her mind kept repeating the terrible sound of the staking." 2000 Topping *Slayer* 202 "Buffy helps them before she can deal with the consequences of Faith's most irresponsible act of all—the staking of the Deputy Mayor." 2000 Holder *Watcher's Guide* 2 49 "It will make the vampire who wears it invincible, to the extent that he/she can survive stakings and sunlight." 2001 Saxey *Reading the Vampire Slayer* 193 "Buffy elaborates this structure with delight but, due to the medium of the TV series, closure is more problematic than a single final staking." 2002 Apr 30 Greenberg *Entropy* "I could take care of this guy if you want…save you the staking." [S]

   1.b: n Activity of killing with a stake
1998 Golden and Holder *Child of the Hunt* 37 "'Leave the staking to us.'" [X] 1999 Odom *Unnatural Selection* 7 "Staking vampires is easy compared with that, and maybe less dangerous." 2000 Dokey *Here Be Monsters* 76 "'I get it. No staking at the present time.'" [B] 2000 Gallagher *Prime Evil* 187 "Buffy headed back to the van like a Slayer bent on some serious staking."

   2a: n *attrib* Pertaining to the act of killing vampires. Pertaining to killing with a stake
2000 Dokey *Here Be Monsters* 61 "'I just love that sound, don't you?' they said, as they danced backward, out of staking range." [Percy]

   2b: n *attrib* Pertaining to the act of killing vampires
2002 Overbey and Preston-Matto *Fighting the Forces* 77 "[Xander] lacks Buffy's staking skills." [STAKE + -ing² suff in sense 1.a]

stake-free *adj* Without a stake
1999 Summer Stokes *Buffy the Vampire Slayer* 6/2 "From the bottom of our stake-free hearts, we thank you." [fr. *stake* n in sense 1 + -*free* suff, fr. *free* adj in sense 4.a & 4.b]

stammery *adj* Unable to speak without repetitive pauses and sounds
2002 Overbey and Preston-Matto *Fighting the Forces* 81 "Giles becomes stammery again." [*stammer* vi + -*y*¹ suff in sense 1]

stay iny *adj* Unwilling to reveal a secret or private matter publicly
2002 Feb 12 Greenberg *Older and Far Away* "[Buffy:] 'I'm definitely not ready to…' [Tara:] 'Come out.' [Buffy:] 'Yeah. I'm all stay iny.'" [*stay*¹ v intr in sense 1 + *in* adv in sense 1 + -*y*¹ suff in sense 1; fr. *in 'in the

closet' as antonym of *out* adj in sense 9 'openly gay, lesbian'; see also *HDAS out* adj in sense 6 and *DAS3 out* adj in sense 3]

stealage   n   Stealing
1999 Oct 13 The Bronze "How much of her reaction to Kathy was a result of the soul stealage and how much was the genuine Buffy reaction." [*steal* vt in sense 1 + -*age* suff in sense 4.a]

Stepford   adj   Subject to mind-control
1997 Dec 8 Greenwalt and Whedon *Ted* "[Buffy:] 'Mom has been totally different since he's been around.' [Willow:] 'Different like happy?' [Buffy:] 'Like Stepford.'"   2000 Nov Watson *Pale Reflections* [37] "[Willow:] 'She's late...again.' [Giles:] 'What do you mean, again?' [Xander:] 'Ever since she became Stepford Buffy.'"   [fr. *The Stepford Wives* 'title of a film dir. Brian Forbes (1975)']

sticking-upness   n   Defense
2002 Jul 31 Bronze: Beta "Thanks for sticking up for me, even if there was no sticking-upness needed." [fr. *stick up for* phr v sv stick, stick + -*ing*[1] suff in sense 1 + up + -*ness* suff]

stiff upper-lippy   adj   Stoic; unemotional
2001 Oct 2 Fury *Bargaining* 2 "[Giles:] 'Willow, I don't know where to start.' [Willow:] 'Well, maybe you shouldn't...I'm trying to be stiff upper-lippy.'" [*ADH4 stiff upper lip* n + -*y*[1] suff in sense 1]

still   adv   Nevertheless (elliptical)
1998 Jan 27 Des Hotel and Batali *Phases* "[Willow:] 'So I'd still, if you'd still.' [Oz:] 'I'd still. I'd very still.'" [*still* adv in sense 2.a]   See LIKE

stompy   adj   Disciplinary
2001 May 8 Kirshner *Tough Love* "Me the grown up, the authority figure, the strong guiding hand and stompy foot that is me." [B] [*stomp* vi + *y*[1] suff in sense 1]

stretchy   adj   Attractively lithe
1997 Mar 17 Reston *The Witch* "Oooh, stretchy! [of a girl trying out for the cheerleading squad]." [X] [*stretch* vi in sense 1 + -*y*[1] suff in sense 1]

stripy *adj* Striped
2000 Topping *Slayer* 95 "Giles claims not to have any clothes other than those he wears to school (which, judging by the stripy tie he takes to his date with Jenny, seems to be true)." 2002 Jul 29 Bronze: Beta "[W]ell, I'm at work, so I'll have to search the home computer for funky-haired images […] Were you referring to stripey red? Or the fuschia?" [*stripe* n in sense 1.b + -*y*¹ suff in sense 1]

suckage 1: n Awful things
1999 Jun 26 The Bronze "Oh eye = serious suckage." 2000 Sep 1 The Bronze "Geometry is of the greatest suckage alive." [*suck* vi in sense 4 + -*age* suff in sense 1.a]
  2: n Feeding from
2001 Shuttleworth *Reading the Vampire Slayer* 222 "The week of the completion of my draft, however, saw the US and UK broadcast of 'Tough Love' (5.19), in which Tara, in Benson's words, 'suffers some brain suckage' by Glory." [*suck* vt in sense 3 + -*age* suff in sense 4.b]

suckfest n Orgy of murders by vampires
1997 Mar 10 Whedon *The Harvest* "If this Harvest thing is such a suckfest, why don't you stop it?" [B] 1997 Golden and Holder *Halloween Rain* 46 "'Well, I'm way sorry to interrupt the suckfest,' Buffy sneered, 'but haven't you leeches ever heard of the Red Cross.'" [*suck* vi in sense in sense 1 + -*fest*, fr. *fest* n] See BITE-FEST, SLAYERFEST, and VIDFEST

Support-o-gal n A reliable friend
1998 Dec 8 Noxon *The Wish* "I'm here for you, Xand. I'm Support-o-gal." [B] [*support* vt in sense 7.a + -*o*- + *gal*¹ n] See DUMP-O-GRAM, SLAYER-O-METER, and SLUT-O-RAMA

surfacey *adj* Superficial
2002 Feb 5 De Knight *Dead Things* "But it's all just surfacey, physical stuff." [Tara] [*surface* n in sense 3 + -*y*¹ suff in sense 1]

suspicious n A questionable, unanswerable, or unnerving sensation
1999 Gilman and Sherman *Visitors* 106 "'Long story, short of which is this Sheila chick knows way more about supernatural stuff than she should. Which gives me a bad case of the suspicious.'" [B] [fr. *suspicious* adj in sense 2] Cf. WIGGINS

swappage n Exchange
2000 Sep 1 The Bronze "And he says it's a go. All up for some swappage."
[*swap* vi + - *age* suff in sense 4.a]

taggage n HTML or formatting code
2002 Jul 28 Bronze: Beta "And Thoin wades in with a humongous post
(with hopefully no more dropped taggage)." [*tag* n in sense 11.b + -*age*
suff in sense 1.a] See DROPPAGE

team v Become a team
1998 Oct 20 Noxon *All Men Are Beasts* "Faith, you and I team. Willow,
stick with Buffy." [G] [*team* vi in sense 1 (also DAS3 *team* [*up*])]

ten adv Extremely
2001 Apr 24 Espenson *Intervention* "[Giles:] 'How strongly do you feel
about this?' [Buffy:] '10. Serious to the amount of 10.'" [*ten* n in sense
1; fr. *on a scale from one to ten*]

teutonic adj Inclined toward a traditional male attitude about women
1999 Nov 16 Petrie *The Initiative* "[Xander:] 'I'm sure he'd pick another
night, if he knew you were busy with teutonic boy toy.' [Buffy:] 'Riley's
a doof; he's not teutonic.'" 1999 Nov 16 Petrie *The Initiative* "[Buffy:]
'What, you think that boys can take care of themselves and girls need
help?' [Riley:] 'Yeah.' [Buffy:] 'That's so teutonic.'" 2000 Holder *Watcher's
Guide* 2 73 "As she accuses him of being Teutonic, and tells him to shoo,
they both leave in opposite directions when they hear a scream for help."
[fr. *Teutonic* n]

therapy-land n Confusion, anger, or other conflicted emotions
1997 Dec 8 Greenwalt and Whedon *Ted* "Seeing my mother frenching a
guy is definitely a ticket to therapy-land." [B] [*therapy* n in sense 2 +
land n in sense 7]

-thing n Situation, tendency, or predilection
1997 Mar 10 Whedon *Welcome to the Hellmouth* "To make you a vampire
they have to suck your blood. And then you have to suck their blood. It's
like a whole big sucking thing." [B] 1998 Oct 20 Noxon *All Men Are
Beasts* "I've been at Mr. Donut since the TV did that snowy thing." [W]
1998 Oct 20 Noxon *All Men Are Beasts* "I want you to do the guy thing."

1998 Dec 15 Whedon *Amends* "Must be that Angel-killed-his-girlfriend-and-tortured-him thing. Giles is really petty about stuff like that." [X] 1998 Golden and Holder *Child of the Hunt* 50 "Willow was glad she and Oz both did the cazh thing together, she in cords and a brown sweater, he in one of his many very cool bowling shirts." 1998 Golden and Holder *Blooded* 40 "[Giles:] '[I]t does still seem an odd confluence of events, wouldn't you say?' [...] [Buffy:] 'Then, oh, yeah, Giles. Definitely super-odd, the um, conflue-thing.'" 1999 Jan 19 Fury *Helpless* "Maybe we're on the wrong track with the whole spell, curse, and whammy thing." [X] 1999 Jun 26 The Bronze "Does anybody know about an Interactive Game? Heard something from someone about one coming out. Rumor or fact? Or middle thing. Or something. Anyone heard a thing?" 1999 Jun 26 The Bronze "I[']m in full agreeance over the Xander thing." 1999 Nov 30 Forbes *Something Blue* "Sorry. Duty thing." [B] 1999 Gilman and Sherman *Visitors* 13 "'And my grades are going up, so can't we ease up on the twenty-four/seven study thing.'" [B] 1999 Gilman and Sherman *Visitors* 161 "That's what Slayers had Watchers for, to do the Knowing Stuff thing." 1999 Golden and Holder *Immortal* 112 "'If you don't count the whole trapped-for-hours-with-a-bunch-of dead-corpses thing,' Xander added amiably." 1999 Golden and Holder *Sons of Entropy* 175 "'You get used to it after a while. The surreal part, that is. The screwed thing? When it starts to matter, that's a bummer.'" [O] 2000 Holder *The Evil That Men Do* 40 "'Besides the lying to my parents almost constantly thing; and, well, stuff...' She trailed off." [W] 2000 Garton *Resurrecting Ravana* 38 "'I don't buy cow barn dances or toga parties on the pasture, but yeah, we should do whatever we can to prevent the being-eaten-alive thing.'" [X] 2000 Sep 1 The Bronze "Amber menti[o]ns the Amber is a hottie thing." 2001 Jul Golden *Food Chain* [12] "Okay, I've been in trouble. A lot. But with the whole standing-against-the-darkness thing, there isn't much that I can do about it." [B] 2001 Oct 16 Petrie and Espenson *Flooded* "Since you've been back, you really haven't been big with the whole range of human emotions thing." [W] 2001 Nov *Dreamwatch* 47/3 "[Sarah Michelle Gellar:] 'Joss [Whedon] has an overall creative deal and he's proven that he can create, not one, but two, fabulous shows, and he will go on to create more. Otherwise, it's a personal thing vs. a business corporate thing.'" 2001 Odom *Revenant* 322

"Despite the whole ticking clock thing, Buffy smiled and joined the others in welcoming her friend back." 2002 Feb 5 De Knight *Dead Things* "Come share in the joy of our groove thing." [Anya] 2002 Feb 26 Petrie *As You Were* "So you guys do this often, you know, the whole husband and wife tag team demon fighting thing?" [B] 2002 Apr 30 Greenberg *Entropy* "You know, my whole sticky fingers grabby hands thing." [D] 2002 Jul 28 Bronze: Beta "Eek, I'm doing this awake all night thing again." 2002 Navarro *Tempted Champions* 125 "Maybe they would end up staying in Sunnydale and helping in that never-ending-battle-thing." [fr. thing n in sense 16.b]

thuddage n Skid hitting
2000 Sep 1 The Bronze "I don't recall seeing Leo in the previews but I do predict thuddage." [thud in sense 1 + -age suff in sense 1.a]

timeliness n Characteristic of time
2001 Oct 2 Noxon *Bargaining* 1 "It's time? Like time time? With the timeliness?" [X] [time n in sense 1 + -li- infix + -ness suff]

topicage 1: n Posting board conversation that adheres to current subjects of discussion regarding BTVS
2000 Sep 1 The Bronze "Topicage, ah topicage" 2001 Jun 2 The Bronze "I thought it was just CK toppicage [sic]." 2001 Jun 2 The Bronze "I have lots of topicage for you."
  2: n Activity of conversing about BTVS subjects on a posting board
2002 Jul 25 Bronze: Beta "I am enjoying your Buffy/Spike/Dru posts and wishing I had time to join in the topic-age." [topic n in sense 2 + -age suff in sense 4.a]
  3: adj Topical
2001 Jun 2 The Bronze "And enjoying the topicage marriage, money and Xander/Anya's betrothal." [topic n in sense 2 + -age suff in sense 1.a]

topicy adj On the topic
1999 Oct 13 The Bronze "I'm sleepy and I've not had a chance to re-watch the eps [...] but will rewatch and post tomorrow for better topicy goodness." 2000 Sep 1 The Bronze "I have no topicy goodness to add."

2000 Sep 1 The Bronze "I'm a dismal source of topic-y stuff." 2001 Jun 2 The Bronze "Yum. Topicy goodness." 2002 Jul 23 Bronze: Beta "Nice to see you getting all topiccy [sic]. Good points there." 2002 Jul 30 Bronze: Beta "I may even stick around a bit, but don't expect me to get too topicy." 2002 Jul 30 Bronze: Beta "Topicy poems will be posted the very next day on the board, others will appear when the topic fits." [topic n + -y¹ suff in sense 1]

trancey *adj* As in a trance
2000 Oct 24 Petrie *All in the Family* "I'll go home, I'll get trancey, and I'll see what's affecting my mom." [B] [*trance* n in sense 1 + y¹ suff in sense 1]

tweakos n Geeks
1997 Nov 17 Gordon and Noxon *What's My Line, Part 1* "Oh, right. 'Cause I lie awake at night hoping you tweakos will be my best friends." [C] 1998 Golden and Holder *Child of the Hunt* 54 "'The only people who will be going to that are boring adults and role-playing tweekos.'" [C] [fr. *DAS3* tweaked adj 'odd, crazy' (prob. through *tweako n 'odd, crazy person') + -s¹ suff]

twelve-steppy *adj* Confessional
1999 Mar 16 Petrie *Enemies* "I don't wanna get all twelve-steppy, but remember when you told me that killing people would make me feel like some kind of god? I think I just came down to earth." [F] [*twelve step* adj + -(p)y¹ suff in sense 1]

twitchy *adj* Unnerved
1998 Dec 15 Whedon *Amends* "I don't want to bug Giles. He's still twitchy about the subject of Angel." [B] [fr. *twitchy* adj in sense 2]

überachiever n Super go-getter
2000 Holder *Watcher's Guide 2* 119 "Überachiever Willow has another source of her own private pain: her mother completely ignores her[.]" [German *über-* in sense 'super' + *achiever* n sv *achieve* v] See ÜBERBITCA sv BITCA

übercreepy *adj* The creepiest
2002 *Scooby Doo* "This place is, like, über-creepy." [German über- in sense 'super' + *creepy adj* in sense 1]

überevil n Unsurpassed evil
2000 Feb 15 Noxon *Goodbye, Iowa* "Then I got sucked right back into the überevil." [B] [German über- in sense 'above all' + *evil* n in sense 3]

überexcited *adj* Tremendously excited
2002 Jul 28 Bronze: Beta "For some reason I've been uber excited about my birthday this year." [German über- in sense 'super' + *excited adj* in sense 1]

übernerd *adj* Exceptionally socially inept, technically focused
2001 Dec Andrews *Starburst* 26/1 "They're funny and unusual, but their über-nerd geekiness could start to grate after a while." [German über- in sense 'above all' + *nerd* n in senses 1 & 2]

übersuck n Worst possible thing
1997 Oct 6 Kiene and Reinkemeyer *Inca Mummy Girl* "[Buffy:] 'It's so unfair.' [Willow:] 'I don't think it's that bad.' [Buffy:] 'It's the übersuck.'" 1999 Oct 1 Howard *Entertainment Weekly* 49/4 "**(the) ubersuck** Major bummer." [fr. German über- in sense 'above all' + *suck* vi in sense 4]

übervampire n Worst possible vampire
1999 Oct Watson *Buffy the Vampire Slayer* 14 [Dark Horse Comic] [14] "'The three uber-vampires have left town. My intuition says they'll be back though.'" [X] 2002 Money *Fighting the Forces* 99 "The rehabilitation theme is introduced in the transformations of Angel, soulful vampire extraordinaire, when he loses his soul and reverts to Angelus, evil Über-vampire." [German über- in sense 'super' + *vampire* n in sense 1]

überwitch n Most powerful sorceress
2002 May 21 Fury *The Grave* "You may be a hopped up überwitch, but this carpenter can drywall you into the next century." [X] [German über- in sense 'super' + *witch* n in senses 1 & 2]

unbad *adj* Not bad, but not good
1999 *Official Yearbook* 10/1 "As the undead dude who was un-bad, then ungood, then un-bad again, he's put all our heroes through an emotional roller coaster." [un-[1] *pref* in sense 1 + *bad adj* in sense 2] See UNGOOD

unbeating *adj* Still
2002 Navarro *Tempted Champions* 132 "Harmony had tried hard, you had to give her that, but his little unbeating chunk o' heart just hadn't been in it." [un-[1] *pref* in sense 1 + *beat vi* in sense 2 + *-ing*[1] *suff*]

unbendy *adj* Straight
1999 Nov 30 Forbes *Something Blue* "I will that this Q-tip becomes unbendy again." [W] [un-[1] *pref* in sense 1 + *bend v* in sense 2.a + *-y*[1] *suff* in sense 1]

unbudger *n* One who will not move from or relinquish a point, idea, principle
1997 Oct 6 Kiene and Reinkemeyer *Inca Mummy Girl* "C'mon, Giles, budge. No one like an unbudger." [B] [un-[1] *pref* in sense 2 + *budge*[1] *vi* in sense 2 + *-er*[1] *suff* in sense 1.a]

unchipperness *n* Malaise
2001 Jun 2 The Bronze "Why the unchipperness?" [un-[1] *pref* in sense 1 + *chipper*[3] *adj* + *-ness suff*]

uncommunicated *adj* Unspoken
2001 Odom *Revenant* 4 "'Why is it that guys just never can get the easy things in life? Like basic uncommunicated communication? The things you aren't supposed to know, but do, but also understand you're not supposed to talk about.'" [W] [un-[1] *pref* in sense 1 + *communicate v* in sense 1.a + *-ed*[2] *suff*]

uncomputered *adj* Lacking a computer
2002 Jul 28 Bronze: Beta "I've been un-computered most of the time since hitting the road, oh…weeks ago." [un-[2] *pref* in sense 2.a + *computer n* in sense 1 + *-ed*[2] *suff*]

undead 1.a: n   Vampires or other demons; a vampire or another demon

1994 (1897) Stoker *Dracula* 200 "'Usually when the Un-Dead sleep at home [...] their face show [sic] what they are.'"   1994 (1897) Stoker *Dracula* 201 "'He will think that we may be right, and that his so beloved was, after all, an Un-Dead.'"   1992 Whedon *Buffy the Vampire Slayer* "The world is under attack by legions of the undead." [Pike]   1995 Auerbach *Our Vampires, Ourselves* 1 "Introduction: Living with the Undead." [chapter title]   1997 Sep 15 Whedon *When She Was Bad* "We're still the undead's favorite party town."   1997 Oct 13 Greenwalt *Reptile Boy* "Digging on the undead doesn't exactly do wonders for your social life." [B]   1997 Golden and Holder *Halloween Rain* 7 "It'd be a lot easier to tell the undead from the brain dead."   1998 Apr 2 Dunn *Rolling Stone* 43/2 "[V]iewers began to warm to the adventures of Buffy, a teen from Sunnydale High who has the power to destroy the undead."   1998 May *Spectrum* 10/1 "[I]n both the movie and the series, people other than Buffy 'kill' the undead."   1998 Sep Stoller *George* 110/2 "Buffy the Vampire Slayer [...] represents real girl power, the kind that can kung-fu the undead back into oblivion."   1998 Oct *Details* 149 "Every time the sexy teen scourge of the undead body-slams a vampire, pound a beer."   1998 Oct Brereton *The Dust Waltz* [49] "'Who says the undead don't know how to party?'" [B]   1998 Nov Brody *In Style* 285 "The young actresses are not stalking the undead."   1998 Edwards *Buffy X-Posed* 103/2 "Watching Buffy balance her responsibility with her ongoing battles with the undead doesn't really work here."   1998 Tracy *The Girl's Got Bite* 66 "Rice does subscribe, however, to the long-standing belief that fire is a sure way to kill the undead."   1998 Winter *Buffy the Vampire Slayer* 51 "**undead** [...] *adj.* [sic] vampire or zombie; dead but doesn't act like it." 1998 Nov 17 Petrie *Revelations* "I've had my share of losers, but you, you boinked the undead." [F]   1998 Golden and Holder *Child of the Hunt* 206 "The undead were soulless, and as such, abominations in the eyes of the Erl King and his Huntsmen."   1998 Gardner *Return to Chaos* 203 "The Hellmouth drew the undead to its power, like insects to a flame." 1999 May 13 The Bronze "Dream Buffy Movie Plot? Something really big! I'm thinking...The First Evil (appearing as Jenny) is gathering an army of the undead in a final move to crush humanity." 1999 Golden *Sins of the Father* 177 "Which was, of course, what the families of so many of the undead would say if they were to come face-to-face with their bloodthirsty loved ones." 1999 Oct 1 *Entertainment Weekly* 25/2 "[S]exual healing is not an option for the cursed undead." 1999 Oct 13 The Bronze "I agree with a couple of other Bronzers that don't see any romance going on between Officer Kate and the Undead." 2000 Apr *Sky Magazine* 86/1 "Which, when you're supposed to be kebabing the undead, isn't good news." 2000 Nov Watson *Pale Reflections* [40] "She spends most of her time ramming stakes through the undead." [C] 2000 Sedaris *Me Talk Pretty One Day* 143 "It was my father's dream that one day the people of the world would be connected to one another through a network of blocky, refrigerator-size computers, much like those he was helping develop at IBM. [...] I was hoping the people of the world might be united by something more interesting, like drugs or an armed struggle against the undead." 2000 Gilman and Sherman *Deep Water* 49 "'Oooo, chatting with the undead. My favorite hobby.'" [X] 2000 Topping *Slayer* 94 "After Buffy goes home, Ford returns to a club full of groupies who dream of joining the undead." 2001 Jun 2 The Bronze "Buffy cannot come back as the undead, its too ironic her trying to kill the undead." 2001 Tonkin *Reading the Vampire Slayer* 48 "Buffy [...] hangs out with the undead." 2002 Jul 23 Bronze: Beta "[I]n essence they were his mirror image—the living dead vs the undead." 2002 Jul 30 Bronze: Beta "But please no more BOINKING the undead. Bleech." 2002 Navarro *Tempted Champions* 16 "Sunnydale was infested with the undead." 2002 Overbey and Preston-Matto *Fighting the Forces* 75 "Buffy is punny—even the undead know it." 2002 Krimmer and Raval *Fighting the Forces* 162 "A postmodern reader might suggest that the allure of the series is not based on a maudlin enchantment with the dead (and undead) but lies in the moments that in which the show deconstructs its own premises."

    1.b: n Like a vampire, neither living nor dead
2002 Overbey and Preston-Matto *Fighting the Forces* 74 "So dead metaphors are not so much dead as undead. They die and then are reborn with a different purpose." [un-¹ *pref* in sense 1 + *dead adj* in sense 1]

1.c: n An element in names

2002 Jul 30 Bronze: Beta "Undead" [fr. UNDEAD in sense 3]

2: n *attrib* Pertaining to vampires or other demons

1997 Sep 22 King *Some Assembly Required* "Sorry to interrupt your little undead playgroup, but I need to ask Willow if she'll help me with my science fair project." [C] 1997 Golden and Holder *Halloween Rain* 44 "Maybe Buffy's undead radar was staring to rub off." 1999 Mar 12 Fretts *Entertainment Weekly* 51/1 "Even as she joined Buffy's anti-undead crusade, the seeds of Faith's destructiveness were being planted by the authors." 1999 Sep/Oct *Cinescape* 52 "Plus, when she's not kicking undead butt or cramming for midterms, the Chosen One might have some extra time to go out on dates." 1999 Golden and Holder *Immortal* 40 "Yeah, well, whoever's riding shotgun on this undead posse must have an extra special itch, 'cause they were real concerned about reproducing last night, waiting for a newbie to rise." 1999 Gilman and Sherman *Visitors* 120 "'Giles will know if I need to stake someone before they take up the undead nonlifestyle tomorrow.'" [B] 1999 Gallagher *Obsidian Fate* 81 "The dichotomy he had had to live with, the good and evil that had alternately possessed him during the two hundred and fifty years of his undead existence, had left invisible scars." 2000 Passarella *Ghoul Trouble* 157 "'Maybe Solitaire just found the magic charm in the undead lost and found.'" [B] 2001 Jun 2 The Bronze "No. Just because he is treated like a human does not relieve him of un-dead problems." 2001 Odom *Revenant* 210 "Her mom had brushed up against Sunnydale's undead underbelly a few times and knew it existed, and Buffy hated that." 2002 Jul 23 Bronze: Beta "Xander is about to go off and chop the blond one into tiny undead bits for trying to rape Buffy." 2002 Sep 13 Robischon *Entertainment Weekly* 158/3 "Despite a well-balanced blend of puzzle solving, undead killing, and adventure, the combat system is flawed." 2002 Navarro *Tempted Champions* 22 "And they were always getting their undead butts roundly kicked, too." 2002 Money *Fighting the Forces* 99 "Drusilla, the love of his undead life, has dumped him because he had allied himself with the Slayer."

3: *adj* Not dead, vampiric

1994 (1897) Stoker *Dracula* 205 "'Un-Dead! Not alive!'" 1994 (1897)

Stoker *Dracula* 205 "'I go no further than to say that she might be Un-Dead.'" 1995 Auerbach *Our Vampires, Ourselves* 190 "Undead and in control, she need not defer to male supremacy." 1998 May *Spectrum* 10/1 "Vampires are eternally 'undead' and feed off the blood of humans." 1998 Edwards *Buffy X-Posed* 178 "Quarry remains pleased with his characterization of the undead Count Yorga." 1998 Tracy *The Girl's Got Bite* 53 "What Angel didn't plan on was falling in love with Buffy, which forced him to openly renounce his undead brethren." 1998 Gardner *Return to Chaos* 114 "'That's one of the perks of being undead,' Naomi said brightly." 1998 Golden and Holder *Blooded* 8 "The only thing worse, in her opinion, than a fat, slobbering, undead, bloodsucking show-off was one who was also completely out of his head." 1999 Oct 1 Tucker *Entertainment Weekly* 22/1 "Her good looks and super training don't help her with failing school grades, teachers who've pegged her as a problem child, and a mother who can't fathom the burdens of dating an undead guy." 1999 Oct 13 The Bronze "Every good detective has to have his inside cop buddy—even an undead one." 1999 Oct Watson *Buffy the Vampire Slayer* 14 [Dark Horse Comics] [15] "'We may be undead but we have our pride.'" 1999 Nov 30 Forbes *Something Blue* "[Giles:] 'A truth spell, of course. Why didn't I think of that?' [Willow:] 'Because you had your hands full with the undead English Patient?'" 1999 *Official Yearbook* 10/1 "As the undead dude who was un-bad, then un-good, then un-bad again, he's put all our heroes through an emotional roller coaster." 2000 Gallagher *Doomsday Deck* 34 "[Willow:] 'If the local vampires pig out and a bunch of artists end up dead—' [Oz:] 'Or undead.' [...] [Buffy:] 'Mom will feel responsible.'" 2000 Holder *Watcher's Guide* 2 162 "Unable to persuade Angel to continue to be undead, Buffy moves from pleading to anger." 2001 Sept 8 *TV Guide* 15 "But Angel is a powerful character, and if the show can continue to add fresh meat to his dark universe [...] our undead hero should continue to thrive." 2002 Jul 28 Bronze: Beta "Riley took up with undead hookers." 2002 Navarro *Tempted Champions* 32 "She wasn't really high on the idea of torturing people, alive or undead." 2002 Wilcox *Fighting the Forces* 5 "As Angel points out, he being undead has no breath to offer." 2002 Erickson *Fighting the Forces* 111 "The Victorian vampire is undead, unhuman, and very literally an Antichrist, risen from the dead, offering the possibility of eternal life."

4: *adj* Perennially significant, valorized by tradition
2001 Playden *Reading the Vampire Slayer* 121 "On the one hand is a monumental cemetery filled with undead white males, the grand narrative of Western thought, from Freud back to Plato." [fr. UNDEAD in sense 1.a]

Undead-American n American who is ethnically a vampire
1997 Sep 15 Whedon *When She Was Bad* "You're a vampire. Or is that an offensive term? Should I say 'Undead-American'?" 1999 Oct 1 Howard *Entertainment Weekly* 49/3 "**undead american** Politically correct term for vampire." [UNDEAD + *American* n in sense 1]

unDead Sea Scrolls n Fanciful ancient documents of the underworld
2002 Jul 24 Bronze: Beta "Just for that, those unDead Sea Scrolls will be kept locked up for another century. It's time to pass Satan the A-1." 2002 Jul 24 Bronze: Beta "Judas: Don't worry. I'm sure that as soon as those pertinent unDead Sea Scrolls are publicized, you'll be vindicated and Satan will stop chewing on you." [UNDEAD + Dead *Sea Scrolls* n pl]

undeath n State of being UNDEAD, suspended between life and death
1995 Auerbach *Our Vampires, Ourselves* 3 "I was received with polite revulsion at a Women's Studies symposium when I gave a paper on undeath." 1999 Odom *Unnatural Selection* 186 "Absolute carnage reigned as vampires and changelings battled to the death and undeath." 2000 Garton *Resurrecting Ravana* 126 "'I don't know how Buffy deals with it...y'know, the killing. The death. Or maybe [...] the undeath.'" [W] 2002 *John Carpenter's Vampires: Los Muertos* "Now, Derek, would that be actual death, or undeath?" [un-¹ pref in sense 1 + *death* n in sense 2; by analysis from UNDEAD]

undreaming *adj* Dreamless
2000 Gilman and Sherman *Deep Water* 90 "She'd managed to grab an hour or so of shut-eye after that, thankfully of the undreaming kind." [un-¹ pref in sense 1 + *dream* v in sense 1 + -ing¹ suff in sense 1]

unfriendlies n Demons
2000 Jan 18 Noxon, Fury, and Espenson *Doomed* "You're part of some military monster squad that rounds up demons, vampires—probably have official-sounding euphemisms for them like 'Unfriendlies' or 'Nonsapiens.'" [B] [*unfriendly adj* in sense 1 + *-ies suff*]

unfun 1: n Bad thing, a bad time
1999 Mar 16 Petrie *Enemies* "Graduation Day. There's a big scary unfun." [W] 1999 Gilman and Sherman *Visitors* 83 "'Oh, great,' Xander groused, resigning himself to an afternoon of having unfun." 2001 Odom *Revenant* 3 "Making mistakes equals unfun." [*un-*[1] *pref* in sense 1 + *fun n* in sense 1]
   2: *adj* Disappointing
2002 Jan 13 Robinson *www.theonionavclub.com* 3 "[Joss Whedon:] 'I also have the only poster left with my name still on it. Getting arbitrated off the credits was un-fun.'" [*un-*[1] *pref* in sense 1 + *fun adj*] See FUN

ungood *adj* Not good, but not bad
1999 *Official Yearbook* 10/1 "As the undead dude who was un-bad, then un-good, then un-bad again, he's put all our heroes through an emotional roller coaster." [*un-*[1] *pref* in sense 1 + *good adj* in sense 17.a] See UNBAD

unh 1: n Sex
1999 Feb 9 Petrie *Bad Girls* "I mean, I'm sorry, it's just, all this sweating nightly, side-by-side action, and you never put in for a little after-hours unh?" [F]
   2: n DUSTING
1999 Feb 9 Petrie *Bad Girls* "Tell me that if you don't get in a good slaying, after a while, you just start itching for some vamp to show up so you can give him a good unh." [F] [grunt, accompanied by pumping arm gesture]

unlazy *adj* Without a tendency to idleness
2002 Jan 13 Robinson *www.theonionavclub.com* 8 "[Joss Whedon:] 'I'm not unlazy, and I do procrastinate.'" [*un-*[1] *pref* in sense 1 + *lazy adj* in sense 1]

unlife 1: n Life (for a vampire)
1998 Nov 24 Vebber *Lovers' Walk* "And I said, 'Yeah, I've got an unlife,
you know!'" [S] 1999 Oct 1 Howard *Entertainment Weekly* 49/4 "**unlife**
Living (to the undead)." 2000 Gilman and Sherman *Deep Water* 55
"[W]hat were these green-haired, green-skinned...things? Nothing he
had encountered, not in sixty years of unlife, nor the thirty before then."
2002 Jul 28 Bronze: Beta "Drusilla—she'd be lots of fun and would
probably give me a whole new perspective on life (or unlife)." 2002
Navarro *Tempted Champions* 135 "Here he was, putting his unlife on the
line for the Slayer and all she did was moon over Angel." 2002 Jul 23
Bronze: Beta "But even while possessing this pleasant Buffy, he is willing
to sacrifice himself for the less-pleasant Buffy, not in a unlife-for-a-life
swap, but in order for her to be spared the grief of losing her sister."
[un-¹ *pref* in sense 1 + *life* n in sense 10.a]
   2: n Empty life, life of no quality
1998 Dec 2 The Bronze "I have an un-life ya know!" [signature] [fr. un-
¹ *pref* in sense 2 + *life* n in sense 10.a]

unlive vi Persist in an undead state
1999 Gallagher *Obsidian Fate* 26 "Truth was, the town's underground
contingent—literally, guys who unlive in graves and other equally dark
and disgusting places." 2002 Navarro *Tempted Champions* 99 "'Eternity
is a long time, too long to live—or unlive—without them.'" [W] 2002
Navarro *Tempted Champions* 162 "I think it's pretty clear how she's been
living. Or unliving." [W] [un¹- *pref* in sense 1 + *live* vi in sense 1]

unmad adj Not angry (perhaps with the implication that the person
described is also not happy)
1997 Oct 27 Ellsworth *Halloween* "Actually, he was unmad." [W] [un-¹
pref in sense 1 + *mad* adj in sense 1]

unminiony adj Not subordinated to [something]
2001 Jun 2 The Bronze "Yes, I'm feeling distinctly un-miniony." [un-¹
pref in sense 1 + *minion* n in sense 1 + *y¹* suff in sense 1]

unmixy adj Incompatible
1999 Nov 30 Forbes *Something Blue* "Cars and Buffy are, like, unmixy

things." [B] [un-¹ *pref* in sense 1 + mix *vi* in sense 1.b + -y¹ *suff* in sense 1]

unquality *adj*   Not particularly good
2002 Navarro *Tempted Champions* 215 "[S]he'd spent so much time in this place, quality and unquality time, that she'd come to appreciate the simple, cold beauty of the statues and monuments." [un-¹ *pref* in sense 1 + quality *adj* in sense]

unrelationship n   A friendship neither romantic nor platonic, but almost both
1998 Golden and Holder *Child of the Hunt* 75 "When she'd lived in L.A., her friend Hilly used to say that she liked guys who had a certain something she could never quite put into words. She just called it 'Grrrrr.' Angel had lots and lots of Grrrrr. Sometimes—hell, most of the time— it made their new 'un-relationship' pretty difficult to bear." 2000 Gilman and Sherman *Deep Water* 24 "'When it comes to our un-relationship, he dances around the facts like Fred Astaire,' Buffy thought." [un-¹ *pref* in sense 1 + *relationship* n in sense 4]

unscrolled *adj*   Not yet having reviewed posts on a posting board
2002 Jul 25 Bronze: Beta "Home from dinner, still unscrolled, going to do that now." [un-¹ *pref* in sense 1 + scroll *vi* in sense 1 + -ed² *suff*]

untopicy *adj*   Off the subject
2002 Jul 29 Bronze: Beta "If you think this is now becoming too un-topicy and would prefer to tale it off the board send me an e-[mail]." [un-¹ *pref* in sense 1 + TOPICY]

untopicyness *adj*   Condition of being off the subject
2000 Sep 1 The Bronze "[D]amn your untopicyness (theres a word for anyone haha)." [un-¹ *pref* + TOPICY + -ness *suff*]

unwindy *adj*   Relaxed
2002 Feb 5 DeKnight *Dead Things* "We're thinking of heading to the Bronze later. Wanna come and get all unwindy?" [W]   [unwind *vi* in sense 2 + -y¹ *suff* in sense 1]

unworried *adj* Not afflicted by concern
2001 Oct 9 Espenson *After Life* "[Tara:] 'You don't have to be brave. I still love you. If you're worried, you can be worried.' [Willow:] 'Well, I'm not unworried.'" [un-¹ pref in sense 1 + worry vi in sense 1 + -ed³ suff]

vagueness n Unclear, obscure
1999 Nov 16 Petrie *The Initiative* "I know that sounds lame, that's vagueness." [W] [*vague* adj in sense 1 + -ness suff]

vague up vt Make less clear
1997 Mar 10 Whedon *Welcome to Hellmouth* "Gee, can you vague that up for me?" [B] 2001 Jun 2 The Bronze "Now then, that post made the kind of sense my poor befuddled brain just can't seem to cope with. Could you vague that up for me?" [fr. *vague* adj in sense 1 + up adv in sense 12]

vamp 1.a: n Vampire
1998 Sep Stoller *George* 113 "Her excuse is that he's turned out to be a vamp." 1998 Oct 13 Greenwalt *Faith, Hope, and Trick* "Funny thing about vamps, they'll hit a street even after you've been there. It's like they have no manners." [B] 1998 Dec 8 Noxon *The Wish* "Makes you appreciate vamps, though—no fuss, no muss." [B] 1998 Gardner *Return to Chaos* 8 "The newcomer had something in his hands—it looked like a crossbow—and quickly shot a pair of those little arrow things—bolts, yeah, that's what they were called—at the two nearest vamps." 1998 Golden and Holder *Watcher's Guide* 1 134 "Giles, Buffy, and the Slayerettes all assume that Borba is the Anointed One when he rises from his slab in the Sunnydale Funeral Home as a full-fledged, very crazy vamp." 1998 Edwards *Buffy X-Posed* 119/2 "The vamp's got a point there." 1999 Mar Watson *The Remaining Sunlight* [39] "Hey, vamps seem to get all the chicks." 1999 Summer Iyer *Buffy the Vampire Slayer* 14 "Many of the vamps that Buffy slays on a regular basis are pretty darn old." 1999 Oct 1 *Entertainment Weekly* 25/2 "**Turn-ons** Demon Angel: Darla (the vamp who sired him)." 1999 Oct 13 The Bronze "Lost your reflection? Then call 1-800-IMA-VAMP for a free brochure." 1999 Oct Watson *Buffy the Vampire Slayer* 14 [Dark Horse Comics] [10] "'They were not your com-

mon or garden [sic] vamps.'" [B]   1999 Nov 16 Petrie *The Initiative* "I know I'm not the kinda girl vamps like to sink their teeth into." [W] 1999 Gilman and Sherman *Visitors* 15 "Not a vamp in sight, not even stupid ones." 1999 Massie *Power of Persuasion* 40 "'Besides,' she thought, 'even though it was way unusual, I handled the grab-happy vamps.'" [B] 1999 *Official Yearbook* 8/1 "[A] college hunk tied her up and tried to feed her to Machida, and an old flame from her former school returned to try and turn her over to the vamps." 2000 Jan Sullivan *Teen* 59 "After all, dating vamps can be kinda draining!" 2000 Sep 1 The Bronze "Angel's Angelus[,] My fave little Aussie vamp." 2000 Oct 3 Fury *Real Me* "'Yeah, I got the vamps, and we watched TV.'" [B]   2000 Oct 17 Kirshner *Out of My Mind* "I've got a proposition for you: what about knocking? Seems only fair, since we vamps can't enter your flat without an invite." [S] 2000 Dokey *Here Be Monsters* 55 "As soon as the vamp cleared, Buffy vaulted to her feet and whipped around." 2000 Gilman and Sherman *Deep Water* 4 "'Serves me right for saying I was getting bored with the same old, same old vamps.'" [B]   2000 Gallagher *Prime Evil* 41 "She heard nothing, saw nothing, but sensed a solitary vamp dart out of the shadows behind her." 2000 Navarro *Paleo* 16 "Buffy hated it when the night's vamp turned out to be a child." 2000 Holder *Watcher's Guide* 2 98 "Mr. Trick is a vamp who comes to town in the company of Faith's nemesis, Kaikistos." 2001 Jun 2 The Bronze "So do you think Jennifer Love Hewitt will bring a new dimension to her role as 'Buffy' this fall. Can the 'Brunski' be and [sic] effective fighting technique against vamps?" 2001 Oct 23 Fury and Espenson *Life Serial* "Ah, so it's a set up, i'n't. Squeeze a few quid outta the vamp." [S]   2001 Oct 30 DeKnight *All the Way* "Were you parking…with a vamp?" [B]   2001 Dec Andrews *Starburst* 22 "[W]e see the end of the cue wobble and then slowly swing upwards as the vamp collapses off screen." 2001 Wilson *Reading the Vampire Slayer* 81 "Spike, on the other hand, dispenses with the evil mastermind blather altogether upon destroying the Anointed One and establishing himself (for a time) as the baddest vamp in town." 2002 Feb 26 Petrie *As You Were* "Some vamp get rough with you?" [D]   2002 Mar Espenson *Haunted* [Dark Horse Comics] [4] "But the thing is…the vamp that did it, when he was going to bite, he said, 'I should have done this to the librarian.'" [W]   2002 Jul 24 Bronze: Beta "Strong vamps are older vamps." 2002 Sep 13 Robischon *Entertainment Weekly* 158/2 "You'll also get to wander around The Bronze and other familiar locales, vanquishing vamps with stakes, reaper blades, crossbows, rakes, shovels, and baseball bats." 2002 Navarro *Tempted Champions* 28 "Funny how the vamps always paired or packed together once they made it through the initial survival period." 2002 Krzywinska *Fighting the Forces* 190 "In 'Lie to Me,' Angel visits a 'goth' nightclub and says that none of the vamp-worshiping goths know anything about vampires or what they wear." 2002 Dechert *Fighting the Forces* 221 "As Xander dusts a troublesome vamp at The Bronze, an enraptured Buffy watches."

    1.b: n   An element in names

1998 Dec 2 The Bronze "No katvamp that wasn't your que [i.e. cue] to take a shot at me."   1999 May 13 The Bronze "Hey, tackiVamp!"   1999 Oct 13 The Bronze " 1 Vamp"   1999 Oct 13 The Bronze "vamplet"

    2:   n *attrib*   Pertaining to vampires

1997 Oct 27 Ellsworth *Halloween* "Halloween quiet? I figured it would have been a big ole vamp Scareapalooza." [X]   1997 Golden and Holder *Halloween Rain* 41 "Buffy had gone down there after some vamp tramp several minutes earlier, and hadn't reappeared."   1998 Golden and Holder *Child of the Hunt* 34 "'I thought you said we were dealing with slightly extra-savage vamp attacks.'" [B]   1999 Jun 26 The Bronze "Sorry, I was looking after Angel (she says drooling in full vamp form)."   1999 Golden and Holder *Immortal* 39 "'We've got a rise in vamp activity.'" [B]   2000 Holder *The Evil That Men Do* 132 "'No. It doesn't stop me,' the vampire said, spreading her mouth as she morphed into vamp mode."   2000 Gallagher *Doomsday Deck* 13 "Too bad we can't put up a vamp blockade." [X]   2000 Passarella *Ghoul Trouble* 21 "Angel was probably deep in vamp sleep in his mansion."   2000 Holder *Watcher's Guide* 2 159 "Buffy's successful vamp staking dumps Cordelia in the trash."   2001 Jun 2 The Bronze "I thought, 'that looks like Riley and a vamp prostitute, surely not.'"   2002 Jul 29 Bronze: Beta "So…is this rock/paper/scissors, the vamp version?"   2002 Navarro *Tempted Champions* 65 "[S]he'd been skipped over when it came to vamp radar."

    3:   *adj*   Undead, like a vampire

1999 May 13 The Bronze "[D]o you like Willow? [D]o you like vamp Willow? [D]o you like Willow or vamp Willow in leather?"   1999 Jun 26

The Bronze "I would sooooo be a bad vamp chick." 1999 Jun 26 *http://angelfire.com/in/btvsjade/newbie*.html "**Vampire Board (or Vamp Board)** When no one (or hardly anyone) is posting, the board is dead, because no one is posting, but it's alive, because the board isn't down. Coined by **Grinn** [pseudonym of a frequent participant on the posting board called 'The Bronze']" 1999 Oct 1 *Entertainment Weekly* 45/2 "And we'll not only need, say, Angel in makeup, but vamp Angel." 2001 Jun 2 The Bronze "if any1 has any fan-fiction (esp. vamp Willow or Spike…could you send it to WatcherGiles2000@yahoo.co.uk?)." 2001 Kaveney *Reading the Vampire Slayer* 248 "Vamp Willow is sent back and staked." 2002 Jul 30 Bronze: Beta "I had no problem with Angel helping either human Darla or vamp Darla." [*vampire* n in sense 1]

   —**bedvamp** n Bedbug
1999 Jun 26 The Bronze "Nite, Crash ;-) Don't let the bedvamps bite." [*bedbug* n + VAMP]

   —**henchvamp** n Subordinate vampire
1998 Golden and Holder *Watcher's Guide* 1 141/1 "Spike's henchvamps steal back the box." 2000 Holder *Watcher's Guide* 2 145 "Buffy also reports a run-in with Kaikistos's henchvamps." [*henchman* n in sense 1 + VAMP]

   —**nonvamp** n Human
2000 Gilman and Sherman *Deep Water* 89 "'But there aren't any bodies other than these. No nonvamps.'" [B] [*non-* pref + VAMP]

   —**Supervamp** n Vampire of extraordinary powers
1998 Gardner *Return to Chaos* 272 "Otherwise, he might find some new teen queen to make over into Super-vamp." 2000 Nov Watson *Pale Reflections* [12] "[Giles:] 'But Angel's sure he will provide us with some information soon.' [Buffy:] 'Like where these "supervamps" came from?'" [*superman* n in sense 1 + VAMP; parallel to *Superman*]

   —**vampdom** n Condition of being a vampire
2000 Holder *Watcher's Guide* 2 168 "[H]e outsmarts his keepers and sires one into vampdom." [VAMP + -*dom* suff in sense 1]

   —**vamped** 1.a: vi Turned into a vampire
1998 Dec 2 The Bronze "I watch for Faith to be vamped, killed, or possessed." 2000 Sep 1 The Bronze "In true Buffy fashion you will now be vamped." 2001 Shuttleworth *Reading the Vampire Slayer* 226 "This taste

for a good ruck is itself an invented part of Spike's self-definition, part of the new character he fashioned for himself after being vamped by Drusilla." 2002 Jul 23 Bronze: Beta "But if he'd vamped, that's a) attempted murder and b) and indication that Spike is *lethally* out of control."

1.b: vt Turn into a vampire
2001 Shuttleworth *Reading the Vampire Slayer* 231 "His vampiric sire Darla, granted a similar (though not identical) possibility of redemption when restored to humanity, first tries to deny this change of identity by continuing on a path as evil as that of her vampire incarnation, and ultimately seeks to renounce it and return to the reassuringly known selfhood of centuries past by begging Angel to re-vamp her."

2: adj Turned into a vampire
2000 Holder *Watcher's Guide* 2 196 "During patrol, the newly vamped Eddie lures her into a confrontation with the Big Vampire on Campus." 2002 Jul 28 Bronze: Beta "Darla—Angelus—Drusilla—Spike where Darla's hate of vamped Dru [...] created Spike who ruined the first chance they had of restoring Angelus." [*vamp vi + -ed² suff] See VAMPING

—**vamped out** v phr Looking like a vampire
1999 Nov *Toyfare* 42 "The variant figure will be all in black and the exclusive figure also has an alternate head and hands that've been completely vamped out." 2000 Holder *Watcher's Guide* 2 162 "Buffy and Angel share a nightmare, which ends with Angel vamping out and biting her." 2002 Jul 23 Bronze: Beta "He was, in fact, on guard against the thing he believed he had to worry about—vamping out on her." [fr. VAMPED + out adv in sense 10]

—**vamp-face** 1: n Vampiric features into which a vampire's human face transforms when the vampire is about to kill
1998 Golden and Holder *Child of the Hunt* 73 "She had stopped seeing his vamp face when she was in his arms." 1998 Golden and Holder *Child of the Hunt* 180 "Though he was still in vamp-face, Angel seemed to have calmed down somewhat." 1999 Golden and Holder *Immortal* 86 "Even as she spun away, Pepper morphed into vamp face." 1999 Golden and Holder *Ghost Roads* 50 "Angel got out and slipped into the alley, vamp face morphing at the sound of rustling in the restaurant's brimming trash cans." 2000 Holder *The Evil That Men Do* 142 "'I'm

sure it's not the first innocent little boy he's killed,' Angel said, morphing into vamp face." 2000 Garton *Resurrecting Ravana* 143 "A male and female appeared out of the misty darkness [...] the ridges and creases of their vamp faces perfectly etched in deep shadow and the slightly yellowish glow from the streetlights above." 2000 Passarella *Ghoul Trouble* 16 "Nonetheless he tossed the stake to Angel, who was now in full vampface, as often happened when he was in battle." 2000 Holder *Watcher's Guide* 2 155 "Angel rises from the floor in vampface." 2002 Navarro *Tempted Champions* 38 "For a long moment, he let his features slide into vamp-face."

2: n Vampire
2000 Holder *Watcher's Guide* 2 145 "She is distracted by one of the dancers, whose extroverted personality looks doomed to meet an untimely end by an obvious vamp face." [VAMP + *face* n in sense 1.a]

3: adj Into evident vampire mode
2002 Jul 25 Bronze: Beta "I think a good solid physical fight where he went vamp-face might have done it in a way." [fr. sense 1]

—**vamp-free** adj Lacking vampires
2000 Navarro *Paleo* 155 "[Giles:] 'How was patrol?' [Buffy:] 'Amazingly vamp-free.'" [VAMP + *-free* suff, fr. *free* adj in sense 4.a & 4.b]

—**vamp-goon** n See HENCHVAMP
1998 Tracy *The Girl's Got Bite* 233 "When attacked by one of Drusilla's vamp-goons in front of her mother, Buffy is forced to spike the vampire and finally reveals to Joyce her identity as the Slayer." [VAMP + *goon* n in sense 1]

—**vamping** 1: vi Turning into a vampire
2001 Saxey *Reading the Vampire Slayer* 198 "Darla's resurrection as human, and subsequent re-vamping, the extraction from, and return to, the moment of [Buffy's] staking of vamp-Willow, Dracula's endless reformation from dust—all of these complicate the notion of what closure might be." 2002 Jul 30 Bronze: Beta "Spike was at least handsome and worth eating and vamping." See VAMPED

2: n Creation as a vampire
2002 Jul 28 Bronze: Beta "Dru is still psychic (a trait that predated Angel driving her insane, let alone her vamping." [**vamp* vi + *-ing*[1] suff in sense 1]

—**vampnap** *v* Abduct a vampire
1999 Mar 6 The Bronze "They will (vamp)nap me." 1999 Mar 6 The Bronze "The plot is that they (vamp)napp [sic] my boyfriend." 1999 Mar 6 The Bronze "I wish that Spike and Dru would vampnap me!! What a neat word vampnap!" [VAMP + (kid)nap *vt*]

—**vamp-snuffing** *adj* Vampire slaying
2000 Apr *Sky Magazine* 86/1 "Cut to her bedroom, where the vamp-snuffing garlic-queen is rolling around on the floor." [VAMP + snuff² *v* + -ing¹ *suff* in sense 1]

—**vampy** 1: *adj* Pertaining to vampires
1998 Mar Watson *The Remaining Sunlight* [??] "'Ewww, gross. Icky vampy stuff.'" [B] 1998 Golden and Holder *Blooded* 97 "'Good morning, Buffy. You were saying there was a lot of activity this weekend?' 'Vampy only,' she answered." 1999 Oct 1 Tucker *Entertainment Weekly* 22/2 "Actress Alyson Hannigan has been able to occasionally show Willow's vampy side." 1999 Golden and Holder *Immortal* 109 "And yet, after last night's run-in with vampy little Pepper Roback, she knew she had to go to school, if only to see Giles." 1999 Golden and Holder *Ghost Roads* 29 "When Angel got all vampy, it freaked him something fierce." 2002 Sep 13 Robischon *Entertainment Weekly* 158 "The new Buffy game offers plenty of vampy, high-stakes thrills." 2002 Navarro *Tempted Champions* 38 "'So I'm bending over and checking out this find, see, it looks like a good one, some left over fried Mandarin fish from the Chinese place [...] and these two vampy dudes coming strolling [sic] past the alley.'" [VAMP + -y¹ *suff* in sense 1]

2: *n* Diminutive vampire
1999 Gilman and Sherman *Visitors* 141 "'Here vampy,' Buffy called into the night as she stalked, not really expecting an answer. 'Here vampy vampy vampy.'" [VAMP + -y³ *suff* in sense 1]

vampiry *adj* Exhibiting features of a vampire
2000 Topping *Slayer* 26 "Darla's cure until she turns all vampiry." [vampire *n* in sense 1 + -y¹ *suff* in sense 1]

veininess *n* Conspicuous presence of veins
2002 Jan 29 Espenson *Doublemeat Palace* "[Anya:] '[She] was always con-

sidered to be a great beauty.' [Xander:] 'Well, hon, she was a little—there was some veininess.'" [*vein* n in sense 1.b + *-y*¹ suff in sense 1 + *-ness* suff]

veiny *adj* Marked by protuberant veins
2002 May 21 Fury *The Grave* "Yeah, I love you: I love crayon-breaky Willow and I love scary, veiny Willow." [X] [fr. *vein* n in sense 1.b + *-y*¹ suff in sense 1]

vibage n Good feelings
1999 May 13 The Bronze "The better vibage for her to catch." [*vibe* n + *-age* suff in sense 1.a]

vidfest n Session during which many videos are watched
1998 Feb 10 Noxon *Bewitched, Bothered, and Bewildered* "I'll be fine. Mom and I are gonna have a pig-out and vidfest. It's a time-honored tradition among the loveless." [B] [*video* n in sense 3 + *-fest*, fr. *fest* n] See BITE-FEST, SLAYERFEST, and SUCKFEST

viewage n Viewing
1999 Jun 26 The Bronze "Yes, we're still on for CI [i.e., the film, *Cruel Intentions* (1998)] viewage, don't panic!" 2000 Sep 1 The Bronze "Off to do some late-night movie view-age." [*view* vt in sense 1 + *-age* suff in sense 4.a]

Village People *adj* Gay, in the manner stereotypically ascribed to homosexuals
2000 Jan 25 Espenson *A New Man* "Oh, right—very manly—not at all Village People." [B] [fr. *Village People* '1980s pop group, in which all the members were homosexual']

VIPage n Presence of a significant personage
2001 Jun 2 The Bronze "I just wanted to ease your mind and let you enjoy the VIPage." [*VIP* n + *-age* suff in sense 1.a]

visitage 1: n Period of visiting
1999 Jun 26 The Bronze "UK visitage is looking good. UK August visitage isn't." 2000 Sep 1 The Bronze "[Y]up, visitage is indeed the plan." 2000 Sep 1 The Bronze "I can just imagine explaining said visitage to

my parents. 'what mom? Oh no, I'm off to meet some chick who's not my wife who I met on the internet and handcuffed me to a waiter once in DC.'" 2002 Jul 25 Bronze: Beta "Glorificus and I are plotting where to place them in our new digs. How goes it? Visitage soon?"

 2: *n attrib*
2000 Sep 1 The Bronze "You have E m'dear of the L.A. visitage kind." [*visit* n in sense 1.c + *-age* suff in sense 4.a]

wacky n   Strange stuff
1997 Sept 22 King *Some Assembly Required* "Love makes you do the wacky." [B]   1998 Winter *Buffy the Vampire Slayer* 51 "**wacky, the** [...] n. [B] irrational behavior often caused by love."   1999 May 13 The Bronze "'Love makes you do the wacky.'" [quoted in signature]   1999 Oct 1 Howard *Entertainment Weekly* 49/4 "**(the) wacky** Crazy things."   1999 Golden and Holder *Ghost Roads* 76 "'Who was it that said "love makes you do the wacky"?' Cordelia asked."   [fr. *wacky* adj in sense 2 (also DAS3 & NTC)]

Waco *adj*   Bloody, violent
2000 Garton *Resurrecting Ravana* 112 "Oz scratched the back of his head and screwed up his face before asking, 'Little too Waco?'"   [fr. *Waco* 'name of the Texas town near which Federal agents fired on and burned the Branch-Davidian religious cult's compound']

wakey-girl n   Girl kept awake by romantic troubles
1998 Oct 20 Noxon *All Men Are Beasts* "I've been at Mr. Donut since the TV did that snowy thing. How come you're the wakey-girl? I mean, this time it's not your boyfriend who's the cold-blooded...jelly donut?" [W] [*awake* adj in sense 1 + *-y*[1] suff in sense 1 + *girl* n in sense 2]

wannaslay *adj*   Person who wants to be a slayer
1998 Dec 8 Noxon *The Wish* "Had a prime kill—old crush, actually—'til that wannaslay librarian showed up." [X]   [fr. DAS3 *wannabe* n + *slay* v in sense 1]

watchage n   What can be viewed
2000 Sep 1 The Bronze "Watching my monthly season watchage of season three, and can't help but wonder how everybody thinks about each season." [*watch* v in sense 1 + *-age* suff in sense 1.a]

Watcher 1.a: n Mentor to the SLAYER [in sense 1.a]
1992 Whedon *Buffy the Vampire Slayer* "Trained by the Watcher, one
slayer dies and the next is chosen." 1997 Nov 24 Noxon *What's My
Line, Part 2* "My mother and father gave me to my Watcher because they
believed they were doing the right thing for me—and for the world."
[Kendra] 1997 Golden and Holder *Halloween Rain* 19 "He was the
Watcher. His job was to prepare the Slayer for her work, to train and
educate her, to teach her what she needed to know to keep breathing."
1998 Golden and Holder *Child of the Hunt* 34 "Buffy raised an eyebrow
at her Watcher." 1998 Golden and Holder *Child of the Hunt* 176 "'Listen
to me, old man,' the Watcher said." 1998 Edwards *Buffy X-Posed* 42 "Of
portraying Buffy's Watcher, Rupert Giles, he noted to the press, 'Giles
knows so much about vampires and monsters, but he knows nothing
about life.'" 1998 Tracy *The Girl's Got Bite* 12 "Donald Sutherland, whose
credits range from *M*A*S*H* to *JFK*, played the mysterious Watcher,
Merrick." 1999 May 13 The Bronze "The View of the Watcher is what is
important in this case." 1999 Sep DeCandido *American Libraries* 44
"Giles is the Watcher: the source of training, counterintelligence, and
guidance for high-school student Buffy Summers." 1999 Massie *Power
of Persuasion* 22 "Not only was Giles the librarian, he was also her Watcher,
the wise soul who was responsible for her Slayer training and education." 1999 *Official Yearbook* 10/1 "Though Angel tortured Giles for
secrets when he was in his nasty phase, the Watcher eventually recon-
ciled with Angel." 1999 Gilman and Sherman *Visitors* 5 "That reason, of
course, was to be the Watcher to the current Slayer of vampires." 1999
Odom *Unnatural Selection* 5 "Rupert Giles was a librarian and her Watcher."
2000 Sept 27 Noxon *Buffy vs. Dracula* "'You're what? You can't! You're
Buffy's Watcher.'" [W] 2000 Dokey *Here Be Monsters* 92 "She released
the door, heard it click closed behind her. Shutting out her friends, her
Watcher." 2000 Gilman and Sherman *Deep Water* 3 "Giles was her
Watcher—her coach, her mentor, her partner—and her knew her probably better than anyone else." 2000 Gallagher *Prime Evil* 21 "Aside from
taking quiet pride in being the Watcher for a Slayer who always got her
demon, Giles really cared about her." 2000 Garton *Resurrecting Ravana*
11 "'Reality check, Giles,' [Buffy] said. 'You Watcher, me Slayer.'" 2000
Navarro *Paleo* 105 "Me Slayer. You Watcher." [B] 2000 Holder *Watcher's*

Guide 2 9 "But when a Watcher is charged with the care of the Chosen One, he is *the* Watcher." 2002 Jul 31 Bronze: Beta "The Slayer and her Watcher use Bat Sonar and a machete to save the day." 2002 Vowell *The Partly Cloudy Patriot* 112 "You could have gotten some laughs out of an obnoxious, go-go American watcher. But it is off. It doesn't work." 2002 Wilcox *Fighting the Forces* 4 "As she says to her adviser, Watcher Rupert Giles, 'If you don't like the way I'm doing my job, why don't you find someone else?'"

1.b: n   Any of a number of those designated to train or protect Slayers

1997 Nov 10 Batali and Des Hotel *The Dark Age* "Maybe you should consider a career as a Watcher." [B]   1998 Golden and Holder *Child of the Hunt* 169 "'In fact, if you'd look that one over, I can move on to the Watchers' Journals for some mention of a homunculus or of the Hunt.'" [G]   1998 Gardner *Return to Chaos* 44 "And all those Slayers had always had Watchers to guide them on their way."   1998 Cover *Night of the Living Rerun* 47 "'I am convinced, Buffy, that if demons and other ghouls don't do in this particular Watcher someday, his favorite Slayer will manage to do the job for him.'" [G]   1998 Golden and Holder *Watcher's Guide* 1 9 "All Slayers have had a Watcher."   1998 Genge *The Buffy Chronicles* 3 "No more demolition of school property, no more Watchers judging her slaying techniques, right?"   1998 Stafford *Bite Me!* 103 "Giles is great as the very British librarian who, as a watcher, knows of his duties but seems completely unprepared for a rebellious slayer." 1999 Gallagher *Obsidian Fate* 32 "Aside from being born into a family of Watchers and given no choice in his career path either, he had had to improvise and adjust his no-nonsense British approach considerably since being assigned to her." 2000 Topping *Slayer* 18 "But when he's killed by Lothos, there's no evidence of soul transference, so maybe he's simplifying things for Buffy by not telling her there are other Watchers out there." 2001 Oct 2 Noxon and Fury *Bargaining* 2 "Every Slayer needs her Watcher." [Buffybot]   2001 Odom *Revenant* 17 "Who to save? That was a really big thing that a Watcher never trained a Slayer on." 2001 Wall and Zryd *Reading the Vampire Slayer* 71 "Indeed, we have already invoked the Council of Watchers as a representation of a corporate board of directors." 2002 May 21 Fury *The Grave* "Thanks, but I can kill a couple geeks all by myself. But, hey, if you'd like to watch—I mean, that's what you Watchers are good at, right, watching? Butting in on things that don't concern you?" [W]   2002 Navarro *Tempted Champions* 23 "Do-gooders abounded: ex-Watchers, demons who didn't like their own dimensions, those annoying little white witches."   2002 Williams *Fighting the Forces* 61 "Buffy's power is directed by her Watcher, Rupert Giles, and the largely male Watchers' Council."   2002 Money *Fighting the Forces* 104 "Wesley Windham-Pryce, also much improved in *Angel*, first appears in Buffy as Buffy's new Watcher [...], embodying the concept of Watcher-as-jerk, at best."   [fr. *watch* vt in sense 2 + -*er*[1] suff in sense 1.a]

   1.c: n   Someone whose qualities, behaviors, or responsibilities resemble those of a Watcher

2000 Topping *Slayer* iii "For Martin Day. My Watcher. My guru, my brother and my friend."

   1.d: n   An element in names

2002 Jul 25 Bronze: Beta "Watcher's Pet"

   2:   n *atrrib*   Of or pertaining to Watchers

1999 Oct 1 *Entertainment Weekly* 29/1 "Giles dropped out of Oxford to join an occult group before succumbing to his Watcher destiny."   2000 Holder *The Evil That Men Do* 233 "'An undercover Watcher spy?' Buffy asked."   2000 Passarella *Ghoul Trouble* 175 "'All the Watcher books and journals can't be wrong, can they?'" [B]   2000 Topping *Slayer* 194 "However, since Giles demonstrates a relationship with Buffy that the Council deems too close, he is relieved of his Watcher duties."   2000 Holder *Watcher's Guide* 2 86 "[S]he lies to Buffy and Giles, saying that her Watcher went to the annual Watchers Retreat in England."   2001 Apr 24 Espenson *Intervention* "'There is something in the Watcher's Diaries. A quest.'" [G]   2001 Oct 16 Petrie and Espenson *Flooded* "You know Watcher boy doesn't mean anything by it." [S]   2001 Odom *Revenant* 109 "[H]e knew from his Watcher studies that there were thousands of demons."   2002 Jul 26 Bronze: Beta "I'd have Buffy and Spike slowly develop a friendship/partnership over the season. Almost in a slayer/watcher sense."   2002 Navarro *Tempted Champions* 158 "Giles hurried to the counter and began pulling out older volumes of Watcher history from behind it."   2002 Zweerink and Gatson *Fighting the Forces* 253 "Giles becomes Buffy's father and frets about the clash between Watcher duties and his 'own gig.'" [fr. WATCHER in sense 1.a & 1.b]

—**pre-Watcher** *adj* Before becoming a WATCHER
1998 Cover *Night of the Living Rerun* 57 "And even though Giles tried to impress Buffy with the fact that his pre-Watcher existence was none of her business, he nonetheless remarked, 'It's like seeing a ghost, only I've seen ghosts and they're not nearly as attractive.'" [*pre-* pref in sense 1.a + WATCHER]

—**superwatcher** *n* Watcher with abilities in excess of the norm for Watchers
1999 Massie *Power of Persuasion* 40 "[Giles:] 'This isn't a job for the Slayer, it's a job for...' [Buffy:] 'Superwatcher.'" [fr. *super-* pref in sense 2 + WATCHER; formed on *superman* in sense 1]

—**Watcherly** *adv* In the manner of a Watcher
2000 Gilman and Sherman *Deep Water* 72 "'She's putting a severe cramp in your Watcherly behavior.'" [B] [WATCHER + -*ly*[1] suff in sense 1]

—**Watcher-napping** *n* Abduction of the Watcher
1999 Golden *Sins of the Father* 143 "'But what I don't get...I mean, I was sure the way Giles was acting had to do with whoever's behind our little Watcher-napping.'" [B] [WATCHER + (kid)*nap* vt + -*ing*[2] suff in sense 1.b]

weird *n* Uncanny
2000 Navarro *Paleo* 91 "Didn't she herself always try to make sure Joyce was somewhere safe when the weird hit the fan in this town?" [fr. *weird* adj in sense 1]

weirdage *n* Weirdness
2000 Garton *Resurrecting Ravana* 215 "[Xander:] 'So, what do you think?' [Cordelia:] 'What do I think about what?' He lowered his voice almost to a whisper. 'About the current weirdage we're dealing with.'" [*weird* adj in senses 1 & 2 + -*age* suff in sense 1.a]

weirded *adj* Frightened, made to feel uneasy
1999 Odom *Unnatural Selection* 3 "Flicking the toggle off and knowing she was too weirded to calmly sit by without hearing the sound of some-one else's voice, she went upstairs and checked on the baby again." [fr.

DAS3 & NTC *weird* (out) v, fr. *weird* adj in sense 2 + *-ed²* suff]   See
FREAKED and WIGGED

weirdness   n   Strange stuff
1997 Mar 10 Whedon *Welcome to the Hellmouth* "Excuse me…could you
be any weirder? Is there a more weirdness that you could have?" [C]
1999 Golden and Holder *Out of the Madhouse* 62 "With her concern for
Giles battling with the weirdnesses of the Hellmouth for her attention,
Buffy picked up her black bag and went to the drawer where she kept
some of her supplies."   1999 Gilman and Sherman *Visitors* 106 "Giles
had that look on his face, the one he got whenever a new piece of weirdness presented itself to him."   2000 Gallagher *Doomsday Deck* 64 "Among
her friends, weirdness abounded."   2000 Navarro *Paleo* 9 "There the
entry stopped, and Daniel was disappointed when the next pages were
blank. Weirdness, but then it had been sixty years ago, at an isolated dig
site."   2001 Nov 6 Whedon *Once More, with Feeling* "She's easing back
into it. We pulled her out of an untold hell dimension. Ergo the weirdness." [X]   2001 Kaveney *Reading the Vampire Slayer* 256 "Buffy and
Riley's love-making triggers and sustains poltergeist activity which causes
sexual shame and general weirdness."   2002 Odom *Crossings* 162 "'I
knew you hung out with some strange people, X-Man. That old guy that
used to be the librarian at your high school. That girl, Buffy, who always
seemed to be around true weirdness.'"   [*weirdness* n sv *weird* adj + *-ness*
suff]

whack   n   Misfortune; craziness
1997 Jan 19 Noxon *Surprise* "I just think it's some kind of a whack that
we feel we have to hide from all our friends." [X]   [fr. *whack* n in sense
1; NTC in sense 2]

whispery   adj   Engaged in speaking softly
2002 Navarro *Tempted Champions* 114 "'From the way they were all whispery, I'd guess they've known each other for quite some time.'" [S]
[*whisper* n in sense 1 + *-y¹* suff in sense 1]

whupness   n   Work
2000 Sep 1 The Bronze "I'm heavily weighed down with whupness and

getting awfully tired of it." 2000 Sep 1 The Bronze "I'll be needing it once I get away from the whupness." [whup 'work, or other serious responsibilities; what keeps one away from The Bronze' (contemptuous, fr. *HDAS big whoop* 'Who cares?') + *-ness* suff] See WHUPPAGE

whuppage n Work or other serious business
2000 Sep 1 The Bronze "Here I was thinking you were an old timer, I blame whuppage for the indiscretion." [whup 'work, or other serious responsibilities; what keeps one away from The Bronze' (contemptuous, fr. *HDAS big whoop* 'Who cares?') + *-age* suff in sense 3] See WHUPNESS

Wiccapalooza n Festival of witchcraft
2002 May 21 Petrie *Two to Go* "Look, we both know things might get ugly at Wiccapalooza." [X] [*Wicca* n in sense 1 + lollapalooza n (also *HDAS* in sense 1 & NTC in sense 1)]

wicca-y adj Appropriate to the practice of witchcraft
1999 Dec 14 Whedon *Hush* [quoted in 2000 Holder *Watcher's Guide* 2 222] "Her room is wicca-y and also painted black and depressed-y." [fr. *Wicca* n in sense 1 + -y[1] suff in sense 1] See WITCHY

wig 1: vi Become overly excited, agitated, or discomposed, or go crazy
1997 Mar 17 Reston *Witch* "If you're not a picture perfect carbon-copy, they [parents] tend to wig." [B] 1997 Dec 8 Greenwalt and Whedon *Ted* "Yeah, I kicked my ball in, put me in jail, but he totally wigged." [B] 1999 Jan 12 Espenson *Gingerbread* "She's completely wigging." [B] 1999 May 13 The Bronze "Well, if you want me to admit that it wigs me…I won't." 1999 *She's All That* "[Zach:] 'And you can't keep avoiding me. Like the other night. What was that?' [Laney:] 'I was busy.' [Zach:] 'Yeah, busy wigging.' [Laney:] 'Excuse me, I did not wig.'" 1999 Golden and Holder *Sons of Entropy* 302 "Cordelia had wigged many times in the past three years." 2000 Holder *The Evil That Men Do* 90 "'Uh, this is not what I signed up for,' Jordan thought, wigging." 2000 Holder *The Evil That Men Do* 289 "'Mark's gone,' Willow said. 'We can't find him any-where. He must have wigged.'" 2000 Gilman and Sherman *Deep Water* 2 "'It couldn't be a prophecy, or anything? Something I'm wigging to

before you?'" [B]   2002 Feb 4 *Angel* (WB Network) "But ask him to mack on hotties and he wigs." [C]   2002 Odom *Crossings* 46 "[Willow:] 'But we're going back out to the graveyard?' [Buffy:] 'Yes. Willow, don't wig on me.'"

   1.b: vt Make feel frightened or anxious
1995 *Clueless* "Oh, and this whole Josh and Ty thing was wiggin' me more than anything."   1997 Golden and Holder *Halloween Rain* 99 "Clowns wigged her." 2002 Odom *Crossings* 197 "'Being shot at with a rocket launcher tends to wig me.'" [B]

   2: n Creeps, agitation
1997 May 5 Des Hotel and Batali *The Puppet Show* "[Willow]: 'I think dummies are cute. You don't?' [Buffy:] 'No, they give me the wig. Ever since I was little.' [Willow:] 'What happened?' [Buffy:] 'I saw a dummy, it gave me the wig—there isn't really a story there.'" 1999 Oct 1 Howard *Entertainment Weekly* 49/4 "**(the) wig** Creeps; omnipresent term favored by the Scooby gang; usage: wigged, extra wig, (a fair) wiggins, maxi-wig." 2000 Gilman and Sherman *Deep Water* 178 "'You're asking if I'm over my wig about her?'" [B]   2000 Sep 1 The Bronze "They really give me the wig shudder." [*wig* out *phr v sv wig vt* (also *DAS3* in sense 6, and *NTC* in sense 1)]

   —**maxi-wig** n Greatest possible excitement
1998 Jan 19 Noxon *Surprise* "I know, I should keep my slayer cool, but it's Angel, which automatically equals maxi-wig." [B]   [*maxi*(mum) in sense 1.a + WIG]

wiggage n Confusion, disorientation
1999 *She's All That* "[Zach:] 'And you can't keep avoiding me. Like the other night. What was that?' [Laney:] 'I was busy.' [Zach:] 'Yeah, busy wigging.' [Laney:] 'Excuse me, I did not wig.' [Zach:] 'There was major wiggage.'"   [WIG + -*age suff* in sense 4.a]

wigged adj Confused, disoriented
1997 Golden and Holder *Halloween Rain* 121 "Buffy pushed against the invisible barrier, way wigged." 1998 Feb 10 Noxon *Bewitched, Bothered, and Bewildered* "I think she's just so wigged at hitting on one of my friends that she's repressing."   1999 May 13 The Bronze "I was way too wigged to notice much of anything."   1999 Golden *Sins of the Father* 111

"Giles glared at him. 'Define wacky.' Oz frowned. 'Not sure I could, but I can provide synonyms. Wigged, funky, weird, odd, bizarre, creepy, kooky, ooky, nuts, bananas.'" 1999 Golden and Holder *Immortal* 267 "'Oh, you think you're so smart,' [Cordelia] said, but the truth was, she was a little wigged because he had practically read her thoughts." 1999 Golden and Holder *Sons of Entropy* 133 "'It was totally freaky when we got there,' Cordelia told Willow. 'The house was, like, wigged.'" 1999 Golden and Holder *Sons of Entropy* 168 "Then Antoinette Regnier resumed her ghostly form and raised her face. Whoa. Talk about wigged. This lady's hair would turn gray if it hadn't already." 2000 Holder *The Evil That Men Do* 58 "'Hey,' Buffy frowned at her. 'I know you're wigged and I'm really sorry, Willow.'" 2000 Gallagher *Prime Evil* 115 "'Kari tried to pass it off as nothing, but she was wigged because I saw it.'" [B] [WIG + -(g)ed² suff]

wiggins 1a: n Episode of fear, over-excitement, agitation
1997 Mar 10 Whedon *Welcome to the Hellmouth* "That place just gives me the wiggins." [B] 1997 Golden and Holder *Halloween Rain* 48 "'If this thing is giving you guys a wiggins, I'll just put it aside until we're through.'" 1997 Golden and Holder *Halloween Rain* 91 "One was dressed like a clown, and that one gave her the wiggins worst of all." 1998 Jan 20 Whedon *Innocence* "I'm having a thought. And now I'm having a plan. And now I'm having a wiggins." [X] 1998 Fall Carter *Buffy the Vampire Slayer* 44 "Unfortunately, Ms. Carter returned from Sunnydale with a serious case of the wiggins and wasn't able to tell us much about the meeting before checking in to a mid-western mental hospital, where doctors tell us she's resting comfortably in her padded cell and wakes up screaming less than four days per week." 1998 Oct Brereton *The Dust Waltz* [5] "So it was natural for me [...] to be involved in the Buffy comic-book experience [...] I knew I spoke the same language as the show does. I know 'the wiggins' well." 1998 Oct Brereton *The Dust Waltz* [52] "'Oh, major wiggins!'" [B] 1998 Winter *Buffy the Vampire Slayer* 51 "**wiggins** [...] n. [X] the creeps, form of wigged-out—as in *that guy with the nail in his head gives me the wiggins.*" 1998 Genge *The Buffy Chronicles* 129 "'They create language—like "wiggins"—and styles in clothes and body art or even decor [...] but as soon as they create it, it's dated!' So says Peter Walkins, currently studying the remnants of

Cornish language and history in Newfoundland." 1999 Golden *Sins of the Father* 3 "'And, okay, Mom plus dating could at some point equal sex, and that's a giant economy size wiggins.'" [B] 2000 May 2 Noxon *New Moon Rising* "You found out that Willow was in kind of an unconventional relationship, and it gave you a momentary wiggins." [B] 2000 Sep 1 The Bronze "I hate things that float. They give me the wiggings [sic]." 2000 Holder *The Evil That Men Do* 75 "'Some guy takes out his parents, then blows away half the kids on the quad. It makes for a major group wiggins. People are jittery, to say the least.'" [X] 2000 Topping *Slayer* 28 "'The wiggins' is Buffy's personal version of 'the willies.'" 2000 Gilman and Sherman *Deep Water* 62 "Buffy felt a pang go through her that had nothing to do with her dream-induced wiggins." 2001 Jun 2 The Bronze "Have to post late tonight for the British audience. Why shouldn't they get the wiggins as well." 2002 Mar 12 Gutierrez *Normal Again* "So, she's havin' the wiggins, is she? So none of us is real. Bloody self-interested, if you ask me." [S]

1 b: *n*   An element in names
1999 Jun 26 The Bronze "misswiggins." 2000 Sep 1 The Bronze "little wiggins" 2001 Jun 2 The Bronze "Major Wiggins."

2:   *n attrib*   Pertaining to what frightens
1998 Vornholt *Coyote Moon* 57 "'And all that other wiggins stuff about coyotes,' Buffy added."

3:   *adj*   Frightening, unsettling
1998 Vornholt *Coyote Moon* 6 "This bunch looks normal, but there's something wiggins about them." 1998 Vornholt *Coyote Moon* 55 "'I decide what's wiggins, and you decide what it is." [WIG + -(g)ins]

wiggy   1.a   *adj*   Overly excited or agitated, or crazy
1997 Oct 6 Kiene and Reinkemeyer *Inca Mummy Girl* "She was wiggy about the seal from moment one." [W] 1997 Nov 24 Noxon *What's My Line, Part* 2 "Okay, a scenario: you back off, I back off, but you promise not to go all wiggy until we can go to my Watcher and figure this out." [B] 1998 Fall Carter *Buffy the Vampire Slayer* 45 "What should really have Buffy and the gang gettin' wiggy with him is that he seems to be in cahoots with the police in a concerted effort to keep Sunnydale's vampire activity under wraps." 1998 Gardner *Return to Chaos* 152 "Cordelia

had her share of wiggy moments—everybody did, Xander supposed."
1999 Mar 17 *Dawson's Creek* (WB Network) "I always get a little wiggy
this time of night."   1999 May 13 The Bronze "So from time to time over
the next few weeks you may find odd things happening, links getting a
little wiggy, etc."   1999 Gilman and Sherman *Visitors* 16 "'Man,' a voice
said, 'you are getting seriously wiggy.'" [X]   2000 Sep 1 The Bronze
"Then things started to get wiggy."   2000 Holder *The Evil That Men Do*
323 "The ground beneath their feet shook, and everybody got all excited
and wiggy about it."   2002 Helford *Fighting the Forces* 27 "Buffy makes
fun of Kendra's ignorance of U.S. slang, invoking anti-immigrant rac-
ism. When Buffy tells Kendra she must not go 'wiggy,' Kendra does not
understand. Buffy explains, 'You know, no kicko, no fighto,' deriding
Kendra's language skills."
   1.b   adj   Inciting fear or anxiety
1999 Oct 16 *TV Guide* 14 "The series' gifted producer, Moonlighting's
Glenn Gordon Caron, is so protective of what he calls this 'pretty wiggy
stuff' he's created that, to screen a nearly finished episode, I had to trek
to an industrial section of Queens, New York, where the production is
based in a converted cement plant."   2000 Passarella *Ghoul Trouble* 112
"'There's something wiggy about him,' Buffy said."   [WIG + -(g)y¹ suff
in sense 1]

wigout   n   Episode of agitation, hysteria
2000 Holder *The Evil That Men Do* 70 "Giles sent Buffy a note during her
last-period class, which she had spent listening to everyone talk about
Xander Harris's wigout in government."   [fr. *wig out* phr v sv *wig* vt]

Wild Bunch   adj   Like a western rescue
1997 Mar 10 Whedon *Welcome to the Hellmouth* "Get the exit cleared and
the people out. That's all. Don't go Wild Bunch on me." [B]   1999 Oct 1
Howard *Entertainment Weekly* 48/4 **"go wild bunch** Become violent
vigilante group; reference to bloody 1969 Western."   [fr. (The) *Wild
Bunch* 'title of a film dir. Sam Peckinpah (1969)']

Willy Loman   adj   Like a desperate salesman
1998 Nov 10 Espenson *Band Candy* "I'm sure we all love the idea of
going all Willy Loman, but we're not in the band." [B]   1999 Oct 1

Howard *Entertainment Weekly* 48/4 "**going willy loman** Raising money through selling of chocolate bars; reference to *Death of a Salesman*." [fr. *Willy Loman* 'name of the protagonist in Arthur Miller's tragedy, *Death of a Salesman* (1949)']

wimp-free *adj* Lacking any ineffectual people
2000 Holder *The Evil That Men Do* 7 "This house is wimp free." [B] [*wimp* n + *-free* suff, fr. *free* adj in senses 4.a & 4.b]

witchy *adj* Possible for a witch
2002 Odom *Crossings* 23 "'Witchy stuff,' Willow explained. 'Sometimes better than matches.'" 2002 Odom *Crossings* 47 "'Maybe you could use your witchy powers and check on Dawn through a crystal ball or something.'" [B] [*witch* n in sense 1 + -y¹ suff in sense 1] See WICCA-Y

wolfy *adj* Characteristic of a (were)wolf
1999 Golden and Holder *Sons of Entropy* 178 "[Giles] stared hard at Oz. 'You *sense* something?' 'In a wolfy, supernatural kind of way?' Buffy prodded." 2002 Jul 26 Bronze: Beta "From (I think) 'Dead Man's Party'— 'Do you like my mask? It raises the dead! Americans!!' as well as many from 'Band Candy' and the '... Oh priceless...' comment from the episode when he gets shot in the butt by (I think) Willow, when she was trying to use the tranquilizer gun on 'wolfy' Oz." [*wolf* n in sense 1.a + y¹ suff in sense 1]

wow-potential *n* Potential to satisfy romantically
1998 Jan 19 Noxon *Surprise* "Hey, speaking of wow-potential, there's Oz over there." [B] 1999 Oct 1 Howard *Entertainment Weekly* 49/4 "**wow potential** Possible sparkage." [*wow*¹ interj + *potential* n in sense 2]

wrathy *adj* Forcefully, even vindictively angry
2002 May 14 Noxon *Villains* "So Willow's all wrathy. Why don't you go to her? Isn't that your gig?" [Xander to Anya, once and future vengeance demon] [*wrath* n in sense 1 + -y¹ suff in sense 1]

W/X'ness *n* Romantic relationship between the characters Willow and Xander
2001 Jun 2 The Bronze "After all these seasons without even a shred of

W/X'ness." [fr. *Willow* 'name of the character on *Buffy the Vampire Slayer* + X(ANDER) + -*ness* suff]

Xander 1.a: *n* One of Buffy's friends, a member of the SLAYERETTES (see quotations throughout the glossary)

1.b: *n* An element in names

2000 Sep 1 The Bronze "Xanderphile" 2000 Sep 1 The Bronze "Xandman" 2001 Jun 2 The Bronze "Xanderella" [ODFN *Alexander*]

—**Xanderhood** *n* State of being Xander

1999 *Golden Sins of the Father* 22 "'True,' he agreed. 'But I get a bit shy talking about my Xanderhood, so let's move on, shall we?'" [XANDER + -*hood* suff in sense 1.a]

—**Xanderific** *adj* Wonderful in the character's idiosyncratic way

1999 Jun 26 The Bronze "I especially love Xander because he's so Xanderific." [XANDER + -*if*-, by analogy with *terrific, horrific,* etc. + -*ic* suff in sense 1]

—**Xanderish** *adj* Like Xander's manner

1999 Massie *Power of Persuasion* 111 "So he told Calli he thought the Womyn were festering boils on the noble face of feminism. Something Xanderish like that." [XANDER + -*ish* suff in sense 2]

—**Xanderman** *n* Xander, as though he were a superhero

1998 Gardner *Return to Chaos* 125 "'This looks like a job for Xanderman!'" [X] [XANDER + *superman* n]

—**Xandermobile** *n* Xander's car, as though it were a superhero's vehicle

1998 Gardner *Return to Chaos* 125 "'Quick, Oz! To the Xandermobile.'" [X] [XANDER + *Batmobile,* ultimately fr. *automobile* n]

—**Xan-man** *n* Xander

1999 Massie *Power of Persuasion* 15 "'Just humor me. It's for old time's sake. It's a little nostalgia for the Xan-man, to bring back the long legs in the desk next to mine in chemistry class.'" [X] [fr. XAN(DER) + *man* n in sense 3]

—**X-man** *n* Xander

2000 Holder *Watcher's Guide* 2 55 "Big changes in store for the X-man as he moves to center stage in Season Five." 2002 Jul 27 Bronze: Beta "I find your rant about the X-Man being flawed amusing." 2002 Odom *Crossings* 158 "'You sure you don't want anything to eat, X-Man?' Robby asked Xander." See also quotation 2002 Odom *Crossings* 162 sv WEIRD-NESS 2002 Jul 30 Bronze: Beta "Recently, I watched a re-run of Restless, where in one snippet, Anya turns to the X man and tells him that she wants to get back into the revenge biz." [XANDER + man n in sense 3, with attraction to X-Men]

Index

The index gives references both to topics discussed in the text and the words defined in the glossary. Additionally, every episode and screenwriter cited in the glossary is listed, with references to the glossary words for which they have provided evidence.

285